THE ECONOMICS OF ZONING LAWS

THE ECONOMICS OF ZONING LAWS
A Property Rights Approach to American Land Use Controls

William A. Fischel

Professor of Economics
Dartmouth College

THE JOHNS HOPKINS UNIVERSITY PRESS
Baltimore and London

© 1985 The Johns Hopkins University Press
All rights reserved
Printed in the United States of America

Originally published, 1985
Johns Hopkins Paperbacks edition, 1987

The Johns Hopkins University Press
701 West 40th Street, Baltimore, Maryland 21211
The Johns Hopkins Press Ltd., London

Library of Congress Cataloging-in-Publication Data

Fischel, William A.
    The economics of zoning laws.

    Bibliography: p.
    Includes index.
        1. Zoning—United States.   2. Land use—United
States.   3. Zoning law—Economic aspects—United States.
4. Urban economics.   I. Title.
HD260.F57   1985   346.7304'5   84-21840
                           347.30645
ISBN 0-8018-2420-6 (alk. paper)
ISBN 0-8018-3562-3 (pbk.)

To my parents,
LOIS and JACK

Contents

Preface and Acknowledgments

This book is an attempt to persuade my fellow economists that zoning and other local land use controls are most usefully viewed as collective property rights controlled and exchanged by rational economic agents. Such a view allows the application of the modern theory of property rights, which stems from the work of Ronald H. Coase (1959; 1960), to all aspects of current land use issues. This view is thus distinctly different from that usually taken by economists, who see zoning either as an effort by disinterested planners to "internalize externalities" or as irrational rules that impose arbitrary constraints on the land market.

My method of pursuing the primary goal is to demonstrate that the property rights approach provides superior insights into most land use issues. While I was in the process of writing a first draft, two secondary goals appeared. First, the legal and political side of land use decisions requires as much attention by economists as does the private market. Most texts for courses in urban and land use economics devote a chapter to zoning, if that much. I have come to believe that public controls may deserve as much as half of the course. Thus I redrafted this book with an eye towards its employment in courses whose topics include urban economics, land use planning, environment and resources, real estate, and economics of law.

The other secondary goal stems from my discovery that most land use professionals, whose background may be in law, planning, architecture, political science, sociology, or geography, regard economics as largely irrelevant to understanding land use controls. This view stems partly from the highly technical nature of modern economics. Most of it, though, stems from economists' tendency to disregard the institutional structures that land use experts know are important. The property rights approach in this book attempts to remedy both of these problems.

I avoid all mathematical formulations, but there are analytical graphs in most chapters. It is assumed that the reader has some elementary economics background; the professional economist will have to bear with the occasional reviews of basic concepts. Substantial space is also devoted to institutional description and analysis. This is central to the method of the property rights approach, which analyzes the institutions within which exchange takes place to see if they affect the outcomes of exchange.

The book is divided into three parts. Chapters 1–4 deal with the factual, institutional, and legal setting. Zoning may be thought of as a collective property right, but it is not formally recognized as such, and so it is subject to many constraints. One cannot make accurate predictions or realistic reform proposals without some understanding of the land market and the nature of local controls.

Chapters 5–9 develop and apply an analytical model of zoning based on the property rights literature in economics. My principal device is the entitlements diagram, a hybrid of economists' benefit-cost graphs and property law's concept of divisible entitlements. I apply this analysis to three general issues: the siting of noxious industrial activities, the restraints on housing production in residential suburbs, and the fairness of zoning restrictions on individual property owners.

Chapters 10–15 deal with several policy-related issues. These include the influence of the geographic and political structure of local government on zoning; the effects of zoning on the price of housing and the location of economic activity in metropolitan areas; the rationale for the farmland preservation movement; and the relationship between zoning and the provision of local public services. In the last chapter I evaluate current trends and reform proposals.

This book builds on the work of others. The two scholars whose influence is most pervasive are Robert Ellickson and Robert Nelson. Ellickson's several book-length articles, particularly his analysis of suburban growth controls (1977), and the casebook by him and Dan Tarlock (1981) have enlightened the legal and economic analysis of this field immensely. Nelson's *Zoning and Property Rights* (1977) is the first systematic exposition of the fundamental premise of my book.

Many people have contributed to my efforts in writing this book. Marion Clawson, Robert Ellickson, and Robert Nelson read early drafts and provided invaluable comments. Helpful suggestions on one or more chapters or on particular areas were graciously offered by Richard Babcock, Marcia Baldwin, Jonathan Brownell, Robert Cooter, Paul Courant, Carl Dahlman, Ted Frech, Mason Gaffney, Daphne Kenyon, Douglas Kmiec, Daniel Mandelker, Hugh Nourse, Janet Pack, Robert Plotnick, Mitch Polinsky, Edward Rabin, Seymour Schwartz, Julian Simon, Nic Tideman, John Weicher, and Norman Williams. Colleagues within the Departments of Economics at Dartmouth and the University of California at Davis, as well as those at professional meetings, added numerous oral comments about various aspects of my work.

Financial assistance for early drafts of several chapters was received from the Lewis Haney Fund at Dartmouth College and the U.S. Department of Housing and Urban Development. Manuscript preparation was financed in part by the Dartmouth College Faculty Research Fund. Typing was done at various stages by Terry Hall, Elaine Vigneult, Gail Patton and Gail Place. Maps were drawn by Jeanne Childs, and graphs were prepared by Anniken Kloster. My wife Janice provided technical advice on printing as well as conjugal encouragement. I thank them all.

THE ECONOMICS OF ZONING LAWS

1.

Land Use and
Land Economics

In the United States there is more space where nobody is
than anybody is. This is what makes America what it is.
—Gertrude Stein, *The Geographical History of America*, 1936

The fundamental premise of this book is that land use controls
are best analyzed as collective property rights. The present chapter
is devoted to some tasks preliminary to developing this theme.
The first of these is to outline some facts about land use. The
focus is on urban development and population pressure on land
resources. The major conclusion is that we are in no danger of
running out of land for nonurban purposes due to population
growth or development.

The second task of this chapter is to review some elements of
land economics. In order to comprehend the role of public property rights in allocating land, one must understand the basic forces
by which private land uses are determined. This will also enable
us to evaluate some of the arguments against private land ownership, especially that of Henry George.

1.1. HOW MUCH LAND IS URBANIZED?

1.1.1. Paving Over America?

At the beginning of my urban economics course, I pose the
following thought experiment to my students: Divide the current
U.S. population into households of 4 persons and house them at
the "suburban sprawl" density of one acre per household. (An
acre is 1/640 of a square mile, or approximately the size of a

football field without the end zones.) What percentage of the total land area of the forty-eight contiguous states would be taken up?

Answers to this question typically range from 10 percent to 70 percent, with 30 percent a frequent median guess. Even professionals in urban and land use planning usually offer guesses considerably above the correct answer: 3 percent. The high guesses may explain why credence is given to lurid warnings about "running out" of farmland or "paving over" America. Most of us live in or near urban areas, and we tend to project our everyday experience on the entire country. But this is a case where everyday experience is misleading, as looking out of the window of an airplane will usually demonstrate.

One may object to my heuristic calculation. Average household size is smaller than 4 (it was 2.85 in 1980), and other activities besides housing need to be counted. The facts, however, show that my simple calculation is not far off. Table 1 shows that land devoted to built-up uses (urban plus rural transportation) accounts for only 3.2 percent of the land area of the forty-eight states.

Another objection to these figures is that they do not indicate the rate at which rural uses are converted to urban ones. One well-publicized study indicated that this rate had increased alarmingly in the 1970s (National Agricultural Lands Study 1981). The alarm turned out to be false. Subsequent evidence from the 1980 Census and special studies by the Soil Conservation Service proved that there was no acceleration of urban growth in the 1970s.[1]

The issue of urban and suburban development may be put in perspective by looking at table 1, which shows the major classes of land use for the forty-eight contiguous United States. (Including Alaska would increase land area by about one-fifth, most of it in the categories of forests and tundra.) The table shows that the vast majority (87.9 percent) of our land is forest, range, pasture, and cropland. Should an "Earth probe" from an alien planet land in a random spot in the United States, it would be unlikely to encounter human habitation.

One hazard in looking at table 1 is the tendency to view each category as if it were fixed for all time or uniquely suited for its present purpose. This is not true, as but one example will show. From the beginning of this century, cropland expanded from 319 million acres to a peak of 478 million in 1949; it then declined to 434 million acres in 1970. This decline did not occur because the land came to be used for urban or other developed purposes. Most of the loss of cropland has been to other rural uses, most commonly pasture or forest land. This process is of course reversible. When

Table 1. Major Uses of Land in the Contiguous United States

	Millions of Acres	Percentage of 48 States' Area
Forests outside of parks	598.5	31.5%
Grassland pasture and range	595.2	31.4
Cropland	465.7	24.5
Wetlands, bare rock, desert & tundra	90.7	4.8
Rural parks and wildlife reserves	56.9	3.0
Urbanized Areas and Urban Places*	34.6	1.8
Rural roads, railroads, and airports	25.9	1.4
Military and nuclear installations	22.4	1.2
Farmsteads and roads on farms	8.0	0.4
Total land area	1,897.9	100.0%

Source: Frey (1979, 27–33).
* Frey adjusted Urban Place acreage to account for open spaces in many small incorporated places.

world grain prices rose dramatically in the early 1970s, 27 million acres of other rural land were converted to crops to take advantage of the higher prices, so that by 1978 some 461 million acres were classified as cropland (Hart 1984).

1.1.2. U.S. Census Data

In order to evaluate urban land use and its trends, it is necessary to understand some official definitions. The most widely used classification for urban data has been the Standard Metropolitan Statistical Area (SMSA). The SMSA has recently been discontinued as an official definition. It has been replaced by a multiple classification of metropolitan areas by size. However, each of the new categories is, roughly speaking, a repetition or an aggregation of the old SMSA criteria, so it is worth repeating the latter here.

To be included in an SMSA, an urban area must have a population of at least 50,000 people in one or more "central cities." The SMSA includes these cities *and* the *entire area* of surrounding counties that are economically linked to the central city. (The exception is in the New England states, where only surrounding towns are included.) About two-thirds of the U.S. population lives in SMSAs.

As a measure of economic trends in cities, SMSAs have the advantage of including most of the urban population. That they include some rural and small-town population within their counties and that they do not include urban areas with populations of less than 50,000, are not important for most statistical analysis. But they *are* important for calculating population density and other land area data. SMSAs occupied about 10 percent of the U.S. land area in 1970, but this is totally misleading, since *most* land in SMSAs is *not* urban. In fact, the nonurban parts of SMSAs are often important agricultural areas: ranking the 3,000 U.S. counties in order of value of agricultural production, 33 of the top 100 are counties in SMSAs (Brown and Beale 1981, 85).

Because they include so much rural area, SMSAs are not appropriate for measuring population density. I dwell on this seemingly obvious point because it is overlooked by many scholars. In recent years economists have prepared studies purporting to compare the quality of life of metropolitan areas. One of their indicators of quality of life is population density. But the researchers almost invariably calculate density as SMSA population divided by SMSA area. More remarkable than this is that the effect of including such a variable is often significant in explaining wage or housing price variations.[2] Yet there is no correlation between SMSA density and the more reasonable measure of density discussed below.

A better measure of urban land is the Urbanized Area (UA). The UA is, roughly speaking, the built-up, contiguous part of an SMSA. This does not mean just the central city of the SMSA; it includes surrounding suburbs, but its extent is based on population density rather than political boundaries. (Maps of three UAs are in chapter 10.) The density criteria for being included in a UA are not too demanding: a suburban housing development that had one house for every two acres would be included so long as it was adjacent to the rest of the UA.

Urbanized Areas include about 60 percent of the U.S. population, and they take up only 1.2 percent of the land area. But this sanguine statistic does not address the concerns that many express about "suburban sprawl" or about development in smaller towns and rural areas.

Suburban sprawl data can be examined easily. It is true that suburban areas are less densely populated than central cities, but the difference is less than one might suspect. Since the problem of suburban sprawl most frequently focuses on the largest urban areas, I subtracted the population and land area of the central city (or cities, where there were two or more) of the twenty-five largest UAs and computed their gross population density. It turns out to be 4.9 persons per acre. If we all lived at these 1970 suburban densities, we would take up less than 2.5 percent of the forty-eight states' land area.

Another study of urban land use confirms this observation.

Kathryn Zeimetz and others (1976) selected the fifty-three large counties that grew fastest between 1960 and 1970. They then obtained aerial photographs of them from either end of the decade. The sample was dominated by suburban counties of larger SMSAs. By careful examination of aerial photographs, they were able to calculate how much of each county was built-up in various classifications. Using census data for population, they found that population per acre of *all* built-up land was about four persons.

The Zeimetz study also gave a useful breakdown of urban and built-up land use. In their entire sample, about half of such land was used for residential purposes, including residential streets. One-quarter was used for other urban transportation, and only about one-sixth of the built-up land area was used for commercial, industrial, or institutional purposes. (The remainder was recreation or vacant lots.) Housing is thus the dominant land use in urban areas.

1.2. DECENTRALIZATION AND HOUSEHOLD FORMATION

It is clear from the data in the previous section that suburban sprawl does not pose a serious threat to the stock of land for nonurban uses. It has been charged that two demographic trends pose a threat to agricultural land. The first is migration to non-metropolitan areas, where densities are supposedly lower. The second is increased household formation in the 1970s. We shall look first at the available evidence on population densities in smaller urban areas.

1.2.1. Urban Place Density

The major problem in evaluating urban place density is that there are no useful data on which to calculate densities in non-metropolitan areas. The Census Bureau calculates a unit called an Urban Place, which is any reasonably contiguous settlement with a population of at least 2,500. Urban Places include all Urbanized Areas plus smaller units that may or may not be in SMSA counties. Nearly three-quarters of the U.S. population lives in Urban Places. Since about 60 percent of the population lives in UAs, 15 percent of the population lives in an Urban Place outside a UA.

Little is known about the population density of cities and towns smaller than 50,000. Some extrapolations can be made, however, from the available data on UAs. The twenty-five smallest UAs ranged in population from 50,000 to 68,000. In 1970 they had a population density of 3.13 persons per acre. (This probably understates their true density, because many of these UAs are simply the boundaries of a central city, and in many cases the city includes a significant amount of rural area [Frey 1983].) The UAs that are ten times their total population (i.e., the thirteen UAs having a population ranging from 500,000 to 680,000) have an average population density of 3.90 persons per acre. That means that UAs 900 percent larger than the smallest UAs were only 24 percent more densely populated. This suggests that densities in smaller urban areas are not that much less than in the largest areas. Thus it seems reasonable to assume that the decentralization movement to smaller cities will not make an appreciable dent in the stock of nonurban land.

1.2.2. Household Demographics

The second trend that raises concern about land supply is the increased growth in the number of households and a decrease in their average size. The population of the United States in 1980 was about 226 million, representing an increase of 11 percent over 1970. This represents a reduction in population growth rates; population grew by 13 percent in the 1960s. However, the growth in the number of *households* in the 1970s exceeded that in the 1960s. There was a 25 percent increase in households between 1970 and 1980, compared with a 20 percent increase in the previous decade. Average household size has continued to decrease in recent decades, from 3.33 in 1960 to 2.85 in 1980.

The growth in the number of households indicates that land use pressures and the issues they raise are not simply a matter of population growth. Even if there were no increase in population, other factors would cause the demand for new land uses to continue. What requires some discussion, however, is the demand for housing resulting from changes in the age distribution.

The slower rate of population growth in the 1970s (and most probably in the 1980s) is due to the cessation of that demographic aberration called the baby boom. From after World War II to the early 1960s, American fertility rates (computed as the number of children born over a woman's lifetime) discontinued their long secular decline and rose considerably. By the mid–1960s, however, the baby boom was over and birth rates had returned to their pre-World War II levels. The continuation of current fertility rates will lead eventually to zero internal population growth. In the meantime, the children born in the baby boom era have come of age to form their own households. This accounts for much of the increase in housing constructed in recent years. The sudden shift in demand brought about by the larger cohort may also account for some of the housing cost increases.

It is entirely predictable, then, that the shift in housing demand caused by the large birth cohorts of 1946–63 will begin to abate later in this decade. The growth rate of households will most likely decline. Moreover, as people in this young cohort have more children, average household size may rise. Other factors may work against either trend, of course, but this simple demographic analysis holds a lesson about land use issues: they are likely to be less intensive in a decade or so. The problems will not disappear in the near future, but projections of land use catastrophe and capital gains from home ownership based on the last decade's demographic trends are both likely to be overstated.

1.3. THE DISTRIBUTION OF CITY SIZE

We are accustomed to talking about the distribution of population among urban areas as if it were linear: we refer to "big," "medium," and "small" cities. In fact, however, the distribution of urban areas by size class is nonlinear and highly skewed. Here are some illustrations. One-quarter of the population living in UAs in 1980 resided in the four largest—New York, Los Angeles, Chicago, and Philadelphia. The twenty largest UAs contained over half of all UA population.

The distribution of population by size can be seen in figure 1, which plots the twenty-five largest UAs from largest to smallest. The plot can be seen to approximate a rectangular hyperbola, not a straight line. In urban texts, this relation is called the rank-size rule, and it is found to apply to a remarkable degree both across time and across countries (Rosen and Resnick 1980).

A consequence of this skewed population distribution is that aggregate population data for urban areas will be dominated by the largest ones. An example of how this can mislead is the observation that nonmetropolitan areas grew at a rate twice that of metropolitan areas during the 1970s.[3] This observation masks the fact that the major slowdown in metropolitan growth was in the largest SMSAs. If we remove the seventeen largest SMSAs from consideration, we find that the remaining SMSAs grew at exactly

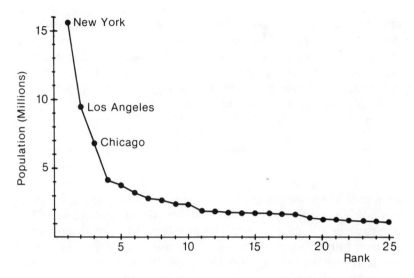

Figure 1.   Rank and Size of the 25 Largest Urbanized Areas in 1980

the same rate as nonmetropolitan areas. Moreover, since more than two-thirds of the population lives in metropolitan areas, the absolute increase in population was 50 percent larger in SMSAs than in non-SMSA counties. The much-discussed shift in population to "rural" America takes on a different perspective when viewed in this light.

1.4. LAND RENT AND LAND TAXES

This section and the following sections will discuss principles of land economics. The urban economics location model and other aspects of land markets will be developed in chapters 12 and 13.

The price of land, computed per unit of time, is usually called rent. Rent is often misunderstood because the same term is applied to income from all real property. It is also used by economists to describe the income from an asset whose supply curve is perfectly inelastic (such as Picasso drawings) or any profits in excess of those required by a firm to continue in business. The latter usage is often called "economic rent." Here I use *rent* in its classical sense: as income derived from selling the services of a unit of land, independent of the services of capital or labor.

Most prices of vacant lots or agricultural plots are not pure rents. There are two causes for the divergence between market prices and rents. The first is that land quality is influenced considerably by past and current investments. Drainage, soil management, grading, utilities, and transportation access are investments that contribute to the value of the asset. Separating these contributions to value from pure rents is very difficult for individual parcels. The second cause is that market prices reflect landowners' market-seeking and risk-bearing activities. Seldom is the most valuable use of land in urban areas evident to the casual observer. Identifying such locations for investments and assuming the risk of loss if one is wrong are important entrepreneurial functions. The reward for such activity is often the capital gain made by reselling the land at a higher price. Thus, even without any tangible physical investments, land prices may include more than just the classical notion of rent.

The usual discussion of land rent proceeds by drawing a vertical supply curve (S_c) and a conventional demand curve, as shown in figure 2. The vertical supply curve is sometimes confusing. For any given parcel of land, the supply is completely inelastic, since land cannot be moved. For all land taken together (that is, the stock of land), the supply is also inelastic—as Will Rogers quipped, they aren't making it anymore. But for land to be used for a particular purpose, the supply is not vertical. As I noted earlier, when prices for wheat and corn rose dramatically in 1972, the demand for cropland shifted to the right, raising its price. This encouraged farmers to convert other land to cropland, as shown in figure 3. The upward sloping supply curve does not contradict the vertical supply curve of figure 2, since more acres of cropland reduces the number of acres for some other use by the same amount.

This distinction is useful in understanding some aspects of land use policy. Economists agree that a tax assessed on specific parcels of land or on immutable characteristics of land (such as "all land within New Hampshire") will be borne entirely by landowners and not shifted to other parties.[4] Precisely because of this incidence, the tax is also efficient: the revenue that the government gets will exactly equal the revenue that the landowners lose. They cannot avoid the tax burden by selling the land, because buyers will offer less as a result of the tax. A landowner can no more pass the tax onto tenants than he can pass on the cost of an operation for his mother. (When there is inflation, either exigency may be used by a landowner to justify an increase in nominal rents.)

Figure 2 demonstrates the previous point graphically. A tax of T dollars per acre of land applied to all parcels making up S_c (say,

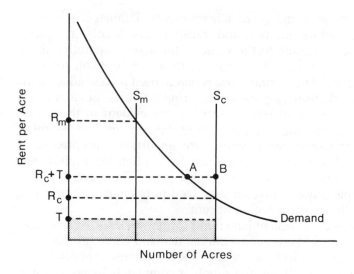

Figure 2. Supply and Demand for Land

all land within a twenty-mile radius of Pittsburgh) will generate revenue indicated by the shaded area. It will not reduce the supply of land for any use. If landowners were to respond by increasing rents to $R_c + T$ in figure 2, a surplus of land (AB in the figure) would develop, because the demanders of land would substitute other factors of production (e.g., building two-story houses instead of one-story houses) for land. This surplus would be eliminated only when landowners reduced rents to R_c. Competition among landowners would ensure that this occurred.

The efficiency characteristics of the land tax just described are sometimes misconstrued to be applicable to *any* type of land tax. Many taxes on land are assessed at different rates according to use. An example is the widespread practice of assessing agricultural, forestry, or open space at a smaller fraction of value than that of developed land (sections 13.1 and 13.8). The supply of land for these purposes is at least somewhat elastic, so the owner can avoid some land taxes by his choice of which use to put his land to. This does not mean that such tax systems are wrong; their very purpose may be to encourage the supply of land for one purpose and to discourage some others. But as such, the classical model of the incidence and efficiency of land taxes cannot be applied.

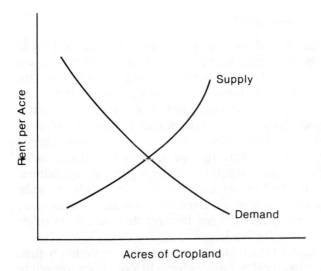

Figure 3. Supply and Demand for Cropland

1.5. LAND OWNERSHIP AND WEALTH

1.5.1. Government Holdings

The largest landowner in the United States is the federal government. It holds title to nearly one-third of the nation's land area (a quarter of the forty-eight states' area and most of Alaska). Its holdings outside Alaska are largely in the dry and mountainous areas west of Denver. The per acre value of this land, with the exception of some mineral holdings, is not large. Most of the valuable farmland and urban land is now in private hands.

At one time, of course, the federal government or the Colonies owned nearly all of the land. The disposition of this land was a major focus of political debate throughout the nineteenth century (Clawson 1968). Questions of private ownership and monopoly were constantly raised. Federal policy was originally aimed at selling land for revenue purposes. Later land policy was more deliberately designed to fulfill the Jeffersonian ideal of independent yeoman farmers. One need not admire the policy or its consequences in order to agree that the idea of fee simple ownership of land was consciously chosen; it was not an accident of history, as is sometimes asserted.

1.5.2. Monopoly Ownership?

Concentration of land ownership in a few hands could lead to a monopoly. The increasing average size of farms and the growth of holdings of land by large corporations have worried some for this reason. But as vast as these land holdings may be, they must be evaluated in terms of the land market of the entire country, and perhaps of much of the rest of the world. In this market, even the largest holdings of agricultural land amount to infinitesimal fractions of the possible substitute sites. Only a national cartel enforced by government sanctions—which is what agricultural price supports enforced by inducing farmers to set aside cropland amount to—can have any effect. Even this program does not work very well as a price support, since farmers then substitute other factors of production for land.

Monopoly of land for urban uses would seem more likely than monopoly for agricultural or forestry uses. In a single metropolitan area, an owner of undeveloped land would need to control far less to affect the price of land for new housing, especially if it were concentrated in the suburbs. There is no evidence, though, that such concentration exists in any metropolitan area. Indeed, reformers often lament that there is little systematic information on land ownership.[5] This could be taken as evidence of the wide diffusion of ownership. In a market with many owners and many small transactions, it is too costly to count them all.

A confusion that seems endemic in the land use literature is the identification of land rent with monopoly returns. This confusion may stem from the modern usage by economists, who classify all supernormal returns, such as those a monopolist might get, as "economic rent." Monopoly returns and land rent are quite different, though. In figure 2, the supply of land is denoted by S_c. Its competitive return is R_c, and no single owner dares to charge more, because his tenants will flee to other sites. If only one owner controlled all sites, he could artificially restrict their supply to, say, S_m, which would result in greater revenues. Although competitive rents are "unearned" in the sense that they are not the result of individual action or forbearance, it is not analytically useful to call such returns the result of a monopoly, since the latter term describes another situation entirely.

Land rent is often referred to as "unearned" income. This does not mean that the income is the result of no *previous* exertion or forbearance on the part of landowners. They or their forebears may have labored and saved for a long time to acquire title to the land. The sense in which rent is "unearned" derives not from a theory of deservingness but from the already observed quality of fixed supply. There is no current activity that the landowner can undertake to increase its rent. (Recall how difficult it is to separate out true rent from capital improvements and such labor as marketseeking and planning.) It is useful to keep in mind that there is no logical connection between "unearned" and "undeserved," unless one's idea of deservingness is founded on economic productivity (sections 9.8 and 9.9).

1.5.3. Land and Inequality

Monopoly power is not the only concern about concentration of land ownership. Many worry that unequal private ownership of land contributes to inequality of income and wealth. There are two statistical issues here. First, how unequally held is land? Second, is income from land a large fraction of national income? Unfortunately, we can offer only tentative answers to both questions. Most aggregate data fail to separate the value of physical capital from the value of land, and no study of which I am aware even attempts to divide land prices into rent and value due to entrepreneurial activity.

We do know that ownership of real estate contributes less to inequality than does ownership of other assets, especially corporate stocks (Smith and Franklin 1974). A large fraction of land's value is in owner-occupied housing and farms. (Although most residential parcels are small, their location in urban areas usually makes them quite valuable.) Nearly two-thirds of all households own their homes, and most farms are owner-managed. Land ownership in the United States is widely dispersed, if not equally distributed.

The most widely cited studies indicate that the share of land rent in national income is only about 6 or 7 percent.[6] (About three-quarters of national income goes to labor; and the remaining one-fifth goes to capital.) If this is true, redistribution of land or national taxation of land rents would not equalize the distribution of income and wealth to a significant degree.

The problem with this conclusion is that Mason Gaffney (1970) has shown that there are serious flaws in the aggregate studies of land value. His study of land values in Milwaukee suggests that the share of land in the national accounts may be understated by a factor of two or three. While I am not prepared to accept his much larger figure, mainly because it is based on what Gaffney admits are some heroic projection assumptions, one must accept the possibility that income from land may be a more significant fraction of national income than is usually believed.

1.6. THE ECONOMICS OF HENRY GEORGE

The most influential critique of private ownership of land was put forth by nineteenth-century American reformer Henry George. His *Progress and Poverty* (1880) was an instant success both in the United States and abroad. It inspired many political movements, and its influence lives on today.

George's best-known proposal is the "single tax." This was to be a tax on the entire rental value of land, whose revenues would provide the sole source of government income. This idea is looked upon with some approval by present-day economists because, as we have seen, a tax on land can be more efficient than other taxes.

Although economists recognize that the basic insight of the land tax proposal is valid, many dismiss Henry George and his followers as eccentrics who just happened to stumble onto a valid economic insight. I think that this view is mistaken for two reasons. First, George was well versed (by self education) in the mainstream of mid-nineteenth-century economic theory. His proposals were based on received economic theory. As such they must be differentiated from the numerous contemporary utopian movements.[7] Second, economists focus on the advantages and disadvantages of the single tax rather than on George's reasons for proposing it. The single tax on land is often criticized for being confiscatory. For Henry George that was its chief virtue. George's primary purpose was to eliminate private ownership of property. The single tax was only an expedient vehicle for accomplishing this end.

Following is an outline of the economic analysis that led George to his reform proposal. I have two reasons for presenting it. One is that many people cannot see what is wrong with George's ideas. In fact, there is nothing wrong with them if one accepts his underlying economic analysis. The critique of his analysis allows us to summarize the modern view of factor shares. The second reason is to point out why George believed that it was entirely fair for the state to expropriate private landholdings by means of taxation. This will allow us in chapters 8 and 9 to evaluate modern expropriation proposals in terms of George's norms.

Henry George came to his radical conclusions by the convergence of two routes. The first was economic theory, particularly as expressed by David Ricardo. The second was his personal observation of economic conditions in the United States, especially in California after the Civil War.[8]

While early nineteenth-century economists made great advances in theories of exchange and production, they never articulated a satisfactory theory of distribution. "Distribution" means the determinants of the general level of wages to labor, interest and profits to capital, and rents to land. It was clear that each factor received more as its quality—skills, productiveness, or fertility— improved, but it was not so clear what determined the proportionate shares of total economic production. Karl Marx's answer to this question was that the capitalists got it all and that labor would become more impoverished as production rose. Marx, perhaps because of his urban European background, had little to say about landowners.

Henry George, amplifying Ricardo, gave a different answer. Landowners would get larger shares of wealth as production rose. And the richer the landowners became, the poorer the workers became.[9] The plight of the working classes was caused by the system of private ownership of land. George rejected with contempt the explanation for poverty offered by Malthus, who said that it was due to the increase in population in the face of fixed land resources. As a newspaperman in California, George saw plenty of want and poverty among workers. It was obvious that it was not for lack of land. The system of private ownership, not the total supply, made the difference to George.

Why did George attack landowners instead of capitalists? He seems to have believed that the supply of capital was highly elastic. Taxing it might discourage its creation. In addition, George saw capital as the embodiment of past labor. For this reason it could not be the source of excessive economic power. Ownership of land seemed to be different. Fortunes were made in land without the least effort by the owner. Moreover, the necessity of all activity to occupy land impressed George. He referred to landowning as a monopoly, although he did not seem to have in mind the conventional notion of a single seller. Rather, it was the monopoly of private ownership as against public ownership that seemed most important. Land rose in value while people went hungry; the evidence seemed unambiguous.

1.7. MARGINAL ANALYSIS AND THE SHARE OF LAND

What is wrong with George's approach? One answer is its theoretical deficiencies, problems that it shared with most other economic theories at the time. The other is empirical observation. George was just wrong in his generalizations about the trend in wages and rents.

The deficiency in George's theory of distribution is its attribution of land as the single crucial factor of production, which enabled its owners to become the recipients of all material progress. The basis for a more satisfactory theory of distribution was being developed even as George wrote *Progress and Poverty*. This was the beginning of the marginalist revolution in economic theory. Its implications were not quickly appreciated even by those most closely involved with it, so it is hardly fair to say that Henry George should have been aware of it.[10]

Marginal analysis rebuts the Georgist (and Ricardian) argument that land will get all of the fruits of economic progress. The marginalist approach contends that each factor of production—land, labor, or capital—will receive the value of its *marginal* product in a competitive economy. The wages of labor, for instance, are determined by the value of the additional unit of output accounted for by the last worker (with a given characteristic such as skill) hired by a profit-maximizing, competitive firm. The rent of land is determined by the value of the additional unit of output accounted for by the last acre (with a given characteristic—location or fertility) purchased or leased by the profit-maximizing firm in a competitive economy. If some workers have skills that are both valuable and scarce, they will earn higher wages than others. Likewise, an acre of land that has a valuable characteristic will command higher rents than other land.

The mechanism that sees to it that land rents, wages, and returns to capital do not exceed value of marginal product is competition among the owners of each factor. A landowner who unilaterally raised the asking price of his land above his neighbor's price would find that no one would want to locate on his land. The potential users (for housing, farms, or factories) would buy other land nearby or in other locations. The rational landowner would lower his price to the competitive price.

How does this theory square with the Ricardian-Georgist view of land as a residual claimant of total output? Surprisingly, it leaves it perfectly intact. Land *does* get the residual. What the marginalists showed, however, was that so do labor and capital. This is because of the "adding-up" theorem in microeconomics. Under conventional restrictive assumptions, this theorem shows that if each factor is paid the value of its marginal product, the total output will be exactly exhausted. There is no surplus to be expropriated. This means that any one of these factors may be thought of as the residual claimant. Thus the only economic difference

between land and the other factors of production is that it is fixed
in supply by virtue of its immobility.

The conclusion of this brief analysis that is relevant to the present problem is that Henry George's fears that land will get all the
increments to national product are not supported by modern economic theory. As the productivity of labor increases, wages will
rise. As new inventions increase the productivity of capital, returns
to capital will rise. All of this is the implication of the neoclassical
analysis, unknown to Henry George.

I should not give the reader the impression that all economists
are satisfied with the marginal productivity theory of distribution.
But there is no reason to have to accept the marginal productivity
approach. The historical facts do not support George's contention
that rents will rise at such a rapid rate as to capture an increasing
share of national product.

In section 1.5.3. I noted that we are uncertain about the share
of land in national income. However biased the estimate is, there
is evidence that the share has not changed much since Henry
George's time.[11] This could be consistent with his theory only if
national income was the same now as it was then, which of course
is not true. Real income per capita has increased at least fivefold
since 1880.[12] One may object that national income and product
are not a true measure of economic well-being, but it is reasonably
clear that this is the measure that Henry George had in mind when
he talked about "material progress."

Corroborating evidence is provided by the trend in real wages.
Average wages—returns to labor, not just income—have risen
at a similarly dramatic rate in the last one hundred years. Even
more disconcerting to the Georgist is that living standards for
workers were probably rising during most of the nineteenth century as well (Andreano 1965, 131). What seemed so obvious to
George from everyday experience is not corroborated by the statistical evidence.

1.8. GEORGISM AND PROPERTY RIGHTS

One should not be too critical of Henry George for these oversights. Economic statistics are largely a product of the twentieth
century. Such evidence as we have about nineteenth-century wages
and national product is based on fragmentary data. The government had few comprehensive statistics on the state of the economy.

In addition, no nineteenth-century reformer had to point out the existence of poverty, and income inequality was more pronounced than it is today.

My reason for paying so much attention to Henry George is that his argument for abolishing private property in land is the best one around. George explicitly rejected the idea that land-owners should be compensated for what amounted to confiscation of land by taxation. He felt that this was entirely just. And who accepting George's analysis could argue otherwise? Private own-ership of land was in his eyes akin to a plague. He attributed to it nearly every economic evil (1880, bk. 4). Not just poverty, but inequality, business depressions, crime, labor strife, unemploy-ment, and protectionism flowed from it. Once this was under-stood, land ownership itself would be regarded as such deviant behavior—he put it in the same class as slaveholding—that even honest expectations of landowners could be put aside as irrelevant. George went so far as to argue that *landowners* would be better off under the nationalization of land.

If we were to accept George's analysis of the consequences of landowning, we would hardly agitate for compensation. No one suggests that thieves should be compensated when they are ap-prehended and their booty is returned to its former owners. But George's analysis is not adequate, and his predictions are contra-dicted by the facts.

Georgism waned as a national movement early in this century. Error has seldom proved fatal to political ideas. A more likely cause of Georgism's decline in national politics is that most ob-servers believed that the single tax would be insufficient to finance government spending. Land rents amount to only one-fifth of the current level of taxes, which take about one-third of national income. Moreover, at the national level, landowners are able to organize to defend their economic interests. For these reasons, Georgist ideas are currently most influential in local government issues, where landowners are sometimes less influential and land taxes would be a significant part of government revenue. As a result, Georgism remains a significant legacy in local land use scholarship. ("Neo-Georgism" is discussed further in sections 9.8 and 9.9.)

1.9. CONCLUSION

The survey of land use in this chapter indicates that there is no danger that development will impinge on the stock of land for nonurban uses. The latter part of the chapter indicated that land has substitutes and that land rent may be only a small fraction of the national economy. This may provoke some readers to wonder why I have written a book about land use controls. The answer is that although *land* may not be crucial, *use* is.

Zoning and other land use controls influence the location and combination of labor and capital. They can have a far greater influence on economic and other social activity than might be indicated by the fraction of land affected or the share of rent in national income. Land *use* controls can affect the quality of the environment, the provision of public services, the distribution of income and wealth, the pattern of commuting, development of natural resources, and the growth of the national economy. The notion that zoning is just a matter of local concern is incorrect when the cumulative effect of these regulations is considered.

NOTES

1. The data that refute the National Agricultural Lands Study (NALS) statistics are in Frey (1983) and U.S. Department of Agriculture (1984). For a review and critique of the NALS data and conclusions, see Fischel (1982) and sources in chapter 13, n. 2.

2. For example, Nordhaus and Tobin (1972) find density to be a significant disamenity, while Rosen (1979) finds that higher density significantly increases an area's attractiveness. It is not my purpose to argue that the Urbanized Area density, discussed below, should be substituted for SMSA density, for it also has (lesser) measurement problems. One might ask what large area density has to do with "quality of life" before doing any comparative amenity study.

3. National Agricultural Lands Study (1981). Census Bureau estimates for 1980–82 indicate, however, that nonmetropolitan growth is slowing (Forstall and Engles 1984).

4. There is, however, renewed debate about how much farther one can extend this proposition. Bentick (1979) argues that a tax on land *value* may not be efficient, since value changes over time and may vary according to the type of use contemplated in the future. This view is strongly disputed by Tideman (1982). The crucially related problem of assessment of land value is plumbed in essays and discussion in Holland (1970).

5. Raup (1982) confirms the lack of knowledge about land ownership at an aggregate level. A detailed study of the Baltimore area rural fringe land markets indicates that sellers of land appear to be operating in competitive markets (Peterson 1978, 67). A study of metropolitan Toronto concludes that land ownership is not concentrated and that land monopoly is a canard

(Markusen and Scheffman 1977). Healy and Short (1981) find little evidence of monopoly in rural land markets.

6. Keiper et al. (1961, 102). Their more precise estimate of land's share of national income in 1956 was 6.4 percent. The lack of importance of land in American economic growth is confirmed by Lindert (1974).

7. Schumpeter (1954) commends George for his mastery of current economic doctrines. Of the single tax, Schumpeter observes, "If Ricardo's vision of economic evolution had been correct, it would even have been obvious wisdom" (p. 865).

8. My source on George's life and thought is Barker (1955).

9. George's theory of wages allowed that they could rise even as rents rose but that they could not rise as *fast* as rents. Thus while the share of wages would fall, their level would not necessarily decline. George, however, also attributed business cycles and other economic ills that lowered wages to the evil effects of land speculation. Thus in this indirect sense the statement in the text is correct, and it is generally true to George's rhetoric in *Progress and Poverty*.

10. Philip Wicksteed, one of the major contributors to the new theory, was an enthusiastic supporter of Henry George (Barker 1955, 381–82). John Bates Clark was also influenced by George.

11. Keiper et al. (1961) found that the share of land did not change significantly over the past century. These estimates may be biased for a given year, but the same methods were used in all periods, so they are probably consistent.

12. Between 1880 and 1970 real per capita product grew between 1.6 percent and 1.8 percent per year, implying that it increased by a factor of 5 or 6 over the century (Kuznets 1977, 5). This experience was more or less shared by most European countries and Australia, Canada, and Japan (Kuznets 1966, 64–65).

2.

The Structure and Administration of Zoning Laws

It is my thesis that zoning should be thought of as a collective property right. This view allows us to make analogies between zoning and other property rights that will in turn facilitate the application of the economic literature on property rights to zoning. The problem with this approach is that there is no law that simply grants property rights in land to the community authorities. Zoning evolved without any conscious decision to reassign ownership of property (Nelson 1977). As a result, the structure and administration of zoning law require special attention to glean the ways in which property rights have been altered.

2.1. ZONING: AN OVERVIEW AND INVENTORY

Zoning is the division of a community into districts or zones in which certain activities are prohibited and others are permitted.[1] The original zoning laws implied a hierarchy of land uses to be protected. At the pinnacle is residential use, especially the single-family home. The hierarchy was most obvious in the older, "cumulative" zoning regulations. In these, commerce and industry were prohibited in certain residential zones, but residential uses were permitted anywhere. This is no longer typical of modern local ordinances. In most, homes are prohibited from being built in industrial areas, just as industry is prohibited from locating in residential zones.[2] The underlying idea that residential use is to be protected from other economic activities nonetheless persists.

The image of a "hierarchy" or "pyramid" of land use is perhaps responsible for the term *downzoning*. To eastern U.S. land use experts, downzoning means reclassifying a parcel of land for more intensive use; it is being moved down on the hierarchy of land use, which usually means that its value is increased. To a western U.S. lawyer or planner, downzoning means just the opposite: rezoning land for a less intensive use, such as single family houses on larger lots, which often reduces its value. In an effort to appeal to a national audience, I shall avoid the term and its equally ambiguous converse, *upzoning*.

Zoning is one of the community's "police powers." This broad regulatory authority is derived by the municipality from the state government. In most cases a special enabling act, patterned after a standard act promulgated in the 1920s, gives the locality the power to zone. States can withdraw this authority: the "Quiet Revolution" in land use controls described by Bosselman and Callies (1971), in which a few states have taken over some traditionally local zoning matters, is simply a resumption of authority.[3]

The establishment of zoning and any substantial changes in the original law are carried out by the local legislative body, such as the town or city council, or the county supervisors. Administration and minor adjustments (variances and special permits) are delegated to the zoning board of adjustment (the official title varies by state; I refer to it as the ZBA). In most states both the council and the ZBA are supposed to be guided by the planning commission. This body, like the ZBA, is usually appointed by the local legislature, though sometimes either office may be elective. In larger communities, the ZBA and the planning commission are advised by a professional staff of city planners. The planning commission draws up and occasionally amends a general statement of the goals that zoning is to implement. This statement is called the master plan or the comprehensive plan.

Some books on zoning give a count of the types of jurisdictions that have zoning laws. I shall spare the reader this because there is little reason to give such a count. Virtually every general-purpose local government in the United States has the authority to adopt zoning and related police power regulations.[4] Which governments zone, then, simply depends on what types of government are important in the area. In New England, counties do not zone, but that is because cities, towns, and townships all have the authority. In the South and the West, counties are more important governmental units, so they often do the zoning. In Pennsylvania and New Jersey, townships are often granted the power to zone as independent units, while in much of the Midwest, townships are just subdivisions of counties and thus usually lack zoning authority.

It is likewise unnecessary to count the number of zoning jurisdictions. Many rural communities have no zoning, and many that do have very weak controls. Some observers take this to mean that zoning is not much of a constraint on development. This is not necessarily true. In many cases, an unzoned community that is confronted by plans for some extraordinary development can legally forestall it by a hastily enacted interim zoning law. (It can also use public service moratoria to accomplish the same thing.) This allows the community plenty of time to enact a strict zoning law. The major restriction on such actions is that they apply to the entire community, not just to the threatened area. Furthermore, a community may make existing zoning laws more restrictive in response to some unexpected development proposal.

For these reasons, we may practically assume, without even investigating the existence of particular ordinances, that all general-purpose governments have zoning. Zoning may be our most common example of ex post facto laws. This may oversimplify the issue, but it often appears that the only time a developer has a true "vested right" to develop is after he has literally established that right in concrete, the concrete of a building's foundation.

2.2. OTHER LOCAL POLICE POWER CONTROLS

2.2.1. Subdivision Regulations

Within a zoning district, builders are subject to subdivision regulations. In order to proceed with their projects, developers must meet certain requirements set by the planning commission. These subdivision regulations may demand that the developer put in roads, sidewalks, sewers, water mains, utility lines, and recreation areas. An alternative to having the developers do these on their own is to have them pay the community a special fee, called a subdivision exaction, for the costs of expansion.

The importance of subdivision regulation is that it enables the community to force the developers to pay for some of the community infrastructure occasioned by development. There is, however, a substantial difference between these regulations and zoning. Zoning is a more powerful device because it permits the community to exclude many uses altogether. Under subdivision regulations, developers must bear certain costs, but having done so, they usually have the right to build. Under a valid zoning ordinance, developers do not have the right to erect any structure not in conformance with the zoning district, regardless of what they are willing to pay. The main point is that the community may refuse any attempt to alter a valid zoning ordinance, while it may not impose arbitrarily large subdivision exactions on permitted uses.[5]

2.2.2. Building and Housing Codes

Rather than prescribing the developer's contribution to community infrastructure, which subdivision regulations deal with, the building code designates the standards for materials and procedures to be used in new structures. These codes may require copper pipe for water and sanitation flow, insulation of a particular quality, and the use of plaster in certain areas. Such regulations can add to the cost of any structure, and they have been criticized for retarding the use of new building technologies (Colwell and Kau 1982). Their effects on housing costs do not seem to be large, though (Muth and Wetzler 1976). Their use has not generated the same kind of controversy as zoning perhaps because, like subdivision regulations, the range of costs to be borne by the developer is more specific.

Housing codes differ from building codes in that the former apply to existing structures, while the latter apply only to new ones. Housing codes set standards for the continuing maintenance of units, such as having hot water available and fixing stairs. These codes are not important exclusionary devices, since they apply to people who already live and vote in the community. They are mainly constraints on rental housing units, and they are most controversial when the community imposes rent controls. When rents are limited, landlords have an incentive to reduce maintenance, and housing codes are a means by which tenants can force them to keep up the rental units.[6]

2.2.3. Provision of Municipal Services

A final control of highly variable importance is the community's willingness to provide municipal services such as roads and water and sewer lines. Provision of municipal services obviously is mixed in with zoning and subdivision regulations, but it is a device of considerable importance in recent years (Tabors, Shapiro, and

Rogers 1976). Communities may limit development by refusing to extend water or sewer lines to certain areas or by refusing to annex unincorporated areas adjacent to them, which would deny new developments' access to all municipal services. This is an especially important constraint in areas where septic tanks and individual wells are not feasible. It should be noted that decisions about providing such services frequently are made not by a local government or its agencies but by metropolitan or county commissions or special districts. This may be the most important example of metropolitan land use control in the United States, even though it may not have been intended to function in this way.

2.3. FEDERAL, STATE, AND PRIVATE CONTROLS

2.3.1. The Federal Government and NEPA

Federal agencies have a variety of regulations that may be interpreted as land use controls. Examples are laws that pertain to soil conservation, navigable waterways, mining, air and water pollution, transportation rights of way, and forestry. These are largely neglected in this book, even though the amount of land affected is considerable and the economic activities involved are important.[7] Most of these controls are directed at particular activities rather than at controlling all potential aspects of land use. For example, pollution control may affect land use in many communities, but an industrial firm that meets federal air and water quality standards is not usually further restricted in its location decisions by the federal government. Such a firm may, however, meet all such standards and still be excluded from any number of communities by local zoning laws.

The major federal law regarding land use issues is the National Environmental Policy Act (NEPA). NEPA requires federal agencies to conduct environmental impact studies for their development activities. Since federal money often is involved in local projects, such as airport development, low-income housing, and road construction, their developers must conduct such studies. This gives communities or groups who object to these developments an opportunity to challenge them. The challenges may end up in court, where the opponents may obtain substantial concessions from the developer or even halt the project altogether.

Despite the importance of federal environmental laws and procedures, I am reluctant to call them federal land use controls, because the decision to use them as described comes from local governments or local citizen groups. During the mid–1970s it seemed likely that the federal government would establish something analogous to a land use planning commission, if not a national zoning board. It did not happen. Neither house of Congress approved the bills that would have moved in this direction. The federal government has confined itself to encouraging and subsidizing local planning activities.

2.3.2. State Governments

In the late 1960s and early 1970s, state legislatures began reasserting their police power authority over the use of land. This took a number of forms. A handful of states (Vermont and Oregon most prominent among them) set up statewide regional land use commissions. These commissions reviewed many of the decisions of local governments for their regional impacts. Other states established similar commissions, but only for a special area of the state. Examples include New York's Adirondack Park Agency and the California Coastal Commission. A third approach has been state establishment of metropolitan federations to coordinate land use policies among the many local governments that constitute most large urban areas. Well-known examples are the Minneapolis and St. Paul Metropolitan Council and the assumption of land use powers in the Miami, Florida, area by Dade County.

Despite their appearance, these new agencies have not greatly supplanted local autonomy. The local governments within the regions covered by the agencies seldom give up the power to zone and regulate subdivisions. The chief impact of the agencies is to provide a "double-veto" power to residents who oppose a particular development. If the shopping center passes the local zoning and planning board, it may still be rejected by the regional or metropolitan commission. It seldom works the other way: few if any of these commissions have told local governments that they must accept developments that they do not want.

The Quiet Revolution has taken a new twist in the last few years. There have been few initiatives towards pro-environment state and regional land use controls since about 1976 (Callies 1980). Several states, however, have attempted to preempt local authority over the location of especially noxious but necessary projects such as hazardous waste dumps (Tarlock 1983). Even in these cases, though, local governments retain substantial control.

The land use controls outlined so far are part of the community's police powers. Two of the more important alternatives are briefly described below.

2.3.3. Nuisance Law

Nuisance law is the branch of tort law that deals with specific harms by one activity on another nearby. The law of nuisance was a predecessor of zoning, but it is not a land use control in the modern sense. A nuisance is defined as a specific activity, and it must be shown to exist and actually cause some harm before a court will hear the case. It becomes a land use control only as a result of the effect of spatial proximity of incompatible activities, such as hog farms and most anything else.

Nuisance law has largely been superseded by zoning and other police power controls. The reasons for this include the somewhat narrow definition of what constitutes a nuisance, the lack of prospective control, the high cost of litigation, and the tendency to use the extreme remedy of the injunction rather than award damages.[8] More important than these, I suspect, is that zoning allows communities to control activities that no court has ever found to constitute a nuisance. In other words, zoning represents a far more generous distribution of entitlements to the community than does nuisance law, even though the latter does not require the community to pay compensation either.

2.3.4. Covenants

Another major alternative to land use control is the protective covenant.[9] In this category I include, as a lawyer might not, all private agreements between landowners. These include a remarkable variety of legal devices, generally called servitudes, which illustrate the extent to which property rights can be divided and sold. One can acquire air, mineral, and travel rights to another's land. Neighbors can agree to restrict architecture, landscaping, or conditions for occupancy. The former practice of using covenants to restrict ownership by race probably accounts for the disrepute into which they have fallen.

Among the practical objections to protective covenants is the difficulty of changing the rules as conditions change unexpectedly. For a homeowner to alter the conditions of the covenant to allow, say, a home business office, would normally require unanimous written consent of all those subject to the covenant. An alternative to the covenant is the residential private government (RPG), whose most common forms are condominium and homeowner associations (Reichman 1976). The RPG has the same purposes as ordinary covenants, but instead of particular conditions being imposed in the deed to each property, the conditions are delegated to a property owners' association. This association then can alter, usually by a supermajority rather than by unanimity, various common conditions in the neighborhood.

Some observers regard zoning and private covenants as essentially the same thing, since they are directed towards the same types of issues. The crucial difference is that under covenants some price must be paid for the exercise of controls over other people's land. This is true even of private covenants that a developer imposes on buyers of lots. The price paid by the developer is the opportunity cost of allowing the land to be used for some activity not permitted by the covenant. Since it is the landowners who plight their own assets by imposing such controls, they are led to at least consider the alternatives.

A valid zoning ordinance, or a legal change in one, does not usually require any compensation to property owners (chapter 3). Since the affected land is not owned directly by the community, the opportunity cost is not perceived by local authorities. As we shall see (in section 4.8), some opportunity cost might be perceived in the form of fiscal, convenience, or employment benefits from certain types of activities, but only under rather special conditions would this be the same as market opportunity cost.

2.4. STATUTORY AUTHORITY AND FISCAL ZONING

Local governments in the United States are created solely by the states. In order to enact zoning laws and subdivision regulations, communities must obtain authority from the state. This authority ordinarily comes in the form of enabling legislation passed by the state legislature, but sometimes the authority derives from home rule charter provisions or state constitutional amendments. The latter seem to have occurred where state courts initially struck down zoning on constitutional grounds. The states—Georgia and New Jersey were two—simply amended their constitutions to override the judicial veto.

This possibility may be one reason why courts skeptical of zoning are nonetheless reluctant to curb its excesses. The courts may realize that their actions may engender a state constitutional amendment that gives them even less control over the police power. Such seems to have been the perception by the Georgia Supreme Court in 1960: "But the people by their votes amended or changed this constitutional guardianship of private property, and in the process stripped their judiciary of power to protect it."[10]

Statutory authorization for zoning was for many years remarkably similar throughout the United States. This was the result of the widespread adoption of the Standard State Zoning Enabling Act (SZEA), drawn up by the U.S. Department of Commerce in 1926. Nearly every state adopted enabling legislation that was either taken verbatim from this model statute or heavily influenced by it. This in itself would make the SZEA remarkable in the history of state government. More surprising is the durability of the act. In many states it survived for fifty years with only minor amendments.

State enabling acts and local laws are no longer as uniform as they once were. Some of the changes came about to accommodate the aforementioned regional authorities, and some to allow for new zoning devices. In response to these pressures, the American Law Institute published *A Model Land Development Code* in 1975. This has not created the same response that the SZEA did in the 1920s. One reason is that in the intervening half-century most courts abandoned their narrow interpretation of the proper scope of local police powers. This made explicit legislation authorizing novel regulations less necessary. Despite this erosion, the SZEA deserves the attention of any student of zoning. It still forms the basis of many states' zoning laws, and even in states where new enabling legislation has been enacted the influence of the SZEA is clearly perceptible.

What accounts for the popularity of the SZEA? I believe that it is the broad and vaguely defined powers that it grants to local governments. There seems to be no better way to convey the sense of these powers than simply to reprint the first three sections of the act. (These sections are about one-fifth of the entire act, the rest being devoted to procedural matters.) Some often repeated phrases are in italics.

Section 1. Grant of Power.—*For the purpose of promoting health, safety, morals, or the general welfare of the community,* the legislative body of cities and incorporated villages is hereby empowered to regulate and restrict the height, number of stories, and size of buildings and other structures, the percentage of lot that may be occupied, the size of yards, courts, and other open spaces, the density of population, and the location and use of buildings, structures, and land for trade, industry, residence, or other purposes.

Section 2. Districts.—For any or all of said purposes the local legislative body may divide the municipality into districts of such number, shape, and area as may be deemed best suited to carry out the purposes of this act; and within such districts it may regulate and restrict the erection, construction, reconstruction, alteration, repair, or use of buildings, structures, or land. *All such regulations shall be uniform for each class or kind of buildings throughout each district, but the regulations in one district may differ from those in other districts.*

Section 3. Purposes in View.—*Such regulations shall be made in accordance with a comprehensive plan* and designed to lessen congestion in the streets; to secure safety from fire, panic, and other dangers; to promote health and the general welfare; to provide adequate light and air; to prevent the overcrowding of land; to avoid undue concentration of population; to facilitate the adequate provision of transportation, water, sewerage, schools, parks, and other public requirements. Such regulations shall be made with reasonable consideration, among other things, to the character of the district and its peculiar suitability for particular uses, and with a view to conserving the value of buildings and encouraging the most appropriate use of land throughout such municipality.

I find it difficult to imagine any government's desiring more authority than is granted by a literal interpretation of section 1. The catch is that it cannot be interpreted outside the context of the limitation on the police powers of the state imposed by the federal and most state constitutions. (These are discussed in chapter 3.) Even in this context, however, the grant of power is quite broad, and remarkably so for the 1920s.

Given such a broad grant of power, one might suspect that zoning would have had many opponents in state legislatures. The key to overcoming this opposition was the lack of coercion of the municipality by the state. In most cases, adoption of zoning and other controls was a matter of local discretion. This tradition continues to this day, though there has been some erosion of it in several states.

The purposes of zoning mentioned in section 3 of the SZEA relate to virtually every municipal function. This undermines the distinction that planners, lawyers, and economists make between "fiscal zoning" and some other types of zoning. The purposes of zoning expressed in the SZEA are frankly aimed at concern with the community's fiscal functions. The clause "to facilitate the adequate provision of transportation, water, sewerage, schools, parks, and other public requirements" may be read as an invitation to use zoning as a means of avoiding expensive municipal services. Just how much substitution of police power for fiscal power may be permitted is not clear, but a community's attempts to limit the number of bedrooms in a residential development in order to keep school enrollments (and thus local taxes) down are not obviously inconsistent with the purposes of zoning expressed in this act.[11] In a sense, then, nearly all zoning may be said to be fiscal zoning.

2.5. PLANNING AND ZONING

The other interesting clause in section 3 of the SZEA is the requirement that zoning be done "in accordance with a comprehensive plan." What most commentators thought this clause would require was a document by a local planning commission that would state the goals of the community in regulating land use. These goals would then be implemented, perhaps over a long period of time, by zoning laws.

Most large communities do have a planning commission and a master plan. But often the planning commission and master plan came *after* the first zoning ordinances were enacted. Some small communities that have zoning continue to operate without a master plan. (Some have no zoning but do have subdivision regulations, so that they have a planning commission but not a ZBA.)

The lack of formal planning before zoning may be attributed to two factors. First, the per capita cost of a professional planning consultant may be substantial in rural communities on the edge of an expanding metropolitan area. Such communities often find that they want to enact or amend a zoning law in response to the proposal of a large development. In their haste, the niceties of planning are often forgone.

Second and more important, most courts have been unwilling to hold a zoning ordinance invalid simply because the community lacked a formal master plan. They interpret "in accordance with a comprehensive plan" as requiring only that all of the community, rather than selected parts of it, be zoned. Communitywide zoning must embody a plan of some sort, they reason, even if it is not written down. The existence of a master plan is often helpful to the community in that it provides evidence that the community did not act arbitrarily, but the plan itself has little force of law.

Both of these factors have been changing. The federal and state governments have provided grants to communities to be used for planning, so presumably the cost of doing so is reduced. Many federal programs for local governments are contingent on some planning and zoning. The courts have also become more hostile to ad hoc planning to rationalize zoning ordinances, and communities have thus been encouraged to be more careful. In addition, the American Law Institute model code attempts to tie zoning more closely to formal planning, though it declines to mandate planning prior to zoning.

The movement towards encouraging a formal planning process seems to have been engendered by conflicting motives (Mandelker

1976; Tarlock 1975). One concern has been that zoning is not sufficiently restrictive and that more planning is necessary to take into account longer-range environmental effects. Thus communities were encouraged to plan to preserve sensitive environments and conserve natural resources (Reilly 1973). The other concern has been that zoning is too restrictive, especially with regard to exclusion of lower-income groups. Several states have adopted legislation requiring communities to plan for their share of the region's low-income housing. It was hoped that planning could induce communities to open their gates a little wider.

Most planning documents written since 1970 seem to reflect both of these concerns. There is little evidence, however, that the latter concern has been affected by its being stated in the master plan. The breadth of the purposes of zoning as stated in such plans, as well as in the SZEA, makes it very difficult to isolate one motive as a controlling factor. The community may glibly mention the need for low-cost housing, but in actually providing for it the goal is overshadowed by concern for protecting the environment, preserving historic areas, preventing sprawl, and reducing congestion. Establishing a closer relationship between planning and zoning may have some advantages, but making low cost suburban housing more available does not seem to be one of them.

2.6. WHO CONTROLS ZONING?

2.6.1. Planners versus Politics

The establishment of zoning and similar land use regulations is clearly the function of the local governing body. So too are major alterations in the zoning laws, although other agencies have some influence on minor changes. It is important to emphasize this point, because it clearly puts zoning and rezoning in the local political arena. Some theories of zoning seem to suppose that it is established by an independent authority whose goal is the efficient use of land. This notion is perhaps engendered by some of the planning literature, which paints a picture of a farseeing planning office attempting to correct the misdeeds of the private market or to supplant it altogether.[12]

The idea that planners and the planning profession in general should control zoning stems in part from movements early in this century. One placed a great deal of faith in the ability of technically trained people to solve social problems. The other was the attempt to remove municipal decisions from party politics. Their conjunction gave us the city manager and the nonpartisan elections of many local governments. City planning was to be part of the same technocratic process, removed from partisan politics and pressures (Nelson 1977).

Despite this tradition, zoning is an eminently political process; and it may be the most important municipal function in many communities.[13] Most of the modern planning literature recognizes this. Professional planners whose ideas of good planning and zoning are often at odds with those of elected officials who appoint them usually have little job security. This is not to say that planners are unimportant. Insofar as they are often the only source of technical information, they can use this position to further their own goals. There is a good deal written about "advocacy planning," in which planners set their own preferences as the agenda rather than attempt to distill the preferences of the local citizens.[14] Planners are said to have preferences that differ from the general population. My impression is that they like rail transit and dislike autos; like public housing for low-income people and dislike mobile homes; like downtown shopping and industry and dislike suburban malls; like high-density central cities and dislike suburban sprawl.

To the extent that planners can set the agenda, they can exercise some control over zoning decisions. The trouble is that most planners who do have such discretion are employed in jurisdictions whose politics match their preferences. The better local-government planning jobs are in large central cities where mayors usually like rail transit, public housing, downtown shopping, and lots of constituents. As to reforming the suburbs, most are independent of their central city, and many developing suburbs, where zoning is most important, do not employ any full-time professional planners.

2.6.2. Citizen Participation

In an attempt to keep zoning decisions out of partisan politics, the early authors of zoning acts tried to get as much citizen participation as possible. This attempt continues to this day. To establish a zoning law or to make major amendments, most state enabling acts require at least two public hearings. The local government appoints a committee to recommend zoning boundaries, and this committee is required to hold hearings. In the case of rezonings, the ZBA and/or the planning commission must make recommendations and hold hearings. Once their recommendation is made, the legislative body must hold hearings before its decision. Each of these steps provides a forum for neighbors who may be affected by the zoning proposal. Local officials are at some pains to accommodate their objections.[15]

Still another entitlement to neighbors is the "20 percent protest clause" of the SZEA. In several states, a petition by 20 percent of the neighbors of a tract proposed for rezoning requires that three-quarters of the local legislature must vote in favor of the change in order for it to pass. It is not clear how important this clause actually is, but it does illustrate the tendency to give neighboring property owners more weight than other members of the community.

I emphasize these procedural aspects of zoning because it is sometimes alleged that zoning is heavily influenced by developers and that neighborhood interests are disregarded. In some cases this may be true, but it is most likely invalid in places where zoning matters most: in suburban residential communities. All evidence suggests that in these places the preferences of homeowning voters are given the most careful consideration. If the "majoritarian" model of politics has any validity at all, it is in suburban zoning issues.[16]

2.7. ZONING BOARDS AND PLANNING COMMISSIONS

Zoning requires two continuing tasks: interpretation and exceptions. These are undertaken by the ZBA. The interpretation function is largely to clarify ambiguities in the text of a law. These may arise when a developer disagrees with a zoning administrator. The latter may often serve in this capacity as an adjunct to some other position, such as that of building inspector.

The more important function of the zoning board is to grant exceptions to the ordinance. This does not include major *rezonings*, which are done by the legislature. There are two kinds of exceptions: the variance and the special permit. (The special permit is often administered by the planning commission.) A variance is an exception to the strict application of the zoning ordinance to a particular lot. It is designed to account for hardships inherent in the lot itself, such as steepness or water problems, not financial hardship of the owner or developer. The hardship cannot be just that the land might be more valuable in some other use.

Many readers may be familiar with cases where such standards did not seem to apply. Some studies have shown that zoning boards may grant variances for almost any cause. In many such cases, however, the neighboring residents or property owners do not object, or they are placated with modifications promised by the developer. Absence of opposition may be taken by the practical volunteers who are the ZBA to mean that the request is harmless to the neighbors and thus reasonable to grant (Rose 1983; Sussna 1961). Variances may be a source of petty corruption in some places, but looseness of application is not by itself evidence of misrule by the ZBA.

Zoning laws are often couched in terms of uses permitted by right and uses permitted by special permit. Many communities have general residential districts in which single-family homes are permitted as of right. Other uses, such as apartment houses, may be authorized by special permit only. In considering an application for a special permit, the ZBA or the planning commission decides whether the proposed use will have an undesirable impact on the neighborhood.

Special permits and variances may be issued with conditions attached to them. The board may, for example, authorize apartments only if there is screening, garage parking, or other conditions designed to mitigate their effects on the neighborhood. In this respect, the ZBA acts as a mediator between the developer and the neighbors.

The use of the special permit is growing. The logical culmination of the idea is the Planned Unit Development, in which the developer and community authorities (often the legislature rather than the ZBA) negotiate every feature of the project. While such procedures allow for more community discretion, they also permit more opportunity for the developer to strike deals and compromises with the community.

The other major administrative agency is the planning commission (or board). A major responsibility of the planning commission is to review subdivision proposals. The developer and the planning commission often go over the proposed plats in detail. Two considerations seem paramount in these negotiations: the existing neighbors are to be disturbed as little as possible, and the community is not to take over control of low-quality infrastructure (sewer pipes, water mains, streets) after the project is completed. The latter purpose is to avoid future fiscal costs.

The other role of the planning commission is making and changing the master plan, which in some states the local legislature must then accept or reject. As noted above, zoning often proceeds initially without any such plan; its main influence, then, is on rezonings. The master plan is useful in making the rezoning process more legitimate in the eyes of a judge. A rezoning that appears haphazard or involves only a few tracts may be condemned as *spot zoning*, the opposite of zoning "in accordance with a comprehensive plan" and thus invalid.

It is easy to exaggerate the influence of the ZBA and the planning commission. Major changes in land use can be accomplished only through amendments to the zoning law or by comprehensive rezoning of the community. These amount to changes in the local government's laws and thus must be enacted by elected officials.

This section shows that it is not appropriate to examine only the actions of a single board in studying the effects of land use controls. The ZBA and the planning commission have influence, and often the local legislature must act in a rezoning. There are many stages at which the community gets a chance to review new land uses. Proposals to change this with "one-stop" development permits overlook that multiple hurdles are regarded as an advantage by the beneficiaries of zoning. A community that is thoroughly opposed to a particular project has several brigades to defend its fortress.

2.8. CONCLUSION: ZONING AS A PROPERTY RIGHT

It is a truism in zoning law that no individual property owner or resident has a legal right to a particular zoning ordinance. Zoning is not a personal property right; it is a community property right. In this chapter I have limned the major aspects of this right. It is not the same as owning one's car or home or personal effects, but there are enough similarities to begin to draw some analogies.

No zoning law says that the community has a legal right to control undeveloped land or to prevent redevelopment. The very broad, vague, and difficult-to-monitor purposes of zoning nonetheless provide an effective arsenal to accomplish as much. No law allows the community to sell this property right in the way one might sell his house. It is clear, though, that zoning can be changed at the discretion of community authorities. Zoning laws nominally vest authority in elected officials and hope that they will pay attention to planners, but every zoning procedure guarantees a great deal of public participation, especially by neighbors. Thus even though resident homeowners have no vested right to zoning, they appear to have a reliable political entitlement to the status quo in land use.

The major difference between these public rights (zoning) and their closest private analog, private homeowners' associations, is that the latter do not include any property owners who have not agreed to the rules in advance (Ellickson 1982). Zoning is enacted by a local government, which usually has some involuntary members. The one-resident, one-vote rule and majority voting procedures open the possibility that public property rights might be expanded at the expense of politically effete members of the community. The constitutional constraints on this are explored in the next chapter.

NOTES

1. My generalizations about zoning law can be supported by the appropriate sections of the works noted below. That contrary examples can be found is not sufficiently remarkable in this diffuse field to warrant a footnote to every claim. Where there is more than the usual debate about some comment, or where the legal climate is in flux, I shall note the differences and refer the reader to secondary sources and sometimes a leading case. This procedure will apply for subsequent chapters as well.

The best one-volume source of information on the structure, laws, and administration of land use controls is Ellickson and Tarlock (1981). Ellickson and Tarlock have the unusual advantage among casebook authors of considerable economic literacy, and their materials and commentary reflect this. Their book is a strong complement to (I hope not a substitute for!) my own. Another fine one-volume work is Hagman (1971). A comprehensive, multivolume work on zoning law is by Norman Williams (1975), who undertook the Herculean task of reading the land use decisions of every state and federal appellate court. His work is kept up to date with annual supplements. Williams is somewhat skeptical of economic analysis (see his sec. 7.03) and thus may provide a useful contrast to Ellickson and Tarlock. A useful collection of essays on modern issues is *Management and Control of Growth*, published by the Urban Land Institute, in Washington, D.C., at various dates since 1975. Discussions of zoning in the context of statewide controls are Bosselman and Callies (1971) and Healy and Rosenberg (1979).

2. Pollard (1931, 20) indicates that protection of industry from homeowner suits was one of the reasons for adoption of zoning. Zoning thus avoids the moral hazard of moving to the nuisance (section 13.7). It is in this way similar to a rationale for the Occupational Safety and Health Act regulations described in Posner (1977, 247).

3. Judges have had no compunctions about the states' withdrawing local authority. "Local control" is a political cry, not a constitutional issue (Hess 1977).

4. U.S. Deptartment of Agriculture (1972) and U.S. Federal Insurance Administration (1976) summarize state enabling laws.

5. What is arbitrarily large is a matter of some debate. See Adelstein and Edelson (1976), Ellickson (1977, 475), and sections 4.1.1 and 15.3.2.

6. Tenants' power to use housing codes in this way was established in Javins v. First National Realty Corp., 428 F2d 1071 (1971), discussed by Rabin (1984).

7. One book that does construe these broader environmental controls as land use controls is Natural Resource Defense Council (1977). Although I resist their classification, it is significant that an organization that regularly opposes growth regards the national regulations as land use controls. This reflects the increased ability of parties in "neighbors' cases" (section 3.2) to intervene in land use decisions using rationales generally not available before the 1970s. See also Mandelker (1981).

8. Ellickson (1973, 720). This article is the major brief for substituting a rejuvenated law of nuisance for many (not all) zoning regulations.

9. The most vigorous and articulate advocate of substituting convenants for all local zoning is law professor Bernard Siegan (1972, 1976). His paradigm is Houston, Texas, which has no zoning but lots of covenants. See also section 11.1.

10. Vulcan Material Co. v. Griffeth, 114 SE 2d at 31 (1955), discussed (and dismissed as an aberration among the states) by Williams (1975, sec. 6.25).

11. Ellickson and Tarlock (1981, 884) cite two court cases in which the number of bedrooms in apartments was limited. The New Jersey courts disapproved of such limitation, but the Maryland courts upheld one.

12. On planning generally see Chapin and Kaiser (1979) and essays in So et al. (1979). The terms "externality" and "market failure," on which economists typically base their rationale for planning and zoning, are absent from both books. On the latter point, see section 6.7.

13. Political scientists who have investigated zoning controversies emphatically confirm the central role of local politics (Allensworth 1974; Danielson 1976; and Linowes and Allensworth 1973). Siegan (1976, 79) reports that "it has been variously estimated that municipal councils spend 60 to 90 percent of their time on zoning." Hagman (1971, 61) notes that desire for zoning has motivated several instances of municipal incorporations.

14. Leading advocates are Davidoff, Davidoff, and Gold (1970). A recounting of how Cleveland planners pursued advocacy goals is Krumholz (1982).

15. An interesting example of the influence of neighbors on zoning exceptions is documented in Tideman (1969). He found that in Cicero, Illinois, it typically took only three or four neighbors' objections at a zoning hearing to cause the authorities to turn down proposed commercial or industrial developments.

16. "Majoritarian" is a neologism that I first encountered in Ellickson (1977, 405) and Komesar (1978, 221). It differs from "democratic" and "majority-rule" by the implication that the majority is not constrained by constitutional or other checks on the political process. I shall take up the issue of political structure and zoning in more detail in chapter 10.

3.

The Role of the Courts:
The Limits of Zoning

Given the delicate and difficult task of local and regional planning, one might expect that the bulk of the professional literature on zoning would be written by city planners, engineers, and various social scientists. To the contrary, it seems that the majority of books on zoning are written by lawyers.[1] This is a hint that zoning is not really about planning: it is about legal entitlements.

I believe that the person who best understands the essential nature of zoning is a practicing lawyer with a client. The client may be a developer, a landowner, a municipality, a neighbor to a proposed development, or an outsider who wants to live in the community. In all cases, the question is, What entitlement do I have to the use of some property? If I am a developer, can I build on it? If a municipal official, how much or how little can I regulate it? If a neighbor, can I prevent it from being developed or alter it to protect my property's values? If an outsider, how can I get the community to rezone it to accommodate housing I might buy?

This chapter reviews some of the considerations that lawyers face in determining these entitlements. There are so many works on the subject by lawyers that it is hardly the comparative advantage of this book to add to them. Instead, I shall attempt to describe some of the more important judicial rules, especially their interpretation of constitutional protections, so as to point out their economic implications.

3.1. CONFLICT RESOLUTION: STATE AND FEDERAL COURTS

The previous chapter indicated that the powers granted to local governments by state zoning enabling acts are broad and vague.

This sets the stage for conflict between the local government and owners and users of the land that is regulated. Such conflicts may be resolved by the political process. If local officials offend enough owners and users of land, they may be voted out of office and replaced by those more sympathetic to the goals of their constituents.

Political resolution of conflicts is more likely in governmental units whose populations are large and heterogeneous. This is because the political process in such places will tend to balance the interests of all parties in a zoning dispute, and there is an opportunity to express the strength of one's preferences. I shall elaborate on this theme in chapter 10, but for now it will do to indicate that most central city jurisdictions are large and heterogeneous, while most suburban jurisdictions are smaller and more homogeneous. Thus suburbs and small towns are less likely to achieve an internal political resolution of land use disputes that balances the interests of current residents and landowner-developers, the latter acting in response to outsiders' demands.

The other method of conflict resolution is to go to court. The judicial system ultimately defines the limits of the police power. In contrast to the statutory authority for zoning, however, there is considerable variation among the states as to what the limits of community power should be. Some generalizations may be safely made, but the attitudes of the judges vary not just from state to state but also over periods of time (often with no obvious trend) and occasionally from court to court within a state (Williams 1975, chap. 2; 1982).

One reason for the variation from state to state is the reluctance of the U.S. Supreme Court (and consequently the federal courts in general) to become involved in local land use issues. Between the landmark *Euclid* case in 1926 (discussed in section 3.4) and 1974, the Supreme Court issued only a handful of decisions pertaining to zoning.[2]

Since 1974, however, the Supreme Court has stepped into zoning again. Following, in chronological order, are some of the more important cases:

1. Village of Belle Terre v. Boraas, 416 U.S. 1 (1974), ruled that a Long Island suburb could regulate home occupancy by family relationship, effectively excluding rental of single-family homes to college students.

2. Warth v. Selden, 422 U.S. 490 (1975), denied standing in federal courts to persons outside a Rochester, New York, suburb who sought to challenge its "exclusionary" zoning.

3. City of Eastlake v. Forest City Enterprises, 426 U.S. 668 (1976), upheld a Cleveland suburb's practice of requiring referenda for rezonings, reversing the Ohio Supreme Court.

4. Young v. American Mini Theaters, 427 U.S. 50 (1976), upheld Detroit's use of zoning to limit concentration of pornographic movie houses.

5. Village of Arlington Heights v. Metropolitan Housing Development Corp., 429 U.S. 252 (1977), refused to find that a Chicago suburb's denial of a low-income housing project violated Fourteenth Amendment rights.

6. Penn Central Transportation Co. v. City of New York, 438 U.S. 104 (1978), held that the city's designation of Grand Central Terminal as a historic landmark, which prevented substantial redevelopment on its site, was not a taking of property.

7. Agins v. Tiburon, 447 U.S. 255 (1980), refused to overturn a California court decison that payment of damages for excessive lot size regulations in a Marin County community was never an appropriate remedy. (Some doubt on the U.S. Court's direction was subsequently raised in San Diego Gas and Electric v. City of San Diego, 450 U.S. 621 (1981), where a minority that might be a future majority argued that compensation was the appropriate remedy for excessively burdensome regulations [section 9.7].)

The thread that holds these cases together is that the Court did not overturn local-government decisions. Despite the renewed attention to zoning by the Court in the 1970s, the message remains the same as it has been since *Euclid*: the Court will seldom interfere with local-government decisions on zoning and related land use controls.

A note on the relation of the U.S. Supreme Court to the state courts may be in order. State courts apply both federal and state constitutional provisions, but U.S. constitutional doctrine, as interpreted by the U.S. Supreme Court, is binding on the states. However, a state may apply its constitutional provisions more strictly (or differently) than the federal courts would apply analogous provisions of the U.S. Constitution unless the state courts are specifically overruled by the federal courts. Thus the holding in *Belle Terre* is not necessarily binding on the states, and several state courts have ruled that zoning by family relationship is not constitutional (e.g., State v. Baker, 405 A.2d 388 [N.J. 1979]). Sager (1978) worried that the *Eastlake* decision overruled the Ohio Supreme Court and would become a national rule. Many state courts had ruled against such referenda.

3.2. NEIGHBORS' CASES

Economists tend to think of only one kind of court case in zoning conflicts: when landowner-developers sue community authorities for refusal to accommodate their proposals. These are known in the zoning literature as *developers' cases*. There is, however, another type of suit called the *neighbors' case*. This distinction, drawn most clearly by Norman Williams (1975, sec. 2.01), is crucial to understanding zoning cases. In neighbors' cases, the zoning authorities are sued for having allowed some development that residents near the project believe will be detrimental to their interests. Neighbors may thus sue over variances, special permits, or rezonings for property near their own.

The existence of neighbors' cases draws attention to the facts that zoning is the exercise of governmental authority and that a government's actions may often displease at least some of its constituents. Within most communities, protection of neighbors from unfavorable decisions by zoning authorities is offered by the political process and the procedural rights of neighbors in zoning decisions (sections 2.6 and 2.7). Perhaps as a result, most neighbors' cases in the past did not succeed unless there was some violation of procedures. The remedy in such cases is simply to redo the proceedings.

The rule that "neighbors usually lose" has a hollow ring to it these days, not because of changes in the legal status of neighbors, but because the number of procedures that local authorities must go through has increased greatly since 1970. Increased procedures have been occasioned by both statute and judge-made law.

Premier among new statutory procedures is the Environmental Impact Statement (EIS). Although an EIS is required at the federal level only for government projects (a list of which is longer than one might think, since it includes projects even partially financed or licensed by the government), several states require them for almost any local project. The cost of the EIS and the delay from subsequent administrative and legal challenges give neighbors a powerful entitlement.

The judge-made cause for the rise of neighbors' power is that a few courts have begun to attach less deference to local legislatures as representatives of a "coequal" branch of government. For example, local changes in zoning may be viewed as a "quasi-judicial" function and thus put to closer scrutiny and a more exacting procedural standard by appellate courts.[3] By forcing the community authorities to go through more elaborate and costly

procedures and increasing the number of points where the neighbors' arguments against the rezoning may be heard, the neighbors
can wear down the authorities and delay development. In developers' cases, on the other hand, plaintiffs usually are dissatisfied
with current zoning and seek an exception to allow a more intensive use. More elaborate procedures and judicial review are for
them usually a cost rather than a benefit.

Even if the developer succeeds in obtaining a decision that
overturns the local authorities' refusal to rezone his property, in
very few states will the court's remedy be an order to rezone the
plaintiff's property. Instead, the community may be ordered just
to redo the proceedings. The delay and uncertainty occasioned by
this is costly to the developer but works to the general benefit of
neighbors who oppose the project.

3.3. THE CONSTITUTIONAL ISSUES

3.3.1. The Three Clauses

Although many zoning cases involve statutory law, I believe
that the significant challenges to zoning laws, especially in developers' cases, raise constitutional claims. Statute law is less important because the state legislature can change it. For instance,
when courts find that a local practice is beyond the scope of the
enabling legislation (an adventuresome practice, indeed, given the
breadth of most enabling acts), the legislature may change the act
to be more accommodating to the community.

There are three constitutional clauses on which litigation is
based: (1) due process, (2) equal protection, and (3) takings or
just compensation (the last is sometimes called the eminent domain clause). The Fourteenth Amendment concludes, "Nor shall
any State deprive any person of life, liberty or property, without
due process of law; nor deny to any person within its jurisdiction
the equal protection of the laws." (Note that this applies to the
states and hence to all local governments, which are creatures of
the states.) The Fourteenth Amendment has also been construed
to apply the Fifth Amendment to the states. The Fifth Amendment
concludes, "Nor shall private property be taken for public use,
without just compensation."

All state constitutions but one (North Carolina's) have a taking
clause similar to the Fifth Amendment's, and most also have due
process and equal protection clauses. Thus a developer who wants

to sue on any of these grounds may choose state or federal courts. States may interpret their clauses differently from the federal courts in some instances. This is especially important in zoning because of the hands-off attitude of the federal judiciary.

The nature of zoning issues will be easier to understand if we distinguish among the three clauses. The problem in distinguishing one clause from the other is that plaintiffs often invoke them simultaneously. Appellate courts are not always careful to say which clause (or, sometimes, which constitution) they are basing their decision on. Part of this may be inevitable, since the clauses are closely related both in text and in purpose. I shall nonetheless try to differentiate them below. The following sections will then examine each clause individually.

Due process.   Legal treatment of due process is divided into two parts: procedural due process and substantive due process. The first asks whether the legislative or administrative body in question followed the rules in processing the claim of the plaintiff. In zoning cases, this means inquiring whether appropriate notice was given, whether hearings were held, and whether permits were issued on schedule. Substantive due process, on the other hand, asks whether the rules themselves are reasonable. A developer challenging the zoning of his land for, say, farmland only may argue that the law itself is not reasonably related to the purposes of the police power of the community. This is a substantive question.

Equal protection.   Equal protection implies, at minimum, that the law applies impersonally to everyone. Laws may classify by situation but not by name. This affords some protection of landowners from arbitrary treatment. The community cannot allow Jones to build in a district in which it has denied permission to Smith, assuming that both had planned to erect similar structures under similar conditions. But it does not protect Smith from being treated differently from Jones if they own property in different zoning districts, provided that the community can withstand Smith's due process charge that it drew the district lines arbitrarily and capriciously. A law might pass muster on due process grounds but still be a denial of equal protection. It could involve a legitimate public purpose but be applied unequally.

The more recent use of the equal protection clause is to argue that outsiders who are excluded by a zoning ordinance are being treated unequally. This is an outgrowth of the judicial activism in the use of the equal protection clause in the 1960s. As we shall see, a few states, most notably New Jersey, have used this doctrine

in all but name to attempt to reduce barriers to low-income housing.[4] (The federal courts have rejected it, but they have not forbidden the states to accept such arguments.) The claim is that
local ordinances restricting such housing are a denial of equal
protection to poor outsiders, even though they may provide public
benefits to insiders.

Takings.   The taking clause requires that the government pay
for the resources that it takes for public use. The easy application
is land acquisition for a public road or structure. Even though the
project meets the due process criterion that it is reasonably related
to a public purpose, the agency cannot simply expropriate the
land. The purpose of this rule seems to have been to prevent the
government from burdening particular individuals.

Applied to zoning, a taking might be found if a regulation so
restricted the use of one's property that it might be deemed analogous to expropriation. The demarcation of this point will occupy
us at some length. For now, it will suffice to note that no legal
authority argues that a taking must always be found if a regulation
reduces property values by some amount. In practice, substantial
decreases in property values due to zoning laws are routinely
upheld without compensation.

3.3.2. Takings Compared with Equal Protection and Due Process

The taking clause differs from equal protection in two respects:
First, a taking may be found even though the law does not seem
to have been the result of any invidious distinction among individuals or distinct classes of persons (e.g., by race or sex). Second,
a violation of equal protection would always require that the ordinance be suspended; a finding that an ordinance was a taking
would allow the government to continue to do it if it was willing
to pay just compensation.

Due process is preliminary to a taking. In principle, judges ask
first whether a law meets due process criteria; if it does not, the
community is told to get rid of or modify the law, and no inquiry
into a taking is necessary. But a law might pass muster on due
process grounds but still be ruled a taking. A court could rule that
an ordinance that zoned an area for "open space" was reasonably
connected to police power purposes, but nonetheless the burden
on landowners of not being able to develop at all would be great
enough to constitute a taking, for which they would have to be
compensated.

There are also differences in remedies. A court that finds a
violation of due process always requires that the community repeal

its law or redo it using the right procedures. Violation of the taking clause may require only that the community pay damages, though a community unwilling to pay would then have to rescind its ordinance.

3.3.3. The First Amendment

The First Amendment is sometimes invoked in controversies involving zoning of movie theaters, bookstores, churches, and outdoor signs. There are also some interesting cases involving political protests that ran afoul of zoning laws. Land use seems to be an area where the Supreme Court is willing to allow more latitude for governmental regulation of speech and other protected categories than would be allowed under more direct regulation. Communities cannot ban pornographic bookstores, but they can regulate their location to a significant degree. These issues are not, in any event, at the center of most zoning controversies.

3.4. DUE PROCESS: EUCLIDIAN ZONING AND ITS IMPLICATIONS

Due process is the most frequently used of the constitutional grounds for zoning review. I have already described the major trend in procedural due process cases in section 3.2. New statutes and some court decisions have increased judicial scrutiny of local decisions. This section will deal with substantive due process.

3.4.1. Euclidian Zoning

The major substantive due process case, which remains the leading zoning case, is Euclid v. Ambler, 272 U.S. 365, decided by the Supreme Court in 1926. The case is analyzed in every legal treatise on zoning, so we shall not examine it too closely.[5] The facts of the case do provide a convenient description of the U.S. judicial approach to zoning that continues today.

Euclid is an independent suburb of Cleveland, about ten miles from its central business district. In the early 1920s the town was still a largely undeveloped residential community. During this time it adopted its first zoning ordinance, based largely on the New York City ordinance of 1916. (Though proponents of zoning conceived of it as regulating city land use, it quickly spread to the suburbs,[6] and Euclid was not unusual.) This ordinance zoned an important part of the property owned by the Ambler Realty Company for residential use only. Ambler had purchased the property, which was situated between a railroad and a major thoroughfare, in the expectation of selling it for industrial use. The company argued—and its argument was not seriously contested—that zoning exclusively for residential use substantially reduced the value of its property. Ambler asked that the entire ordinance be invalidated as a violation of due process. (A taking was also alleged, but Ambler sought no damages, and the Court did not reach the issue in its opinion.)

The U.S. Supreme Court reversed the federal district court, apparently disagreeing with Judge Westenhaver's appraisal that "the result to be accomplished [by Euclid's law] is to classify the population and segregate them according to their income or situation in life."[7] Drawing analogies to nuisance law and noting the growing acceptance of zoning by state courts, the Court ruled that zoning was a legitimate exercise of the police power—it did not violate due process—so long as it had some "reasonable relation" to the promotion of the purposes mentioned in the SZEA, "health, safety, morals, and general welfare" (section 2.4).

3.4.2. Reasonable Relation and Efficiency

The "reasonable relation" criterion is one focus of substantive due process. Some writers attempt to differentiate due process from takings by saying that takings are about fairness and due process is about efficiency (Ellickson and Tarlock 1981, 62–64). One might then conclude that reasonable relation would require that the ordinance in question meet some notion of benefit-cost analysis. (This would imply not the Pareto criterion, unless a taking was subsequently found, but the Kaldor-Hicks principle that those who benefit *could* compensate those on whom the costs fall.)

My own reading of zoning decisions, however, suggests that the efficiency interpretation of the due process criterion is strained. Few decisions manifest even the most casual attention to benefit-cost principles. Reasonable relation seems to mean that zoning cannot be completely arbitrary, advancing no recognizable public purpose. But it does not require that zoning be shown to be the best means of accomplishing the public purpose or that the public benefit exceeded private loss. (Section 8.6 contains some reasons for the courts' reluctance to do this.) If one had to characterize the reasonableness standard in economic terms, I would call it "benefit-" analysis, that is, benefits without the costs.

However, this may be extreme. In practice, the due process rule is bound up with the taking criterion. Most cases rule that owners must not be deprived of *all* income from their land, so *some* cost must be accounted for in the public's calculus. This inhibits some of the broader zoning arrangements. A community cannot ordinarily provide for preservation of open spaces just by zoning vacant land for that purpose, though there are some instances of this being upheld.[8]

3.4.3. Public Purposes

The other important due process check on zoning is the requirement that it be used to promote some legitimate public purpose. The definition of a legitimate purpose is, it seems, very much up to the court trying the case. Enabling legislation is of relatively little help here, since it is so broad. The increased attention to planning rationales to determine community intentions is one manifestation of the concern about purposes. But it is also clear that the scope of "public purpose" has been expanded greatly over the years. A passage (for the majority) by Justice William O. Douglas in a 1954 eminent domain case is frequently quoted: "The concept of the public welfare is broad and inclusive . . . the values it represents are spiritual as well as physical, aesthetic as well as monetary. It is within the power of the legislature to determine that the community should be beautiful as well as healthy, spacious as well as clean, well-balanced as well as carefully patrolled."[9]

An example of the changing view of the courts towards the extent of public purpose is their attitude towards aesthetics. Earlier in this century, most courts were hostile to zoning whose only apparent purpose was improvement of aesthetic conditions. This was particularly evident in cases involving limitations on billboards, and even sympathetic judges had to search for some other rationale to uphold them. Nowadays aesthetic considerations are usually accepted as legitimate, and arguments proceed on whether the standards are reasonable, not on whether they should be a valid point for regulation.

Recognition of aesthetics as a legitimate public interest nonetheless leaves unresolved whose taste shall prevail. The New York City Landmarks Preservation Commission designated a church as a landmark against the wishes of the congregation, who wished to tear it down and sell the property. The commission cited the church's exterior as an example of "scientific eclecticism," which the church's minister translated as "architectural mishmash" not worthy of preservation (*New York Times* 2 March 1982, 39).

3.4.4. Burden of Proof

A significant result of judicial recognition of zoning is the "presumption of validity." This means that the community authorities need not bear the burden of proof in zoning cases brought either by developers or by neighbors. If developers want to challenge some action by the authorities—say, a rezoning of land from commercial to residential—they must prove that the rezoning is unreasonable. The benefit of any doubt is given to the community. This makes zoning much easier to administer, but it also enables the community to push the margins of restrictiveness further than it would if it had to make the case to justify them. With the lower perceived return on mounting an expensive court case, developers are more likely to tolerate costly restrictions on the use of their land.

3.4.5. Trends

The foregoing judge-made laws have been an important force enabling communities to prevail in developers' cases. The rules, however, are subject to exceptions by both time and place. Judges, especially those in lower state courts, were more sympathetic to landowners' and developers' interests in earlier times than they are today. This concern with the rights of landowners continued well after the *Euclid* decision in many states. The spread of judicial precedent is not instantaneous, especially when judges do not like it.

This has implications for economic studies of zoning. The pattern of land use in older communities was established either before zoning or when communities exercised their power very gingerly. Only since perhaps the 1950s could communities impose substantial restrictions without fear of hostility in the courts.

There are also variations among the states today. On occasion a court will overturn some local restrictions on the grounds (usually implied) that the loss of the landowner is too great in relation to the benefit to the community. Illinois courts often make use of this argument. California represents the opposite extreme, for its courts pay little attention to landowner complaints. National studies of zoning should be aware of these differences.

3.5. TAKING LESSONS FROM *PENNSYLVANIA COAL*

It seems to be a requirement for law journal articles on takings to begin by admitting that the issue is tangled, confused, inconsistent, and intractable. For every legal rule for determining a taking inferred from leading cases, one can find numerous examples that seem to defy it, often in the same court of law. I shall devote chapters 8 and 9 to showing what economic analysis can do to unravel the taking conundrum. The purpose of this section is to give an overview of the issue by examining the leading case in which the taking clause was invoked.

3.5.1. Holmes and Brandeis on Taking Theory

The case is Pennsylvania Coal v. Mahon, 260 U.S. 393 (1922). It appears to be a leading case not so much because its holding is followed closely but because the opinion by Holmes and the dissent by Brandeis articulated the issues so well.

Ownership of surface and mineral rights in Pennsylvania could, by statute, be divorced in two ways. The surface owner could have the right of support from the mine (by leaving timbers or pillars of unmined coal in place), assuring that when coal was mined, land above would not subside. Alternatively, the surface owner could surrender his right to such support and take his chances when the coal beneath was removed. Mr. and Mrs. Mahon purchased their home subject to the latter disability in their deed. (Presumably this made it less expensive than otherwise.)

Pennsylvania subsequently passed a law, the Kohler Act, effectively eliminating the second kind of right in most urban and built-up areas. Its purpose was to protect these areas from subsidence. The Mahons attempted to force Pennsylvania Coal Company, which owned mineral rights beneath their house, to provide support to prevent subsidence of their land. They argued that this was required under the new law, even though it was contrary to their deed. The company argued that the Kohler Act was invalid because it took their property without just compensation. The U.S. Supreme Court agreed with the coal company and reversed the Pennsylvania Supreme Court, which had upheld the Kohler Act and ruled for the Mahons.

Justice Holmes's opinion provides numerous insights into the taking issue. First, the standard for a taking is imprecise and varies by case: "The general rule at least is that while property may be regulated to a certain extent, if regulation goes too far it will be

recognized as a taking" (p. 415). How far is too far? The clues
are not definitive. The extent of the diminution of value caused
by the regulation is one test. But as Brandeis pointed out in dissent, the separability of property rights makes this problematic.
If the coal company had owned surface as well as mining rights,
would the regulation have substantially reduced the combined
value of the surface and mining rights?

One can point to cases before and after *Pennsylvania Coal* in
which nearly complete elimination of property value was upheld
by the same court. One case was Hadecheck v. Sebastian, 239
U.S. 394 (1915), in which the expanding city of Los Angeles zoned
an area containing a preexisting brick factory for residential use
and then ordered the immediate discontinuance of the factory,
without compensation. The ordinance was upheld.

Another clue given by Holmes was "average reciprocity of advantage" (p. 415). He distinguished *Pennsylvania Coal* from another mining case in which coal pillars had to be left in place to
prevent dangers in other mines. Such a regulation would redound
to the general benefit of all mining companies, even though it
might be to the profit of one not to have it.

Holmes indicated that the taking issue hinges on fairness considerations. His remarks about encroachment on private property
suggest this. More explicitly, he notes that "it is not plain that a
man's misfortunes or necessities will justify his shifting the damages to his neighbor's shoulders" (p. 416). Thus the taking issue
is distinguished from due process considerations, where the reasonableness of the law with respect to some public purpose is at
issue: "We assume, of course, that the statute was passed upon
the conviction that an exigency exists that would warrant the exercise of eminent domain. But the question at bottom is upon
whom the loss of the changes desired should fall" (p. 416).[10]

Despite this nice distinction, due process considerations do seem
to have crept into the evaluation of a taking. Holmes noted that
in the case presented, the harm dealt with was a private one,
falling solely on the Mahons and not on the public, and that simple
notice of intent to mine would serve to preserve public safety. In
his dissent Brandeis seized upon this, saying that the public harm
might be very great and that the Court should defer to the state
legislature and state courts in such matters. Brandeis went on to
argue that reciprocity of advantage might be an acceptable criterion when legislation involved conferring benefits upon property
but not when it involved preventing harms.[11]

3.5.2. Taking Law in Practice

I shall attempt to fuse these considerations into what I hope is a coherent view of the taking issue in chapter 8. This section concludes with a few generalizations about the practical, existing approaches to the taking issue.

1. Land and immovable natural resources are more likely to raise the taking issue and judicial scrutiny than are other types of assets. The literature is filled with mines and quarries and zoning regulations. Movable assets like stills and handguns seem to receive less protection.

2. Government trespass or appropriation of title almost always will be ruled a taking. A 1982 U.S. Supreme Court decision (Loretto v. Teleprompter, 458 U.S. 419) ruled that a law requiring the landlord to permit the trivial (perhaps even beneficial) invasion of a TV cable in apartment buildings was a taking. The same court has upheld rent controls that impose a great and obvious burden on building owners.

3. Courts seldom award damages, perhaps because plaintiffs seldom ask for them. The usual remedy for a taking is an injunction against the offending agency, despite the explicit constitutional authorization of "just compensation." (But see the *San Diego Gas* case cited in section 3.1.)

4. The more noxious or dangerous the use within its neighborhood context, the less judicial protection it seems to receive. Brandeis seems to have carried the day here.

5. Financial loss by the landowner must be very large for a regulation to be declared a taking on this ground alone. The word *confiscatory* crops up again and again in the cases. Regulations are usually upheld unless they leave the owner with "no reasonable use" of his property.

6. Despite the supposed differences among takings, due process, and equal protection, a law that fails on one is likely to fail on the others as well. Epstein (1982, 360) offers a reason for this: "In my view, they [the equal protection and due process clauses] are, and can be shown to be, variations on the deeper eminent domain questions." Pat distinctions may not be reliable.

3.6. EQUAL PROTECTION: INSIDERS AND OUTSIDERS

Equal protection of the laws means that zoning cannot be applied in a discriminatory fashion. The traditional problem is possible unequal treatment of landowners and, to a lesser extent, neighbors within the community. The new equal protection involves claims by people outside the community that the zoning law treats them unfairly.

3.6.1. Equal Protection within the Community

Within established zoning districts, zoning laws must treat landowner A the same as landowner B. The problem this sometimes raises is that some nonconforming uses may be desirable, while a lot of them may be undesirable. Suppose that within an isolated residential zone someone proposes to convert a house into a local convenience store that would serve the neighborhood. Suppose also that the developer satisfies immediate neighbors that such a development will not harm them. The zoning authorities may still reject such a proposal on the grounds that someone else may want to do the same thing. The second store may not be welcome, yet its developer might claim a denial of equal protection if he is denied permission.

In fact, such claims do not seem to have inhibited minor developments. More problematic is the method of satisfying immediate neighbors. The absence of specific devices to compensate neighbors for localized nuisance is a defect of zoning that has led to proposals, such as Ellickson's (1973), that would resurrect nuisance law to deal with such cases.

Equal protection comes up more often when community authorities adopt spot zoning or "floating zones." These and similar devices allow developers to make an offer to community authorities to allow some use anywhere within largely undeveloped zones. Until recently, most courts were inclined to rule against such flexible arrangements.

Although judges often ruled against them on the grounds that they were not authorized by the enabling statute (especially that they were not "in accordance with a comprehensive plan"), the fears expressed about their use related to equal protection concerns: neighbors did not know what to expect from zoning, and developers might be treated differently by community authorities in such cases. Possibilities for unequal treatment seemed restricted if district lines appeared on the map before a use was proposed. Lines at least afforded the basis of attack by citizens, even though the burden of proof that they were arbitrary and capricious fell on the plaintiff and could rarely be sustained.

The change in judicial concern for lines has occurred slowly, but there is growing acceptance of regulations that are tantamount to floating zones, which invite the developer to make an offer to authorities. State legislative authorization of these non-Euclidean approaches under new names like Planned Unit Development seems to assuage the courts' concern. Increased attention to master plans and other verbal, rather than cartographic, indications of zoning intentions has probably helped the courts to accept what they once condemned as the antithesis of a comprehensive plan.

3.6.2. Outsiders and Equal Protection

Whose interests are the public interest in local zoning laws? The *Euclid* court decided that they were the interests of those currently residing in the municipality. (The opinion did hedge: "It is not meant by this, however, to exclude the possibility of cases where the general public interest would so far outweigh the interest of the municipality that the municipality would not be allowed to stand in the way" [272 U.S. 390]). It remains so to this day, in fact if not always in law, in most states.

The equal protection arguments of the civil rights movement spilled inevitably into zoning litigation. The equal protection doctrines set certain groups or interests apart as "suspect classifications" that invoked special judicial scrutiny. This opened up a new area of litigation. The new plaintiffs were people outside the community, not necessarily the traditional developer (though they were often allies in this effort). They argued that the community's laws effectively excluded them on the basis of race, sex, or national origin or infringed upon some specially protected right. The equal protection provisions of the Constitution would then be invoked to invalidate the restrictions. Once a suspect classification was shown, the community would have to show a compelling state interest in maintaining its laws. The burden of proof was shifted then to the community, and in practice it could seldom be met.

The equal protection argument in these cases was buttressed by national and sometimes state legislation such as the civil rights acts. The attack on exclusionary zoning received the support of many groups representing the interests of blacks, low-income people, and civil rights advocates generally.

The movement has been stymied in the federal courts. In Warth v. Selden, 422 U.S. 490 (1974), a motley group of plaintiffs alleged damage by the zoning ordinance of Penfield, New York, a suburb of Rochester. They were denied standing to sue because the Supreme Court decided that they could not show damages specific to themselves. In Village of Arlington Heights v. Metropolitan Housing Corp., 429 U.S. 252 (1976), the court declined to rule that the denial of a rezoning for a low-income housing project in an all-white Chicago suburb was invalid merely because the ordinance had the effect of excluding many blacks from the community. To many observers, the case effectively closed off the use of the Fourteenth Amendment as a basis for attacking exclusionary zoning. Its ruling that the plaintiffs had failed to show racially discriminatory *intent* on the part of village authorities set up a nearly impossible barrier to surmount for this type of litigation. (A subsequent suit based on federal civil rights legislation was successful in inducing the community to accept the housing project.)

The Supreme Court ruled in other cases that housing is not a fundamental right, and it has backed away from declaring income a suspect classification on the same order as race or national origin. In brief, the court decided to maintain its traditional noninterventionist attitude towards local zoning decisions.

A few state courts, most notably New Jersey, have not been so reticent. The New Jersey courts have accepted, on state constitutional and legal grounds, nearly every argument that the federal courts have rejected or avoided.[12] The landmark case is Southern Burlington County NAACP v. Mount Laurel, 336 A.2d 713 (1975). This experiment in judicial policy making is still going on, but it is sufficiently instructive to deserve substantial treatment in chapter 15, after we have developed the themes of this book. Briefly, the New Jersey Court found that the township of Mount Laurel, a suburb of Philadelphia, was guilty of exclusionary zoning, to the detriment of outsiders in general and the poor in particular. It ordered the community to rezone to accommodate its "fair share" of the regional housing needs of all segments of society.

Mount Laurel did not eagerly comply with the court's order, and the New Jersey Supreme Court recently decided to take extraordinary measures to get it and other communities to comply. More important, however, is that most other state courts have not followed New Jersey's lead in this matter. *Mount Laurel* is noted widely and approvingly, but in terms of altering zoning practices, it has not yet become, as Professor Norman Williams proclaimed, "the new *Euclid*" for residential housing types.[13]

3.7. SUMMARY AND CONCLUSION

Zoning is a collective property right, vested in community authorities. People who do not like a particular zoning decision may use the political process to defeat it. They may also use the courts. Neighbors to a site that is rezoned have no legal rights to prevent it, but their political influence and the use of procedural delays may accomplish as much.

Developers are protected from regulatory expropriation by provisions in the U.S. and state constitutions involving due process of law, taking without just compensation, and, to a lesser extent, equal protection of the laws. These do not guarantee benefit-cost analysis of regulations, nor do they protect landowners from any but the most extreme regulations. As a collective property right, zoning can impinge on private property to a substantial degree.

The more recent use of the equal protection clause has to do with the status of "third parties" to zoning controversies. The traditional zoning cases involve either neighbors or developers against the local government or its agencies. However, there is obviously another party at interest: the people who might live, work, or shop in the community if the zoning laws permitted the development to occur. To an economist, it may seem peculiar to want to give such parties standing. This is because the interests of these parties are what motivates the developer. A developer would not want to build houses, factories, or stores if there were not a very strong possibility that someone would want to live in the houses, work in the factories, and shop at the stores. Ordinarily, we would expect developers' desire for profit to serve these demands.

It has occurred to many people that these demands are not especially well served. This is not necessarily because of a failure of the profit motive on the part of developers but because of its limitation by communities. Developers' entitlements have been curtailed by zoning, and this makes it difficult, if not impossible, for them to reacquire the right to build in a community. This theme will be extended in the next chapter.

NOTES

1. For sources, see chap. 2, n. 1. Current issues are covered in the monthly periodical, *Land Use Law and Zoning Digest*. General developments are chronicled in the American Planning Association's *Land Use Controls Annual*. Law reviews print occasional student surveys of the field. An excellent one is [*Harvard Law Rev.*] (1978).

2. Soon after the *Euclid* case, the Court ruled that a zoning boundary was drawn arbitrarily and held the ordinance invalid. Nectow v. Cambridge, 277 U.S. 183 (1928), encouraged the belief that the Court would supervise

zoning very closely. But the other shoe never dropped; the Court has not accepted another case like it.

3. The leading case is Fasano v. Board of Commissioners of Washington County, 264 Or. 574, 507 P.2d 23 (1973). The case has been influential in other states, but many have rejected it. A critique and reformulation of *Fasano* is Rose (1983).

4. This is best recounted approvingly by Sager (1969) and skeptically by Michelman (1969). A post-mortem of the Supreme Court's refusal to extend the "new equal protection" to zoning issues is Sager (1978).

5. An entertaining social history is Toll (1969, chaps. 8 and 9). Tarlock (1982) reviews Alfred Bettman's influential amicus brief. A succinct constitutional review that puts the *Euclid* case in the context of earlier and subsequent decisions is Johnson (1955).

6. The legal pioneer in zoning, Edward Basset, observed that "townships have been almost as active as cities in adopting zoning ordinances" (1936, 48).

7. Ambler v. Euclid, 297 F. 307 (1924). Williams (1975, sec. 83.03) denigrates Westenhaver's seeming solicitude for the poor by pointing out that elsewhere in the opinion the judge alluded to the "fact" that blacks lowered neighboring property values. This is not convincing, since Westenhaver seemed to be repeating, without approval, the "facts" accepted by social scientists of his day (e.g., McMichael and Bingham 1923, 181).

8. As I shall discuss in the next chapter, these instances arise mainly where the government has cloaked its "open space" zoning under an acceptable category, such as agricultural land or wetlands. The leading case of recent years is Just v. Marinette County, 201 N.W. 2d 761 (1972), upholding a Wisconsin landowner's conviction for unauthorized construction near wetlands.

9. Berman v. Parker, 348 U.S. 26 (1954). In case there was any doubt, Justice Douglas took the opportunity to apply similar language to a zoning case, Village of Belle Terre v. Borass, 416 U.S. 1 (1974). Because *Belle Terre* involved claims of civil liberties (college students were excluded from renting homes in the village because they were not a "family" under its ordinance) against claims of (very local) environmental protection, both of which Justice Douglas championed, the case was jokingly referred to in legal circles as "Douglas v. Douglas."

10. In a later case, the Court, in an opinion by Hugo Black, was more explicit that "the Fifth Amendment's guarantee [is] designed to bar Government from forcing some people alone to bear public burdens which, in all fairness and justice, should be borne by the public as a whole" (Armstrong v. United States, 364 U.S. 40 at 49 [1960]).

11. In chapter 8 I adopt the principle that regulations preventing harms— read as "subnormal behavior"—should not require compensation. Thus the question is whether subsidence is subnormal behavior (the pun is unavoidable). That in turn depends on how bad the subsidence is. There is a suggestion in the arguments of the case that new mining technology made subsidence a much more serious problem over the years, since it became possible

to safely mine the coal pillars which had previously prevented cave-ins. That coal mining subsidence can cause drastic problems years later is amply demonstrated by the experience of Rock Springs, Wyoming, much of which is literally falling into its labyrinth of old coal mines. One estimate of the cost of rectifying the problem was put at $300 million (*New York Times*, 27 April 1983, A18).

12. The New Jersey Court did not base its decision on the equal protection clause of the state or federal constitution, apparently to avoid reversal by the federal courts. Its entire argument, however, is parallel to the "new equal protection" as described by Sager (1969; 1978) and Lamb and Lustig (1979).

13. Williams (1975 [1980 suppl., sec. 66.13a]). Insights into the *Mount Laurel* decision may be had by studying Williams's book. He dedicated his treatise to, among others, the now retired Justice Frederick Hall, who wrote the first *Mount Laurel* opinion. Justice Hall in turn frequently quoted Williams in his opinions. The latest *Mount Laurel* opinion, 456 A.2d 390, 413 (1983), concedes that other courts have yet to implement the fair share requirement that is the lynchpin of New Jersey's remedy.

4.

Zoning Law in Practice

The purpose of this chapter is to delineate the extent to which communities can control land use in actual practice. After wading through two chapters on administrative structure and legal rules, the reader may wonder why a separate chapter on "actual practice" is necessary. It is offered because zoning practice can differ substantially from what the law says.[1] This does not necessarily imply illegality. It is more often the result of the ability to obtain the same result by many different means.

The chapter is organized around five questions that I believe are most important in understanding zoning issues: (1) To what extent can a community require new development to finance municipal services? (2) How much social and economic segregation can be accomplished? (3) How well can a community control changes in its environment, particularly those resulting from non-residential use? (4) How effectively can the community control the density of residential development and total population? (5) To what extent is it possible for the community to exchange its control over land use for other goods?

The answers to these questions affect not only our perceptions of the desirability of zoning but also the way that zoning can be characterized in various economic models. I hope that this discussion will nudge economists and other analysts to examine the realism of their working assumptions about land use laws.

4.1. FINANCING MUNICIPAL SERVICES

4.1.1. Capital Costs and Subdivision Regulation

It is well settled that subdivision regulations can be used to ensure that new residential development does not impose substantial *capital* costs on the community. This means at least that new sewers, water mains, and roads that serve the development will be built by the developer or financed by him through subdivision exactions. In many cases, developers may also have to contribute land for building new schools and parks, especially if the subdivision is large; however, developers can seldom be required to pay for construction of the schools themselves (Ellickson and Tarlock 1981, chap. 5A; Hagman 1971, 99, 253; Williams 1975, chap. 156).

The major controversy in subdivision regulation is how to assign the costs occasioned by a new development.[2] Two problems must be distinguished.

1. If capital improvements benefit the subdivision alone, it is efficient for developers or subsequent residents to face the costs directly. Subdivision exactions are one way to do it. The problem here is that previous developments' infrastructure may have been financed by municipal bonds, not subdivision exactions, and these bonds are paid off through general local property taxes. Thus new residents end up paying for other people's infrastructure through property taxes and then paying for their own infrastructure through exactions. This seems unfair, but it may be necessary to promote location efficiency when there are rising costs (section 15.3.2).

2. The other case is where the new subdivision occasions new capital costs for the entire community—say, a new water system. In this case, economic efficiency requires that all users of the facility face the same price per unit of water. There should be a uniform price based on marginal costs rather than, as is frequently proposed, a lower price for existing residents and a higher price for new ones (Hanke and Wenders 1982). But to avoid increased costs, existing residents may withhold subdivision permission. The efficient response is a subdivision exaction at least equal to the consumer surplus lost by longtime residents when water (and other) prices rise. Thus exactions may be more efficient than the proposed discriminatory pricing of public utilities.

Both of the foregoing problems are compounded by inflation, the consequences of which are examined in section 15.3. The law regarding subdivision exactions is unsettled, but it seems to have generated less litigation than have general zoning restrictions.

4.1.2. Operating Costs and "Fiscal" Zoning

The problem for the community is that capital costs are a relatively small part (10–20 percent) of the local budget. They would be much larger, of course, without subdivision regulations. The

major costs are operating expenses. Attempts by the community
to control these are more controversial. By far the largest of these
costs is for public education. Until recently, municipalities have
had an incentive to use zoning to ensure that new development
would "pay its own way" in property taxes for education expenditures. Since many states have, under court pressure, reduced
reliance on local taxes for school finance, this incentive has been
reduced in recent years (sections 15.2 and 15.4).

Economists sometimes assume that communities can actually
state that new development must have some minimum value per
dwelling unit in order to ensure that it will pay enough in property
taxes. This it certainly cannot do. Another blatant device is the
limitation on the number of bedrooms, sometimes coupled with
a maximum number of occupants. This is sometimes tolerated in
apartments, where a special permit may require that most units
have only one bedroom, but it is not ordinarily tolerated for single-
family homes. For single-family homes the major fiscal device is
to add construction costs to raise its assessment. These "quantity"
(as opposed to price) regulations are usually an acceptable sub-
terfuge if rationalized in the appropriate "health, safety, and welfare" language.

The most popular devices to ensure some minimum housing
value are the minimum lot size and various bulk requirements that
may be related to lot size. The latter are important to prevent the
construction of a low-cost house on a large lot. Sometimes these
involve turning the usual density controls on their heads. One
means of controlling density is to limit the floor area (or perhaps
the volume or number of rooms) of a dwelling to no more than,
say, 50 percent of the lot. For fiscal purposes, this is often turned
into a minimum requirement—that is, the dwelling unit can cover
no less than some percentage of the lot—to ensure that a small
home cannot be constructed. Other devices, such as an absolute
minimum floor area per dwelling,[3] or a prohibition on mobile
homes, also add to the property-tax base per household.

The use of these devices is not universally tolerated by the
courts, especially when their sole apparent rationale is control of
fiscal costs. An increasing number of courts, for example, do not
permit total exclusion of mobile homes, as is common in many
suburbs (Kmiec 1983). There does seem to be increasing acceptance of minimum building-size regulations, but the minima in
many cases do not seem to be very large and acceptance is still
not universal.

What is curious to me about fiscal zoning is that the actual
devices for enforcing minimum standards do not seem to be much

of a constraint. The minimum lot size is actually rather small, and the bulk requirements seem to allow rather large families.[4] One explanation may be that real cost-creating zoning is applied only to relatively large-scale projects. A rational strategy for a community concerned about fiscal impact may be to allow small-scale, local builders considerable latitude but to impose more stringent standards on large-scale builders, who would have a substantial impact on the local fisc. For example, Vermont's statewide review process exempts housing developments of fewer than ten units. Exempting the smaller projects from such regulations helps to assuage local builders and landowners, who may have some local political power. These small projects are probably below the scale economies necessary to build moderate-cost housing anyway, so there is likely to be little influence on the fisc.

4.2. SOCIAL AND ECONOMIC SEGREGATION

In many ways social and economic segregation is closely connected with financing municipal services, since one's economic status is likely to be related to one's demand for housing and thus the local property-tax base. In this way fiscal zoning encourages income segregation.

Direct regulation of social, racial, or income status is completely forbidden by the courts and usually by legislatures. Racial zoning was struck down by the U.S. Supreme Court in 1917 (Buchanan v. Warley, 245 U.S. 60). Racial covenants have not been legally enforceable since 1948 (Shelley v. Kraemer, 334 U.S. 1). Zoning by direct reference to income, religion, or national origin is likewise unacceptable.

More important than direct regulations by race are the indirect effects of zoning. It is well known that it is more difficult to enforce antidiscrimination laws in owner-occupied housing. A consequence, perhaps unforeseen, of the acceptance of the primacy of the single-family housing district is the perpetuation of racial segregation in areas hostile to minorities (Yinger 1979).

While de jure discrimination is barred, there remains a question of how much de facto economic segregation may be accomplished. As I pointed out in section 3.6, it depends on which courts one looks at. The federal courts have avoided the issue, but some state courts have moved to deal with zoning whose effects exclude the poor. Prodded by these decisions and by state legislation, many local master plans now mention low-income housing as a goal (section 2.5). So many other goals are mentioned in these plans, however, that there is no reason to expect that low-income housing would receive priority. Case studies by the Stanford Environmental Law Society (1982) confirm this for several California suburbs. Although California statutes require accommodation of low-income housing in master plans, many communities used environmental goals to gain exceptions to this mandate. We shall return to this theme in chapters 14 and 15. My conclusion for now is that de facto segregation by social class has become more difficult to accomplish by zoning but that suburban communities can do it if they are careful to rationalize their policies as pursuing more innocent goals.

4.3. ENVIRONMENTAL EFFECTS OF NONRESIDENTIAL DEVELOPMENT

Economists seem not to realize the extent to which nonresidential activities can be regulated. I once attended a seminar at which a distinguished economist talked about the problem (which he'd just begun to investigate) of a large industrial firm moving into a town and taking over the place. I later learned that he had dropped the project, and I speculate that he did so for lack of examples of this occurring.

This is not because large firms lack influence in town politics and planning. After they have arrived, their employment and fiscal effects on the town make local officials solicitous of their financial health. In many cases the firms are invited into the town by local officials to alleviate unemployment or fiscal problems. In others, the firm's location was a considered decision by local officials not to oppose it. A town that opposes a large-scale commercial and industrial development in its midst will most likely succeed.[5]

As a rule, larger and more noxious facilities are more easily excluded than are smaller or more benign ones. Large plants usually require some zoning exceptions and special public services even on land zoned for industry, and community discretion can be exercised here. Noxious activities usually require special permits if they are not prohibited outright. It is in fact possible for a community to require the discontinuance of firms (and some types of residential structures) in areas zoned or rezoned for other uses. The discontinuance of such "nonconforming" uses does not necessarily require compensation, nor is there any settled rule of law that states how long the firm may be allowed to operate before it must be removed. In some cases the firm may be ordered to cease operations immediately.[6]

The treatment of nonconforming uses is important in economic studies of the effects of zoning and nuisances on residential property values (section 11.3). Several studies have found that the presence of nonconforming uses in residential neighborhoods seems to have little effect on residential property values. The reason for this may be quite simple: zoning law permits the termination of nonconforming uses that are genuinely harmful, leaving behind only the ones that are benign or innocuous.

All of this is not to argue that nonresidential activities have no rights at all. When a firm desires to locate in a place that is appropriately zoned and can show that it will meet whatever performance standards exist, it usually can get the location. The point is that the community can establish whatever standards it wants, so that it is possible, with a little forethought (and sometimes just afterthought), to exclude most industrial or commerical activities.

There is an exception to the right to exclude nonresidential activities. If the proposal is not an ordinary commerical or industrial firm but a community facility, such as a school, hospital, or recreation area, the courts tend to be much more skeptical of such exclusion, especially if the facility is publicly owned or operated (Williams 1975, sec. 76.06). In cases involving exclusion of such facilities, the courts often have found for the promoters of the facility rather than for the community. The reasoning usually involves the judges' wondering aloud what "general welfare" is being served by a zoning ordinance that excludes a facility that is publicly supported for the general welfare. The differences in the treatment of public and private activities is perhaps attributable to the courts' deference to a coequal branch of government. It is otherwise difficult to explain the apparent differences in treatment of public schools and private schools, the latter obtaining less protection from exclusion in many states.

It may come as a surprise to economists that there is litigation about the location of schools and parks. The presence of such facilities is generally thought to enhance residential property values. They usually do, but not necessarily for the immediate neighbors. It is good to have an elementary school *nearby*, but it is less desirable to live right next to it (Ellickson and Tarlock 1981, 562). This points up the importance of distinguishing between developers' cases and neighbors' cases in zoning litigation. Litigation on community facilities almost always involves neighbors against the community's decision.

While communities can prospectively control local industries, in most cases they cannot control noxious effects of industry located outside their borders. A few states allow extraterritorial zoning and subdivision regulations, but these apply mostly to unorganized townships beyond the city limits, areas that the city may annex sometime in the future. Nor are provisions for intercommunity cooperation widespread. This leads to an incentive for communities to pursue a beggar-thy-neighbor policy with respect to noxious land uses: they may be placed near borders, downwind, downstream, and out of sight of the voting population (but see section 5.6).

4.4. RESIDENTIAL DENSITY AND POPULATION CONTROL

4.4.1. The Prima Facie Case

The analysis of the legal constraints on zoning in the previous chapters provides what I think is a prima facie case for the proposition that communities *can* have a substantial impact on the overall density of population. The major reason is that courts of law are willing to sustain zoning laws (or, more frequently, amendments to zoning laws) that substantially reduce the value of undeveloped land. This allows the community to reap the benefits of restrictive zoning (to current homeowners and other voters) without having to confront the cost that these regulations impose on developers and prospective residents. Nonmarket substitutes for compelling the community to account for costs of regulation are seldom required by the courts. Communities do not have to do anything approximating benefit-cost analysis before imposing land use regulations. This condition leads to overregulation and residential densities that are too low. (A more formal derivation of this result is given in chapter 7.)

This prima facie case—that communities can ignore losses in land values—requires at least one qualification: a zoning regulation is not necessarily unreasonable just because it causes some reduction in the value of undeveloped land. Suppose that a general-residence district that allows apartments as well as single-family homes becomes largely developed with the latter type of housing. The owner of a remaining tract then applies for a building permit to erect a high-rise apartment house. The neighbors petition the local authorities for a change in the zoning laws so as to allow only single-family houses on the remaining lots. This lowers the value of those lots, but it may well raise the value of the existing single-family homes by an even larger amount. Thus simply because zoning may lower property values of undeveloped land does not mean that it will result in inefficiently low population densities (section 11.6).

The fact that zoning *can* be too restrictive does not mean that it will in fact be used that way. One criticism of my prima facie case is that zoning laws actually adopted by most communities are not really very restrictive, so that they create land use patterns that are not very different from those that unregulated private developers would have created (Weicher 1980, 150). Zoning, according to this critique, may matter for individual landowners but not for the community as a whole, or at least not for the larger region or metropolitan area of which the community is but a small part.

One problem with this critique is that inspection of zoning ordinances gives little information about how restrictive a community actually is. A town with land zoned for apartments or moderately priced housing might in fact put many additional constraints in the form of special conditions, or it might even rezone the land for another use in the face of a bona fide developer's application. This argument works both ways, of course: apparently restrictive communities might actually be willing to rezone to accommodate all developers.

4.4.2. Increasing Community Resistance

The more important response is that community zoning restrictions increase over time. There are two independent causes for communities' adoption of increasingly restrictive zoning ordinances. The first, which affects all communities more or less equally, has been the greater incentive in recent years. Some states now require all local governments to zone. Several federal programs, notably flood insurance, require some local zoning for eligibility, and others subsidize local planning. Most important, however, is the increasingly permissive attitude of the state and federal courts towards communities' exercise of the police power (sections 3.1 and 3.4). With zoning no longer required to be "strictly construed" within a narrow scope of health, safety, or other specific concerns, communities have found that a broad range of public benefits secured by land use restrictions is inexpensive to establish and defend. This is also why one cannot dismiss the increasing restrictions of a single small community: other towns in the region tend to imitate the more restrictive one once they see that its regulations will hold up in court (chapter 7, n. 5; and section 11.5).

The second reason why zoning has become more restrictive is the increase in development itself. Many observers have noted that as a rural township becomes a suburban development, the zoning restrictions become more stringent. This is partly due to a desire to deal with the nuisances of development itself, but it is more frequently caused, I believe, by the demands of more affluent newcomers whose taste for open space and other benefits of zoning is matched by their knowledge of the system of land use controls. For whatever reason, the jurisdiction does become more restrictive, and it does so independently of the secular trend in zoning laws mentioned above.[7]

Both of these trends make it hard to assess a given community's zoning restrictions. A suburb may indeed harbor a number of quarter-acre or smaller lots; there may be some areas zoned for apartments as well. But my experience has been that most of the smaller lots are already built upon, and they were developed well before the community became a suburb or otherwise extensively developed. The zoning that matters to developers is zoning of undeveloped lots. It is there that the standards for development are likely to cause the land to be used much less intensively than in the older parts of the community.

4.5. THE PANOPLY OF RESIDENTIAL GROWTH CONTROLS

A problem with studies showing that zoning is not very restrictive is that they too frequently focus on the workhorse of residential zoning restrictions, the minimum lot size. Lot size is important, but there are a number of other ways by which community authorities can restrict development. A nonexhaustive survey of these devices is presented here to give the reader a sense of the range of ways by which residential development may be curtailed.

Minimum lot size is the most frequently used means of regulating density. There is no judicial consensus as to how large the minimum can be before the ordinance becomes a taking of property or invalid on other grounds. One can find instances of courts tolerating minimum lot sizes as large as 160 acres, while others have struck down some as small as one acre.[8] Litigation is often about attempts by the community to increase the minimum lot size after a developer has proposed a substantial development on the land in question. That such cases are often decided for the community suggests that lot size is not a trivial constraint.

Subdivision regulations do not usually specify lot size, but they can be used to lower the amount of housing on a given parcel of land by requiring that the developer devote a substantial amount of it to parks or other common lands.

Delaying development is the next best thing to eliminating it altogether. A number of approaches have been used. The most common is a zoning or subdivision moratorium, according to which the community simply declines to issue building permits until it reevaluates its master plan or zoning ordinances. Sewer or water hookups for new developments have also been suspended for similar motives. This buys a little time, but more effective in the long run is systematic rationing of building permits or tying residential development to a plan of future community capital improvements such as roads and sewers.[9] These devices are often carefully worded to avoid the appearance of excluding only low-income housing.

Annexation policy is an important means of controlling residential development in much of the western United States. In many places the refusal of a suburb or small town to annex undeveloped, unincorporated land adjacent to it may be tantamount to eliminating development if water and other services cannot be provided by the county or an independent district.

Zoning for commercial or industrial use is another means of controlling residential development. The widespread adoption of mutually exclusive zoning districts can provide an effective barrier to residential development. The problem with this is that the community may not want the nonresidential development either. This would work only if there were no demand for industrial or commercial space in the community or if the community were to place such stringent performance standards on all firms that very few would be able to locate there. This tactic is limited by courts in some states. They may find a taking if no development occurs for several years.

Municipal referenda are a new means of controlling growth in a community; the U.S. Supreme Court has approved the practice of submitting rezoning requests to a local referendum.[10] The result has been a much more effective means of excluding residential development. This is because voters need not be required, as are planning and zoning boards or local legislatures, to hear both sides of the story and at least go through the motions of disinterested evaluation of a developer's plans. Although it is likely that public officials attempt to act in the voters' interests, they are restrained to some extent by principles of good planning, procedural fairness, and judicial review of their actions (section 10.8.2). Thus the practice of putting zoning changes up to voters' decisions is apt to reduce further the residential density of a community whose voters find new development inconvenient to themselves.

Zoning for "open space" is the ultimate means of restricting residential development. This classification is likely to be successfully challenged by landowners as a taking. Communities have taken two approaches to get around this problem. The first is to offer some form of compensation to the landowner, short of actually purchasing the land. Communities may seek to acquire the development rights or "scenic easements" to the land. They may attempt to pay for such restrictions with the promise that the affected landowner can use his development rights elsewhere. These promises are called transferrable development rights (TDRs). Many states also have programs that offer substantially reduced local property taxes in exchange for a landowner's promise to the community not to develop the land for some period of time.

The problem with compensation mechanisms is that the community has to give up some of its collective resources in order to get what it wants. Less expensive is the second means of avoiding a constitutional challenge: invoking new rationales for the public purpose to which the police power is supposed to bear some reasonable relation. These rationales include preservation of rare environments, endangered species, and historic areas. The discovery that a tract is ecologically fragile or harbors an endangered species or was the locus of some historic event, however, often seems to follow soon after development is proposed (Frieden 1979).

Such actions can restrict development and retain much land in open space, but usually a lot of open land still remains. Most of it is farmland. A recent technique of restricting residential growth is to zone open space exclusively and (unlike in older agricultural districts) permanently for agriculture. Since it is arguable that crops can be grown almost anywhere, the acceptance of the preservation of farmland as a legitimate motive of local zoning ordinances represents an extraordinary leap in the ability of partly developed communities to exclude new housing (section 13.1).

4.6. ZONING FOR SALE?

The second criticism of my prima facie case that zoning tends to systematically reduce residential density (section 4.4.1) is that developers ought to be able to buy their way out of excessive restrictions. Even though a community's zoning laws are very restrictive, the owners of the affected land should be able to compensate the community in some way so as to get back the right to use their land as they wish. The *ultimate* use of the land would be no different under zoning than in its absence, though at any given moment zoning may appear to be very restrictive.

This argument is a sophisticated "property rights" idea, and it will require several chapters to develop it adequately. My primary refutation of it rests on the idea that it is difficult for the affected landowners to buy back their development rights. This is elaborated in the following sections of this chapter and then applied to a formal model in sections 7.3 and 7.4.

More than one observer (including myself) has suggested that communities be allowed to sell zoning entitlements. Several others suggest that this is actually done by various devices.[11] However, planners and lawyers are often puzzled or horrified by the idea. Before discussing the extent to which such sales actually occur, I want to suggest to my fellow economists that there are some reasons for this reaction beyond simple hostility to exchange, although there is certainly plenty of that too.

Zoning is part of the community's police power. This authority is the power to make the rules of public life. One can hardly imagine a government lacking this authority and still functioning as a government. The police power is often said to be the least limitable of state powers. This is problematic in a liberal democracy. Besides judicial review under the doctrines described in chapter 3, one way of ensuring some limitation is to require that police power regulations not be used solely as an expedient for raising public revenue or reducing expenditures. This does not mean that the government cannot incidentally use police powers as a substitute for taxes; it just cannot be the primary purpose of the regulation. For example, a government cannot make some activity illegal simply in order to collect fines from violators or sell exceptions to high bidders.

One can certainly think of marginal cases. One example was the New York City practice, recently discontinued, of granting developers zoning exceptions if they contributed to a special fund for the maintenance of Central Park. (The examples I know of all come from central cities, where zoning practices often are more freewheeling than elsewhere.) But it is clear that the courts are uncomfortable with these exchanges, and the receipts from such sales are invariably earmarked for some special public purpose rather than used for general revenues.

The reasoning behind discomfort over selling the police power ought to be spelled out. A longstanding, if highly variable, constitutional issue is the "public purpose" doctrine (Horwitz 1982). This was created by the Supreme Court in the nineteenth century to limit governmental activity by creating distinct spheres of public and private activities. Police power regulations must be related to a valid *public* purpose.

If a zoning regulation *does* serve the public welfare, then an exception to the rule cannot be sold.[12] The economist would say that selling an exception to a regulation shows only that the cash (or whatever else is gained by the community in exchange for exceptions to zoning regulations) serves the public welfare better than the regulation does. This may be true, but it misses the point about limitations on the scope of the police power. If the economist's argument were accepted, *any* regulation could be passed and the exceptions sold to the highest bidder. A government that did that would appear more like a protection racket, and not one that operated for the benefit of its citizens. (There is more discussion of this issue in chapters 8 and 9.)

Despite the above observations, some observers regard zoning as perfectly fungible. A landowner or developer who does not have the appropriate zoning simply purchases an exception to it, just as he would purchase construction materials needed for the project. Others believe that most developers have significant problems in arranging for changes in zoning laws, and even those who succeed do so at a substantial cost. I lean towards the latter view: zoning laws should not be thought of as fungible in the ordinary sense. I shall press my point of view by adopting the tactic that the two positions do not disagree on the facts so much as they approach the facts with different expectations. In other words, the debate is like arguing whether a glass is half-empty or half-full.

Zoning cannot be simply auctioned off. But there are some subtle and not-so-subtle subterfuges. Two classes of these will be described in the following sections, along with reasons why these subterfuges are not perfect substitutes for an auction of zoning entitlements.

4.7. PRIVATE SALES: PAYMENT WITHOUT CONTRACTS

Just because the community does not advertise "zoning for sale" does not mean that developers and landowners will not attempt to purchase exceptions to current zoning laws when it appears that they will not be altered on request. A private agreement between the developer and a public official who has the authority to change the laws is one method. This is illegal, but in some places bribes may be a common way to change zoning laws. We might briefly consider what is wrong with this, since some observers occasionally imply that it is not such a bad arrangement.[13]

The problem with bribing the official is not that money is being paid but that it is being paid to the wrong party. Zoning is a collective community entitlement, not a personal one. If the developer is willing to pay for a rezoning, he should pay the proper owners of the entitlement. Aside from the inequity of a system of bribes, there is an efficiency problem. The bribe to a single person will usually be too small. This is because there are neighborhood effects from most developments, so that many people will be affected simultaneously. The well-being of all of those affected must be considered. In technical terms, demand for public amenities (or lack of disamenities) must be summed vertically, not horizontally. If we are to have a market for zoning, the market must be arranged so that some approximation of a solution to the public goods problem must be reached. Just compensating one party, who may not even be affected by the development, is insufficient.

In defense of bribes, one might point out that politicians who take bribes and make unpopular decisions get voted out of office. This does happen (Gardner and Lyman 1978), but it does not remedy the harm if the project is already done. One might also argue that the feasible devices for compensating citizens are so cumbersome that a system of bribes should be tolerated as a second-best but workable means of getting socially useful developments. I hope to persuade the reader in chapter 9 that legal transactions are not so difficult to arrange that we must concede such demoralizing arguments.

There is a more legitimate, private means of compensation. This is to have private agreements between the developer and those neighbors who are likely to appear at the public meeting that considers the exception. Such agreements could be made where the number of neighbors is small and where the proposed change is not very controversial. In its most blatant form the developer, who is most likely asking for a variance or special exception, simply offers the neighbors a certain amount of cash either for not showing up or for speaking in favor of the proposed project (Geller 1983, chap. 14). Since the ZBA normally weighs the opinions of neighbors quite heavily in issuing variances or special exceptions, this would be one means by which zoning is fungible.

Though it would obviously be hard to get data on such practices, I have heard of only a handful (Ellickson and Tarlock 1981, 358). But cash is not the only compensation that could be offered. Far more likely are informal, "good neighbor" arrangements. In cases where a minor exception to a zoning regulation is applied for, the applicants capitalize on their stock of good will. In the case of a commercial development that wants to expand, the owner may have issued some preferential credit terms or other favors to neighbors over the years. In the case of residential changes, the owner-occupant or landlord may have been extra solicitous of the well-being of the neighbors. Such good will can facilitate the negotiations between neighbors and the developer that take place quite openly before many zoning and planning boards. To couch these transactions in economic terms may seem crass, but it is no less an exchange than paying cash. Such exchanges are usually invisible to outsiders. They may help explain the existence of the numerous variances and special exceptions that vex many observers of zoning.

There are three problems with such private arrangements.

1. In the early years of zoning, some communities attempted to forestall neighbors' cases by delegating legal authority over development to nearby landowners. A landowner-developer could obtain a rezoning for particular parcels of land only if the consent of a certain percentage of neighboring property owners was obtained. Many courts, however, are very wary of such delegation of the police power, perhaps because it nearly eliminates the distinction between private and public described above.

This is important because it discourages negotiations between developers and neighbors, since they cannot make a final contract. The developer of a gas station may be willing to pay his neighbors to accept the inconvenience it may create (without the liquidity problems of actually buying his neighbors' property). However, the negotiations are inhibited if such an arrangement is only advisory rather than a legal contract. This is because third parties (who may be on the ZBA or may live more distant from the proposed use) may object as well. This adds uncertainty to the potential developer. Even if he goes to the trouble of satisfying his neighbors, he may still end up without permission to undertake his project.

2. A second problem is that most exceptions to zoning laws are expected to apply to the property rather than to a given owner. This inhibits transactions based on good-neighbor policies. The current owner's reputation for neighborliness might cause neighbors to support a proposed change but for one problem: they have

no control over who will be the subsequent owner of the property. This must inhibit some of the changes that might otherwise be made. (I may be making too much of this. Richard Babcock, a zoning lawyer of national experience, assured me that many special exceptions are issued for a limited period of time, so that the property owner's behavior can be periodically reassessed and, if necessary, permits can be revoked for unacceptable behavior.)

3. The most serious problem is that for large projects, there are likely to be too many neighbors for any transaction to be made or for the force of reputation to carry much weight. It is one thing for your neighbor to apply for a permit to conduct a small real estate business at home and quite another for someone in the next block to want to develop a shopping center. The latter has effects that are far-reaching and potentially more harmful. Only the most optimistic would suggest that the latter be handled strictly by private agreements. This does not mean that no transactions can or should be made. It simply means that the parties to the exchange must be the developer and public officials, rather than the developer and private individuals.

4.8. PUBLIC DEALS: THE BARRIERS TO SALES

Several compensation mechanisms are available in the public sector. Some of these were reviewed in section 4.1, which considered the extent to which a community could force newcomers to finance municipal services. Such fiscal considerations represent an important aspect of the fungibility of zoning. We will see in chapter 14 that this exchange mechanism has important implications for judgments about the efficiency of local property taxes in a fragmented metropolitan area. For now I want to consider the variations in these methods and the extent to which they make zoning truly fungible.

4.8.1. Negotiated Settlements

The simplest means of compensating public officials (and through them the community at large) would be to negotiate property-tax assessments for each new development. Another means is to negotiate various gifts in kind with the developer. The developer could be required to dedicate a certain amount of land to public use or simply to give it to the local government. Developers might also be required to supply certain public works which would benefit not only those occupying the new project but the larger community as well. A simpler way is to get the developer to pay subdivision exactions in excess of those actually beneficial to the subdivision itself. Still another means of inducing community acceptance of the project is for the developer to make gifts to local charities with strong hints that there is more to come if he gets his project accepted.

I have found examples of each of these exchange mechanisms at work. In this sense, I seem to be agreeing with those observers who believe that zoning is completely fungible. But I have seen as many instances where these mechanisms seem to have broken down. One cannot be sure what caused the breakdown—it might have occurred in any case—but there are many instances where it appears that potential gains from trade were lost because of the legal and institutional restrictions inherent in zoning law. It is these issues that I will consider presently.

Two qualifications need to be made. First, it must be understood that all the mechanisms described above by which zoning is exchanged involve a "leasing" of zoning rather than a "sale" of it. The distinction is that under a lease final control of the property rests with the owner, while under a sale final control is transferred. Zoning can never be "sold" in the sense that the community can just give up its authority over a given parcel of land. The only way that this could happen would be for the parcel of land to become incorporated as a separate municipality.

The other qualification is that the rules seem to be different for nonresidential development. Each of the means by which zoning can be made fungible—negotiated tax assessments, required gifts in kind, subdivision exactions—are easier and less controversial to apply to commercial and industrial development than to residential projects. That is to say, zoning for commerce and industry is very close to being perfectly fungible.

This is sometimes encouraged explicitly in state laws, especially the newer statewide land use controls. Moreover, nonresidential development frequently confers substantial fiscal and employment benefits on the community, and the negotiations are often reversed. The developer may demand special tax abatements, more public services at a lower cost, or other concessions from the community to induce him to locate there rather than somewhere else. These may not always be granted but they do establish a tradition of negotiation.

4.8.2. Housing and Contract Zoning

Housing development represents about twice the value of commercial and industrial property in most areas, but deal making is more difficult. Housing developers can be made to supply various gifts in kind to the community. Even if these are sufficient to satisfy community authorities, there is a problem of mutual assurance involved. If a developer wants to put up a tract of houses in a town generally opposed to it, he may propose financing a community recreation center in exchange for permission to develop. The logical means of assuring each party that the exchange will be consummated is a contract between the zoning authorities and the developer providing that if the developer does not finance the recreation center, his zoning will be rescinded; or financial penalties could be applied if the developer had already begun.

The constitutional problem with contract zoning is the "reserved power doctrine," which precludes contracts for the police power (but not for taxing or spending powers) by holding such contracts to be unenforceable. Douglas Kmiec (1981) finds recent signs that the federal courts are no longer as concerned with the reserved power doctrine, and he makes contract zoning a central aspect of a proposed zoning reform. State courts are nonetheless divided on the issue. Many will not enforce the contract or will allow third parties (such as disaffected neighbors) to overturn it (Liebermann 1981).

Lack of legal enforcement of contracts does not preclude their existence. There are many instances of such arrangements' being consummated. But lack of legality introduces yet another degree of uncertainty into an already uncertain business, and it must deter some transactions that would otherwise have taken place. There are instances of communities that rezoned a property in the expectation that the developer would perform some task only to discover that the developer understood differently. Likewise, there are developers who have offered compensation in advance to preclude the former concern, only to find that the community authorities had changed their minds. (Or perhaps as the result of an intervening election the authorities were now different people.) Legal contracts are useful devices.

The other problem that residential developments have is that they change the political makeup of the community. People in factories and stores do not vote; people in houses do. This means that new residents can unite politically to rescind any special burdens placed on their homes, such as higher tax assessments. The way to avoid this would be to have lump-sum payments made prior to the actual construction of the development. Such explicit arrangements are more likely than others to fall afoul of the state's zoning case law, however, which may account for their scarcity.

4.8.3. Other Constraints on Bargaining

As I mentioned earlier, some of the new statewide land use laws explicitly encourage fiscal bargaining, so that their use is not much inhibited by the courts. The problem with these arrangements, though, is that such laws also increase the number of parties entitled to participate in the proceedings. This may mean that agreement is nearly impossible. A developer who wants to build in a certain town may be explicitly empowered to negotiate about fiscal matters, but under most of the statewide laws, he must satisfy not just the host town but also numerous other parties who may be hypersensitive, eager to make a largely unrelated political point, or just plain protectionist (section 10.9). Thus although such laws overcome some of the legal barriers to exchange, they usually erect more substantial practical barriers to negotiations. They may be important, however, in establishing the legal precedent for fungibility of zoning regulations.

The restraints on exchange in land use controls are not just legal. The traditional outlook of the planning profession is hostile to it (Nelson 1977, chap. 3). The traditional goal of planning is to get development to go where the planning authorities want it to go. This is shown by the general attitude towards devices such as spot zoning and floating zones. The floating-zone concept does not initially establish zoning boundaries. The community waits until a developer proposes one or more projects and then establishes zones consistent with those developments. The zoning purpose of district separation is served by these devices, and project review is reserved for the planning board, but there are no initial districts and no master plan to decide what will go where.

To an economist, this approach makes sense because it is hard to know what the best use of property is going to be until someone proposes one. But there is nonetheless considerable hostility to this idea by planners, perhaps because it reduces (but hardly eliminates) their role in public life. The attitude is softening somewhat, but there are many who remain convinced that such flexibility is the antithesis of the comprehensive plan doctrine. As long as the idea persists, the exchange of zoning authority will be further limited.

4.8.4. Barter and Subsidies

The final barrier to fungibility for zoning is the necessity of using goods in kind, and a limited range of goods, rather than cash as the medium of exchange. Even if the barriers to trade described above did not exist, exchange of zoning would be inhibited as long as only barter were permitted.

We use cash so frequently that we often forget how useful it is compared with barter. Barter's disadvantages are the indivisibility of goods offered and the lack of coincidence of wants between parties. The latter is basically an information problem: the developer has to spend a great deal of time and other resources to find out exactly what the community wants.

The problem of barter is compounded in that the range of goods that a developer can offer tends to be restricted. He cannot, for example, promise to provide everyone in town with some private good like a turkey or a bicycle. He is usually confined to some collectively consumed good like a park, a school, or some other service.

This latter condition—restriction on the range of goods—suggests that the developer is limited in effect to public sector subsidies. Most economists have concluded that public sector subsidies can be as inefficient as private sector subsidies. A subsidy causes the price of some good to be too low compared with its marginal cost of production. Thus people will overconsume it relative to other goods. Unless there are compelling reasons to encourage this overconsumption, there is a net loss to society for redistributing income in this way. This is not because the party being subsidized is worse off from the low price but because the recipient could be made better off, at a lower cost to the donor, by using unrestricted cash grants.[14]

4.9. CONCLUSION

My conclusion from the previous two sections is that there are substantial barriers to trade in zoning entitlements. The reason that some scholars regard zoning as fungible is this: if one looks at zoning laws initially and takes them and their rationale literally, one does not expect to find any exchange going on at all. Those observers who move beyond the words on the page discover that in practice there is plenty of exchange, so much so that zoning looks perfectly fungible. But if one looks at zoning entitlements as just another factor of production, where permission to build is as useful to a developer as bricks and mortar, zoning appears far less salable. Thus disagreements about fungibility result from one's initial expectations of zoning's function rather than from disagreement about the facts.

The questions I have attempted to answer in this chapter have implications for several policy issues, each of which will be examined in a later chapter. At the risk of (further?) oversimplification, this chapter is summarized with short answers to each question.

1. To what extent can a community require newcomers to finance municipal services? The community typically can avoid most infrastructure costs, but the most important burdens—operating costs for public schools and general municipal services—seldom can be directly apportioned to new developments.

2. How much social and economic segregation can be accomplished? A considerable amount, although the community must be quite circumspect in doing it.

3. How well can the community control changes in its environment resulting from nonresidential uses? Within its own borders, almost completely; outside its borders, hardly at all.

4. How effectively can the community control the density or intensity of residential development? It can certainly press the density well below what the unregulated market would allow, but how much below is an open question. The more recent environmental and resource preservation rationales for zoning do provide additional means by which a community can control population growth.

5. To what extent is it possible for the community to exchange its control over land use for other goods? It can do so in rather limited ways, and then only under what to an economist appear to be highly artificial rationales. Compared with other economic entitlements, zoning cannot be sold.

NOTES

1. Babcock (1966) is an entertaining and insightful review of the realities of zoning practice. Other useful sources are Geller (1983); Mandelker (1971); and Siegan (1972).

2. Adelstein and Edelson (1976) review subdivision exactions in economic theory. For a legal and economic critique of subdivision exactions see Ellickson (1977, 465). An interesting alternative to subdivision exactions for infrastructure is the municipal utility district (Peiser 1983).

3. A pioneering legal review of the minimum floor area standard and its relatives is Haar (1953), which criticizes a New Jersey decision, Lionshead Lake, Inc. v. Wayne Township, 89 A.2d 693 (1952).

4. The New Jersey Bureau of Local Planning (1967) surveyed all localities for minimum lot size; they did not seem to me to be especially large.

5. Nonresidential land use was the focus of my doctoral dissertation, most of which is in Fischel (1975). See also sections 5.7, 5.8, and 14.8.

6. This is not a new doctrine, and it is consistent with the common law of nuisance. An example is Hadacheck v. Sebastian, 239 U.S. 394 (1915), discussed in section 3.5, in which a Los Angeles brick factory was ordered closed after the city rezoned the area for residential use. State courts are still squeamish about applying this rule and there is considerable variation in practice (Ellickson and Tarlock 1981, sec. 2C; Williams 1975, chap. 116).

7. A survey of the adoption of zoning in rural townships and municipalities in Ohio concluded that "as communities grew and made the transition from a population of 1000 to 2000, problems apparently develop which cause communities to adopt zoning ordinances" (Ohio Department of Economic and Community Development 1974). This suggests the cross section effect of development. The secular trend is indicated by New Hampshire, which has no statewide mandates or controls but nonetheless had 160 (of 212) local governments with zoning laws in 1973 compared with only 52 in 1956 (New Hampshire League of Women Voters 1975). Both trends are discernible from data in Manvel (1968), which used a national sample.

8. Ellickson and Tarlock (1981, 828) caution against a search for constants: "In no state can one identify a threshold (e.g., three acres) at which a lot size requirement will *always* be declared invalid." The 160–acre minimum was in an agricultural preservation zone, which was upheld in Wilson v. County of McHenry, 416 N.E.2d 426 (Ill. App. 1981). The landowner in that case had his property rezoned from one and one-eighth acres to five acres in 1974 and from five acres to 160 acres in 1979.

9. The two pioneering communities in this area were Ramapo, New York, and Petaluma, California. Several essays on them constitute chapters 9 and 10 of Scott (1975). Both plans were upheld by the courts, but Ramapo has since abandoned its plan. On the effects of Petaluma's plan, see section 11.5.

10. City of Eastlake [Ohio] v. Forest City Enterprises, Inc., 426 U.S. 668 (1976). The case is cogently criticized in Wolfstone (1978). Such referenda are not confined to Ohio. In California in 1978 and 1979 there were 32 city or county ballots to limit growth, of which 19 passed (*Davis* [Cal.] *Enterprise*, 15 October 1980, 5). I know from experience that particular rezoning proposals are often voted upon in Vermont and New Hampshire town meetings. Ellickson and Tarlock (1981, 307) note, however, that "judicial hostility [among the states] to popular elections on small-scale rezoning is widespread."

11. Favoring sales are Clawson (1971), Fischel (1979b), Kmiec (1981), Nelson (1977) and Tarlock (1973). A review of "zoning on the auction block" is in Glickfeld (1978, chap. 16). Suggesting that they happen anyway are Ellickson (1977, 427) and James and Gale (1977). Ellickson and Tarlock (1981, 234–81) discuss "deals between local governments and private developers" in which they note an increasing judicial acceptance of deal making. They also note the rise of special development taxes that may, if the amounts are negotiable, serve as a means of payment to consummate these deals (pp. 728–61). Transferable development rights programs are essentially a means

of exchanging zoning entitlements, though usually not for cash. Economic analyses that suggest this are David Mills (1980) and Carpenter and Heffley (1982).

12. This may be an underlying rationale for the "harm-benefit" rule for distinguishing takings from acceptable police powers, discussed in chapter 8. Its classic statement is in Freund (1904): "Under the police power, rights of property are impaired not because they become useful or necessary to the public. . .but because their free exercise is believed to be detrimental to public interests" (p. 546). "The exercise of the police power can hardly result in appropriation of property by the public. . .for if the property is dangerous, it is dangerous in the hands of the public as well as of the private owner, and if the danger can be met by regulation, such regulation is possible while the property is left to the owner" (p. 547).

13. This seems to be implied by Siegan (1972, 196), but corruption is elsewhere condemned (p. 172). Buchanan (1973) finds that bribes may promote government efficiency in theory, and Rashid (1981) finds this to be true in practice in less developed countries. Ellickson and Tarlock (1981, 247) conclude their discussion of corruption by asking, "Would the successful suppression of zoning graft have the unfortunate side effect of ending the communication of economic signals that are important to the welfare of consumers of controversial land-use activities?"

14. An exception is when a higher (subsidizing) government attempts to encourage the local (recipient) government to provide services that have interjurisdictional spillovers. As a means of just making a payment, however, subsidies or grants in kind are inferior to lump sum cash grants. On intergovernmental grants theory see Oates (1972, chap. 3).

5.

The Analytics of Land Use: The Property Rights Approach

This chapter develops an analytical apparatus with which to examine land use controversies. The analysis is motivated in terms of a specific problem: obtaining a rezoning for a large industrial plant in a residential community. The model essentially applies economists' marginal benefit/marginal cost calculus to property law's idea of divisible property interests. This allows for diagrammatic exposition of the establishment and exchange of entitlements.

With this model, the Coase theorem—that the initial distribution of entitlements will not alter the final allocation of resources—is demonstrated and generalized to apply to any land use controversy. The chief problem in such issues is obtaining information about valuations of public amenities. The proposed analytical solution to this problem is political economy's median voter model. Within this context, the primary assumptions of the model are reexamined. This reevaluation is continued in chapter 6, in which I shall also look at some general criticisms of the property rights approach and contrast it to the conventional externality approach.

5.1. THE PULP MILL EXAMPLE AND EFFICIENCY

5.1.1. The Controversy

The Coase theorem will be developed using an example based on a real controversy that I studied in some detail (Fischel 1979a). A wood pulp manufacturing company sought to locate a mill along the Connecticut River in New Hampshire. After briefly testing the political sentiments of several towns, it purchased an option to buy a large farm in a town of about three thousand people. The town is largely residential and isolated from population centers; most residents work in small towns nearby. The company needed the town government to rezone the property from agricultural to industrial. It also had to meet current federal air- and water-pollution standards. The mill made no attempt to seek exceptions to the federal standards, and I will not discuss their influence further. I also assume, as is realistic, that the mill sells its product in a competitive national and international market. Local demand is unimportant to it.

Even though the mill might not have contributed to regional air or water pollution, it would still have created a number of *localized* nuisances that caused many townspeople to object to the rezoning proposal. These nuisances included the odors from the mill, the heavy truck traffic, and the disruptions to small-town life occasioned by the influx of newcomers who would work in the mill.

The initial focus is on just one of these nuisances, the sulfurous odors of the mill. There are two further simplifying assumptions: the odors are available equally to all citizens of the town, and the odors do not affect any people outside the town.[1] The first assumption eliminates all "neighbors' cases" (section 3.2). All residents are neighbors as far as odors are concerned. (This does not ensure unanimity, since people have different preferences and sensitivities.) The second assumption allows us to ignore parties not represented by the town officials.

5.1.2. The Mill's Valuations

People who are not economists tend to assume that this controversy is an either/or situation: either the mill comes in and stinks up the place, or the mill may not and the site is unused. Economists' training, however, encourages them to think in terms of alternative outcomes in between these extremes. Let us first consider the alternatives from the mill owner's point of view.

The mill's production process generates some fumes that must be disposed of somehow. An inexpensive way for the mill owner is to deposit them in the atmosphere. In this sense, the atmosphere is an input to producing pulp, just as trees, labor, trucks, and chemicals are inputs to producing the product. Like the use of other resources, the use of the atmosphere can be conserved if the mill's owner has some incentive to do so. I will leave the incentives for

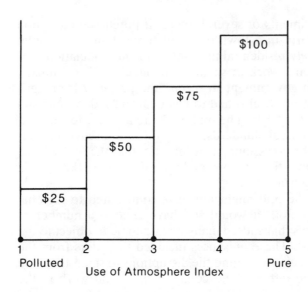

Figure 4. The Mill Owner's Valuation of the Atmosphere

the next section and consider here some technological changes the owner might make to reduce the use of the atmosphere, and what they might cost. Since I will use numerical examples, it will be useful to keep track of them on a graph, figure 4.

Figure 4's horizontal axis is labeled "Use of Atmosphere Index." On the left side, it is as polluted (in the sense of foul odors) as is profitable for the mill; on the right it is perfectly pure. If we assume that degrees of pollution, the complement of air purity, can be measured accurately and easily, then there are, for the sake of argument, five degrees of air pollution or purity. To move from point 1 to point 2 (i.e., to reduce odors around the village) the mill owner takes some relatively inexpensive steps: he attaches some filters to major smokestacks and reduces some of the chemical spillage around the factory. Let us say that these steps cost $25. Now consider a further reduction in pollution, from point 2 to point 3. This requires a more costly adjustment. (It cannot be less costly; if it were, the firm would have done it first.) The factory may try a more expensive process using less sulfuric acid, it may pay a premium for types of wood that do not need so much processing, and it may cut back operations during temperature inversions. This costs an *additional* $50. To move from point 2 to point 3 costs the mill $50, but to move from point 1 to point 3 costs the mill $75 (= $25 + $50).

This and subsequent calculations are based on the assumption that the plant is built from the ground up to obtain any degree of air quality. Thus it does not have to modify existing equipment in order to achieve a given point on the index. This assumption makes movement up the index subject to the same cost schedule as movement down the index. This is realistic for a prospective activity, since all modifications occur prior to construction.

Moving from point 3 to point 4 involves still greater expense (special precipitators, severely reduced operating hours, hiring more labor to monitor containments), of $75 extra. Moving from point 4 to point 5 involves looking for the next-best site—not locating there at all—at a cost of an additional $100.

5.1.3. The Village's Valuations

Now consider the village residents who (alone) are affected by the atmospheric pollution. What is good-smelling air worth to them? Using figure 5, whose axes are the same as those in figure 4, begin at the left side again, where the air is (hypothetically)

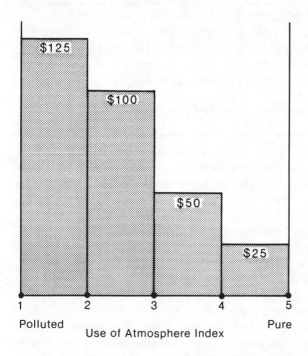

Figure 5.   Village Residents' Valuation of the Atmosphere

heavily polluted by the mill's fumes. What would it be worth to the villagers, all together, to reduce pollution from point 1 to point 2? Let us say $125. This might be inferred from increased housing values as the place became more pleasant (assuming the mill had already located there), but one must confess even at this early stage in the analysis that the collective value is difficult to determine: "I'd give one dollar to have a little less of those fumes," says one of the 125 villagers, and the sentiment is unanimous.

Suppose now that the villagers desire to have the factory reduce the pollution still more, from point 2 to point 3. That is worth $100. Why less than $125? Because of the law of diminishing marginal utility: reducing pollution when the air is usually pure is less compelling than reducing pollution when the air is palpably foul.

Using the same hypothetical procedure, we arrive at the remaining dollar values in figure 5. One further assumption must be added here: the villagers' willingness *to pay* to reduce pollution by a given degree is the same as the minimum the villagers would *accept* as payment for increased pollution. For example, in moving from point 3 to point 4, the villagers are assumed to be willing to *pay* someone as much as $50 for the odor reduction. The assumption introduced here is that they would willingly accept $50 (or more) from the mill to move from point 4 to point 3, voluntarily accepting more pollution in exchange for more money. (This assumption is reexamined in sections 6.2 and 7.5.)

5.1.4. Value Maximization, Cost Minimization

The next step in the analysis is to superimpose figure 4 on figure 5, which is done in figure 6. This allows us to determine the point on the use of the atmosphere index that produces maximum valuation of air resources. The villagers would prefer point 5, the pure atmosphere. Their total valuation of point 5, as compared with point 1, is $300 (= $125 + $100 + $50 + $25).

The mill owners would prefer an entitlement to point 1. Their valuation of the right to unrestrained use of the village's air (point 1) as compared with point 5, is $250 (= $25 + $50 + $75 + $100). This is less than the $300 valuation the residents would put on the opposite extremum. If points 1 and 5 were the only choices, the mill should not locate there.

If all of the points were realistic choices, then point 3 would produce the maximum valuation of the atmosphere. The mill's preference for point 3 as opposed to point 5, is $175, and the villagers' valuation of point 3 as opposed to point 1 is $225. The

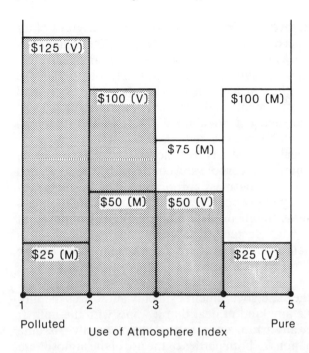

Figure 6. Mills' (M) versus Villagers' (V) Valuation of the Atmosphere

total valuation is thus $400 (= $175 + $225), greater than that of either point 1 or point 5. It is also greater than the total valuation at point 4 ($375) or point 2 ($350), though either of these is preferable to the endpoints.

Point 3 also minimizes the costs of using the atmosphere as a resource. The cost to the villagers of moving from point 5 to point 3 is the value of pure air they give up to get there: $25 + $50 = $75. The cost to the mill of point 3 is the loss of the use of the air as a disposal for smells, or $25 + $50 = $75. Thus the total costs are: $75 + $75 = $150, which is lower than similarly calculated costs at any other point. This shows the duality principle in economics: what maximizes resource value minimizes the costs of production.

5.2. ENTITLEMENTS AND EXCHANGE: THE COASE THEOREM

The last section treated the problem of the pulp mill as an engineering exercise. The technically feasible trade-offs are determined, people reveal their valuations of various degrees of air quality, and the maximum dollar values can be determined. Altogether ignored was the issue of what degree of air quality villagers or mill owners are *entitled* to, and how they might *exchange* entitlements after they have been set. In what follows, I shall investigate both entitlements and exchange. A political/legal system will be added, and the possibilities for self-interested, voluntary exchange will be investigated.

The political/legal situation is as follows. The village will be assumed to be a municipal corporation chartered by the state, and the mill's owner to be a business corporation. The business corporation is owned by many people who have authorized the managers to do business for them. The municipality is composed of many people who have elected officials to conduct public business for them. We shall assume that there are mechanisms to ensure that both sets of representatives act in the best interest of their constituents.

Assume that the state government explicitly authorizes the municipality to make any kind of deal that it wants with the mill. It will freely enforce any arrangement settled on voluntarily. Assume also that the valuations of both parties of the use of the atmosphere (figure 6) are known to both sides.

Now we state a seemingly remarkable result, known as the Coase theorem.[2] Point 3 in figure 6, the use of the atmosphere that produces the maximum valuation, will be obtained regardless of whether the factory is initially entitled to pollute (point 1) or the villagers are originally entitled to pure air (point 5). Under our assumptions, in other words, the initial distribution of resource entitlements has no effect on the outcome, and the outcome maximizes the social valuation of the resource.

To show this, let us consider first a state legislature (or a court system) that wants to encourage industry.[3] Acting on this inclination, it gives all firms an entitlement to use the atmosphere as intensively as possible (point 1). (The same result would be obtained if the legislature were less permissive and entitled the mill to point 2.) In terms of our example, this would imply that the village had no authority to deny the mill a rezoning from agricultural to industrial.

In this situation, consider the motivations of both the mill managers ("the mill") and the municipal government officials ("the village"). According to our previous calculations, it would be worth a total of $225 to the village for the mill to adopt pollution abatement procedures that would improve air quality to point 3. It would cost the mill only $75 to do so. Surely some kind of deal could be worked out. In the baldest kind of exchange, the village could just tax its citizens an extra $75 to bribe the mill to adopt pollution abatement. Equivalently, the mill might petition for a local property-tax abatement worth $75, or it might ask for some "free" municipal services worth $75. (If the mill wanted to be nasty about it, it might demand almost as much as $225 to reduce its pollution to point 3, since it knows that the villagers will pay *up to* this amount. I will take up this "entitlement protection" problem in section 6.4.)

Consider a second initial position in which a state legislature (or court system) says that its citizens are entitled to pure air (point 5 in figure 6). Now the mill must do the compensating if it is to locate in the village. Again, it can and will get to point 3. It is worth $175 to the mill to go from point 5 to point 3, while the villagers value that sacrifice in pure air at only $75. There is plenty of room to make a deal. This time the villagers may bargain hard, and instead of accepting only $75, they may extract up to $175 from the mill for permission to use their atmosphere at intensity point 3. Regardless of how the surplus is allocated, though, the same result is obtained as before.

Why will the mill stop at point 3 in paying for entitlements? Clearly point 2 or point 1 would be advantageous to the mill. It will not go there, because in moving from point 3 to point 2, the villagers will ask for $100, while the mill will be willing to pay no more than $50. The transaction, though legally possible, will not happen, because the parties cannot come to an agreement.

5.3. THE COASE THEOREM GENERALIZED: THE ENTITLEMENTS DIAGRAM

5.3.1. Divisible Entitlements

The result in the previous section may be generalized by acknowledging the following possibilities:

a. One can discuss entitlements to *any* resource or activity, not just use of the atmosphere.

b. Any number of divisions of the resource could be considered, not just the five air-quality points.

c. Any two parties might be involved in the exchange process, not just a private corporation and a municipality.

I noted earlier that economists' training makes them think of several alternative assignments. A lawyer's training suggests much

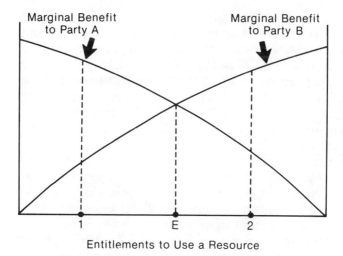

Figure 7.   The Entitlements Diagram

the same thing. A common metaphor in property law is that property is a "bundle of sticks." The implication is that one can split up entitlement bundles in many ways: private agreements to divide property can involve covenants, easements, and other "equitable servitudes" that divide an interest. Nuisance law and zoning law can also be thought of as dividing up entitlements between the public and private landowners. The property metaphor and the economists' idea of continuous production functions provide the base for a similar outlook and analysis.

The Coase theorem, then, can be analysed more generally with reference to figure 7. This diagram is the same as figure 6, except that it is modified according to the generalizations listed above. We will subsequently use this diagram to discuss land use issues. I will henceforth refer to it as the "entitlements diagram."[4]

The efficient use of entitlements, point E in figure 7, will be obtained regardless of the initial distribution of entitlements between parties A and B, provided that:

1. entitlements are completely defined (i.e., they can be measured in some way);

2. entitlements are exclusively assigned so that their owners can prevent others from using them adversely to their interests;

3. entitlements may be legally and costlessly transferred from one party to the other so that there are no barriers to trade; and

4. the initial distribution of entitlements does not itself affect the demand for any subsequent exchange.

Provided that each of these assumptions holds,[5] the process of self-interested exchange can be depended upon to yield a unique and economically efficient allocation of resources. In particular, it does not matter whether initial entitlements are at point 1 or point 2 in figure 7; the unique and efficient equilibrium point E will be attained in either case. This is the Coase theorem. Reexamination of assumptions 2, 3, and 4 will be the focus of much of the rest of this chapter and the next.

The curves in figure 7 are both labeled "marginal benefit," rather than one being a cost and the other a benefit. This is to emphasize the frequently neglected point that the resource is useful to *both* parties, but in mutually exclusive ways. (If they were not mutually exclusive, there would be no controversy.) But one could label either or both curves as "marginal *cost*." The advantage of my notation is that it shows the symmetry of the controversy more clearly and thus focuses discussion on more alternatives than the standard analysis might.

5.3.2. Indivisibilities, Corner Solutions, and Instability

Both curves in figure 7 are drawn as a smooth, continuous line. This implies that there are no technical discontinuities in using the resource. Whether this is valid must be considered on a case-by-case basis, but I would make two points in favor of usually assuming continuity. One is that disputes about entitlements are assumed to take place in advance of any construction. For most zoning issues I think that this is realistic. Second, many problems that are identified as technical discontinuities are really information costs, not technically indivisible techniques.

The reason why industrial siting issues appear to be decided on an either/or basis is that it is too time-consuming to draw up and consider many alternatives. But that does not mean that the alternatives are not implicitly considered. A mill may make an estimate of what kinds of conditions a community may accept and then lobby for them to be approved by local officials. This strategy may result in approval more quickly than would presenting the full panoply of options to the authorities. Thus it may appear to be a discontinuous (either/or) decision, but in fact the discontinuity is not technical in the sense that planners and engineers have no choices with respect to input combinations.

Two alternative marginal benefit schedule shapes require some

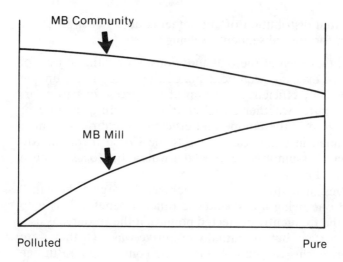

Figure 8.   Corner Solution

comment. In figure 8, one benefit schedule, in this case the community's, dominates the other party's (the mill's) in all areas in which entitlements are defined. As drawn, this gives a corner solution. The villagers would not be willing to give up any of their entitlement to clean air for anything the mill might profitably pay.

Corner solutions are common in most ordinary property transactions; one party buys out the other entirely. Precisely because this situation requires no splitting of entitlements, however, it is of little interest for policy. What may be more interesting is that the village's marginal benefit schedule can rise over time.

Because it is a public good, demand for air quality should be summed vertically. As more people arrive in the community, the value of such amenities increases. The mill's valuation of atmosphere is unlikely to increase, since having more people in a community does not affect demand for its product. In this situation it would be efficient to have the mill adopt more stringent standards, perhaps even shut down (as in figure 8).[6]

The previous analysis assumes, contrary to experience, that the villagers do not work in the mill. If they do work in the mill, a merger of interests is achieved, and one would expect the disamenity affects of living there to be reflected in wages. The mill managers thus have an incentive to reduce pollution to save on wages, and voters have an incentive to tolerate some pollution to maintain employment (section 6.7).

The pathological situation is shown in figure 9. Here the mar-

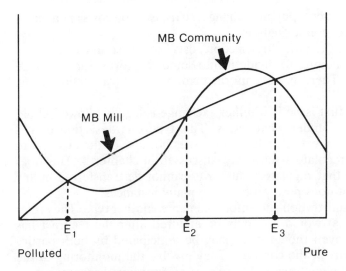

Figure 9. Multiple Equilibria

ginal benefit (MB) schedule of the community first decreases, then increases, then decreases again. It intersects the mill's MB schedule in three places. Point E_2 is unstable: the villagers would be willing to pay the mill either to have less pollution, thus moving to E_3, or to accept payment to have more pollution, thus moving to E_1. The unstable, multiple equilibrium situation illustrated here is the source of several arguments about market failure.[7] I leave it alone in this book because I cannot think of any zoning situations in which it applies.

5.4. TRANSACTION COSTS AND
THE PROBLEM OF PUBLIC GOODS

Universal definition and exclusive assignment of control are necessary conditions for the Coase theorem, but they are not sufficient. The third condition is that entitlements be costlessly transferable from one party to another. If all property were inalienable, the initial entitlements would be the final ones, and the gains from trade and specialization that exchange allows would be lost. Trade requires various pre- and post-exchange arrangements. They involve what are referred to as "transaction costs," or the resources involved in exchanging entitlements. Exchanges are pervasive in a modern economy, and so are the limitations that governments put on exchange, so transaction costs are a major focus of economic analysis.

Because the term "transaction costs" covers so much territory, it may be helpful to divide it into some categories for analytical purposes. There is no uniform taxonomy for transaction costs, though.

1. The first issue is whether exchange is legally allowed at all, and if it is, under what terms. This type of transaction cost is especially important in land use issues because of the hostility to "selling" regulatory authority, discussed in chapter 4. This does not mean that regulatory authority cannot be transferred in any way, but it does pose problems in many instances.

2. Administration and enforcement are another type. They refer to costs that would normally be endured after the contract has been set, even though they may be anticipated by both parties and are part of the contract. They involve the monitoring of the terms of the contract and the process of settling disputes.

There is an extensive economic literature on the costs of administering and enforcing contracts (Goldberg 1976). Economic theories that seek to explain the existence of firms and the nature of contract law focus on this type of cost. But it is less important in property law and land use issues, because the things that are exchanged are (relatively) stationary. One can literally go out and see, for example, whether curbing is being installed in the subdivision. (Might this be a reason for distinguishing contract law from property law?)

3. In land use issues, the crucial transaction cost is the cost of *prior* information. In order to make an exchange, the parties to it must determine what it is worth to them. The problem is one of knowledge of valuations. For our purposes, two aspects of information costs are especially important. One is the means by which preferences for collectively consumed goods are to be measured and aggregated. The second, which is considered in chapter 6, is the need to measure the other party's valuations in order to forestall strategic bargaining.

A public good is one that can be enjoyed by additional people without reducing the consumption of others. Such a good is said to be "nonrival"; it allows others to consume the same "unit" as I do without reducing my enjoyment of it. Obviously, these are matters of degree; one can think of goods that begin as public goods but, with sufficient numbers of consumers, become more like private or rival goods. Space on the beach is one example.

The public goods problem, to refer to the pulp mill example, means that a community's willingness to pay for entitlements is the result of a vertical summation of willingness to pay for each degree of air quality. Each resident must be thought of as having some demand for an increment to a given entitlement, and each of these amounts is added up to get the village's marginal benefit schedule.

The *problem* of public goods is to get people to reveal their willingness to pay for them so as to provide the correct amount. Because everyone gets the same amount regardless of one's own contribution, the temptation is to understate one's preferences, thus becoming a "free rider." For the decision maker, this is an information cost and hence a transaction cost. It would also be the problem for private goods but for the fact that the providers of private goods can withhold them if they are not paid. "Free riders" are thus the classic problem in determining the appropriate level of public goods.

The crucial assumption of the Coase theorem is that this knowledge is easy to obtain. This leads us to inquire about the methods by which various institutions induce people to reveal knowledge, especially about public goods.[8] This is the subject of the next section.

5.5. PUBLIC GOODS AND MAJORITY VOTING

Public goods and their consequence, free riders, are a lesson that economists find so neatly intriguing that they often neglect the not-so-neat ways that governments deal with them every day. The problem created by nonrival, nonexclusive goods is that there is no *voluntary*, *market* mechanism by which preferences can be reliably revealed. But local government actions are *not* based on voluntary, market preferences; they are based, ultimately, on the results of the ballot box.

Economists have begun to deal with the problem of democratic provision of public goods. The model most frequently advanced is the median voter model. Its premise is that government officials act "as if" there were a referendum held on every public issue. It has been shown that under some rather restrictive assumptions, the median voter model can result in an efficient allocation of public goods in a community.[9]

The "as if" assumption of majority rule seems to be reasonable for communitywide land use issues. This is due to the extensive citizen participation (open meetings, referenda) that zoning law encourages (section 2.6).

A potential defect of the median voter model is that it would appear that a developer might be able to bribe the 51 percent of the voters who are least affected by it to vote for it, to the detriment of the other 49 percent. Aside from logrolling and the transaction costs of vote buying, this possibility is substantially reduced by the weight that zoning law and practices give to neighbors when variances, special permits, and rezonings are being considered. This is an important check on majoritarian excesses.

A practical defense of the applicability of the majority voting model to land use decisions is that the same process allocates most *other* local public goods. There is evidence that the median voter model gives reasonable empirical estimates of the levels of such local public goods as public schools, roads, police protection, and recreation services (Bergstrom and Goodman 1973; Rubinfeld 1977). There is also (weaker) evidence that these levels are efficient (section 14.11).

The reason for investigating the relation of local public decisions to individual preferences is that it is crucial to the application of the property rights model to zoning issues. The property rights approach is often criticized as "valid but not applicable" because of the large-numbers problems in bargaining.[10] Bargaining cannot occur if more than a few parties attempt to strike a deal. What the critics overlook is the possibility that many people may delegate authority to bargain on their behalf. In business the premier means of doing this is to form a corporation. In public life the obvious way is to elect a representative government. Once the organization has been completed, though, the large-numbers problem disappears.

5.6. THE PULP MILL REVISITED: SPILLOVER PROBLEMS

The second assumption of the Coase theorem was that entitlements were exclusively assigned. This is one function of a political/ legal system: both common law and statute law may assign public resource entitlements. This does not mean that the job is complete, though.

An important problem of unassigned entitlements in zoning cases is the spillover from one jurisdiction to another. Zoning law typically permits community discretion in controlling industry within its borders, but it is almost silent on the issue of intermunicipal (or interstate) spillovers (section 4.3). In my example, I have suggested that the federalization of air- and water-pollution issues reduces the intermunicipal spillover problem, so that the location of a pulp mill is more likely to be a local issue, involving only one or two communities in its nuisance effects. Despite this, there is reason for concern about spillovers among a few communities.

One approach, suggested by Ellickson (1979), might be to establish a common-law set of nuisance rules that entitle neighboring or downstream communities to collect damages for such spillovers. Another option is tax-base sharing among communities, in which the taxes generated by fiscally profitable activities are shared with other communities in proportion to the damages caused by the intermunicipal spillovers.[11] (On the other hand, some uses may create desirable spillovers that in a rough way compensate for the undesirable ones. In my study of the pulp mill, respondents who favored the mill indicated that employment opportunities were an important intermunicipal spillover.)

While such options have their merits, there is a third to consider. This is forbearance. My experience with local officials in rural areas suggests that they are not eager to despoil their neighbors in other communities. Generally speaking, people in one community take some account of the well-being of people in nearby communities. This can be seen in mutual aid agreements for fire and police protection.

Such arrangements suggest a self-interested reason for neighborliness: foisting nuisances onto another community invites retaliation, and there are a number of ways to retaliate. If this is a reasonable approach, it suggests that some intermunicipal spillovers may be internalized after all. Explicit provision for intervention by one community into the decisions of another by the methods described above could upset the "neighborliness" balance that may already restrain community actions.

Many observers have suggested that industrial siting gives rise to another kind of spillover (Bergman 1974). New business attracts new workers to the area. The town that gets the commercial or industrial tax base may not be willing to rezone itself to accommodate new workers, who must then live in other towns. This imposes a fiscal burden on the nearby communities that is not offset by additional tax bases.

It is not clear that this effect, if it occurs, should be called a spillover. The neighboring towns in the above example generally have the same zoning entitlements as the one in which the mill proposes to locate. If they, too, wish not to accommodate new residential development, they can exclude it as well as the mill town can. To the extent that neighboring towns are capable of seeing to it that newcomers pay marginal costs of public services (via "fiscal" zoning or other devices described in section 4.1), the newcomers cannot be said to be a fiscal burden.

It may be argued that *no* nearby town wants to accommodate residential development. But then one might ask why a mill would locate in the area in the first place. If towns will only accommodate workers with high incomes, then the mill will find that it has either to hire from the existing labor force or to induce new workers to move in with such high wages that they, too, will have high incomes. This cost is one that the mill will have to consider in evaluating the merits of various sites.[12] Thus it can be seen that this is not necessarily an "externality" at all. The location of prospective employees is something that both town officials and mill managers will have to consider and bear the consequences of.

5.7. INFORMATION COSTS IN THE PULP MILL CONTROVERSY

Despite the problems just mentioned, the law of zoning does assign a reasonably complete set of entitlements to community residents. The most important problems with zoning stem from the restrictions on transferring these entitlements.

The legal restrictions on exchange of entitlements were discussed at length in chapter 4. It was found that some indirect types of exchange are permitted, but direct cash transfers generally were not. I did qualify that for decisions about commercial and industrial property. In these the legality of direct user charges and other development fees seems less controversial than in the construction of homes, apartments, and public facilities. Thus the legal inhibitions on exchange probably were not important in the pulp mill example.

The more important transaction costs are those of information about the valuation of public goods. My response to that was that the democratic process is a reasonable means of revealing preferences. The town elects officials to make decisions, and they often have the option of having a referendum on the issue. The median voter prevails by definition in the latter case.

Voters also elect a representative government whose small numbers enable negotiations to take place. My argument in section 5.5 was that the large-numbers problem in bargaining is solved by the use of representative government. This must be qualified. One of the problems that the local government officials in my actual example encountered was *excessive* public participation. Representatives for the mill proposed having a closed meeting with town officials to iron out differences that had become apparent and to resolve, presumably by haggling and compromise, problems that had been aired in the extensive public debate. Town officials were agreeable to such a meeting, but the opponents of the mill obtained a court injunction against any closed meeting.

Anyone even casually familiar with analogous situations, such as collective bargaining or corporate mergers, knows that such negotiations cannot take place in public. If they did, few participants would be inclined to air the whole range of options and compromises, and little testing of the other side's sentiments would be possible. The requirement of open meetings effectively precluded the exchange of information.

It may appear to the reader that I have just contradicted myself. I urged that political economy's median voter model be adopted in zoning matters in part because citizen participation made public officials sensitive to the desires of their constituents. Yet I then suggested that such participation can be a barrier to achieving an efficient outcome. But this contradiction is more apparent than real: one can have a public decision-making system that allows for both substantial citizen input and closed negotiations between small numbers of representatives. There is time and room for both; it is not necessary to choose only between pure democracy and smoke-filled rooms.

In the instance cited, I suspect that the opponents of the mill knew that requiring an open meeting would preclude negotiations. They realized that while a majority of the town's voters preferred no mill to one that was initially proposed, some of them might be swung over to favoring the mill if modifications to the initial plan were made and guaranteed. Since the mill representatives seemed genuinely perplexed by the opposition, the only way such modifications could have been made was by consultation with knowledgeable officials. This was precluded by the court injunction.

Another information problem is understanding the technical alternatives available. However diligent and honest local officials are, they cannot be expected to comprehend the technical information necessary to exchange the kinds of entitlements that they are expected to exchange in this system. But this is a problem hardly unique to land use issues. No one expects elected officials to design sewers, build bridges, evaluate school services, or apprehend criminals. They hire experts to perform these services. In evaluating the work of their own experts, they may hire independent consultants. So although the local land use authorities may not comprehend the technical issues, they ought to be able to hire someone who can.

The problem with this approach is that hiring your own expert may be costly. This returns to the original point that information is costly; it is the major transaction cost. As a result, community authorities may choose to trade on limited information. This means that the community must accept some risk that the benefits might turn out to be illusory. Public officials are probably more risk averse than other economic agents, so the danger of their making this kind of miscalculation seems low (Buchanan and Faith 1981). The main point is that there is no compelling reason to make land use entitlements inalienable when they are held by a community. There may be good reasons to limit the terms under which exchange is allowed, but these need not make zoning entitlements inalienable (sections 6.5 and 9.1).

5.8. CONCLUSION AND POSTSCRIPT

In this chapter I showed that by looking at zoning as a collectively held entitlement, one can examine it in terms of the framework of the Coase theorem. This led to an examination of the nature of resource entitlements and the transaction costs involved in their exchange. I argue that representative governments can overcome the problem of free riders that make purely private negotiations unlikely. Elected officials may be able to exchange community entitlements to public goods resources to the mutual advantage of resident voters and outside producers and consumers. While this process is complicated by intermunicipal spillovers, they do not seem so formidable as to preclude the possibility that such bargaining can promote an efficient balance between local environmental amenities and production of other goods and services.

The reader might want to know what happened to the pulp mill. After intensive debate, the town of Walpole, New Hampshire, held a town meeting in March 1976 and voted 866 to 690 not to rezone the land as the mill's developers had requested. The Parsons and Whittemore Company, prospective builders of the mill, made no further efforts to locate in New England. They were reported to have found a suitable site in Alabama.

What was wrong with this outcome? In my opinion, nothing; this was most likely a true corner solution. Walpole's main village contains some of the finest examples of nineteenth-century classical revival architecture in northern New England, and the amount its residents would have had to be paid to accept the mill might well have exceeded the mill's value of location in that town. If my conjecture is valid, the decision against the mill maximizes the value of society's resources. But two problems with the decision process stand out.

First, the mill developers did seem uninformed, not to say naive, about the preferences of the citizens. There were several towns nearby whose citizens would seem to have been far more willing than Walpole's to accommodate a large pulp mill. Perhaps engineering considerations caused them to choose the site they wanted, but with the advantage of hindsight, one can suggest that a somewhat less technically favored site in a more welcoming community might have been cheaper. Maybe that community was indeed in Alabama, but the company and members of the community did engage in substantial expense to find that out.

Not much can be done about the previous point except to urge that state or regional development commissions try to gauge in advance the sentiments of the communities to which they guide industrial development. A second problem bears more consideration. This is the laws that permit factions to manipulate the decision making process. The example in this instance was the injunction against closed meetings between elected officials and company representatives. I would not dwell on it were it not pandemic in major land use controversies. It is a major feature of the newer statewide land use laws. Open meetings and sunshine laws have their merits, but improving the quality of complicated contractual arrangements is not one of them.

NOTES

1. Even the classic nuisances of railways, major highways, and industrial locations are found to be localized. Their effects on residential property seem to be undetectable at more than a quarter mile from the nuisance (Langley 1976, Poon 1978, Tideman 1972). See also sections 11.2 and 11.3.

2. The seminal articles are Coase (1959; 1960). One will look in vain for anything labeled a theorem in these works. Reference to the Coase "theorem" was made by others such as Harold Demsetz (1964) who developed the implications of Coase's critique of modern welfare economics. For a survey of this literature see Furubotn and Pejovich (1972). A collection of many important articles that develop the Coase theorem is Manne (1975). Many critical essays are in [Coase] (1973–74). Examples of recent critiques

are Cooter (1982) and Dahlman (1979). A succinct and sympathetic textbook development of the property rights approach is Posner (1977, chap. 3).

3. This appears to have been the purpose of the nineteenth-century English courts, which modified the common law of nuisance to accommodate the factory system (Brenner 1974).

4. The first use of a diagram like this to analyze the Coase theorem seems to have been by Turvey (1963). It is not quite standard analysis in the property rights literature, but it does crop up almost as frequently as diagrams marked "Supply and Demand." More recent examples are Feldman (1974) and Polinsky (1979). The first applications of it to zoning were a paper I wrote on zoning reform (Fischel 1979b) and an independent paper on zoning by David Mills (1979).

5. The major focus of the Coase theorem is assumption 3, zero transaction costs. The first two are often stated differently. Posner (1977, 29) states the assumptions as (1) "universality," (2) "exclusivity," and (3) "transferability." His term "exclusivity," however, seems to mean what I would call an extreme initial entitlement point on the entitlements diagram; one begins either at the far left side of the horizontal index or at the far right. But this is not necessary when entitlements can be easily separated and defined along a continuous line. See also section 6.5.

6. Corner solutions might also occur because of limited information about the marginal benefit schedules. For example, the villagers might take the costs of pollution abatement to be constant rather than rising (as is assumed in this analysis). They might then insist on pollution abatement standards that would lead to a shutdown (corner solution) of the mill even when that is not the efficient outcome (Polinsky 1979).

7. Multiple equilibrium may result from nonconvexities in the production set, examined by Baumol and Oates (1975, chap. 8). Keep in mind that they consider national pollution, while zoning is largely confined to local issues. Crone (1983) applies a nonconvexity argument to zoning. His empirical results do not support the existence of nonconvexities in single-family and multifamily housing zones in Foster City, California.

8. Robert Cooter (1982), in a review and extension of the literature on the Coase theorem, makes a case against its applicability. He notes that additional communication between parties in a controversy may as likely induce them to adopt bargaining strategies that would retard the exchange of entitlements as it would promote exchange. This is an important point, and it helps delineate the nature of transaction costs. But it does not itself dispose of the Coase theorem as an analytic device. The crucial aspect of transaction cost is *knowledge*. Communication is not synonymous with knowledge, as most instructors know.

9. The original statement of the conditions for efficiency of majority voting is Bowen (1943). (I do not review them here.) Evidence for the median voter hypothesis is in Inman (1978) and Holcombe (1980). I argue in chapter 7 that the median voter model is especially appropriate for suburban communities. The model is examined in a more general theory of politics in chapter 10. The efficiency of local government decisions is augmented by

residents' ability to vote with their feet, as suggested by Tiebout (1956). See also chapter 14.

10. See, for example, Baumol and Oates (1975, 10–13) and Mandelker (1971, 26). Coase mentions zoning in both of his seminal articles (1959; 1960), but not in terms of a collective property right. It is perhaps significant that the first major work to analyze zoning as a collective property right makes no mention of the Coase theorem (Nelson 1977). While elements of the Coasian analysis were incorporated in several earlier articles, I believe that I was the first to make a formal connection between the Coase theorem and zoning as a collective property right (Fischel 1978).

11. This was at least part of the rationale of the Minnesota Fiscal Disparities Act, analyzed in Fischel (1976) and Fisher (1982).

12. In section 14.10.3, I show that a firm that has to pay its workers above-market wages might exploit the resulting labor queue by moving to a community that is remote from its workers. Thus some firms may appear to be unconcerned with their employees' ability to locate near their place of work.

6.

The Property Rights
Approach in Perspective

This chapter continues the last by examining and qualifying the property rights approach. It deals first with criticisms that monetary values and marketlike exchanges are inappropriate for dealing with land use questions. Some of these criticisms have merit, but I argue that most are based on a misunderstanding of economics and the land market. I shall also answer the charge that adoption of the property rights approach would have regressive effects on wealth distribution. The opposite is more nearly true.

The middle sections deal with several theoretical criticisms of the Coase theorem: that it is not valid in the long run because of excess entry by those who seek entitlements; that strategic bargaining precludes many settlements; and that it is trivial because the parties in conflict can merge their interests. None of these is formally dispositive, but each introduces some necessary qualifications and provides insights to the application of the Coase theorem to the real world.

The final sections discuss the differences between the property rights approach and the more standard externality approach to land use controversies suggested by A. C. Pigou. They differ in their approach to public policy rather than in their formal economic analysis.

6.1. CRITICISMS OF ECONOMIC CALCULATIONS

That land use issues ought to be decided on the basis of economic calculations is not a popular proposition. Economics is thought by many observers to be either irrelevant or wrong-headed when dealing with questions of community environment. This attitude is more pervasive in land use issues than in any other economic domain. Many people who normally approve of free exchange draw the line at the land market.[1] This section evaluates some of these arguments.

6.1.1. Defects of the Land Market

It is sometimes argued that economics has a limited role in land use planning because of the defects of the land market. Compared with other markets, the land market is said to be unresponsive, random, or perverse. (Part of the blame is put on speculators, whose function is examined in section 12.7.) Even if this were well established, it would not itself eliminate the application of economic reasoning to land use issues. Economics has expanded in recent years into many areas of behavior where there appear to be no direct markets. Examination of marriage and family relationships is one example (Becker 1976).

Unlike spouses and children, however, land is indeed sold on the market. It simply is not true that this market fails to reflect underlying conditions of supply and demand. There are many empirical studies of land markets. These are usually investigations into housing markets, but since their method is to hold constant the influence of building characteristics, they tell a great deal about the land market.

What they find is that the land market is sensitive to most of the things to which we expect it to be sensitive. Residential land values are influenced by distance from employment, access to schools (and quality of schools), the presence of pleasant views, neighborhood nuisances, the presence of utilities, air quality, aircraft noise, property taxes, and the type of zoning.[2] I shall discuss the last finding in section 11.3, where I am critical of the interpretation of of such studies. But that the market for land responds to such influences seems almost incontrovertible.

Some may find the last assertion dubious because it is frequently observed that the land market is characterized by limited information (Healy and Short 1981). Limited information need not be a barrier to efficient markets, though. Vernon L. Smith (1982) has shown experimentally that market equilibrium is achieved quickly even though participants know only their own reservation prices.

6.1.2. "Subjective" versus "Objective" Values

A distinction is sometimes made between the "objective" monetary values of everyday goods that are purchased in the market, and the "subjective" values of the environment and other goods not commonly sold on the market. This may reflect misunderstanding of value theory in economics, which holds that all values are subjective. More charitably, it reflects a consumer's surplus doctrine, in which people put a value above the market price of particular amenities. This is not satisfactory, though, since consumer's surplus applies to all goods. People may get consumer's surplus from their clothes or automobiles, but arguments that either good should be allocated by anything but the market are heard less frequently.

I think that the subjective values argument for environmental amenities is caused by a lack of experience with an explicit market for them. In buying a house or renting an apartment, one must evaluate the worth of various amenities. But the evaluation is almost always part of a tie-in sale. What is bought is a composite good, housing and amenities. The latter are never explicitly priced. Never having paid the price explicitly but nonetheless knowing that they are valuable, people may refer to the values as subjective.

A variation on the subjective values argument comes from the environmental movement. The argument here is that economic values do not give sufficient weight to environmental values. This is true in the sense that environmental amenities are often public goods, so that ascertaining their value is more difficult than it is in the case of private goods. Formation of collective property rights, such as zoning, is a means of dealing with this problem.

Aspects of the environmental argument, however, go much farther than economists' conventional market failure problem. It is argued that the preferences of nonhuman species and even inanimate objects should be counted. The proposition that trees should have legal standing—one given serious consideration in some circles—is not viewed solely as an expedient by which the preferences of that diffuse group of people who like to look at standing trees can have their preferences counted.[3] Whatever the philosophical merits of this argument, it must be understood that the tools of economics are valid only for preferences that can be expressed in some way. Perhaps the higher primates can do this, but the values of rivers and trees are only those that human beings impute to them.

6.1.3. Information Costs

Another reason for aversion to economic calculation in land use issues may be that it is so difficult to get the necessary information to make decisions that it is not worth the effort. This is an objection with which economists can surely sympathize. It is rational for people to exclude economic calculations from certain aspects of their lives (Schelling 1980).

The appeal of this argument must be tempered by its *reductio ad absurdum* consequence: never take economic values into account in making land use decisions. Since such decisions can have effects of considerable magnitude, this argument becomes a justification for arbitrariness. At best, then, information costs could be an argument against a complete restructuring of a zoning ordinance, say, just because someone can show that the total value of land may be increased by 1 percent.

6.1.4. Rent Seeking

An important function of antimarket arguments is to obtain a superior set of entitlements or to protect those one already possesses. The search for new entitlements by individuals or groups with a common interest is referred to in economics as "rent seeking" (Krueger 1974). It typically involves convincing political or judicial authorities to grant individuals or groups a right to receive some stream of benefits or to control some resource. It is not necessarily an unjust or inefficient activity, though many economists regard it as such (Bhagwati 1982).

Rent seeking may be the objective of a community that invents new types of restrictions on development. These restrictions are valuable to the community in that they may enhance the value of property not so restricted, such as existing homes, or they may enable preexisting residents to shift tax burdens onto newcomers. It would be difficult to justify such a redistribution of entitlements to legislative or judicial bodies on economic grounds. To say that one person may not sell his land to a developer just because the rest of the community would like to take some of that value for itself is not appealing in our society. A way of masking such a purpose is to argue that the economic values that the landowner is forgoing are inappropriate for the community to consider.

Rent seeking need not involve complete expropriation of property. Something owned by one party may benefit others. A way for the latter to ensure their entitlements is to make the owner's entitlements inalienable. This is the effect, if not the conscious intention, of arguments that land is a "resource," not a "commodity." Commodities can be sold; resources, according to this rhetoric, cannot.[4]

6.2. THE WEALTH EFFECT OF INITIAL ENTITLEMENTS

There is another argument that people who dislike the property rights approach to land use issues often employ. This is the invocation of income or wealth distribution issues, with the assertion or implication that such economic approaches are regressive.[5] This argument is worth special attention because, first, it does raise an issue that is important in land use controls, and second, it has the conclusion about wealth distribution backwards.

The strong version of the Coase theorem asserts that initial entitlements, a form of wealth, will not influence the demand for exchanging entitlements. The resulting equilibrium will be identical regardless of initial entitlements. This obviously is not true in most land use issues that involve residential housing. In the pulp mill controversy the outcome would have been different if the residents had had to compensate the mill for the cost of nuisance abatement rather than vice versa. A large amount of personal wealth is tied up in residential real estate. The initial entitlement to be free of nuisances is valuable to most voters.

What, then, are we to make of the fairness of the initial entitlements if fairness is to refer to wealth distribution effects? Economists have no special insight into the desirability of one wealth distribution versus another. The economist's task is to point out the consequences of a given system of regulations or taxes. It is a commonplace that the answer to the question, Who pays the tax? is often different from the answer to, Who is assessed the tax? Seemingly progressive taxes on "rich" firms may ultimately be borne by not-so-rich employees, suppliers, or consumers.

The same analysis of incidence must be applied to the distribution of various environmental entitlements. By most accounts, environmental regulations have inadvertently had a regressive effect on the distribution of income and wealth. In terms of employment and wage effects, compliance costs tend to be shifted to low-income people. In terms of benefits received, nearly every serious study shows that they redound disproportionately to the rich and that the rich value them more.[6]

One should not expect noneconomists to pay much attention to the literature on the incidence of land use and environmental controls. What is curious to me is that people persist in asserting the opposite even in cases where the evidence is obvious to the casual observer. In the pulp mill case of chapter 5 the local division in the debate about its desirability was obvious: the affluent, well-educated professional and managerial residents fought the mill,

while the lower-income, less educated, blue-collar people generally favored it. The situation becomes even more obvious when
one turns from industrial uses to low-income housing. Trailer parks
and public housing for the poor are often the objects of intense
community opposition.

One cannot jump from the incidence studies to the conclusion
that pulp mills and other nuisance-producing activities ought to
be entitled to move to any spot they please. Just because burglary
may, on balance, redistribute wealth from rich to poor does not
mean that it should be tolerated. There may be other reasons to
assign a generous set of land use entitlements to current residents
(chapters 8 and 9).

The regressivity of initial land use entitlements may be compounded by making them inalienable. Regressiveness of the initial
distribution is diminished if free trade in entitlements is encouraged. (Section 9.1 offers other arguments for alienability.) Although it may cost a firm more to obtain a suitable site if it must
compensate neighbors, the impact of this is not nearly as great as
it would be if the firm were *not allowed* to compensate residents,
since the supply of sites would be more restricted. Yet wealth
distribution remains the focus of much of the antimarket criticism
of exchange of land use entitlements. One satire of a proposal to
sell effluent permits concluded, "It just means the rich can get
away with crimes like poisoning people's lungs that the poor can't
afford to commit" (Hoppe 1975).

6.3. THE PROBLEM OF THE LONG RUN
AND EXCESSIVE ENTRY

The Coase theorem has generated a large literature concerning
its theoretical validity. Several objections to it have implications
for the problems of land use. This section considers whether the
Coase theorem is valid in the long run.[7]

To see the "long-run" argument, return to the example of the
pulp mill. Under the assumptions of the Coase theorem, the air
quality was shown to be the same in the village, regardless of
whether the mill was entitled to pollute the air or the villagers
were entitled to have pure air. Some have argued that this is not
true when one considers incentives that are created for *additional*
mills to enter the village.

Suppose that *any* mill is entitled to pollute the air and that one
mill has just been paid to agree to reduce its pollution. Will this

not encourage other mills to enter the village, partly drawn by the prospect of being paid *not* to pollute? And will this not then result in more total pollution (and firms) than if the mill did not have the right to pollute?

Another way to look at this is to consider the problem from the other side. Suppose that villagers had the right to pure air. Mill owners pay the villagers for the right to emit some pollution. Will this not encourage migration into the village by new residents, partly seeking to benefit from the compensatory payments offered by the mill? With all these new recipients, would the mills then decide to reduce pollution (and production) even further so as to avoid having to make the payments?

The answer to both these "nonsymmetry" objections is, Not as long as the original assumptions of the Coase theorem are adhered to. The problem with both of these plausible-sounding sequences is that entitlements have not been exclusively assigned. The first example assumes implicitly that the bargain that the town strikes with the first mill is with that mill only and that other mills need not respect it. This does not need to be the case, and it would clearly be a faulty contract if the village did so.

What the village must do is contract with all *owners of land* on which a mill might feasibly locate and acquire the rights to use the atmosphere from all of them.[8] These atmospheric entitlements would then have to be purchased by other mills that wanted to locate in the village. They could purchase them from the villagers if the villagers were willing to surrender some more of their pure air, or they could be purchased from the original mill provided that it was willing to reduce its own pollution to leave air quality unchanged.

The key to this problem, then, is that entitlements must *run with the land*. An entitlement runs with the land if, when the real estate is sold, the new owner is subject to it just as the former owner was (Dunham 1965). Entitlements cannot be specific to each firm, for the supply of potential firms is indefinitely large. (The direct relation of this principle of law to the debate about the long-run validity of the Coase theorem does not seem to be widely recognized.)

The case best illustrating this is Lewis v. Gollner, 14 N.Y.S. 362 (City Court of Brooklyn 1891). Lewis and some neighbors paid Gollner to desist from erecting a tenement in their high-class Brooklyn neighborhood. Gollner stopped that project but then acquired a site across the street and, under his wife's name, started building again. The trial court refused Lewis's request to enjoin

Gollner from doing so, for the original contract was not specific to a piece of property.[9]

The same caution applies on the alternative assignment problem, in which the village grows too large as immigrants move in to seek payments from the mill. If people in a village are to have an entitlement, it must be specific to them or their assigned successors, not to all potential entrants.

The "long-run" objection is thus not dispositive, but it does point to the importance of establishing a well-defined and exclusive set of entitlements in land use. Zoning approximates such entitlements; it usually permits a community to exclude commercial development on virtually all of its land (section 4.3). This entitlement applies to land, not to specific firms. A factory that has gained permission to enter a community has obtained an entitlement that may be transferred to another owner of the same factory, but it cannot be sold to an owner of another parcel of land. Only the community can grant the latter entitlement. The community in addition can control, although far less perfectly, the flow of immigrants through restrictions on new housing construction. This tends to mitigate the problem of excessive entry of people to collect compensatory payments from the firms (see also section 14.10.2).

6.4. STRATEGIC BARGAINING AND ENTITLEMENT PROTECTION

Another objection to the Coase theorem is that it neglects the possibility that strategic bargaining might prevent, or at least inefficiently delay, the mutually advantageous exchange of entitlements.[10] Chapter 5's pulp mill example can be used to show this. Suppose that initial entitlements are such that the village can have pure air (i.e., point 5 in figure 6 in section 5.1.4). The villagers would accept as little as $75 to allow the mill to use the atmosphere to point 3. The mill, however, would be willing to *pay up to* $175 to obtain this privilege. There is latitude for bargaining here, and the strategies and delays caused by taking various bargaining positions might lead to some result other than point 3 in figure 6, which was deemed most desirable.

Bargaining normally takes place when one party does not know the position of the other. For example, the mill might try to convince the village that if it had to pay more than $75, it would choose to locate in another area. Likewise, the town might overstate its true valuation of air quality in order to convince the mill that it would accept no less than $175. But both of these positions assume an information constraint, contrary to the assumptions of the Coase theorem. Zero transaction costs mean that each party knows everything relevant to the exchange, which includes the other party's reservation prices.

Still, it might seem that the monetary difference would be some cause for negotiation, even in the absence of information costs. The solution is in the assignment of entitlements. Not only must initial entitlements be assigned, but rules by which the entitlements are legally protected must also be established.

There are at least three possible means for protecting entitlements: property rules, liability rules, or inalienability. These were explored in a classic article by Guido Calabresi and A. Douglas Melamed (1972). Unambiguous assignment of one of these rules will avoid the bargaining problem.

Inalienability simply means that the entitlement cannot be transferred, so there is nothing to bargain about. This rule will be examined (unfavorably) in section 9.1.

A liability rule to protect an entitlement requires payment of "damages" for the loss of the entitlement. These damages are some valuation made by a distinterested third party, and they may be based on market values. The crucial aspect, however, is that the owner may not refuse to trade under a liability rule. An example of a "damages" rule is the protection of one's home from a government agency that wants to demolish it for some public project under eminent domain. The owner may not refuse or ask for some arbitrarily large compensation, but he is entitled to be paid the market value of his home.

A property rule, on the other hand, allows an owner to refuse all offers, holding out for any price or for no exchange at all. For example, ownership of personal belongings is typically protected by a property rule. An owner may ask any price that he wants, or he may refuse to sell at all.

If either of these rules is applied in the previous situation, there is no room for bargaining. Under a property rule, the village can extract all of the mill's valuation of the right to use the atmosphere. (Recall that it knows exactly how much it is worth to the mill under the zero-transaction-cost assumption.) The mill has no latitude to bargain. Under a well-defined liability rule there is no scope for bargaining, either. Suppose that the liability rule specified as damages the collective valuation by the village for the use of the atmosphere. Since this was known, the village would, as before, have no room for bargaining. Bargaining is forestalled in the Coase theorem by perfect information and a complete prior specification of entitlements and rules protecting them. (Section 9.5 considers which rules are preferable when information is in fact costly.)

6.5. A DIGRESSION ON ENTITLEMENT PROTECTION

The difference between property and liability rules was developed by Calabresi and Melamed (1972). I wish to clear up a point about their exposition that may otherwise cloud understanding of their important contribution. They propose four rules of entitlement protection besides inalienability. I shall argue that these are not really four rules, but N times two rules, where N is the number of initial entitlement positions.

Consider Calabresi and Melamed's distinctions in terms of the entitlements diagram. I shall use their own words and example. Marshall, the homeowner, is prospectively damaged by Taney, the mill owner. Their marginal benefit schedules are shown in figure 10. This presents a problem for which Calabresi and Melamed propose four rules:

Rule one: "Taney may not pollute unless his neighbor, Marshall . . . allows it." This implies that Marshall is initially entitled to

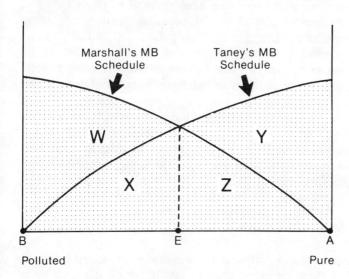

Figure 10.   Calabresi-Melamed Entitlement Protection Rules

pure air, point *A* in figure 10, and that he has property rule protection: he can refuse to trade. This implies that Marshall could *potentially* extract amounts *Z* and *Y* from Taney in an exchange that moved from *A* to *E*. The terms of trade, in other words, all favor Marshall.

Rule two: "Taney may pollute but must compensate Marshall for damages caused. . . ." Marshall still has an initial entitlement to pure air (point *A* again), but now the terms of trade are different. Marshall may not refuse to trade his air rights, but he must be paid damages. If we assume that damages are measured as the area under Marshall's *MB* schedule, Marshall gets amount *Z* from a movement from point *A* to point *E*. He cannot collect any (or much of) amount *Y*.

Rule three: "Taney may pollute at will and can only be stopped by Marshall if Marshall pays him off." This is a shift of initial entitlements to point *B* in figure 10. Taney has the right to pollute. Moreover, this right is protected by a property rule, and so Taney can refuse to trade. This superior bargaining position gives him the potential ability to extract amounts *X* and *W* from Marshall in an exchange moving from point *B* to point *E*.

Rule four: "Marshall may stop Taney from polluting, but if he does he must compensate Taney." Taney has an initial entitlement to pollute (point *B*), but now it is protected only by a liability rule. Marshall only has to pay him damages of amount *X* (the cost of pollution abatement) to move from point *B* to point *E*.[11]

Under my formulation of a continuum of entitlements, there exist not just two initial entitlement points (*A* and *B*) but an indefinite number of them. Thus the number of rules that can be posited is not just four (two entitlement points times two protection rules) but two rules times an indefinite number of entitlement points.

This is not, I believe, a splitting of hairs. It shows that Calabresi and Melamed's analysis opens up an even richer set of approaches to nuisance and other spillover problems. Looking for only four alternatives might cause analysts to overlook some preferable solutions to the problem at hand.

6.6. THE MERGER OPTION

The Coase theorem approach is sometimes criticized by pointing out that there are few cases in law in which it seems to be invoked. Appellate court opinions in nuisance law suggest a breakdown of bargaining rather than a prevalence of it. But this is not evidence against the Coase theorem. It would be interesting to know how many nuisance disputes are settled out of court, as well as how many adjudicated nuisance cases subsequently result in an exchange of entitlements that modifies the decision. Sometimes a judge will suggest just such a modification: Learned Hand, issuing an injunction against pollution of a small stream, suggested that the defendant "make its peace with the plaintiff as best it can" (Smith v. Staso, 18 F.2d 736, 738 [2d Cir. 1927]).

A more subtle critique of the property rights approach is to point out that the conflicts can always be resolved by merger of the two parties, so that splitting entitlements never needs to be negotiated or adjudicated. An example is the conflict between the owners of the Copley Plaza Hotel and the owners of the John Hancock Building in Boston. When the foundations for the Hancock Building were being dug, the hotel next-door began to show cracks in its foundations and walls. Rather than go through the litigation that was sure to follow, the Hancock Company simply bought the hotel. After that it had internal incentives to take the proper degree of care not to damage the hotel, and it avoided some costly litigation.

The same argument applies to benefit spillovers as well as nuisances. Disneyland, in Anaheim, California, provided significant spillover benefits to nearby landowners, who erected hotels to accommodate visitors. When the Disney company later built a similar park in Florida, it was careful to acquire a parcel of land sufficiently large that it would reap all the benefits of the park's attractions. Shopping malls are a less grand example of the same principle.

As these examples suggest, there are barriers to the merger solution. The obvious one is the economist's stand-by: capital markets are imperfect and thus borrowing enough funds to make such a transaction is difficult. A possibly more important reason why merger is not the proper solution was suggested in an early article by Professor Coase (1937; Alchian and Demsetz 1972). He asked why, if the market was efficient, any activities were conducted within firms. Why does a corporation have an accounting department instead of hiring an accounting firm?

The answer is that some activities are more easily controlled within firms; the arm's-length market does not allow for sufficient monitoring of certain activities that are best done by teams of workers. Conversely, Coase's thesis offers a reason why *all* activities are not administered within firms: some types of activities are not easily controlled within firms, and the discipline of market competition makes it possible to buy them from external sources at lower cost.

This may explain why all land use conflicts are not resolved by mergers. It may be inefficient for one firm to operate some lines of business. For example, insurance company executives may not be able to evaluate the performance of hotel employees very well. The value of production would decrease if there were random mergers of different lines of business.

Mergers need not be complete, however, to be effective. One may simply establish a congruence of interests. A pulp mill in an isolated area (Millinocket, Maine, comes to mind) may employ most of the people in the town. If it does, it will have to take into account residents' distaste for pollution. This is because the mill will need to pay workers more to live in the area (or to commute a long way) if there is excessive local pollution. This solution may be true of isolated, one-industry towns, but it seems unlikely to apply in most other areas, in which community residents are unlikely to be employed by the firms whose pollution affects them.

6.7. THE PROPERTY RIGHTS APPROACH VERSUS THE EXTERNALITY APPROACH

The previous discussion may have convinced the reader that the assumptions of the Coase theorem are extreme. Entitlements are *not* universally defined and exclusively assigned, and most transactions are complicated and costly to arrange. What is the use of such a theorem?

The actual theorem itself is of little significance. It can be thought of as a restatement of the conditions for achieving Pareto optimality in terms of alternative legal entitlements. As a formal theorem it is small beer compared with the elaborate and (for economists) sophisticated mathematical derivations of the fundamental theorem of welfare economics. (The theorem, best known for Adam Smith's "invisible-hand" formulation of it, is that competitive markets, among other conditions, ensure an efficient economy.)

The importance of the Coase theorem is the *approach* that it suggests for examining public issues.[12] The framework of the Coase theorem points more clearly than do other economic approaches to the alternatives for dealing with land use controversies. It is more useful in focusing on the problems attendant to alternative policies. If the defect in zoning is seen to be an incomplete assignment of entitlements, the property rights approach leads one to ask how entitlements ought to be assigned. If the defect is high transaction costs, the approach leads one to ask how to reduce such costs. If the defect is one of fairness, it leads one to ask how entitlements should be distributed or protected so as to promote fairness.

This point has been emphasized recently by Coase (1981). After responding to yet another disproof of the Coase theorem, he says: "I would not wish to conclude without observing that, while considerations of what would happen in a world of zero transaction costs can give us valuable insights, these insights are, in my view, without value except as steps on the way to the analysis of the real world of positive transaction costs. We do not do well to devote ourselves to a detailed study of the world of zero transactions costs, like augers divining the future by the minute inspection of the entrails of a goose."

The difference between the property rights theory and the more widely known externality theory is one of approach and focus. The Coase theorem is not a new economic theory. Using it as the beginning of a discussion of land use issues does not necessarily mean that one will come to different conclusions than will someone using externality as the framework. Yet I believe that the property rights approach is more useful than the externality approach, at least for discussion of land use controversies. The reason is that one is *more likely* to come to a better analysis and make more useful policy prescriptions using this approach.

To see the differences between the approaches, consider the problem of the polluting factory in terms of the externality analysis suggested by A. C. Pigou.[13] He would make a distinction between the mill's private costs and its social costs. The private costs are those factors of production that the mill purchases and for which it fully compensates the owners: labor, capital, land, and raw materials. Social costs are private costs *plus* any resources, such as air quality, that are used without payment in the mill's production. In the situation posited, private costs are less than social costs, so that the mill overuses its unpriced input (the atmosphere) and also produces too much of its output.

In latter-day "Pigovian" analysis, the excessive smoke, or other consequence of overusing an unpriced factor, is designated a negative externality. When externalities are present, there is evidence of "market failure." This means that society's resources are inefficiently used, because the private sector cannot be expected to take into account its externalities.

The conventional Pigovian solution for this problem is to pass a law assigning some government agency to regulate the firms creating the problem. It may do this by taxing or fining the firm in some proportion to its pollution or by adopting direct regulations. The level of the taxes or fines, or the configuration of the regulation to be applied, is to be established by objective and fair-minded legislators or by administrators acting at the behest of the legislators. The implication is that this will eliminate (to the fullest extent possible) the market's failure.

6.8. PIGOVIAN SOPHISTRIES

There is nothing formally wrong with Pigou's approach. In the hands of a truly expert economist it can be used to analyze a situation and suggest a policy that will be the best obtainable. But for the rest of us this approach is apt to lead to some errors that the property rights approach may avoid.

6.8.1. Incomplete Analysis

One is liable to make an incomplete analysis of the situation using the externality approach. The language of the term "negative externality" is conducive to a one-sided view of the situation. The problem is seen solely as a matter of a firm's harming the residents by polluting their pure air. But as the Coase theorem shows, who is harming whom is not so obvious. Would not the village be harming the firm—and consumers of its product—by forbidding the location of the mill on an advantageous site? And as far as policy goes, should we not at least consider the possibility that the villagers ought to shield themselves from the effects of the smoke if this can be done without much expense? These are questions that are often overlooked in discussing land use issues.

The externality approach does not inevitably lead to these oversights. The modern Pigovian would say that the focus should be on externalities, but the remedies should balance marginal benefits against marginal costs of taxation, fines, or regulations. Yet this latter calculus is usually done well after the establishment of some regulation. The externality argument has been used to justify wholesale adoption of regulations, with only the briefest thought that entitlements ought to be distributed in some other way.

A related problem is that the externality approach does not encourage one to ask about the source of the externality. Its language seizes upon the consequences of unpriced resources but does not ask why they are unpriced (or underpriced). Is it incomplete assignment of entitlements? If so, policy can be directed to assign them. Is it because entitlements are assigned but not easily exchanged? If so, policies might be designed to reduce barriers to trade. Again, there is nothing in the externality approach to prevent one from thinking of these, but they are seldom a matter of analytical priority.

6.8.2. Criterion for Success

Another problem with externalities is the criterion for success in dealing with them. Economists often speak of "eliminating" or "internalizing" externalities as the goal of public policy. Without a more sophisticated understanding of what this means, this can lead to harmful policies. In the context of the mill example, it might be taken to mean that the mill should not be allowed to use the atmosphere as a disposal medium at all.

A more subtle error is that the externality approach is apt to find fault in situations where there is none. Suppose that the mill had in fact paid compensation to use the atmosphere and emitted some sulphurous fumes periodically. The visiting economists might be unable to detect the original, mutually satisfactory agreement. But they could smell the fumes, which might lead them to declare that this is an externality for which higher government intervention is needed. Only by an inquiry that the externality approach does not encourage them to undertake would they discover that there was in fact no externality involved.[14]

If the reader needs any evidence that the error described in this section is pandemic, just consult almost any introductory textbook on economics (e.g., Samuelson 1976, 477). Under the term "externality" will be given an example of the smoky factory or a nuisance of some sort. For the most part, the word *nuisance* will be used interchangeably with the term "negative externality" or "external cost." But to do so misses the essence of the problem of externality.

For a nuisance to be an externality there must be some barrier to making a contractual arrangement between the creator of the nuisance and the receiver of the nuisance.[15] If such barriers do not exist, that is, if it is perfectly possible for the several parties to get together to make a contract, the nuisance may persist (perhaps with lessened intensity), but it is *not* a negative externality.

That barriers to such contractual arrangements may be common is a dubious excuse for persisting in an error that deflects from the essential aspect of the problem to be examined.

6.8.3. Information Costs and Policy

For the purposes of formulating policy, the key difference between the property rights approach and the externality approach is the assumption about information. Many Pigovian discussions of environmental policy assume that the damage and benefit schedules are well known or at least easily ascertained. They then proceed to discuss which policies might best achieve the optimum. (It gives a ring of truth to the standard economist's joke: Three thirsty castaways contemplate how to open a case of beer. One asks the economist, deep in thought, for his suggestion. He responds, "Well, let's assume we have a can opener. . . .")

The property rights analysis does not assume that policymakers know the right answer. Knowledge is costly, and people will not reveal it without some incentive to do so. Establishing individual or collective property rights and allowing their exchange is one way to reward people for acquiring and revealing information (section 9.2).

6.8.4. Market Failure and Perfectionism

A final objection to the externality approach is summed up in an objection to the term "market failure." For something to fail there must be some criterion for success, and the Pigovian criterion appears to be nothing short of a world of one in which all resources are priced at their full marginal cost. In such a world the assumptions of the Coase theorem apply. It is not the one in which we live.

The externality approach gives us no indication of how close to market perfection is close enough. Governmental intervention can always be made to seem attractive, since no market can meet its criterion for success. The property rights approach, on the other hand, leads one to a "comparative institutions" approach (Demsetz 1969). Of the various arrangements by which we can allocate resources, which will lead to the more productive or fair outcome? It may well be that taxes on industrial effluents are the most efficient approach, but this conclusion must take account of several possible governmental failures, such as rent seeking by various political groups and high information costs for government agencies. These must be weighed against alternative assignment of rights among members of the public and improved institutions to arrange for their voluntary exchange.

6.9. CONCLUSION: WHY TWO SCHOOLS?

I have argued in this chapter that the Coase theorem is less interesting as a theoretical proposition than as a focus for policy analysis. In qualifying the theorem to take account of objections to its applicability, I developed several aspects of property rights that need to be emphasized in designing land use policies. For example, strategic bargaining must be accounted for, and rules for protecting entitlements are one way of dealing with this.

Despite my claim that there is little fundamentally separating Pigovian from Coasian analysis, two schools of thought on this persist. I shall conclude by suggesting some reasons for this, in the spirit of promoting more understanding of both schools.

Proponents of the property rights approach tend to be politically conservative or libertarian, while proponents of the externality approach tend to be modern liberals or socialists. It is perhaps true that something labeled "the property rights approach" tends to make one regard private property more seriously than does an approach that talks about pervasive market failure. It seems possible nonetheless that modern liberals could construct as many arguments for state intervention based on transaction costs as they can based on externality.

Some critiques of the property rights approach imply that the Coase theorem is a conservative manifesto, since it seems to "prove" the efficiency of market approaches. This is not true. The Coase theorem proves nothing about the efficiency of the market. Under its assumption of zero transaction costs, socialism could perform as well as the system of private property. Since all relevant information about costs and preferences is assumed to be known, *anyone* could identify the set of efficient points and command that resources be allocated so as to achieve one of them.

The Coase theorem focuses attention on the role of markets— and governments or other nonvoluntary institutions—in gathering information. One might thereby compare the efficacy of different institutions, private property among them, to obtain information and apply it correctly. Whether the market's performance is superior to alternative arrangements is thus an empirical question, not a matter of dogma.

Another difference between the externality and property rights approaches is the mode of exposition. The property rights literature is largely verbal, while the externality literature is more often mathematical. I think that there are good reasons for this. The property rights approach emphasizes institutional analysis. Property rights theorists dwell upon legal relationships and thus attempt to present their ideas to legal scholars who may have little formal training in economics.

The externalities literature is more mathematical because it provides a tractable benchmark model—the world of perfect competition and zero transaction costs—into which various causes of market failure can be introduced and examined. The distinctly different modes of expression are beneficial, since they widen the field of skills that can be applied to economic issues. The current trend in professional journals, however, seems to be towards merging the two schools, or at least towards increased borrowing of the other's attributes.

If the externalities approach can be criticized for being perfectionist or utopian, the property rights approach can come dangerously close to a Panglossian outlook: whatever exists has evolved because alternative arrangements seemed too difficult to adopt, so this must be the best of all possible worlds. The emphasis is on *possible*, not *best*.

My response to this is that economists should be modest in the application of their trade. Using their tools of analysis to create a deterministic analysis of society seems dangerous and wrongheaded. To tell people, for example, that pollution is not a problem because private transactions might have handled it would be the epitome of presumptuousness. Economics is a means of analyzing social relationships, and it can provide a basis for suggesting alternative means of accomplishing social objectives. This may sometimes mean concluding that a given problem is not worth the sacrifice involved in solving it. But to assert this as a prior expectation, as the Panglossian outlook does, is to vitiate the entire application of economics to social issues. One does not need to be a perfectionist to acknowledge that most things could be improved.

NOTES

1. The Georgist inclinations of Winston Churchill are often quoted as an example of this (Hagman and Misczynski 1978, 18). He is not an unimpeachable source: "Yet all his life, Churchill was a babe in the woods when it came to economics" (Samuelson 1976, 5, citing the blunder he made as Chancellor of the Exchequer).

2. An extensive study showing most of these effects is King (1973). Essays on many types of neighborhood effects are in Diamond and Tolley (1982). The sensitivity of the property market is suggested by Portney (1981), who inferred from the Pittsburgh housing market plausible estimates of the risks of mortality from air pollution.

3. In an influential article entitled "Should Trees Have Standing?" Stone (1972) treads very closely to this line. He urges inalienability for environmental features and suggests that "we may have to consider subordinating some human claims to those of the environment per se" (p. 490). Justice Douglas, in his dissent in Sierra Club v. Morton, 405 U.S. 727 (1972), also adopts this theme.

4. The "resource, not commodity" distinction is from Aldo Leopold (1949), whose work has much influenced the contemporary environmental movement (e.g., Reilly 1973). A variation of it appeared in an advertisement in *The New Yorker* (21 September 1981, 65). Headed "A letter from Kennedy Galleries," the director begins loftily, "As you no doubt have read in numerous forums, I am candid about my feeling that art is not a commodity." The advertisement concludes, however: "It hardly needs repeating that great art does not decline in value. Kennedy Galleries has been providing art and advice to its clients for more than a century. I am at your service."

5. A representative example is Randall (1974): "It seems likely that emitters (industrialists and their stockholders) may be more wealthy than the ordinary citizens who are the receptors" (p. 41). "Surely decent people could see a moral problem in poor citizens bribing an affluent producer of effluents, or accepting pollution in defenseless silence, while Coasians looked on benignly" (p. 53).

6. Studies indicating regressivity include Baumol (1974); Chickering (1975); Dorfman (1977); Dunlap and Allen (1976); Fischel (1979a); Goetz and Brady (1975); Goodchild (1974); and Hollenbeck (1979). Finkler, Toner, and Popper (1976) nonetheless devote an entire book to the proposition that nongrowth strategies will help the poor as well as provide better environment.

7. For a review of this debate and a resolution of the issue see Frech (1979). An earlier and less technical approach is by Calabresi, who first argued that long- and short-run implications were different (1965) and then concluded that they were the same as long as the assumptions of the Coase theorem were rigorously adhered to (1968).

8. The importance of making the contract with landowners was pointed out by Frech (1973). Kneese and Maler (1973) show that the Coase theorem is valid as long as payments are made to all potential entrants. Despite their claim that this is impractical, payments to landowners that run with the land would have the same effect.

9. The New York Court of Appeals subsequently reversed the trial court's decision and did enjoin Gollner, who was candid about his extortionist motives (Lewis v. Gollner, 29 NE 81 [1891]). The point remains, however, that Lewis's contract would not have prevented any other builder from erecting tenements.

10. Rothenberg (1970) and Cooter (1982) both address strategic bargaining. Demsetz (1972) argues that strategic bargaining is just a manifestation

of monopoly, but Feldman (1974) shows that strategic threats can apply to bargaining over competitive rents.

11. Rule four was Calabresi and Melamed's advance over Michelman (1971), who had proposed the previous three rules. The only example of rule four in nuisance disputes is Spur Industries v. Del Webb Devel. Co., 494 P.2d 700 (1972), in which the Arizona court ruled that a resort town that had located near a noxious, preexisting cattle feed lot could enjoin the lot only if it paid the cattleman's relocation expenses (section 13.7.2). Discussion of these rules is also in Bromley (1978); Buchanan and Faith (1981); and Polinsky (1980).

12. My discussion of this issue (to the end of this chapter) was much influenced by Dahlman (1979) and, to a lesser extent, by Cheung (1970).

13. Pigou (1932, esp. pt. 2, chap. 9). He did not use the term "externality," and Goldberg (1981) has argued that Pigou had elements of the property rights approach in mind. Probably the fullest expression of a "Pigovian" analysis is Baumol (1969), whose approach to environmental issues is present in Baumol and Oates (1975).

14. An example of this externality fallacy is examined in detail by Cheung (1973). He shows that a widely believed example of market failure—the pollination of apple orchards by bees—in fact had an apparently successful market after all. My analysis of the location of firms in suburban communities suggests that the externalities (i.e., nuisances) that they are widely believed to create for residents may actually be compensated through the property tax system (Fischel 1975, 164; and section 14.8 below).

15. This is clear in Baumol (1969, 25): "An externality consists of the interdependence together with the lack of accompanying compensation." However, Baumol and Oates (1975, 18) back off from this second condition. What I refer to as an externality is a Pareto relevant externality, to use a term from Buchanan and Stubblebine (1962). Baumol and Oates deal almost exclusively with pervasive and widespread environmental disamenities, to which the second condition—lack of a contractual mechanism—is almost certain to apply.

7.

Suburban Zoning and Housing Supply: A Property Rights Analysis

The previous two chapters developed the property rights model of land use controls with an example that involved a controversy over the location of an industrial plant. Such controversies are neither the most frequent nor the most important zoning issues. The latter distinction belongs, I submit, to the panoply of restrictions on the development of new housing in suburban jurisdictions.[1] The purpose of this chapter is to employ the property rights approach to analyze suburban development controls.

The first sections will fit suburban zoning issues into the framework of the property rights model developed in chapter 5. The next sections will examine four reasons why suburban zoning may be too restrictive. The reasons are (1) high transaction costs caused by legal restraints on exchange and by the political process; (2) the wealth effect of the entitlements that zoning bestows upon suburban communities; (3) the vague definition of entitlements and the resulting problem of distinguishing "illegitimate" motives for zoning from more acceptable ones; and (4) the possibility that zoning may be used to promote monopoly in the local housing market. The conclusion discusses the importance of distinguishing these cases.

7.1. THE NATURE OF SUBURBAN ZONING CONTROVERSIES

The typical setting for the controversies discussed in this chapter is a partially developed suburb or a small town in or near a metropolitan area. The community is assumed to be small and independent of the central city. The parties in the dispute are a representative landowner-developer who wants to put up new housing on vacant land and the preexisting residents of the community. The latter group are homeowners or, less conventionally, renters who get a large amount of consumer's surplus from their current location, so that they would be willing to pay not to have to move. (Appropriation of this surplus by landlords may be prevented by rent control or other tenants'-rights legislation.)

The term "landowner-developer" is used to emphasize that this is a party who both wants to develop the land and stands to profit from any increased land values. We do not consider the developer-contractor, who may seek to erect the houses, or whatever is built, but only after the requisite zoning, subdivision, and other permits are obtained. It is a continuing source of confusion in this field that the owner of the land and the contractor who erects the houses are often the same firm. The reason for this combination of functions is probably that local authorities usually want detailed construction plans before granting permission to develop. There is much give and take between developers and authorities, and it would be cumbersome and time-consuming for a landowner to relay all modification requests to an independent contractor.

The political power of the suburb or small town is entirely in the hands of current residents. They may have differing views about the benefits of various land use entitlements, but I assume that their preferences regarding any prospective development can be ranked along a one-dimensional scale and that this ranking is "single-peaked." This allows us to apply the median voter model described in section 5.5 to deal with the public goods problem. Government is conducted by elected representatives who are faithful to the preferences of the median voter.

Landowner-developers have little influence on the political process. In most suburban communities they are a tiny minority. This is one reason why I differentiate suburban from rural and big city zoning. In rural communities landowners may form a significant minority, and their preferences must be taken into account. Central city politics also gives landowner-developers more weight because of the city's more heterogeneous makeup (section 10.5). I also rule out direct political influence by people who might want to live in the proposed housing. Few are community residents, and they probably could not be organized politically if they were.[2]

Many studies of the economics of zoning founder on the motivation of local officials. Zoning authorities are variously assumed to minimize taxes, maximize fiscal dividends, preserve social homogeneity, maintain residential real estate values, or minimize nuisance costs. Each of these motivations seems plausible in a given situation, but they are only partial theories of zoning. Some of them conflict with one another. Maximizing fiscal dividends may be inconsistent with both minimizing nuisance costs and preserving social homogeneity.

These ad hoc theories of zoning are rejected in this work. Given the political process, I propose that local authorities attempt to maximize the net worth of the median voter.[3] This assumption allows for broader objectives than just maximizing certain aspects of residents' wealth, such as own property value. The latter objective is too narrow, since it may increase a voter's wealth to allow the location of a noxious use next to his home, which would lower his property value, if a sufficiently large side payment is offered (section 11.3). I defend the realism of this assumption by pointing to the numerous empirical studies (noted in section 5.5) confirming it when applied to other local government activities.

As in chapter 5, the benchmark model assumes that any adverse effects from development are pure local public goods. No one outside the community is affected by its actions, and all people in the community are affected equally. This assumption precludes the purely neighborhood controversies in which a landowner has sought an exception via the variance or special permit. Although such controversies are important to the participants, I doubt that they have much effect on housing supply.

The pure local public goods assumption is a strong one, but it is not as unrealistic as it may seem. Many of the objections that people voice towards large residential developments are based on perceived adverse effects that have little to do with physical proximity to the project itself. These include objections that the project would overburden public services or necessitate a tax increase and that the project would change the character of the town.

7.2. SUBURBAN ZONING IN THE ENTITLEMENTS DIAGRAM

7.2.1. Zoning Restrictions as Entitlements

The model for analyzing suburban zoning is the entitlements diagram developed in chapter 5 (figure 7). Here it is modified to deal with housing rather than industrial nuisances. One modification is that I consider the entitlements of a particular parcel of land owned by a single party. This is realistic in that most controversies occur one at a time.

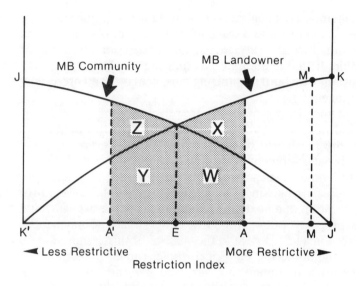

Figure 11.   Entitlements to Suburban Land Use

Despite the focus on a single parcel, there are collective implications. Rules that can be placed on one landowner can be
placed on others. Thus we may think of the landowner as a "representative" owner of undeveloped land. Consider as an example
an undeveloped 160–acre (one-fourth of a square mile) parcel
that was formerly a farm but whose economic viability is now
solely for residential housing.

The issue may now be framed in terms of the entitlements
diagram in figure 11. On the horizontal axis is a restriction index
for the 160–acre parcel. At the far left side, the landowner is
entitled to do anything he pleases with the undeveloped land. He
may, for example, put up very high-density housing. At the right
side, the landowner is not permitted to do anything with his open
land.

The curves JJ' and KK' in figure 11 are the marginal benefit
schedules for restrictions to the community and to the landowner,
respectively. They may also be thought of as demand curves for
the right to use the land in particular ways. It is assumed (for
stability and uniqueness) that both schedules intersect only once,
and then when both are sloping downward.

7.2.2. The Landowner's Benefit Schedule

The landowner's marginal benefit schedule is read from right
to left. At point J' in figure 11 the landowner gets no benefit from

the land that he owns because he cannot use it at all. It would be worth the dollar amount of the area $J'KM'M$ to have an entitlement to point M, so that some use could be made of the land. For example, it would be worth this amount for the landowner to develop his land for single-family homes on, say, ten-acre lots. For a further reduction in restrictiveness, such as allowing development on five-acre lots, the total benefits to the landowner increase. However, the *additional* value of these benefits is assumed to be lower than the initial reduction in restrictiveness.

The height of KK' in figure 11 is determined by the demand for land for housing by outsiders. This will vary directly with access to jobs and shopping and with community amenities such as school quality and recreation opportunities. I emphasize that KK' is a demand curve, not for housing itself, but for the community's *permission* to allow the landowner-developer to build housing on lots of various sizes with various restrictions on them. It should also be noted that this is the only way that outsiders register their preferences. The landowner is the intermediary between existing homeowners and outsiders who may want to enter the community as net additions to the population.

7.2.3. The Community's Benefit Schedule

The community's marginal benefit schedule is JJ'. It is read from left to right. It is drawn so that the total benefits to the current residents increase with additional restrictions on vacant land, but at a diminishing rate. This means that preventing the land from being used for a high-density apartment complex is more valuable than preventing its use for single family homes on half-acre lots but that community residents put a positive value on both restrictions. The median voter's net worth increases when initial entitlements are moved to the right in figure 11.

The height and shape of JJ' are perhaps the most problematic aspects of zoning. In some instances it might be argued that community residents place no value on some restrictions and perhaps negative values on others. Some voters welcome new development in the community in order to have more people with whom to socialize (e.g., more children in the neighborhood) or to have a larger tax base over which to spread the costs of basic public services. Thus JJ' might be negative (below the horizontal axis) towards the right side and perhaps upward-sloping for a time at the far left side. The reason for drawing JJ' as in figure 11 is that in the range of restrictions in which most zoning controversies occur, preexisting residents seem to prefer more restrictions (e.g., larger lots, lower density, and requiring developers to provide more services on their own) rather than fewer. Indeed, if they did not, there would be no controversy.

The benefits of restrictions to the community remain to be specified. Here the ad hoc theories of zoning, that emphasized social, fiscal, or environmental goals provide some insights. In this model, the community's benefits are whatever the median voter thinks they are. They may be direct benefits, such as preservation of open land that current residents enjoy for the view,[4] or indirect benefits in the form of costs avoided by the community. The latter benefits include not having to educate the children of people who may pay less than average property taxes, avoiding congestion of public facilities which may be expensive to expand, or keeping at a distance people of a different race or economic class.

An important assumption of this approach to zoning is that voters are capable of evaluating the *net* benefits of each restriction. This is necessary because, as was mentioned earlier, some motives will conflict with others. For example, suppose that the issue is whether to allow apartment houses. Apartments often have fewer school children per unit of taxable property than do single-family homes, so they may be more advantageous in terms of fiscal gains (James and Windsor 1976). However, they also house transients, who may reduce the perceived level of personal safety of residents. If the benefit of preventing the latter cost exceeds the former fiscal benefits, then a restriction on apartments will be valued by existing residents.

The vertical elevation of JJ' will depend on a number of factors that vary among communities. Preferences for environmental quality will vary with personal income of the communities' residents. There may also be differences in geography, climate, and topography that cause the perceived impact of development to vary among communities. So also will its level of development. A community that is already intensively developed may value restrictions more highly than do sparsely developed communities.

7.2.4. The Coase Theorem Restated

Having set out the issue in terms of the entitlements diagram, I shall restate the Coase theorem. This will serve both as a review of its conditions and implications and as a benchmark for analyzing the reasons for which suburban zoning may be "too restrictive."

The assumptions of the Coase theorem are: (1) all entitlements are defined (measurable and exchangeable); (2) entitlements, as well as the rules by which entitlements are protected, are exclusively assigned (presumably by legislatures and courts); (3) transaction costs are nil (no legal restraints or information costs); and (4) initial distribution of entitlements does not affect subsequent demand for their exchange.

Given these assumptions, it does not matter where on the restriction index of figure 11 entitlements are initially assigned. If point A' were the initial entitlement, which would be favorable to the landowner, the community would attempt to pay the landowner to accept additional restrictions. Whether it must pay him amount Y (damages) or $Y + Z$ (its entire consumer surplus) would depend upon whether the landowner's entitlement was protected by a liability rule (the usual case) or a property rule.

If point A were initially assigned (as I argue below is typically the case), the landowner would have to pay the community to escape some of the restrictions. If the community were protected by a property rule, as is common, it might extract up to amount $X + W$ in figure 11. In any case, point E is obtained after all transactions have taken place.

7.2.5. The Initial Entitlement Favors the Community

It will be useful for subsequent analysis to submit here an empirical characterization of the initial entitlement point in this controversy. My analysis in section 4.4 leads me to believe that zoning offers initial entitlements well to the right of point E, so that a point like A is a reasonable one from which to begin discussion. A community of the type outlined above will attempt to establish as many restrictions as it can. We saw that zoning enabling acts grant a very broad set of powers to the community and that court decisions on zoning have adopted an increasingly broad view of the police power. Communities are seldom compelled to compensate landowners whose property values are reduced by zoning, nor is any special benefit-cost calculation required. Courts may, however, protect a landowner whose land value is completely eliminated by zoning, so we exclude point J' as an initial entitlement.

7.3. TRANSACTION COSTS FROM LEGAL INHIBITIONS ON TRADE

The latter part of chapter 4 was devoted to advocating the view that zoning is not truly fungible. The main reasons for this are that contractual arrangements are either forbidden or limited in

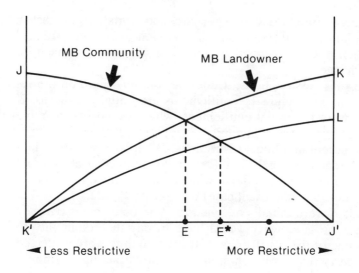

Figure 12.   Entitlements and Transaction Costs under Property Rule Protection

their terms and that most trade is limited to barterlike subsidies in the public sector. I submit that there is substantial divergence between existing methods of exchange and the generally disapproved method of cash compensation.

The question now is, How does this result in "excessive" restrictions? There are two cases to consider. Figure 12 shows the distortion presented by noncash compensation when the community's initial entitlement (point *A*) is protected by a property rule. Recall that property rule protection means that the community can set any terms it wants for the exchange of entitlements and so can extract the full rental value from the landowner. Thus *KK'* is the full opportunity cost to the community. In the absence of transaction costs, the community will proceed to point *E*. But if the compensation to be extracted from the landowner comes via barter or subsidies, so that it is valued at say, 75 cents on the dollar, the community's *perceived* opportunity cost will be *LK'* (which is drawn to be 75 percent of the height of *KK'*), and trading will halt at point *E**, not at *E*.

Point *E** in figure 12 is more restrictive than point *E*. The reader might object that this does not show much restriction, since the diagram is for one landowner and one community. But the same problems will occur when the community deals with *any* landowner, and the same problem will arise in *every* suburban community.[5] Thus the restrictions caused by such transaction costs are pervasive.

In the previous example we assumed that the community was protected by a property rule. This is in fact what communities have in most cases. Once a community has established a valid zoning law, a landowner must satisfy whatever conditions the community wishes to impose. (In reality, the community may only ask for damages [section 9.5]).

It can be shown that the outcome is not altered by switching to a liability rule. Under the latter protection, the community is entitled to "damages" from the developer, but it cannot collect more than that. This means that the landower-developer must pay the community for the value of losses under JJ' in figure 13. In the world of zero transaction costs this will lead again to point E. But when the value of compensation perceived by the community exceeds the cost to the landowner, the "damages" curve is shifted upward from JJ' to MJ' in figure 13. This is because it costs the landower, say, $1.25 to make the community feel compensated by $1.00. As can be seen by inspection of the diagram, the resulting equilibrium (E') is again to the right of the optimal equilibrium (E), and it ends up being "too restrictive" in the same sense as before.

7.4. TRANSACTION COSTS FROM PUBLIC DECISION PROCESSES

The other transaction cost examined in this chapter is making public decisions. Two types of these costs seem important. The first is that local officials may not know what the median voter actually wants, and the second is that various parties may attempt to thwart the preferences of the majority to use zoning for their own purposes. Both of these problems tend to be more important in large communities than in small ones. To the extent that the suburban jurisdictions are smaller than others, these arguments apply there with less force.

Local government officials contemplating a rezoning request do not have a direct pipeline to majority opinion, and even where they do, the opinion may change rapidly. On the other hand, zoning decisions do require more public comment than most other local public-sector decisions. Moreover, in many communities it is possible—sometimes even required—to hold a formal referendum on certain rezoning requests. Thus the first type of public

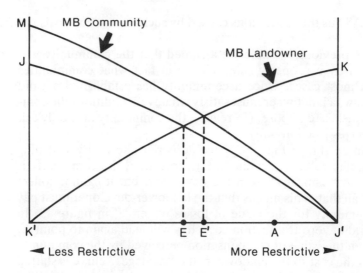

Figure 13. Entitlements and Transaction Costs under Liability Rule Protection

transaction cost, information about voters' desires, is not important in the jurisdictions considered here. (But see chapter 10 on other jurisdictions.)

The other problem is the attempt to thwart the preferences of the median voter. This is probably a more important source of restrictiveness. Some such attempts tend to make zoning excessively permissive (i.e., to the left of point E in figure 12 or figure 13). These include developers' illegally bribing local officials and special lobbying efforts by developers and their allies. These may be important in some jurisdictions, but there is little evidence that they are pervasive in suburban communities.

More common are antidevelopment efforts to thwart majority rule. In some situations this raises no question. We saw in chapter 2 that zoning procedures give special attention to the feelings of those immediately abutting the proposed project. However, the present chapter is about a substantial development, not a one- or two-lot exception, and its effects are felt throughout the community. There is little objection to giving into minority preferences when only that minority near the project is affected, but the case seems weaker when the benefits are communitywide.

I argued in section 3.2 that these minority preferences are a more important factor in zoning decisions than they once were.

The major vehicles for exercising this control are court suits that allege that zoning authorities erred in some procedure. The increased success of these suits is largely due to the expansion of procedural requirements, which can so delay projects as to make them uneconomical.

To put this more formally, the prospective economic value of a proposed project may be so reduced by delays as to make full compensation to the community impossible. The effect is thus analogous to the one depicted in figure 12, where $K'L$ is in this instance the reduced expected value of the landowner's entitlement as a result of procedural delays and uncertainties. The resulting equilibrium does not deter all trade but does end up more restrictive (at point E^* rather than point E in figure 12) than otherwise.

There are many special-interest groups that may attempt to block transactions beneficial to the median voter. These include people outside the community who dislike its developments and commercial interests within or outside the community who do not want competition from the proposed development. (Examples are in sections 5.7, 10.9, and 13.1.) The point now is that the power of special-interest groups to thwart exchanges seems to increase as the degree of restrictiveness of initial zoning entitlements increases. The farther to the right we are on the entitlements diagram, the more likely it is that special interests will attempt to divert the potential stream of income to their own purposes.

The reason for this is that there are start-up costs for special interests to become organized. It is not worth lobbying for something unless there exists an entitlement large enough to justify the effort (section 10.1). Thus it may be that transaction costs are greater as entitlements are moved farther away from the theoretically efficient point. This is one reason why reforms that seek to make zoning more efficient should exercise some control over initial entitlements, as well as permit free exchange of them.

7.5. THE WEALTH EFFECT

The Coase theorem assumes that the initial distribution of entitlements does not affect the demand for the goods being traded. This assumption may be close to reality for exchange between two firms that operate in a competitive economy (Demsetz 1972). In the context of land use controls, however, it does make a differ-

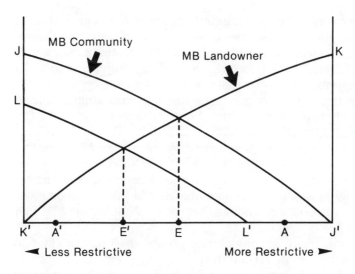

Figure 14. Wealth, Preference, and Monopoly Effects

ence whether point *A* or point *A'* is the initial entitlement in figure 14, even if there are no transaction costs. There are several reasons for this.

One is that there seems to be a systematic behavioral bias towards holding on to entitlements that one already possesses. Experiments have shown that the amount that people will offer for agood is significantly less than the amount that they are willing toaccept for the same good, if they already possess it (Knetsch and Sinden 1984). This result seems independent of the "wealth effect," since it arises even when trivial amounts are involved.

More important for our present purposes, however, is that the assignment of rights under zoning is an important form of homeowners' wealth. The goods that zoning provides for residents, such as neighborhood ambiance, are surely wealth-elastic in demand. This means that the quantity demanded increases as one's wealth increases. In this instance wealth includes both personal assets and collective entitlements.

To show the wealth effect, figure 14 is drawn with two different marginal benefit schedules for the community. Line *JJ'* is the demand for restrictiveness when there is a generous entitlement granted to the community, such as at point *A*. Line *LL'* is the demand for restrictiveness when the community begins at point *A'*, where it must purchase most additional restrictions from landowners. The vertical distance between *JJ'* and *LL'* represents the differences attributable to the initial assignment of entitlements, or the wealth effect.

The wealth effect will cause a difference in the equilibrium trading point, even assuming zero transaction costs. For example, in figure 14, if initial entitlements were at point *A*, the resulting equilibrium would be at point *E*, while if trade began at point *A'*, the result would be less restrictive, such as at point *E'*. (There are many more initial entitlement points than *A* and *A'*, and hence there are many more equilibrium points. The collection of all of the latter points would make up a contract curve on an Edgeworth-Boley box. The entitlements diagram may be thought of as a reduced form of this common expository diagram.)

Thus an "overgenerous" assignment of rights to (original) homeowners may result in more restrictive land use controls. Because this assignment is widespread, it will restrict the supply of housing in the metropolitan area, though we cannot call such restrictions inefficient. Because most zoning controversies occur in the suburbs, the wealth effect would seem most important there. The earliest residents of most developing suburbs (aside from farmers who were there long before any development took place) were more affluent than average.[6] It is typically these people who enact the first planning and zoning laws that are significant constraints on development. This suggests that the wealth effect of zoning accrues chiefly to some of the wealthiest members of our society.

When I am feeling demagogic about this issue, I argue that the free entitlements that zoning offers to suburban residents are like offers of free memberships to the best country clubs to the rich, while all others must pay to get in. The analogy is not exact, since most current suburban residents paid for the entitlements when they purchased existing houses. The point is that the "free" entitlements of zoning do not do much to make the distribution of income or wealth more equal.

Although I believe that the wealth effect adds to the restrictions on housing, it is easy to exaggerate its influence.The demand for land use controls is greatest in the richest communities. But this would be true even if all restrictions had to be purchased (that is, if everyone had to start at point *A'* in figure 14). Where restrictions are purchased, as in residential covenants (section 2.3.4), the greatest degree of restriction is found in the most affluent neighborhoods. The wealth effect of zoning entitlements should be observed among all income classes, though. Even a poor community that is given the right to restrict open land will be more restrictive than it would if it had to purchase such entitlements.[7]

7.6. ILLEGITIMATE PREFERENCES AND ZONING ENTITLEMENTS

The Coase theorem assumes that entitlements are clearly defined. This section shows how overly broad definition of entitlements might make zoning too restrictive by some standards.

Section 2.4 showed that zoning presents communities with a broad set of vaguely defined entitlements to control the use of land in the community. This condition could result in excessive restriction if we adopt a distinction between "legitimate" and "illegitimate" purposes for land use controls. Such a distinction is assumed to be made by those who authorize and supervise the use of zoning by individual communities. Legislatures and the courts, in other words, decide what the division will be. Individual communities, on the other hand, are assumed not to be concerned with the distinction.

To use the most controversial example of this conflict, legislatures and courts may decide that it is unacceptable to use zoning to exclude poor people via exclusion of low-income public housing. The Massachusetts legislature passed the "Anti-Snob Zoning Act," which attempted to override some municipal zoning laws excluding low-income apartment development. There are few other examples among states, but as we saw in section 3.6.2, some state courts, most notably New Jersey's, have taken up this issue.

Before analyzing the consequences of this distinction, we should at least raise the issue of how it can exist. State legislatures are voted in by the same people who vote in local elections, and we have not explicitly assumed that local governments are especially mean-minded. The persistence of "illegitimate" preferences may be attributed to two sources.

One is that the issue is raised mainly in the suburbs, while state legislatures are composed of people elected from central cities as well. The latter may not be a majority in the legislature, and the attractions of local control for other reasons may make them less than effective on this issue.

The other explanation is the large-number problem (Downs 1973). Each individual suburb (in an area where there are many) may feel that its "illegitimate" motives are in fact undesirable. But each may also think that if it and only it becomes less restrictive, all of the problems associated with low-income housing will fall upon it alone. If only one suburb becomes less restrictive, it will do little to alleviate the problem but will put a very high cost on the accommodating community.

One might ask why we do not assume that the landowner has some illegitimate preferences that may affect the disposition of his property. The reason is that the landowner can take the money and run; he does not have to live with the people to whom he sells his land. Even if he did have some aversion to dealing with certain types of people, he could easily sell his property to someone who has no such aversion. Note that we are considering an owner of undeveloped land here, not owners of apartments or houses or real estate brokers. These other parties' illegitimate aversions may indeed affect the housing market.

The problem may be illustrated by again referring to figure 14. Now line LL' is intended to show the community's valuation of the "legitimate" uses for zoning. Such legitimate purposes may be to prevent traditional physical nuisances, promote reasonable levels of public safety, and provide for orderly growth of the community.

Line JJ' shows the legitimate *plus* "illegitimate" valuations of zoning restrictions. (Recall that since both are public goods, demand is summed vertically.) The vertical distance between JJ' and LL' is thus the value of these illegitimate preferences. The nature of illegitimate preferences may vary from state to state and from one era to another. The preference most widely regarded as illegitimate is the desire to exclude people on the basis of race. Beyond this, however, there is no consensus as to what constitutes an illegitimate motive. For the present analysis, we assume that the distinction between legitimate and illegitimate motives or purposes is not a matter of debate.

If we begin at entitlement point A in figure 14 and assume that it is protected by a property rule, the community in question will, if left to its own devices, exchange entitlements until it reaches point E. To the left of point E the community values the restrictions at more than the landowner is willing to pay to be rid of them. Although point E is an equilibrium, it is not socially optimal. This is because it is arrived at by allowing the community to exercise both legitimate and illegitimate public purposes. The social optimum would be point E', which would be arrived at if the community did not place any collective value on illegitimate purposes.

The problem of excessive zoning restrictions is the result of both overly broad definition of entitlements and the difficulty that courts or legislatures have in monitoring the use of these entitlements by individual communities. Monitoring is mainly an information problem: How does the court or the legislature *know* what the purpose of any given aspect of zoning is? How can it prevent the community from overstating its desire for legitimate zoning purposes in order to serve illegitimate purposes?[8] As an information problem, this perhaps belongs more properly in the class of transaction costs. But this particular transaction cost arises largely because of the very broad purposes of zoning, which enable communities to substitute one rationale for another. The problem would not disappear completely if zoning's purposes were more precisely stated in the state zoning enabling acts, but monitoring such illegitimate purposes would be easier. (See also section 15.4, which concludes that some attempts by courts to monitor the illegitimate use of zoning by communities may have the perverse effect of making zoning even more restrictive.)

It is important to differentiate the overbroad definition and assignment of entitlements from the wealth effect described in the previous section. Both effects tend to make zoning more restrictive than it would be in their absence, but for different reasons. The wealth effect makes for more restrictions because zoning adds to the community's collective wealth, so current residents will demand more of many things. The wealth effect would exist even if there were no distinction made between legitimate and illegitimate purposes for zoning. Conversely, if we assumed away the wealth effect, the community would still demand more restrictions (point E in figure 14) rather than fewer (point E') even if it were to start at an entitlement point like A'. In other words, a community would be willing to pay to acquire certain illegitimate restrictions even if they were not part of zoning.

This suggests an advantage of "nonzoning" as a cure for illegitimate motives. If the community had to start at point A' in figure 14, it would have to acquire restrictions from landowners. The resulting contracts or convenants presumably would spell out the restrictions. This would give the courts an opportunity to scrutinize them if they involved unconstitutional restrictions. Such contracts, in other words, would have less of the vagueness that gives rise to the monitoring problem discussed here.

7.7. MONOPOLY CONTROL OF DEVELOPMENT

The Coase theorem's assumptions say nothing about the competitiveness of the agents to whom entitlements are assigned. This is in strong contrast to most economic discussions, which explicitly assume that agents must have no ability to affect prices if one is to reach a welfare-maximizing position. The reason for the difference is that the Coase theorem buries the same assumption in zero transaction costs.

If there are truly no costs to making *any* potential transaction, then monopolistic behavior cannot exist. This is because all those who are harmed by monopolies will be able to bribe the potential monopolist to forswear any monopolistic behavior (Calabresi 1968). The necessity of making the bribe, of course, leaves people worse off, but this is "just" a matter of wealth distribution.

For readers who find this departure from the conventional economic assumptions hard to take, let me quickly add that I shall not make it here. I am going to consider the case where the *community* has some potential monopoly power over the supply of land suitable for residential development. It is assumed, though, that neither landowners nor potential residents are capable of persuading the community to desist from monopolistic behavior. Thus monopoly power by the community enables it to raise land prices, and thus housing prices, above the market equilibrium by restricting the supply of sites more than either landowners or a competitive set of communities would. This increases the wealth of community residents who are homeowners prior to the adoption of the restrictions.[9]

To examine this cause of excessive zoning restrictions, return to the original model, again assuming away transaction costs, wealth effects, and considerations of illegitimate preferences, except as noted in the foregoing paragraph. Assume also, as before, that the initial entitlement in figure 14 is point A, which gives the community more than the optimal degree of restriction.

The LL' schedule in our present modification of figure 14 refers to a competitive situation in which the community has no market power over the supply of sites. This was assumed to exist in all the cases considered in previous sections. The JJ' schedule applies in a monopoly situation in which the community does have some power.

For there to be a monopoly in any market, the demand curve that the supplier faces must be inelastic, and there must be some barrier to entry by potential competitors. In this case, it is the demand for housing sites that is inelastic. The source of this inelasticity is the comparative advantage that the entire metropolitan area (or other housing market) has relative to the rest of the world.[10] The metropolitan area must have a special characteristic that makes some firms or households prefer it to all others. If one does not assume this, then the demand for location in the area would be perfectly elastic, since other metropolitan areas would be perfect substitutes for the one in question. Any increase in land prices would simply cause potential immigrants, who want to live on the undeveloped land, to move elsewhere. (This would be an "open city," discussed in section 12.5.)

The pure monopoly, in the case above, refers to control of the entire supply of land in a metropolitan area. Vernon Henderson (1980) has suggested another kind of monopoly that may exist even when there are numerous communities. There may be a shortage of certain *kinds* of communities because it is difficult for developers to form new ones or for existing towns to modify their services to imitate the ones for which there is excess demand.[11] Henderson shows that the development of such monopoly communities is not impaired so long as zoning entitlements are transferable. This is, of course, another manifestation of the Coase theorem, this time in a two-period development model.

For purposes of discussion in the balance of this chapter, let us assume that a single government has control over planning, zoning, and public services in developing suburbs. In the competitive case, by contrast, planning, zoning, and public services are provided by a large number of small communities. Any attempt by a single community to reap monopoly profits in the exchange of entitlements would be undercut by neighboring communities, and the excess profits would be eliminated.

The potential supply of sites in figure 15 within the boundaries of the metropolitan area is S_c, and the rent is R_c. The demand for location in this area by outsiders is inelastic up to Q_m. With a large number of communities and landowners in the metropolitan area, S_c is made up of many suppliers, who perceive (accurately) that the amount of land they supply will have only the smallest effect on rents.

With a single metropolitan community, however, additional restrictions on all land do have some effect on the rent of land. Thus to increase total rents, the monopoly community may restrict the supply of sites to something like S_m. The rent received by the

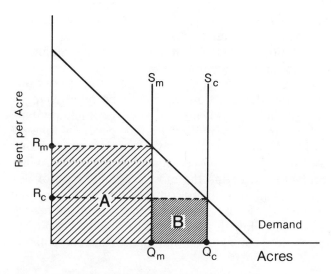

Figure 15. Monopoly Supply of Land

community for selling its rezonings is now higher per acre (R_m) than it was before, and this is due to monopoly restrictions.

The manifestation of this monopoly power in the entitlements diagram is again shown by reference to figure 14. The greater height of JJ' is caused by the community's perception that restrictions not only provide them with certain residential benefits as represented by LL' (e.g., pleasant views of open land, lack of congestion of local services) but also provide a means to expropriate the rents for location in the metropolitan area as a whole. This means not just that there are higher rents per land unit but also that there are, in equilibrium, more restrictions. In figure 14, the monopoly equilibrium is represented by point E, where JJ' and KK' intersect. This is to the right of point E', the equilibrium that would have been achieved in the absence of the monopoly premium demanded by current homeowners. The greater restrictiveness is necessary to keep the supply of land at S_m in figure 15. (Section 14.4 offers another demonstration of the monopoly effect.)

7.8. MONOPOLY AND DURABILITY

There are two theoretical objections to the "monopoly" conclusion of greater restrictiveness. Both involve the fact that land is a *durable* resource, so that one must take into account the behavior of its owners over time.

The previous section showed that the monopoly community is too restrictive. The implicit assumption was that all of the undeveloped land controlled by the community had to be disposed of at once and that after this decision was made, no other changes in land use were possible. This is not realistic. A community typically makes development decisions over a long period of time. If it decides to withhold some land from development in the present, it has that land available for development in the future. This creates two problems: to define the most profitable path of development for the community and to convince present buyers that their asset will not go down in value in the future. For the reader who does not care to follow this somewhat arcane discussion, let me give the conclusion: zoning under monopoly control is still too restrictive.

7.8.1. Resource Depletion over Time

The first problem, defining the maximum-profit time path of development, is related to the literature on the depletion of nonrenewable natural resources. The problem is often framed in the context of the prices of petroleum and other minerals. It is clear that the prices of such products *ought* to increase over time to reflect their increasing scarcity value and to provide incentives for the development of substitutes. This will happen at a socially desirable rate if ownership is competitive and several other conditions are met (section 13.4). But what if monopoly is present? In this case, the monopolist may diverge from the optimal path of price increases.

The consensus in the literature is that the monopolist will *at first* have prices higher than the competitive alternative; however, *later* the monopolist will have lower prices than the competitive alternative (Devarajan and Fisher 1981). This odd result stems from the monopolist's initially higher prices. They cause consumers to seek substitutes even faster, so that there is more of the monopolized resource left over in the future. With greater amounts left over, the price will naturally be lower. To see this, consider the case where the competitive price eventually becomes infinite because the resource is totally exhausted. If the monopolist has one ounce of the stuff leftover, it will sell for a price less than infinity.

How does this apply to land use controls in the suburbs? If a community controls much undeveloped land, it has the power to ration it over time. Once development does occur on a parcel of land, the resource is "used up" as far as the community is concerned. Thus community authorities are in a position similar to that of the monopolist-owner of a natural resource, and assuming away other transaction costs, their behavior should be the same.[12] Thus it may be that in 1985 zoning in the monopoly community is excessively restrictive, but in 2005 it may be less restrictive— compared to the competitive case—simply because it has more land left over.

This argument does not prove that the analysis of monopoly zoning earlier in this section is wrong. This is because consumers of housing, like consumers of everything else, prefer to have goods now rather than later. Pushing the lower prices off until later is no bargain. Thus monopoly zoning is still inefficiently restrictive even though at some later time it may appear to be less restrictive than competitive situations.

The analysis in this section is relevant to the contention that removing a large fraction of a community's open land from development does not affect housing prices because enough land remains available to accommodate independently projected needs. This erroneously equates potential supply, a stock, with annual supply, a flow (section 1.4). Potential supply is all the land that might be brought to market at any price. By removing a large fraction of the potential supply from development, remaining landowners may be given some monopoly power over development, since they realize that buyers have fewer alternative sites. It would be rational for them to reduce the annual number of lots they would bring to market. This implies an inward shift in each year's supply curve, which drives up the price of housing per year. Landowners' ability to do this is still dependent on the community's having some monopoly power; otherwise buyers would simply seek alternative sites in other communities.

7.8.2. Anticipation and Contractual Guarantees

The other amendment to the monopoly case also stems from land's durability (Coase 1972). Suppose that the zoning authority faces the demand curve shown in figure 15 and has available to it the quantity of land Q_c. Its profit-maximizing procedure in the first instance might be to sell Q_m at price R_m, earning profits identified by the shaded area labeled A. Having done that, the town has some land left over (Q_c minus Q_m). What is to prevent the town from then selling off that amount at price R_c, making profit labeled B? (If it does this in small increments, it is a discriminating monopolist; the number of increments is not the point here.)

What *might* stop this process are the expectations by the initial buyers of land (who bought Q_m) that if they just held out for a while, the price of the land would go down. If buyers always anticipated the behavior of the zoning authority, the zoning authority could not reap any monopoly profits.

In order to gain from its monopoly position, then, the zoning authority must convince buyers that it will not engage in any subsequent sales after the first ones. One way is to "waste" the excess land by such devices as large lot sizes or dedications of much undeveloped land for parks or greenbelts. This effectively prevents the zoning authorities in a community with fixed borders from rezoning that land for development at some later time.

Another constraint on the zoning authorities is that the land initially sold at the high price was used to build houses for people who now live *and vote* in the community. The newcomers will put pressure on the zoning authorities to prevent subsequent sales of development permits that would reduce the resale value of their own homes. (This assumes that the potential gains from selling more development rights cannot be used to compensate the newcomers. This kind of transaction cost was explicitly invoked at the beginning of section 7.7 in order to explain the existence of monopolies.)

The conclusion about zoning thus remains the same even when we consider monopoly over time and the problem of durability. Monopoly zoning will be excessively restrictive when compared with the competitive case. The durability factor can explain some zoning behavior, such as wasteful lot sizes and behavior of zoning over time.

7.9. CONCLUSION: EXCLUSIONARY ZONING

The term "exclusionary zoning" is widely used but seldom precisely defined. Although it is denotatively empty—all zoning excludes something—the connotation is that certain zoning outcomes are too restrictive in some sense. The discussion in this chapter attempts to identify the sources of excessive restrictiveness.

Zoning may be held up to the economists' efficiency standard: it is too restrictive if, with a given endowment of entitlements, there are potential net welfare gains from some reduction in zoning restrictions. These welfare gains may be lost because of monopoly government structure or because transaction costs prevent further exchange. Legal impediments and public choice problems were identified as the primary sources of transaction costs.

Two situations where zoning may be regarded as too restrictive had little to do with efficiency. These were the wealth effect of granting zoning entitlements to early residents and the exercise of illegitimate preferences through zoning. In these cases the community and the landowner could achieve no voluntary gains from trade, but outsiders were harmed. The landowner-developer might want to build and sell housing for those outsiders, but he is prevented from doing so because he cannot compensate the community and still make a profit. The community, because of its initially free entitlements to exclude or because of its antisocial preferences, asks for too much.

Since there are a number of different reasons why people will regard zoning as excessively restrictive, there is apt to be substantial disagreement on the remedies to exclusionary zoning. This is most obvious in the different approaches of the "open-suburbs" movement, as exemplified by the *Mount Laurel* decison in New Jersey (sections 3.6 and 15.2), and the deregulation-of-housing approach, as exemplified by the President's Commission on Housing (1982). The latter is concerned with efficiency problems, while the former seems largely motivated by equity issues. I shall take this issue up again in chapter 15.

A specific lesson of this chapter for economists is to avoid equating restrictiveness in the land market caused by zoning with conventional monopoly motives. The training of most economists encourages this confusion. This is because in most private markets, property rights are fully assigned and transferable, so that the only plausible reason for restraint of trade is monopoly or its cousins. But in the case of public entitlements such as zoning, monopoly is only one of several reasons for restraint of trade. Modeling zoning as analogous to private monopoly may at times be correct, but it may overlook other important or contributing problems.

NOTES

1. The major article on suburban zoning is Ellickson (1977). A shorter overview of the same issues is Zumbrun and Hookano (1977). An excellent set of case studies and a political analysis of such zoning is Frieden (1979). The techniques were described in section 4.5.

2. See Frieden (1979). Work by my colleague, Daphne Kenyon (1984) on zoning board decisions in Ann Arbor, Michigan, indicated that prospective tenants of apartments sometimes appeared at zoning hearings. Ann Arbor is a "central city" of its SMSA, and there are several tenants' organizations that developers can call upon for support. It is hard to imagine this happening in suburban jurisdictions; in my regular reading of zoning controversies in newspapers I cannot recall any. Further discussion is in section 10.2.

3. Analyses of zoning that make a similar assumption are Bender and Shwiff (1982), Cooley and LaCivita (1982), Downing (1977), Nelson (1977), and Sonstelie and Portney (1978; 1980). The last two articles explore the profit (wealth) maximization assumption in more detail.

4. A survey by Knight and Menchick (1974, 73) indicated that "environmental features such as open views of undeveloped land and direct access to natural areas such as woods are valued highly enough by substantial proportions of potential homebuyers that they may be willing to give up substantial proportions of their private lot, or pay a substantial money premium in order to obtain these features."

5. For example, the city of Petaluma's novel plan to limit growth by means of a quota system for building permits was quickly adopted by other California cities once the legal challenges were settled in favor of the community (Ellickson and Tarlock 1981, 853). Another example was the rapid spread of minimum floor-area standards once the New Jersey Supreme Court upheld them in one case (Haar 1954, 991). The rapid spread of zoning after the *Euclid* decision in 1926 likewise supports this position.

6. This has been the case since the last century. For an example from Boston see Warner (1971, chap. 4): In the late-nineteenth-century suburban expansion occasioned by the development of the streetcar early residents were wealthier than average. This income segregation was created without zoning laws. Section 12.3 discusses economic reasons for this.

7. Questionnaire surveys of Philadelphia suburbs found low-income communities as opposed to development of small houses on small lots as high-income places (Coke and Liebman 1961; Williams 1965).

8. Reasons for the courts' impotence in these matters are discussed in Babcock (1976), Fischel (1979, 317), and E. Mills (1979, 519).

9. I neglect economic models premised on developer monopoly because of a lack of evidence. Section 1.5 noted that there is no evidence of landowner monopoly in developing suburbs. The homebuilding industry, especially for single-family houses, is likewise competitive. The community monopoly proposed in the text works for the benefit of local homeowners (i.e., the voters), not for the benefit of the officials of those governments. Other theories of local government monopoly have seen community monopolies as a means by which bureaucrats increase spending to feather their nests at the expense of voters (e.g., Wagner and Weber 1975).

10. These conditions for a zoning monopoly were developed by Hamilton (1978). While I accept Hamilton's theory here, I am skeptical of the empirical evidence for either monopolistic structure or monopolistic effects (Fischel 1980c; and section 10.7 below).

11. I will deal with the issue of different kinds of communities in chapter 14. Goetz and Wofford (1979) suggest that zoning is an attempt by home-owners to create a monopoly. However, they do not indicate how home-owners in different communities coordinate their efforts, which would be to naught if there were many communities in the relevant housing market.

12. Markusen and Scheffman (1978) examine the timing of development under monopoly control. Their monopolist is assumed to be a private de-veloper, but the results would seem to be the same for a monopoly com-munity. They indicate that the monopolist-developer may earn subnormal profits in an early period in order to obtain supernormal profits at a later time.

8.

The Taking Issue and Zoning

After all, if a policeman must know the Constitution,
then why not a planner?
—Justice Brennan, dissenting in San Diego Gas and Electric
v. City of San Diego, 450 U.S. 621, 661 (1981)

The last chapter addressed problems with zoning that arose from economic efficiency and broad social equity concerns. This chapter will continue to examine normative issues. The topic here is fairness to individuals. The focus will be on the constitutional prohibition against "taking" property for public use without "just compensation." I choose to scrutinize the taking clause rather than the due process and equal protection clauses. My discussion is relevant to the latter clauses in that all three address the larger concern of the relationship of the individual to the state in a democratic society. The reason for focusing on the taking clause is that its "just compensation" command provides a remedy for the defects in zoning noted in the conclusion of the last chapter. My hope is to stimulate students and scholars to think of the problem from a new perspective.

My view of takings has been greatly influenced by Frank Michelman's classic (1967), which was modified and applied to zoning by Robert Ellickson (1973; 1977). It diverges from these by developing the argument in an economics framework that emphasizes property rights. The plan is first to identify the ethical norm underlying the issue. I will then outline four classes of rules that courts have actually used to differentiate a taking from a legitimate exercise of the police power. These will then be analyzed in terms of the entitlements diagram developed in previous chapters. Each set of rules by itself will be found wanting, but taken together they can be synthesized into a legal approach that is consistent with the ethical norm. The keys to this synthesis are the concepts of normal behavior and transaction costs. The remaining sections explore the question of when and where such rules ought to be applied.

8.1. MICHELMAN'S FAIRNESS CRITERION

As I noted in the discussion of Pennsylvania Coal v. Mahon in section 3.5, the underlying concern of the taking issue is principles of fairness. The basic ethical norm that undergirds Michelman's (1967, 1166) philosophical discussion is that civilized people should not sacrifice the well-being of identifiable individuals for the benefit of the majority. It is this norm, I believe, that motivates the taking clauses in the federal and state constitutions. The authors of these clauses and the citizens who approved them wanted to prevent democratic governments from putting special public burdens on particular individuals or politically defenseless minorities (Nedelsky 1982, Pulliam 1983).

Michelman's philosophical approach, which rests in part on early work by John Rawls, has been criticized as insufficient to bear the weight of the taking issue. While I reject this criticism,[1] it may be more persuasive to the reader to point out that Michelman's approach seems congruent with the normative theory of constitutional interpretation advanced by J. H. Ely in his influential book *Democracy and Distrust* (1980). Ely makes two points that are relevant to the approach to the taking issue advocated here.

First, it is not necessary to elevate property to any special status. Ely argues that the Fifth Amendment's taking clause was not adopted to advance private property beyond the reach of democratic decisions: "On the contrary, the amendment assumes that property will sometimes be taken and provides instead for compensation. Read through it thus emerges—and this account fits the historical situation like a glove—as yet another protection of the few against the many" (pp. 97–98). Besides this, elevating property to a special status would make the argument for its protection both too easy and unpersuasive. I suspect that most people would agree with Milton Friedman on this: "Property rights cannot be absolute precisely because of their neighborhood effects. They are not 'natural' because so many arise only because of the existence of society (e.g., property value of privilege of 'limited liability.') What such rights should be can only be decided collectively" (Friedman and Robertson 1973, 1038).

The more important reason to tie the taking issue to Ely's essay

is that he is concerned with broad issues of constitutional interpretation, not just the taking issue. This grounds his reading of
the purpose of the taking clause in a wider judicial interpretation
of the Constitution rather than just imputing some intent to the
authors of the Fifth Amendment.

Ely's theory of the interpretation of the "open-ended" clauses
of the Constitution is that they are invitations for the courts to
protect individuals and minorities from the excesses of democracy
and to keep open the avenues of democratic political discourse.
Thus the standard of fairness that underlies the taking clause is
consistent with the Warren Court decisions on desegregation, protection of aliens, voting rights, and legislative apportionment.

The ethical norm discussed here requires further explication to
fit particular cases. An intermediate step to this goal is Frank
Michelman's fairness standard: "A decision not to compensate is
not unfair as long as the disappointed claimant ought to be able
to appreciate how such decisions might fit into a consistent practice
which holds forth a lesser long run risk to people like him than
would any consistent practice which is naturally suggested by the
opposite decision" (1967, 1223).

A paraphrase of this standard for zoning might be as follows:
"A landowner ought to be able to see that uniform application of
a zoning restriction is in the long-run interests of himself and other
landowners in the community." Note that this assumes that the
landowner is rational ("ought to be able to see") and does not
have a very high discount rate ("in the long-run interests"). Both
qualifications allow that the landowner may well be disappointed
by a decision that is nonetheless consistent with the ethical norm.

It may help to narrow our discussion of the taking clause to
note that the fairness test does not preclude deliberate redistribution of income by governments. A progressive tax and special
aid to the poor can be thought of as a public good, in the technical
sense (Hochman and Rodgers 1969; Orr 1976). Thus one can argue
that those who lose from income redistribution programs ought
to be able to see that it is in their long-run best interests. Ely's
interpretation of the constitutional purposes of the taking clause
also would not preclude income redistribution. The rich are not
a politically defenseless minority, and it is arguable that they are
not even a distinct class. (If the poor cannot be so classified, as
the Supreme Court has ruled, we can hardly say that the rich
can.)[2] Michelman's normative approach to the taking clause thus
leaves a broad scope for governmental authority.

8.2. SAX'S APPROACH

Before we look at the operational rules that courts have devised to determine a taking, we will briefly consider another approach that has been widely cited. Joseph Sax's two articles on takings evince a growing concern that the taking clause might undermine policies needed for environmental protection.[3]

In his earlier article (1964), Sax argues that compensation should be paid when the government acts in an enterprise capacity, acquiring property rights through regulation for its own use, but not when it is acting as a disinterested mediator of private disputes. The paradigm in such an instance might be the zoning board of adjustment that rules on a variance or special exception. This pits neighbor against neighbor when there is a dispute. Here two parties of approximately equal political influence in the community are at odds, and it appears that ZBAs do often act as disinterested mediators (Rose 1983). It may also be the case, as is suggested in section 10.8, that land use decisions by the state, federal or other large area government may approximate such a balance of political interests, so that local authorities may be viewed as mediators.

The entire thrust of my present work, however, is that this distinction is unsatisfactory for zoning disputes involving undeveloped tracts in suburbs and small towns. Here the local government acts in the interests of the resident voters and against those of the owners of the land. It is plainly not a disinterested mediator.

Sax's second article (1971) urges even fewer instances in which compensation should be paid. His rule is that government can deny compensation whenever its regulations deal with spillover effects. I can find no workable distinction in his work between land uses that create spillovers and those that do not. *Every* economic activity can be argued to affect someone else. Sax is aware of this problem, but his attempts to deal with it nonetheless seem to leave no practical scope remaining for private property. The problem—one Sax shares with other distinguished commentators—is that he seems to have adopted the Pigovian sophistries discussed in section 6.8: spillovers equal externalities, and an externality automatically justifies a particular state action.

In his second article, Sax seems also to have abandoned the concern about majoritarian excesses displayed in his earlier paper. Political checks on the decisions of regulators are now deemed sufficient. But as we have seen (in sections 2.6, 3.7, and 7.1), politics is the problem, not the solution, in suburban zoning. As I shall argue below (section 8.10), there are cases where political checks may be enough, but the more important local zoning decisions aren't among them.

8.3. FOUR LEGAL APPROACHES TO THE TAKING ISSUE

The clearest example of a taking, one where nearly all courts agree that compensation is required, would involve a zoning law that required physical occupation of or public access to a particular property.[4] Planning authorities might legitimately negotiate with landowners who want to develop their land to require them, as a condition for a rezoning, to provide some facilities open to the general public. The authorities cannot, however, zone someone's land to establish parks or school grounds for the benefit of the community without paying for the land. This will be held a taking, even though the damage done to the property owner might be trivial. This is an example of the *physical invasion* standard for determining a taking.

The second standard invoked for determining a taking is the *diminution of value*. This would be applied if the community were to zone someone's land so as to eliminate all or nearly all profitable use of it. Calling this diminution of value is somewhat misleading. It is clear that the community may keep the owner of a parcel of land from using it for the most profitable activity; in that literal sense the diminution of value standard is never taken seriously. However, there are a number of decisions in which the courts emphasized the magnitude of the loss to the landowner, or pointed to the negligible value of the land under zoning, as a reason for overturning the zoning as a taking.

A third standard is only occasionally applied, though it may often be inferred as the basis for many taking decisions. This is the *balancing means* test, which is more aptly called the *benefit-cost* criterion. In using this test, the judge will attempt to determine from the evidence whether the public benefits created or preserved by the ordinance outweigh its costs to the landowner. If they do, the regulation is valid and no taking is said to have occurred. (The balancing means test seems related to the due process criterion that the ordinance must bear some "reasonable relation" to actual community benefits [section 3.4.2].)

The fourth standard is the *harm prevention, benefit extraction* criterion (abbreviated as the *harm-benefit* rule). According to this standard, regulations that prevent a landowner from "harming" the public are valid, regardless of how restrictive they may be, but restrictions used to provide a public "benefit" are invalid takings. The reasoning is that the public at large, not just one small set of the public, should pay for the benefits. On the other hand, it argues that individuals have no right to inflict "harms" on society at large.

This criterion is widely applied as a rationale for all police power activities, and it is implicit in many justifications for zoning. The influence of the harm prevention doctrine is evident in the Standard State Zoning Enabling Act, which talks of zoning's purposes to lessen congestion, secure safety from fire, and prevent overcrowding. The hostility to benefit extraction activity under zoning powers is best illustrated by the judicial attitude towards rezoning land to a less valuable use so that the community can later acquire the land for public facilities at a lower price. Judges will invariably overturn a rezoning whose primary purpose seems to be such an enterprise use of the police power.

8.4. PROBLEMS WITH EXISTING LEGAL RULES

The problems with each of the approaches to the taking issue outlined in the previous section can be illustrated with reference to the entitlements diagram for zoning restrictions (figure 16), developed in the last three chapters. This diagram itself helps to delineate the taking issue. The necessary condition for a taking is the acquisition of some entitlements by the community without compensating the private party whose entitlements are lost. Thus any movement to the *right* in figure 16 might be called a taking, unless the landowners were compensated for the losses, which are determined by the area under their benefit schedule, KK'. This is consistent with Justice Holmes's *Pennsylvania Coal* opinion that takings are to be determined as a matter of degree, along a "continuum of appropriation" (Pulliam 1983, 452).

We can now reexamine the four legal approaches to the taking issue using the entitlements diagram, keeping in mind that the basic question is whether the landowners should be paid for the loss of entitlements.

The first test, the physical invasion criterion, is obviously incomplete. It establishes one reasonably clear boundary—which will later prove to be useful in establishing a more general rule— but in the case of most zoning restrictions, it would not prevent

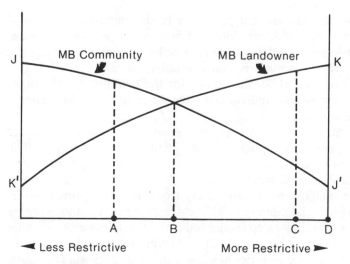

Figure 16. Zoning Entitlements and Takings

the community from moving directly from point *A* to point *D* in figure 16 without paying the landowner a cent. Zoning could prevent all development, reaping for the community gains under the curve *JJ'*, as long as the land was not physically occupied. Of course this violates the basic norm described above. The landowner provides public benefits to the community without receiving any compensation. The basic problem with physical invasion is that the important entitlements in our society are not simple possession of land and other assets but the right to use them in particular ways.

The diminution of value standard also is not helpful by itself. While it would prevent movement from point *A* to point *D* in figure 16, it would not act to prevent a move to point *C*. This would be like telling a landowner whose property is especially suited for housing development that he can still graze cattle on his land, so no taking is involved in denying his development proposal. This is not apt to seem like fair compensation to him.

A variation on the diminution of value standard is to compare the relative magnitudes of the losses. A regulation that reduced a property's value by 20 percent might be tolerated, but one that cut it by 70 percent might not. The trouble with this approach is that it could be used to require compensation for denial of truly noxious activities, while a denial of inoffensive uses might not require compensation. The general objection to this standard is that it says nothing about the *benefits* of regulation. A 70 percent loss in value might be reasonable if the benefits were of a similar magnitude, while a 20 percent loss might be unconscionable in the face of negligible community benefits. In terms of figure 16, the trouble with the diminution of value standard is that it takes no account of whether one is to the right or the left of the optimal degree of restriction (point B), since it pays attention only to KK', the landowner benefit schedule, not JJ', the community benefit schedule.

The standard that is apt to be most appealing to economists is the benefit-cost comparison, or balancing means test. Applying it would allow movements from A to B, but not from B to C or D in figure 16. This might promote efficiency (depending on the quality of the benefit-cost analysis), but it has serious drawbacks as a normative rule in taking cases.

To see the drawbacks, suppose that this were not a zoning issue but a highway building problem. The question is which land to acquire for a new road. The benefits of acquiring your land for this route clearly outweigh the cost of acquisition. Normally, this would mean that payment would actually be made by the community to you. But by the benefit-cost standard for a taking, no payment would have to be made, since the proposed acquisition provided benefits to the community greater than the costs. This is a violation of our most basic normative notion of the compensation principle. Identifiable individuals ought not to be made to bear burdens for general community benefits when compensation can be made.

If the government is not required to pay compensation to individuals in the physical invasion case, it is difficult to think of any other situation where it would have to. It was suggested previously, though, that physical ownership should not be fundamentally different from other entitlements. If we insist on paying landowners when their land is physically occupied, even though the occupation may meet the benefit-cost test, why deny payment for other types of public acquisition of entitlements?

Economists typically favor applying benefit-cost criteria to zoning, and one gets the sense that they believe that adoption of this standard would dispose of the taking issue. There is, however, an efficiency-based argument against the sole use of the benefit-cost criterion. This is that public agencies will not accurately account for private costs unless they actually have to pay them.[5] As most economists who have done benefit-cost analysis will concede, the process is as much art as science. Government agencies do not have unlimited budgets to accomplish goals mandated by legislatures. The temptation to understate private costs as well as to overstate public benefits would become irresistible for many. To put it another way, any poker player knows that the quality of the game is immensely improved when real money is used.

The harm-benefit criterion makes the least sense to economists. It appears to be just a connotative distinction. This is because any harm may be thought of as a benefit that is forgone, while any benefit can be thought of as a harm that is prevented (Dunham 1958, 644). The benefit of eating food is the prevention of the harm of hunger. The harm of breathing polluted air is forgoing the benefit of pure air. The labeling of the entitlements diagram (e.g., figure 16) illustrates this. Both schedules are labeled "benefit" curves, but as was demonstrated in section 5.1, either could be called a "cost" curve.

8.5. EXPECTATIONS, EFFICIENCY, AND NORMAL BEHAVIOR

Although the formal logic of the harm-benefit criterion is deficient, its connotation is important. The reader may be surprised to learn that I adopt a version of the harm prevention, benefit extraction rule, called the "normal behavior" standard, for determining when compensation for zoning regulations should be made.[6] The reasons are that it promotes economic efficiency by stabilizing expectations and reducing transaction costs of providing for public goods. These reasons, I shall argue, promote Michelman's fairness criterion.

A criterion for a taking that may seem attractive to economists is the following: a taking will be found if the landowner had a reasonable expectation that he would be able to use his land in a certain way but the community used its police powers to stop him. This may be one interpretation of the "investment backed expectations" sometimes said to be protected from destruction by regulation. The economic appeal of this rule is that it reduces the uncertainties of planning an investment and thus increases the value of resources.

But what is a *reasonable* expectation? It cannot mean a purely personal or empirical estimation of the consequences of one's actions. For example, people who jog in Central Park in New York at midnight have, as an empirical matter, some expectation that they will be mugged or worse. We nonetheless do not condone mugging, nor do we think that a person who is mugged is not entitled to legal protection.

By the same token, a landowner-developer might appear before a zoning board and claim, perhaps quite honestly, that he expected to be able to build his pulp mill in the midst of the residential district and had made plans and invested substantial funds in order to do so. He is not entitled to legal redress if he should have known to inquire into the land use norms of the community. A system of laws must get individuals to accommodate the norms of society (see also section 9.3).

The standards for "reasonable expectation" must, for the foregoing reasons, be based on social norms, not individual empirical estimations. It is such a norm that the harm-benefit criterion connotes. A harm is some subnormal behavior as judged by prevailing social, not individual, standards. Conferring a benefit, on the other hand, implies some above-normal behavior. A reasonable expectation is thus one that conforms to prevailing social standards of acceptable behavior.[7]

We begin, then, with one rule for resolving the taking issue: a taking may be argued to have occurred when a regulation requires a landowner to exceed prevailing social standards of behavior. The landowner should not be forced to "confer a benefit" on the community. No taking occurs when the regulation simply forces the landowner to conform to prevailing community standards or prevents him from adopting subnormal land uses.

A standard of normal behavior promotes economic efficiency by reducing the transaction costs of providing for public goods. In a world of zero transaction costs, we could negotiate with all potential litterers to persuade them not to throw trash in public places. But when the costs of negotiating and enforcing such contracts are considered, it becomes clear that it is worthwhile to establish a zero compensation point (i.e., normal behavior) of not littering. This is because most people are *not* strongly inclined to litter, in part because of a distaste for other people's littering. Thus only a few transactions need to be made to extract a price (a fine) from those who are inclined to litter. On the other side of the zero compensation point, we would expect that people who systematically clean up litter ought to be paid for the service. Most people are not inclined to clean up after strangers, and attempting to enforce a supernormal standard on passers-by, penalizing them for not cleaning up others' trash, would usually involve far greater transaction costs than would hiring a sanitation worker to do the job.

The littering example suggests that normal behavior can vary by place and by community. Those who attend an outdoor rock concert do not regard (most) litter as subnormal behavior. Members of some hiking clubs, on the other hand, consider it normal to pick up (minor) litter left by others on the trail: leaving it lie is considered just a little below standard behavior. Thus the "normal behavior" approach differs from one interpretation of the harm-benefit rule, which sees it as prohibiting "noxious uses." The latter is unsatisfactory because, as Sax (1964) points out, many noxious uses are beneficial and should be allowed at least somewhere. "Normal behavior" may be superior as a rule because it allows for spatial and situational variations in normality: a place for everything, but everything in its place.

The standard of normal behavior can be used to provide a necessary reference point for the diminution of value standard. A problem with this latter approach, it will be recalled, is that it applies with more force the more outrageous the proposed land use. A landowner whose proposed pulp mill is excluded might argue a greater diminution of value than would a landowner whose more reasonable tract of one-family homes is excluded. If a common standard of normal social behavior is applied, however, this distinction evaporates. The former landowner would be entitled to charge a taking only if pulp mills were a normal activity in the community.

If a parcel of land were uniquely suited for some activity deemed subnormal or unneighborly, the rule suggested here would allow a valid zoning ordinance to leave the owner with zero return on his land. If zoning entitlements are tradeable, however, it seems unlikely that the land would remain unused. The developer would pay the community or the neighbors to allow the subnormal use.

8.6. TRANSACTION COSTS AND BENEFIT-COST AS TAKING CRITERIA

8.6.1. Transaction Costs

The normal behavior standard establishes a static point for determining a taking but by itself does not provide satisfactory criteria for most zoning controversies. This is because zoning laws change over time, often because the community wants more restrictions. To deal with this, the concept of transaction costs is brought into the analysis.

Let us reconsider figure 16. Suppose that originally point A was considered normal behavior in the community and that, moreover, point A was also efficient: the marginal benefits schedule of the community intersected the landowner's benefit schedule at this point. (These schedules are not shown in figure 16.) Now, because of exogenous factors—growth in other areas of the community, increased income, or greater information about effects of pollution or crowding—there is a collective demand to restrict remaining landowner-developers to a greater degree. That is, the benefit schedule of the community shifts upward to JJ', so that the new optimum is point B. It is assumed that the best way of achieving point B is to establish more stringent land use regulations. These reduce the value of the landowner's property by the area under the KK' curve between points A and B. Should the landowner be paid for this loss?

The case against compensation is this: Suppose that a move from A to B in figure 16 causes "damages" to the landowner of $100, the area beneath the KK' schedule between A and B. However, the costs of identifying the affected parties, winnowing out false claims, and adjudicating the damages (since landowners may overstate losses) and disbursing the funds amount to $120. This amount (not shown on the diagram) is the *transaction cost* of making the $100 payment. The community would have to pay $220, not $100, to reap its benefits. Application of the taking clause in this instance might reduce total well-being if the total cost ($220) would deter the community from undertaking the regulation.

8.6.2. Benefits and Costs

If high transaction costs are a justification for not compensating landowners in moving from A to B in figure 16, what prevents the community from moving to C or D by the same rationale? It is in this context that the rudimentary benefit-cost calculations would seem necessary. It should be insufficient for the community to argue that transaction costs are large relative to costs imposed on landowners; they must also be large relative to the benefits reaped by the community.

The harm prevention, benefit extraction distinction can be helpful here in lieu of a costly and perhaps empirically dubious formal study. If the regulation in question moved the community to a position that was still consistent with "normal behavior," then there would be some presumption that the net benefits were substantial. (The region of normal behavior is developed in section

8.9.) If the regulation moved towards *super*normal standards, however, it would be appropriate for the community to bear the burden of proof that public benefits outweighed the cost to the landowners, as well as to show that transaction costs of compensation were very high. Thus a move from A to B in figure 16 would probably be upheld with little effort, but a move from B to C or D would more probably involve supernormal standards, and it would be more difficult to meet the burden that public benefits exceed private losses. The argument that transaction costs of making compensation were relatively high would thus not be dispositive in the latter situations.

In summary, the rule for determining takings is as follows: Government authorities respect the entitlements of individual landowners insofar as these entitlements are not subnormal by community standards. When standards change, or when normal behavior is inconsistent with demands by the community, governments that propose regulations to restrict the use of property *should compensate* affected property owners *unless both* of the following conditions are present: (1) The costs of actually making the compensation (i.e., the transaction costs, *not* including the compensation itself) are excessive relative to the amount of compensation; and (2) the public benefits of the restriction can be demonstrated to be larger than the costs to landowners.

8.7. LOCAL PUBLIC GOODS AS SUBSTANTIVE CRITERIA

There is a paradox that arises when benefit-cost criteria are applied to regulations: it is easier to calculate the benefits of regulations that produce private transfers of wealth than those that provide for public goods. The latter cannot ordinarily be provided by private exchanges (section 5.4). But precisely because of this characteristic, it is very difficult to calculate the value of such goods. Regulations that are straightforward appropriations of private wealth, however, are more easily evaluated. Thus in courtroom testimony about the public benefits versus the private costs of a regulation alleged to be a taking, rent-seeking regulations may make a better show than those that provide local public goods.

This paradox, combined with the indeterminacy of most actual benefit-cost calculations, explains why reliance on a "normal behavior" criterion seems economically preferable in most situations. But we cannot dispense with benefit-cost ideas altogether. There are many situations where the proposed regulations are "supernormal" and transaction costs are high. Some judicial evaluation of benefits to costs, at least for local land use disputes, will be necessary.

The following suggestions may provide some guidance through this problem. Zoning should be used only to provide local public goods. This statement contains two key words: *local* and *public*. Substantive review of zoning laws should ask whether the regulations provide for public goods rather than just redistribute private wealth. This provides a more precise definition of zoning entitlements than the traditional "health, safety and general welfare," while it is consistent with its intention.[8]

This recommendation is not itself an attempt to limit the scope of the police power, for the range of public goods may well be very expansive: not just safety from fire and disease but security and aesthetic pleasures from an orderly community may be included. What the public goods requirement limits are some purely rent-seeking rationales for zoning. Protecting business firms from competition or preserving land to provide goods sold on the private market (e.g., agricultural products) would be suspect goals under this rule.

This does not mean that the existence of some incidental private wealth transfers should necessarily be fatal to the ordinance in question. If this were the case, almost no regulations could be passed. My argument is simply that these private transfers ought not to be counted as part of the community benefits in evaluating the benefits and costs.

The "local" side of this criterion confines zoning to local issues. This is to inihibit the use of national issues as a rationale for highly restrictive zoning. Requiring that new housing meet costly standards of energy efficiency is an example. (This assumes that conservation will reduce dependence on imported oil and thus arguably provide for national security.) Several communities have adopted such standards, which can add substantially to the cost of a home in these jurisdictions.

There is no reason to believe that the independent decisions of local governments will provide the correct level of national public goods (Oates 1972). The free rider problem is as great among 80,000 units of government as among 226 million people. Moreover, the amount of conservation affected by the few communities that adopt these regulations is very small, and the regulations may have perverse effects on metropolitan development, since it will be pushed to communities farther away from employment centers. Energy conservation would look less like an exclusionary smoke screen if it imposed retrofitting standards on existing houses. It seldom does.

One exception to counting only local public goods must be admitted. If local governments are acting in a ministerial capacity to implement a plan enacted by a higher government, this argument does not apply. Examples are the federal government's flood plain zoning requirements and state-mandated air-pollution standards. The key difference in such programs is that local governments lack discretion to use such regulations as exclusionary devices.

Attention to local public goods as the basis for zoning also may promote more serious consideration of less intrusive means of providing for them. Nuisance law and the various refinements of servitudes—covenants, easements, and residential private governments—may in some instances be helpful substitutes for zoning (section 2.3.3). They cannot, however, be used to deal with fiscal issues or spillovers that have pervasive, communitywide effects because of the transaction costs of dealing with a large number of people in already developed communities. I am sympathetic to reforms that increase reliance on these devices, but I remain skeptical of them as complete replacements for zoning regulations.

8.8. EFFICIENCY AND FAIRNESS

The previous sections developed a dual.criterion for takings based on efficiency considerations. The taking issue is not about efficiency; it is about fairness. I shall argue here that these criteria are consistent with the standards of fairness developed in section 8.1.

My paraphrase of Michelman's fairness principle was that a landowner whose property is reduced in value by a zoning regulation ought to be able to see that requiring compensation for the loss would not be in the long-run best interests of people like himself. What argument might convince the landowner of this? The landowner might accede to the restriction if he were convinced that (1) the new regulation produced substantial community benefits in which he shared and (2) a requirement to pay for his loss would result in the community's not being able to have the benefits at all.

Individual landowners may protest ex post that neither condition is met for their property. It is more appropriate to think of the landowner as participating in a town meeting prior to the promulgation of any zoning laws. People know what assets they hold, but they do not know what *specific* regulations might be adopted. They must each decide what *general* compensation policy should be adopted. I submit that the previous policy would be regarded as fair in such a situation. This is an empirical question whose validity may, with some difficulty, be tested.

Both parts of the criterion are inherent in the efficiency tests stated in the previous sections.[9] They were that the regulation did not need to be compensated for if (1) its public benefits exceeded its costs and (2) transaction costs were large relative to the compensation itself. The first test meets the condition that the landowner must perceive that the regulation produces substantial community benefits in which he shares. (Hence the requirement in section 8.7 that regulations provide local public goods, which are available to all.) The second test, high transaction costs, would indicate that the community might forgo the benefits altogether if it were required to pay. Presented with such an outcome as a result of a universal compensation rule, landowners might decide to accept some uncompensated losses as fair.

Transaction costs of paying compensation rise with the number of parties affected by the regulation. If a regulation affects only one or a handful of easily identifiable landowners, the transaction costs of compensation are apt to be low, and compensation should be made. This is consistent with the practice of paying compensation for physical invasion of property regardless of how trivial the loss. The landowner is easily contacted, and the damage is measurable in square feet.

The normal behavior interpretation of the harm-benefit rule also implies, I believe, equal protection of the laws. Normality must be based on the standards of the society that makes the laws; those who pass the laws must submit themselves to them as well as require that outsiders and newcomers conform to them. We find it unexceptionable to require that all people not litter the sidewalk as they pass by but would object to certain people's being allowed to do it while others are penalized. Likewise, if the norm were for people to clean up sidewalks as they went about their business, we would not object if outsiders and newcomers were to be subjected to the same standard.

8.9. THE RANGE OF NORMAL BEHAVIOR AND THE BURDEN OF PROOF

So far I have avoided the question of how exactly to determine what "normal behavior" and "community standards" are. I do

not promise an exact answer, but there are some guidelines that
may be useful. First and foremost, one should *not* look at the text
of the community's master plan and zoning laws to determine
standards for normal behavior. These are, after all, a manifestation of the problem, not the solution to it.

The reason why the local plan is an inadequate guide is that it
is adopted by a political body that does not adequately represent
potential residents (section 3.7). Remedying this does not mean
that all potential residents must be accommodated. One might,
in the absence of a national (and intergenerational) forum on local
growth policies, formulate a golden rule test: if current residents
were outsiders to their own community, what kinds of policies
would they like to see (as a general rule, not specific to themselves)
in their community? On the one hand, they might want to be
accommodated at reasonable cost; on the other hand, they might
not want to live in a community that was excessively developed
or poorly planned. Balancing these two interests may be regarded
as the function of the normal behavior standard.

A normal behavior guideline better than local master plans is
what the community does, not what it says. Ellickson (1977, 422)
proposes that we examine the standards that existing community
residents have willingly imposed on themselves by looking at the
existing pattern of development. A community composed largely
of single-family homes on quarter-acre lots should be treated as
if quarter-acre lots are a reasonably normal standard for development. If such a community zones undeveloped land for two-
acre lots, it exceeds normal standards and thus should be subject
to scrutiny under the taking issue. Similarly, a developer who
proposes to put up high-density apartments could be regarded as
advancing something that may be below normal standards, and
he would not have a prima facie case for a taking.

There are other ways to define normal behavior. One suggestion
is to look at the pattern of development in large, self-contained
planned communities. In these, the single developer has a strong
incentive to establish a mix of uses that will maximize the land
use benefits of initial residents as well as later ones. This is because
initial residents will not buy houses (or other real estate) in such
a community unless they are assured that subsequent development
will not harm them. But developers will also want to develop the
community as intensively as possible. In planned communities,
the landowner has some incentive to look at both the marginal
benefit schedule of existing residents and that of potential resi-

dents in order to discover the efficient path of development over time (Henderson 1980).

Large planned communities are a growing phenomenon in the United States, and I think that explicit comparisons of the laws of private land use controls (via covenants or residential private governments) with zoning would greatly enrich the latter. But such communities are still rare enough to be dismissed in many instances as exceptions to a given community's circumstances. We are still left with the problem of specifying normal behavior.

It would be desirable to have enabling legislation that defined acceptable community behavior more precisely than is currently done (section 2.4). This is not a likely solution, since state legislatures are responsive to local government demands for autonomy. In any event, it may not be necessary to press for a resolution, because the everyday and common sense language of "normal behavior" will by itself refocus discussion of the issue in a way that will make considerable improvements. Zoning practices in developing communities often involve supernormal standards by *any* conception of the term. The major constraints on suburban development, for example, are not the communities of quarter-acre homes that zone the balance of the community for half-acre and one-acre lots but the communities whose zoning laws and practices forbid or retard development on nearly *all* undeveloped land.

The breadth of the term "normal behavior" suggests that for analytical purposes it is best to depict land use restrictions in terms of three ranges of behavior. In figure 17, entitlements are divided into subnormal, normal, and supernormal standards. The benefit schedules are deliberately withheld, because there is no necessary intersection of them within any one of these areas. I did argue that the intersection (the optimal degree of restriction) would most likely occur in the normal range, but that is not a forgone conclusion.

Normal behavior is depicted as a range along the entitlement spectrum for two reasons: (1) it is difficult to agree on a standard of normality, and (2) standards of normality change over time. Within the normal range the community ought to be given the benefit of the doubt (as is currently the practice in most states) as to the reasonableness of its zoning standards and behavior.

This might suggest that community authorities can automatically obtain the most restrictive of normal standards. This should not be the case. It does mean that it is *easier* for the community

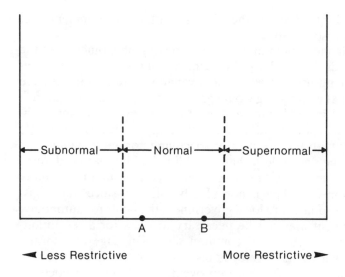

Figure 17. The Range of Community Standards

to establish greater restrictions, moving, say, from point A to point B in figure 17, as long as both are within the range of normal behavior. But landowner plaintiffs in such a situation should be allowed to claim a taking if they can show that the community could make compensation without unduly large administrative (or other transaction) costs. This would protect individual landowners from arbitrary and unfair treatment. Within the normal behavior range, however, the burden of proof remains on the landowner, as under current law.

Once it is established that supernormal standards are being imposed on the landowners, the burden of proof of reasonableness should be placed on the community.[10] The community must then show that transaction costs of making compensation are high and benefits exceed costs. Recall that the community estimates of the value of public benefits are to be given substantial deference as long as they do not include largely private benefits (section 8.7). My recommendation requires, in other words, that when supernormal standards are imposed, the community bears the burden of proof of reasonableness, but that the standard of proof must be something akin to the "preponderance of evidence" favoring its case rather than "clear and convincing evidence" or "proof beyond a reasonable doubt."

8.10. QUALIFICATIONS AND LIMITATIONS ON THE RULES FOR TAKINGS

8.10.1 Economic Due Process Redux?

The suggestions for judicial intervention made in the preceding section may leave the impression that I am advocating a return to the era of "economic due process." This doctrine was adopted by the courts early in this century to strike down much regulatory legislation, including health standards and minimum wages. Its legal basis was a reading of basic market economic principles into the due process clause of the Constitution. However desirable such a reading may seem to economists, it is in fact difficult to discover the precise language that authorized the courts to legislate Adam Smith.[11]

Unlike economic due process, however, the approach to the taking issue advocated here can be rationalized in terms of specific constitutional provisions. This rationalization can also be used to show why the taking problem should focus on local land use issues rather than on national regulations or those not pertaining to real property.

Section 8.1 noted that the taking clause and the equal protection clause seem to have been adopted to prevent oppression of *defenseless* minorities. Minorities in a national or (large) state context may be numerically inferior but they do have the protection of political coalitions (section 10.8). Owners of portable assets have the defense against local regulations of removing themselves and their assets to more favorable jurisdictions. In protecting these minorities the courts need only to be concerned with rights to mobility and free participation in the political process. That indeed seems to have been the thrust of most constitutional interpretation (by academics) of the open-ended clauses. But mobility and participation do not protect owners of land in smaller units of government, where Madison's warning about majoritarian oppression rings most true.[12]

8.10.2. Mobility and Demoralization Costs

My suggestion that the taking issue focus on local, land-related issues may be an unarticulated basis for the historical solicitude for landowners shown by the U.S. Supreme Court. In their influential book *The Taking Issue* (1973), Bosselman, Callies, and Banta note that land use restrictions are "subjected to stricter judicial test than other types of governmental regulation" (p. 232).

They go on to advocate that this distinction be henceforth ignored in order to encourage communities to adopt regulatory measures.[13]

Although one might wonder how much more encouragement communities need in this area, the foregoing discussion may provide a basis for treating land regulations more carefully than others. Land *is* different from the object of most other regulations in that it is not movable and most regulations occur at a local level. The possibilities for owners of this type of asset to "vote with their feet" are obviously limited, and in most communities with stringent land use regulations the possibility of their mitigating their burdens through the political process is almost as remote.

In developing the efficiency rules for a taking, I argued that one condition for not paying compensation is that transaction costs be large relative to the compensatory payment itself. Michelman (1967, 1221) submits a slightly different efficiency criterion here. He says that transaction costs must be larger than "demoralization" costs to justify noncompensation for regulations whose benefits exceed costs. Demoralization costs are the sum of the disutility (producer's surplus?) endured by those who are adversely affected and the long-run efficiency losses (consumer's surplus?) caused by reduced investment in the activity that bears the uncompensated loss. I refrained from adopting this because of measurement problems (especially the possibility of double-counting losses), but they do fit the present argument. Local regulations that affect highly portable activities involve little of either type of demoralization cost because supply is elastic. An example follows.

A community that passes a law prohibiting the sale of alcoholic beverages should not necessarily be deemed to have "taken" the property of bar owners. Alcohol consumption has been shown to cause public harm, and thus its sale may be defined as subnormal behavior. If this is does not seem enough to justify not compensating the bar owners, note that their economic loss can be mitigated by relocating in a different, more permissive community. The land on which the bars were located is reduced in value somewhat, but unless it was uniquely suited for that purpose, it cannot be said to be especially burdened by the regulation.

On the question of politically defenseless minorities the prohibition case would not instantly invoke a taking either. Although the firms affected by a prohibition ordinance may be few, the direct beneficiaries of their activities—consumers of alcohol and suppliers of such firms—are widely dispersed among the population and may be able to effect political compromises with prohibitionists.[14] Neither of these criteria could apply to local regulations establishing broad controls over the use of land. This does not mean that a taking must be found when land is affected; it means only that the taking issue should then be invoked.

8.11. WHERE THE TAKING ISSUE WOULD APPLY

My discussion of the taking issue has focused on local regulation of undeveloped land. There are other landowners who might invoke the taking issue. An owner of already developed property might run into regulatory barriers when he wishes to redevelop it for another use. A neighbor to land on which the authorities have approved a rezoning for an offensive activity might also charge a taking against the community. Both parties might qualify for consideration for compensation, but in each case the plaintiff would run into the normal behavior criterion or the high transaction cost criterion, so that compensation might not have to be made.

An owner who wants to redevelop his property is most likely currently using it for something that is more or less like the use of the rest of the neighborhood. If he wanted to tear down his house and put up apartments or a store, he would be proposing a subnormal activity for that neighborhood. Denial of his opportunity to profit would thus be within the rights of the community. It might be desirable to create a means by which he could compensate his neighbors so that they would willingly tolerate the nuisances he might create, but this would not be a taking issue.

In "neighbors' cases," where abutters object to official decisions, transaction costs are the crucial issue. The authorities have determined that it is in the larger community interest that, say, a shopping center be permitted. Should the immediate neighbors who are adversely affected be compensated? The answer might depend on whether the neighbors were politically powerless; most observers are impressed with how few neighbors it takes to persuade the zoning authorities not to grant a rezoning. But assuming that it has happened, the real issue is whether it would be possible to identify those affected and compensate them without exhausting the entire public benefit. I suspect that transaction costs usually would be excessive, but that is something to be left to individual cases.

The taking issue is most likely to arise, however, when suburban and exurban land that has never been previously developed is burdened with restrictions. It is common for the restrictions to be truly supernormal: minimum lot sizes much larger than those of existing residents' homes, infrastructure requirements of greater real cost than earlier subdivisions, land dedications by developers to provide for activities normally financed by public funds, and procedural delays of many years. The landowners involved are frequently few in number and highly visible, so that the transaction costs of making compensation for increased restrictions would seem to be low.

As was mentioned in chapter 4, just looking at zoning laws themselves may be misleading. Zoning practices may be more important than the laws themselves. Thus I offer below a list of three types of practices that would bring up the taking issue.

1. Often a developer will often acquire land in order to develop something that is perfectly consistent with the zoning laws only to find the community changing the laws in response to his plan. This might involve a formal change in the zoning laws, or it might involve the more informal but equally effective means of resistance to development: excessive subdivision requirements, specious arguments that the proposed development is not exactly that envisioned by the laws, or refusal to grant essential services. Persistent delaying tactics, as well as ad hoc or ad hominum rezonings in the face of specific development plans, would fit into the criteria for a taking. Delay is nearly as expensive as denial in many cases.

2. Communities often decide to change their zoning regulations to make them still more restrictive. (This differs from the previous case in that the community does not just respond to an individual's development proposal.) In this situation, the community has a better defense against a charge that it has taken property, since many owners may be involved and the transaction costs of offering compensation may thus be large. Nonetheless, one does see situations in which a landowner or a group of landowners might successfully argue a taking. Supernormal restrictions, rationalized on the basis of specious reasons or hypersensitive feelings, are widespread. Standards of normal behavior may change, but some attempt can be made to distinguish them from pure rent seeking.

3. It is common in many developing communities to zone large areas of undeveloped land for some low-intensity use, such as agriculture, as a temporary measure. The normal expectation in such cases is that the rural areas will be rezoned, or special exceptions granted, when some acceptable development proposal comes along. In some situations, the municipality may have a time schedule of capital improvements to accommodate development, which also leads to expectations by landowners that they will obtain permission to develop their properties.

In such situations, the taking doctrine might be invoked by a landowner whose application for a rezoning is denied or unreasonably delayed even though the original zoning was acceded to. This is because it had been expected by all involved that at some time in the future a rezoning would be granted. Without such an expectation, the landowners might well have protested the original zoning classification and have had a good case for a taking. For this reason, I would include significant changes in discretionary zoning practices, as well as changes in the text of zoning laws, under the protection of the taking issue. These may be more difficult to identify, but such difficulties may not be a complete bar to remedies where reasonable landowner expectations have been thwarted by community authorities.

8.12. HISTORIC PRESERVATION AND TAKINGS

Most zoning controversies involve suburban restrictions on undeveloped land. Central cities have fewer controversies, because most land is already developed, and redevelopment involves more intensive use of the land. This could involve subnormal behavior, and thus most taking claims would fail.

There is, however, one candidate within developed urban areas for whom a taking might be a successful argument. This is the owner of property that has been designated a historic treasure and thus subject, without compensation, to substantial use restrictions.[15] Why would such a property owner succeed where other owners of developed land were denied?

First, an owner of a historic building meets the criteria for invoking the taking issue. He usually has relatively little political power within his jurisdiction. Moreover, the restriction on conversion or demolition usually means that the capital so invested cannot be moved to another jurisdiction.[16] This absolute immobility is what makes historic preservation a better object for a taking claim than other urban real estate regulations, such as rent control. Under rent control an owner is deprived of substantial income from his property, but he has the option of conversion to other uses (such as condominiums) if regulations become too onerous. But rent control combined with prohibitions on condominium conversion would surely qualify under this approach, contrary to Flynn v. Cambridge, 418 N.E. 2d 335 (Mass. 1981).

What is most important, historic designation of individual properties applies supernormal standards. Most controversies have centered on the preservation of historic treasures, not on the un-neighborliness or subnormality of the proposed new building that is to take its place. This is a case of forcing particular individuals to provide benefits rather than preventing harms. Although it is possible that public benefits normally exceed private costs, the owner burdened by the restriction is almost always easily identified, so that compensation could be made without large transaction costs.

Might a city be sufficiently deterred from uncompensated historic designation by the prospect that such practice will diminish the future supply of architecturally valuable structures? Attractive buildings are more costly to erect than ordinary ones, and a prudent landowner might try to avoid the effect of future regulation by hiring only mediocre architects. (This assumes, contrary to evidence, that public taste in architecture thirty years from now is predictable.) Still another shift in supply may occur: owners of candidates for historic preservation may, when the prospect of full compensation is not likely, quickly destroy their buildings to allow their land to be developed for normal, profitable uses. This is exactly what happened when a Brazilian official, attempting to emulate U.S. rules, gave notice that several São Paulo mansions in a valuable downtown commercial location might be subject to historic preservation. Owners of the structures destroyed several of them overnight (*New York Times*, 18 August 1982, A2).

The foregoing argument usually would not apply to entire historic districts involving many different units. In such cases, the large size of the district would mean that there was some local political power to prevent its restrictive designation if it were undesired. Moreover, there may be substantial mutual benefit to all landowners in most such districts.[17] It would be more difficult to argue that having all the houses in a district conform to similar standards was supernormal behavior.

Proponents of preservation of particular structures may object to the argument that compensation should be paid. The city just cannot afford to make the compensation, it may be argued. This could mean two things. One is that the city is willing to pay for its amenities, but the transaction costs of making compensation are excessive. This argument has some merit where an entire district is so designated, but hardly when only isolated structures are involved. The other meaning of this argument is that the city is unwilling to pay for the historical amenities unless they are offered at the low price of legal fees. This is precisely what the taking clause seems designed to forestall: burdening particular individuals for the benefit of society at large.

A more sophisticated version of the "cannot afford" argument could center on a failure of public choice. The city's voters do truly value the amenities under this theory, but the nature of the political process is such that true preferences are not revealed. But if this is so, by what process are public officials able to discover the community's true willingness to pay when they sit as regulators, while they are unable to find it when they sit as budget makers?

8.13. SUMMARY AND CONCLUSION

Among the legal tests of a regulatory taking, a variation of the traditional harm-benefit criterion appears to be most consistent with the basic norms implied by the taking clause and the efficient exercise of the police power. This variation is called a normal behavior standard. It holds up the community's regulations to judicial review on the basis of whether they are consistent with social norms for communities in their situation.

Standards of normal behavior may change over time. Additional regulations, without compensation for landowners, are then justified when *both* of the following conditions prevail: (1) the transaction costs of making the payment to landowners are large relative to the compensatory payments themselves; and (2) public benefits from the regulations (judged as local public goods, not private transfers) are larger than the private costs of the regulations.

These rules are consistent with economic efficiency in that they promote reasonable expectations on the part of landowner-developers. They are consistent with the standard of fairness expressed by Michelman in that landowners ought to be able to perceive that *not* receiving compensation in the foregoing dual circumstances is in the long-run interest of people like themselves.

Normal behavior is an elastic concept. Standards for individual cases may be discovered by looking at the past behavior of the community or at some aspects of privately planned communities. Normal behavior is also a two-sided criterion. It protects landowners from the community's adoption of supernormal regulations, but it also protects the community from having to pay compensation to a landowner for denying a project that is in the subnormal behavior category.

The ability of governments to unfairly burden identifiable individuals declines when the resources they control are portable. Thus the taking issue should be confined largely to land or to other resources made immobile by the regulation. Modern political economy suggests, in addition, that larger units of government are less likely to commit majoritarian excesses than are smaller units of government. Thus as a practical matter, claims for a taking should be considered more seriously when a local government, especially a small, homogeneous unit, is involved.

Taking could in principle be applied to any landowner adversely affected by public actions, but owners of undeveloped land in suburban communities seem most likely to succeed under the criteria advanced here. Within central cities, the practice of designating isolated structures as historic treasures not to be altered would also raise the taking issue.

Perhaps the major difference between the approach to the taking issue expressed in this chapter and that of much of the legal, economics, and planning literature is its characterization of the local political process. I assume that local authorities are interested in political success. In most suburban communities, this is best achieved by maximizing the net worth of the median voter. Notions of the public interest that are inconsistent with this process are not controlling. There is no disinterested Pigovian planner trying to correct market failures.

While some may regard the public choice model as cynical, it seems necessary to advance it to offset the Pollyannish view that local officials are disinterested planners. The latter view has led many to conclude that the taking issue should not be a serious constraint on land use regulations.

NOTES

1. It is noted in [*Harvard Law Rev.*] (1978, 1483) that Michelman's reliance on Rawls is undermined by the latter's later writings on justice. In later work Rawls (1971) would apply his theories only to "the basic structures of society," of which compensation mechanisms would not be one. Mandelker (1981, 54) invokes this as sufficient to dismiss Michelman's argument. Even if Michelman must be put in lock step with Rawls, it seems to me that the taking issue *is* one of the basic structures of society. Would not the relation of the individual to the state be fundamentally different if it were accepted that governments could appropriate a citizen's assets without compensation?

2. One case rejecting wealth as a "suspect classification" is San Antonio Independent School Dist. v. Rodriguez, 411 U.S. 1 (1972). Earlier evidence comes from the supposed exchange between Fitzgerald and Hemingway: "You know, Ernest, the rich are different from us." "Yes, Scott, they have more money."

3. Most commentaries on the taking issue begin with extensive summaries

and comparisons of Michelman and Sax (Ackerman 1977; Berger 1974; [*Harvard Law Rev.*] 1978). My remarks in the text in this section are critical of the application of Sax's rules to local disputes, but I would agree with him that most federal environmental legislation should not be regarded as a taking.

4. This section and the next follow Michelman (1967, 1183–1201). My major novelty is couching the argument in the entitlements diagram. For a succinct review of these criteria and citations to more recent cases see Ellickson and Tarlock (1981, 133–38).

5. See McKean (1972, 182). Cordes and Weissbrod (1979) found that requirements to pay relocation costs to displaced residents resulted in less highway construction, suggesting that in the absence of such requirements agencies understate costs. Blume, Rubinfeld, and Shapiro (1984) also suggest that governments are apt to calculate biased estimates of benefit-cost ratios that favor their interests.

6. This standard and its justification are lifted from Ellickson (1973, 728–33; 1977, 419–24). See also Wittman (1984). One who has read my earlier commentary (1980a, 95) on Ellickson's proposals might be especially surprised, since I discarded his "normal behavior" standard as too costly to administer. I now think its costs are no greater than other approaches.

7. It also follows that an individual community, one local government within many zoning jurisdictions, must have its standards of behavior scrutinized by the larger society under similar standards of normal behavior. This does not require community uniformity; only that the goals of a given community be consistent with standards of those in similar circumstances. Further discussion is in chapter 15.

8. Jeffrey Strnad, in an unsigned note written as a student ([*Yale Law J.*] 1979), developed a public goods argument for police powers. Epstein (1982, 365) briefly applies it to the taking issue. This approach also seems consistent with the substantive proposals of the President's Commission on Housing (1982), whose list of "vital and pressing" government purposes comprises largely local public goods.

9. The usual merger of and two exceptions to the efficiency and fairness tests are discussed by Michelman (1967, 1223–24). Anecdotal support for the merger of efficiency and fairness criteria is suggested by attitudes towards the military draft. This is a "taking" of the time of those who are subject to it. When it inducts nearly everyone, so that there is an obvious savings in transaction costs of individual bargains, and when the cause for which it is instituted is widely believed to have public benefits in excess of costs, the draft is more readily accepted by those subject to it.

10. This is similar to the recommendation of Ellickson (1977, 469), the President's Commission on Housing (1982, 200) and Sager (1969, 794). The proposal in the text would shift the burden of proof only when supernormal standards were being proposed; those noted here do not make that distinction. Such a reversal has only a few precedents in current zoning law (Ellickson and Tarlock 1981, 76), but it was invoked by the 1983 *Mount Laurel II* decision (452 A.2d at 466), discussed in sections 3.6 and 15.2.

11. A brief for a return to the economic due process courts is Siegan (1980).

12. *The Federalist*, no. 10 (Madison), discussed also by Ellickson (1977, 405–07). Section 10.10 will consider the problem of using constitutional doctrines to *overprotect* well-organized minorities—that is, interest groups. Posner (1977, 49) considers the latter problem exclusively and dismisses the argument that the Constitution tries to protect minorities from majorities. He pays little attention to local regulation in this context, however.

13. Bosselman, Callies, and Banta (1973, chap. 12) would allow takings only for physical invasions. Their contention that a regulatory taking "is wholly inconsistent with the tradition of founding fathers" (p. 325) is contradicted by Ely (1980, 97) and Nedelsky (1982, 347 and 356). Bosselman, Callies, and Banta were commissioned by the President's Council on Environmental Quality, whose natural predisposition is to diminish the scope of regulatory takings. Their report is frankly "designed to assist government officials and attorneys who seek to fashion solutions to environmental problems" (p. v).

14. Similar arguments could buttress decisions denying compensation for local gun controls (the guns are portable) and the military draft (draftees and sympathizers are a politically effective part of the national electorate). This may help distinguish noncompensation situations identified by Posner (1977, 42).

15. The leading case is Penn Central v. City of New York, 438 U.S. 104 (1978), involving preservation of Grand Central Terminal. The court's decision upholding the designation of the terminal as a historic landmark provides imperfect guidance because of the city's willingness to barter rezonings ("transferable development rights") in other parts of the city as partial compensation to the owner. On this case see Marcus (1979) and section 9.8.

16. A regulation making something immobile makes it like land. A leading federal case on compensation for regulation is Pete v. United States, 531 F.2d 1018 (Ct. Cl. 1976), discussed by Hagman (1978, 276). Federal wilderness regulations made Mr. Pete's fishing barges economically valueless. Their size and remote location made them immovable. Pete was paid the replacement value of the barges.

17. This is the "average reciprocity of advantage" of Justice Holmes in Pennsylvania Coal v. Mahon, 260 U.S. 393 (1922), mentioned in Rehnquist's dissent in the *Penn Central* case (n. 15 above), and in section 3.5.

9.

Entitlement Protection and Takings

The central question of the previous chapter was where initial entitlements should be established. The economic problem does not end there. Only by the most felicitous accident would the initial entitlement end all potential voluntary exchange between landowners and the community or other parties with standing in such disputes.

This chapter will explore the conditions under which entitlement exchanges should take place. The fundamental reference is the distinction developed by Calabresi and Melamed between property rules, liability rules, and inalienability (sections 6.4 and 6.5). A property rule allows the possessor of an entitlement to refuse to trade; he can hold out for any price (or no exchange at all). A liability rule requires the owner of the entitlement to exchange it with another party if the offer is considered acceptable by a third party; the owner has no right to refuse all offers. Inalienability means that initial entitlements should not be exchanged under any conditions.

The basic conclusions of each section are as follows: Zoning should be freely alienable; this promotes revelation of values by the community. Capitalization of zoning restrictions in the price of land does not dispose of the taking issue, since acceptance of such an argument makes private rights inalienable. Protection of entitlements is not symmetrical. Community zoning should be protected by property rules except when a clear case can be made that the community's initial entitlement involves regulations that are supernormal. Private landowners, on the other hand, only receive liability rule protection against the community. The reason for the difference is the difficulty that communities have in making collective valuations and decisions about public goods. The choice of liability rule protection for landowners implies that the remedy for a taking should be incremental damages.

I examine and criticize the Neo-Georgist argument that increments to land value should be subject to public appropriation. A summary to the suggested rules for takings and exchange is given in the penultimate section. I conclude that these rules would work for equity and efficiency in suburban zoning disputes.

9.1. REJECTION OF INALIENABILITY

This section presents what seem to me to be the best reasons for making zoning inalienable and then shows what is wrong with them.[1]

9.1.1. Protection of Landowners

I argued in section 7.3 that a cause of excessive zoning restrictions is the judicial hostility towards contract zoning. It was suggested earlier (section 4.6) that courts have a reason for this: making zoning inalienable is a means of protecting landowners from excessive regulations. A community that could sell rezonings might find it profitable to establish restrictive regulations for the sole purpose of selling them to the highest bidder.

It should be apparent, however, that this protection for landowners has not worked well: many zoning restrictions are truly extraordinary. It is thus little protection for a landowner subject to a minimum lot size of 160 acres to forbid him from buying his way out of it. The problem is not the sale of rezonings but the establishment of unreasonable zoning in the first place. The normal behavior standard is one attempt to deal with this initial entitlement problem. Because of the breadth of any such standard, however, it is in the interest of landowners to be allowed to buy their way out of even reasonable-sounding restrictions if community authorities agree to the terms.

9.1.2. Intermunicipal Spillovers

If current zoning arrangements control activities whose harms spill over to other jurisdictions, one would not want the community to rezone in a way that causes more spillovers. One way to ensure against this is to make zoning inalienable. Spillovers may be a problem, but inalienability is an extreme remedy. If interjurisdictional spillovers are pervasive, the root of the problem is that the zoning jurisdiction is too small or that neighboring jurisdictions are not made party to decisions that affect them (section 5.6).

The other problem with the interjurisdictional spillover argument is that there is no reason to believe that an initial zoning entitlement would be optimal for the neighboring jurisdiction. One community's zoning laws may permit many subnormal activities near its borders. In this case, it may be desirable to allow the neighboring community to pay the permissive community to be more restrictive. Alienability may be *desirable* for dealing with intermunicipal spillovers.

9.1.3. Administrative Costs and Myopia

Another argument in favor of inalienability might be that the benefits to undertaking a proposed rezoning are trivial relative to the administrative costs of considering it. This argument may be valid, but the same result can be obtained by granting the community property rule protection. Under such a rule, the community needs to consider only those zoning changes that it chooses to consider.

Community authorities are sometimes said to be myopic in their decisions, taking short-run gains at the expense of long-run benefits. (This view is most often expressed by plaintiffs in neighbors' cases.) A way to correct this tendency may be to make current zoning entitlements inalienable, at least when authorities want to move towards less restriction on new developments. This is an odd argument, since it usually comes from people who think that private landowners also are myopic. But I do not think that either argument is valid.

The pressure on local legislatures in rezoning decisions almost always comes from landowners and homeowners, all of whom own long-lived assets and who thus tend to be future-oriented. Only in large central cities, where renters have more political influence, would this argument have much foundation.

9.1.4. Superiority of Courts

Another argument for inalienability is that the courts, who are the arbiters of initial entitlements, do a better job of determining land use than do community authorities. If this were true, there might be a case for inalienability, since the initial entitlements (as adjudicated by the courts) would be close to an optimal degree of restriction. Subsequent alterations by others would be as likely to move away from the optimum as closer to it. When the masters finish the paintings, their apprentices should not be permitted to alter them.

One might support this position by arguing that judges are probably more intelligent than local authorities. Intelligence, however, is not the issue; the problem is one of knowledge. The question is whether court proceedings are more likely to generate information about the value of land use restrictions by the various parties. Since the problem of knowledge is the heart of the issue of entitlement protection generally, I shall develop it in more detail in the following section.

9.2. ALIENABILITY AND REVELATION OF INFORMATION

Figure 18 is an entitlements diagram that displays the marginal benefit schedules for the landowner-developer and the community as regions rather than lines. The boundaries of these regions have a particular meaning. The upper boundary is the maximum benefit schedule that the community or the landowner could plausibly argue for in front of a reasonable and objective person. The lower boundary is the minimum benefit schedule that might be so argued (by the opposing party) under the same constraint.

This approach illustrates that knowledge of valuations of various land use restrictions is not free and thus can be misrepresented. I shall argue that both of these "bands of ignorance" could be narrowed considerably but that adversarial proceedings in a court of law are not likely to do this.

The community's benefit region in figure 18 is deliberately drawn wider than that of the landowner. The reason is that the benefits of land use entitlements to the community are largely public goods. We know that these are hard to value. Thus the community, if it wants to, can make a sophisticated case for valuing them at a very high rate. But for the same reason, the landowner can plausibly argue that the benefits to the community of any restriction are quite low, which establishes the lower line on the community's marginal benefit schedule. (Recall the indeterminacy of benefit-cost analysis discussed in section 8.4.)

On the other hand, the landowner's benefit region is narrower because it is easier to establish a market value on various degrees of restriction. Similar properties in the community or elsewhere are sold with various degrees of restriction, so that realistic comparisons can be made. This means that the landowner's benefit schedule is easier to determine and monitor, not that it is costless to do so.

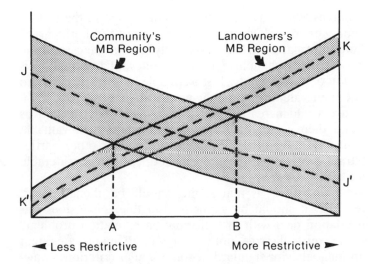

Figure 18. Arguable Regions of Benefits to the Community and the Landowner

In adversarial proceedings, judges will get widely varying information that could cause them to grant an entitlement point anywhere between points A and B in figure 18. The community will argue for point B. It will make a case for the maximum possible public benefits to it, while minimizing the loss to the landowner. The landowner-developer, however, will argue for point A, the least restrictive entitlement, by minimizing the value of the benefits to the community (or arguing that the proposed project will have little adverse impact on the community, which amounts to the same thing) and maximizing the value of his entitlement to that degree of restriction. The wise landowner will not point out his personal profit but instead will emphasize the social value of the development to its ultimate users. That there is a correspondence between the two may be overlooked by many judges.

How would a judge decide which point between points A and B represents the appropriate use of land? In the previous chapter I suggested that the normal behavior standard be used as a guide. But even if this were unambiguous and the judge decided to follow it, there is no guarantee that the true intersection of the marginal benefit schedules, and hence the optimal use of land, is within that range. In any event, is a judge in a good position to determine the optimum from the evidence presented by both parties?

Courts have limited resources; in particular, judges have limited time to decide such issues. Even if they did have the time and other resources, they have a distinct disadvantage in the task of information gathering, because it is in the interest of both parties to withhold information. This is especially true in the case of the community benefit schedule, where the relevant information is the valuation of public goods. Just as people have an incentive to understate their valuation of public goods when a true revelation of preference would increase their tax bills, so they have incentives to overstate them when the result would grant them valuable entitlements. Because of this problem, judges (or other parties who arbitrate entitlements disputes) must operate in considerable ignorance of the relevant facts.

My argument, then, is that zoning should be alienable and, moreover, that it should be explicitly fungible. How does this recommendation deal with the information revelation problem? It allows the courts the freedom to assign entitlements consistent with a normal behavior standard or some similar criterion, knowing that if this is not satisfactory, the parties will change it.

Once an entitlement is established by the court, the motives for exchange will arise if the initial entitlement is not efficient. If the *true* valuations of entitlements in figure 18 were lines JJ' and KK' and the initial entitlement were point B, then landowners would attempt to estimate, perhaps by a series of tentative offers, what the true benefit schedule of the community was in order to buy their way out of excessive restrictions. The community may be induced to respond more accurately because it knows that an overstatement might cause no trade at all, and the landowner's compensation to it will be lost.

Evidence for the efficacy of this process in revealing valuations is provided by the behavior of the National Audubon Society. In administrative proceedings involving wetlands that it does not own, the society usually advocates no development. On wetlands in Louisiana that it does own it leases drilling rights—with environmental safeguards—to oil exploration companies (Baden and Stroup 1981).

9.3. CAPITALIZATION, SPECULATION, AND TAKINGS

The issue of alienability of property is related to an argument that is sometimes used to dismiss the taking issue.[2] This argument is based on the fact that regulations become capitalized in the value of the land when it is sold. Consider the following example.

Landowner A owned a parcel of land zoned for normal uses.

A new zoning law was then passed restricting A's property to a supernormal degree. A then sold his land to B, who was fully aware of the restriction in place. Under the original zoning the land had been worth $2,000. Under the more restrictive zoning it was worth only $500, which B paid to A. The zoning became capitalized into the value of land: its sale value reflects the restrictions placed on it.

The burden of the restriction in this scenario was endured by A, the original landowner, not by B, the buyer. It would appear that awarding damages or less restrictive zoning to B would not be fair, since it seems that A bore the loss. Yet under the taking doctrine suggested in the last chapter, the test would be whether the zoning ordinance was consistent with normal behavior (or met a benefit-cost test) and whether the landowner could be compensated without excessive transactions costs. The identity of the landowner is irrelevant.[3]

Capitalization does not dispose of the taking issue. The reason is as follows. When A sold the property to B, he sold along with the nominal title to the land a legal entitlement to sue the community for a taking of his property. This made the land that much more valuable, and thus A gained from being able to sell it. If A had the right to sue for a taking, but B does not, the right to legal redress is made inalienable. This shifts the burden back to A; he must keep title to the property to retain the right to benefit from the taking clause.

This would be a burden insofar as A might have had a strong time preference, a need for liquidity, or an inability to act as a developer. (Since much undeveloped property is sold upon the death of the owner, all of these would usually apply to the heirs.) Allowing only original owners to sue for a taking, which is the essence of the capitalization argument, is itself a restraint on alienation of property and a taking.

It may be argued from my previous example that new owner B nonetheless paid only $500 for a $2,000 piece of land. If the taking rule were strictly applied, either the land should be rezoned for its previous zoning (if consistent with normal behavior) or the community should pay B $1,500 (the incremental damages [section 9.7]). Should not the community seek out A, the former landowner (or his heirs), to make fair compensation?

My answer is no. The taking criteria are based on community, not private, standards of normal behavior. That landowner A had erroneously thought that he had lost rights worth $1500 is of no importance here. Conversely, we would not compensate the buyer, landowner B, for having bought the land for $30,000 in the erroneous expectation that he could build a profitable but subnormal pulp mill on the site. That buyers and sellers make mistakes is hardly a matter for constitutional litigation.

The appeal of the capitalization argument to economists may be that for once they are put on the side of popular attitudes. Hostility to landowners and speculation is widespread and knows no class. I find it mildly ironic to see well-moneyed suburban homeowners appear at zoning hearings to attack a proposed development as the scheme of a profit-hungry speculator. This objection has an easy answer. The Constitution does not say that just compensation should be paid to everyone except speculators and developers. To argue so would be logically similar to arguing that the First Amendment applies only to people whose views are popular.

Residents who object to development of a particular property often deny that they want to harm the original landowner, who is sometimes a neighbor and long-time resident. The arguments are usually directed against the developer. But developers often have contingent arrangements with landowners; if a developer is denied permission to develop, the landowner loses too (Geller 1983, 119–21). There may be various risk-sharing arrangements between landowners and developers; this does not fundamentally change this argument, since risk shifting is costly (Shavell 1979). It is impossible to make only the speculator pay.

9.4. OLD REGULATIONS

The more reasonable concern behind the capitalization argument is the idea that an old regulation ought to be left alone, even if it is excessive in some sense. This argument has some merit. Planning and zoning decisions involve considerable administrative expense for a community. (Most of this expense is hidden, because most zoning and planning boards are made up of volunteers who could use their time in other community activities.) If charges of a taking are allowed long after the regulatory decision is made, this cost is raised. The landowners might have a good reason for having waited so long, but the burden to show that it was reasonable should be placed on them. There is nothing especially unfair about such a rule. It is analogous to a statute of limitations, a condition placed on harms more serious than most taking cases. Another reason for respecting old regulations is that the standard of what is normal changes over time. This can be shown by an analogy to property law. In many states, a person who crosses another's land persistently and notoriously can acquire a legal right to continue to do so. Such a right could not be acquired if the landowner took some steps to prevent the trespass; but if he did not, the right to exclude others might be lost.

We view this as fair, I believe, because people develop an expectation that they have a right to do something if they are not prevented from doing it. Thus the expectations of the community gradually become founded on the idea that a particular land use control is legitimate. They will make plans based on it. For a landowner to claim compensation for a taking long after such plans have been made hardly seems fair to those other members of the community who acted as if the zoning entitlements were well settled. (A parallel argument could be advanced to justify the common practice of letting old nonconforming land uses persist.)

This argument militates for permitting some apparently super-normal standards to remain in communities that have had them for a long time. (This assumes that the landowner did not press for their removal; the community should not be rewarded for procedural delays.) How much deference should be given this argument would depend on how far from normal the standards are. But note that the argument is based on the length of time that the regulations have been in place, not on change of ownership. It would apply to land whose single owner held the property for fifty years but not to a two-year-old regulation of property that changed hands five times during the period. Who owns the property, in other words, should still be irrelevant.

9.5. PROPERTY RULES OR LIABILITY RULES?

Having argued in the previous sections for both alienable zoning entitlements and alienable legal standing, I return now to consider whether entitlements should be protected by a property rule or a liability rule. The analysis builds on the idea that knowledge, particularly knowledge about public goods, is costly.

Liability rules afford less protection for entitlements than do property rules. There is some confusion about exactly what one means by a liability rule, and there is also doubt whether liability rules such as eminent domain are in fact less costly for the party buying the entitlements than a property rule would be (Munch 1976; Polinsky 1980). But I believe that the distinction remains important. The crucial difference is that under a property rule the owner of an entitlement can simply refuse any and all offers without giving an explanation. Under a liability rule this right of refusal is lost, since some third party monitors offers for reasonableness. The liability rule may in practice result in most offers' being refused, but the owner of the entitlement must undertake some expense in defending his position.

One approach to the question of entitlement protection is to ask why all entitlements in land use are not protected by property rules. If we regard entitlements as important, why should those who possess them be compelled to exchange them? Why would the carrot of financial gain be insufficient to motivate all desirable exchanges? There are two circumstances in which this motive may fail. The first is when many parties must be dealt with and there are economies of scale in completing the project. The second is when other considerations, such as the distribution of wealth, are important. We shall deal with the first of these below and the second in the next section.

The classic argument for liability rule protection of landowners arises when a government agency must assemble many different parcels of land to construct an extensive project, such as a road. After several sites have been purchased, the landowners who have not sold will realize that they are in an excellent position to collect all of the rental value of the road. Were they allowed to do this, few roads might be built, because of the costly negotiations over economic rents in this situation.[4] If zoning regulations provide for public goods in much the same way as rights of way provide for roads, a case could be made for protecting private landowners from the community's regulation by a liability rule. This means that once initial entitlements are settled, the community can establish more restrictive land use regulations, provided that the community is willing to pay for the damages (lost profits or reduction in property value) it imposes on the affected landowners.

One problem with the analogy of zoning with public acquisition of land under eminent domain is that the problem of holdouts in land acquisition applies to private developers as well as public agencies. The developers of private new towns such as Reston, Virginia, and Columbia, Maryland, also had to deal with holdouts. Here we come to an important reason for assigning communities favorable entitlements in land use.

Private developers are single entrepreneurs with an unambiguous motive to make a profit. Public agencies have more ambiguous objectives, so they must conduct much of their work in the open in order to find out whether their constituents approve. Private developers can adopt various subterfuges to avoid strategic holdouts: they can hire straw buyers, form dummy corporations, and make threats to move their project elsewhere. Local governments generally lack such ability.[5]

It is because of this difference in objectives and hence organization between a private corporation and a municipal corporation that I suggest the difference in protection of entitlements in zoning issues. Granting property rule protection to the community in the range of subnormal and normal land uses allows the developer who wants to negotiate for fewer restrictions within this range to be rebuffed. However, as an entrepreneur, the developer has an incentive to *initiate* an exchange of development entitlements. The developer can make a series of offers and counter offers more easily than the community authorities, who must constantly deal with numerous other public objectives and many constituents with different goals.

For these reasons, I do not think that giving the community property rule protection will result in the community's extracting all surplus values from exchanges with landowners, as was suggested in section 6.5. Community authorities are not ordinarily real estate experts; no continuing personal profit results from their learning landowners' reservation prices.[6] As a result, there is little reason to think that property rule protection for the community would frequently lead to the community's collecting all of the increment to land value from removal of restrictions.

The exceptions to the entitlement protection rules occur within the range of supernormal standards for land use. As I pointed out in the last chapter, many communities apply supernormal standards to undeveloped land. Even if the taking doctrine suggested in that chapter were adopted, there would remain numerous parcels of land that, because of the antiquity of the zoning applied to them, would remain subject to supernormal standards. I submit that in this case the entitlement protections should be modified. The community should be protected only by a liability rule. The reason for this will be explained in the next section.

9.6. LIABILITY RULES AND SUPERNORMAL STANDARDS

One reason for not adopting a property rule, besides preventing the high transaction costs of dealing with holdouts, is the desire by public authorities to monitor and, if possible, to vitiate illegitimate motives or advance other public policies. This is true of many entitlements in private transactions. Stockholders of a manufacturing firm may ordinarily sell their shares to others unless such a sale would promote a monopoly in the industry. Similarly, a company found to have monopoly power may be required to sell some properties in order to promote competition. In both cases, full property rule protection—the right to refuse any and all offers—is lifted to promote other public policies. The same might be said about the judge-made rule that racial covenants are unenforceable.

It is because of arguments analogous to these that I propose that supernormal community entitlements—those significantly more restrictive than can be justified by prevailing standards for the community—be protected only by a liability rule. My reasoning assumes that there is a regular, if not invariable, connection between supernormal standards and local public purposes unacceptable to that larger body politic that makes the rules within which communities operate. These illegitimate public purposes include a desire to promote monopoly in the housing (or other) markets and the desire to exclude new residents on the basis of race or some personal characteristic.[7]

Liability rule protection for the community in supernormal land use restrictions promotes the ability of landowners to buy their way out of monopolistic or otherwise inappropriate restrictions. The "damages" that the landowner-developers would have to pay would be monitored by a third party (e.g., the courts), so that they would have to pay compensation, not for destroying monopoly power or desegregating a community, but only for the more legitimate benefits that the community gave up.

Awarding damages may be criticized as simply transferring the community's monopoly profits to landowner-developers, since owing to the community's history of restrictions, the landowner-developers would be able to sell their properties for higher prices. But these profits would be temporary. If all landowner-developers are treated equally, and if there is free entry into that market, subsequent development will lower the selling price of the houses built by the first landowners who broke the community's monopoly restrictions. (The higher temporary profits of initial developers in this case may be viewed as a necessary inducement to challenge the monopoly.)

Why not extend liability rule protection to the community for normal standards as well? Reproducing existing community (normal) standards on undeveloped land may, after all, serve monopoly or exclusionary motives. While this may be true, this extension seems impractical for two reasons. First, it may actually increase transaction costs. I suspect that zoning authorities are far more willing to go to court to preserve normal standards than they are to preserve supernormal standards. Litigation and other transaction costs would increase dramatically.

Second, even in the most affluent suburban communities, existing development occurs at densities that take only a small fraction of the land in a metropolitan area or region. To allow these densities to persist in the rest of the community would not greatly restrict the stock of housing in the metropolitan area if there were many other communities.

The rule proposed here is nearly without precedent in our legal system. It allows the developer to have an eminent-domain-like power to develop in the face of community opposition. Radical as it is, I include it as a serious suggestion because it seems administratively simpler than other remedies for supernormal zoning restrictions. Michelle White's proposal to have a metropolitan wide authority supervise (via taxes or regulations) excessive zoning standards sounds like asking the wolf pack to regulate the killing of sheep.[8] These bodies would most likely be dominated by suburban interests. The courts in New Jersey and some other states have found that direct judicial supervision of zoning is costly and not yet effective (section 15.2.2).

Ellickson's proposal that aggrieved outsiders be allowed as a class to collect damages from communities who engage in monopolistic exclusion will elicit skepticism from those acquainted with antitrust litigation. While he recognizes many of these problems and modifies his proposal so that individual consumers do not actually get the damages, there remains the serious problem of actually determining the existence of a monopoly. His suggestion (1977, 499) that an "an econometrician could be the expert best equipped to detect prices influenced by monopolistic restrictions" is based on optimistic projections of the state of economic science and, more importantly, greatly improved data on local housing markets. Even without these, the objections to benefit-cost analysis in section 8.4 apply to testimony about monopoly power as well.

The major advantage of my proposal to reverse the usual entitlement protection rules in the supernormal range is that supernormality is the only question of fact. No inquiry into exclusionary intentions, racial motives, or monopoly power is necessary. The drawback of the proposal is that communities that desire supernormal regulations for innocent reasons or legitimate public purposes may find them more difficult, but by no means impossible, to establish and maintain.

9.7. REMEDIES: DAMAGES OR INVALIDATION?

9.7.1. Problems with Invalidation

Liability rule protection for the landowner implies the remedy of damages in taking cases where the landowner prevails. That is, if the community rezones a parcel of land to a restrictive degree and the court decides that it is a taking, the community should be given the option of rescinding the regulation or paying damages. The words of the Fifth Amendment "nor shall private property be taken for public use, *without just compensation*," seem the essence of a liability rule: landowners do not have the option of refusing to give up their property as they would under a property rule. This is also explicit in Holmes's opinion in *Pennsylvania Coal*: "A strong public desire to improve the public condition is not enough to warrant achieving the desire by a shorter cut than the *constitutional way of paying the charge*" (260 U.S. at 416 [emphasis added]).

It seems odd, then, that prevailing practice should favor invalidations of the ordinance, which imply property rule protection for landowners, rather than damages. When a taking is found, most courts simply order the community to rescind or amend its ordinance. This has two drawbacks as a remedy.

First, it provides no relief for delay of development. Delay is a cost to the landowner-developer but a benefit to the restrictive community. The latter has no incentive to respond quickly to the court's order. As a result, the landowner may decide to accede to unconstitutional restrictions simply in order to get any practical use from his property.

Second, invalidation usually requires that the community simply redo the ordinance to remove the offensive part. The landowner may not even benefit from this. For example, in Appeal of Girsch, 263 A.2d 395 (Pa. 1970), the plaintiff succeeded in having the community rezone to accommodate apartments, but his property was not included in the apartment zone! Courts can of course be more specific in such developer remedies (as the Pennsylvania court was in a later ruling on *Girsch*), but most are reluctant to do this because of the judicial time that it takes and the usurpation of legislative authority that it involves.

9.7.2. Virtues of Damages

The damages remedy overcomes the above-mentioned problems. It offers relief from delaying tactics and provides an incentive for the developer to pursue his case. The court need not embroil itself in a continuing zoning controversy, because the prospect of paying damages will induce both parties to settle. The objection that damages will inhibit the use of regulation (Agins v. Tiburon, 598 P.2d 25 [Cal. 1979]) seems to miss the point. The purpose of the taking clause is to protect individuals from the the state, not vice-versa.

Another advantage of the damages remedy is that it reduces the harshness of the choices that judges must make in most zoning cases: either to strike down the ordinance or to allow the community to do whatever it pleases. Although subsequent exchanges between communities and landowners can alter either outcome, cooperative exchange is often inhibited by the bitterness of the court battle and the strategies each side has used to establish or protect its position. Judges might be more ready to defend the rights of landowners or to attack local parochialism if their remedies left more flexibility for communities that truly valued their restrictions to pay for them.

The damages remedy recently received support from the U.S. Supreme Court. In San Diego Gas and Electric v. City of San Diego, 450 U.S. 621 (1981), a dissent by Justice Brennan addressed the issues above and came out strongly in favor of a damages remedy for regulatory takings. Brennan was joined in dissent by three other justices, and a fifth justice, Rehnquist, indicated that he agreed with Brennan and would have joined him but for other considerations not germane to the substantive issue. This imputed majority appears to have revived interest in damages both among commentators and in state courts.[9] For this reason, it is worth discussing the implications of a damages remedy in the context of the taking standard that I have advocated here.

9.7.3. The Need for Incremental Calculations

Courts may be reluctant to award damages because they seem to loom so large in the typical case. Appropriate damages may be exaggerated because an aggrieved landowner may ask payment for the total value of his proposed project. One who is denied permission to erect houses on quarter-acre lots may ask for the entire lost profits of this denial.

This would overcompensate him, since he still may be able to use the land for other (presumably less valuable) purposes. The value of the other uses should be subtracted from the loss to the landowner. In other words, the rule should be incremental damages, with the base point of the increment being a use consistent with "normal behavior" or whatever standard is adopted to determine the degree of regulation that would not be judged a taking.[10]

An example may help here. Suppose a five-acre minimum lot size were constitutionally acceptable but a ten-acre minimum were not. A community that zoned an area for ten-acre lots should be given the choice of rezoning the landowner's property for five-acre lots or of paying the *difference* between the value of the land for five-acre minimum lot size and its value for ten-acre lots. The landowner should not calculate his loss as the difference in value between ten-acre lots and quarter-acre lots in this instance.

While such a standard would embroil the court to some degree in the substantive issue of what the appropriate use of land was, it would not need to be excessively careful in determining it. This is because after the court handed down its order, the landowner and the community would most likely negotiate a compromise. The landowner might accept lower compensation in exchange for fewer restrictions. The community, on the other hand, would not need to be ordered to surrender any particular regulation. Moreover, the mere prospect of such outcomes would encourage communities to avoid unconstitutional regulations in a way that the prospect of temporary invalidation would not.

The other area in which damages may be sought but in which judges are reluctant to award them is the costs of delay. Delay costs may be a significant component of a developer's loss. How much should be paid for delay when a landowner-developer succeeds in litigation? The answer again is incremental damages, but this time the increment involves the passage of time.

Suppose a developer plans to build on land that she owns that is zoned for housing. In 1980, after she has applied for a permit, the community rezones her tract for open space. In 1988, the highest court to which an appeal is made rules in her favor. If the court were to follow the remedy urged by Ellickson and Tarlock (1980, 171), it should give the community the choice of rezoning her tract to the original classification or paying permanent damages for the taking. The court should in either case also award interim damages for net income foregone during the period of delay.

Calculating interim damages requires the court to determine when the project would have been completed. The date of permit application cannot be used, because developers might apply for permits prematurely in order to increase damage awards. Suppose experts in the present instance testify that the development was reasonably timed and that the houses could have been completed and sold within a year of obtaining the permit. Assume further that the profits in 1981 would have been $1 million.

The objective of the damages remedy is to leave the landowner's net worth the same as if her project were not denied. If she had been able to do it, she could have invested the $1 million profit at, say, nine percent interest for seven years, and it would have grown to about $1.83 million by 1988. (Note that the total value of the houses, which opponents of the damages remedy might point to as being so large an award as to bankrupt the community, is immaterial in these calculations.) Thus $830,000 is the proper interim award. It excludes the original profit of $1 million, since that would be covered either by the community's permitting the project in 1988 or by payment of permanent damages to keep the tract open.

Although this example ignores some complications, it suggests that interim damages are no harder to calculate for takings than for other areas of the law, such as breach of contract. And if damages do seem costly for the community to pay, think how large they would be for the landowner otherwise to bear.

9.7.4. Transferable Development Rights

There is no obvious reason why "just compensation" should be paid in cash. The community should be able to exchange other assets besides money. For example, it might give the landowner permission to develop elsewhere in the community, if such permission has value equivalent to the rights taken from the landowner.[11] Equivalence of value might be established by making such rights fungible and putting a minimum exchange rate on them, say $100,000 per development right. Credibility of such an exchange rate could be enhanced by the municipality's allowing them to be used for payment of local taxes or fines. The doctrines discussed here are consistent with at least some types of TDR programs experimented with in recent years (James and Gale 1977).

Because TDRs are barter arrangements, they suffer some efficiency drawbacks as a means of compensation (section 4.8). But the taking issue is about fairness, not efficiency. If the community wants to subject itself to an inefficient means of compensating landowners, there should be no objection as long as two conditions are met: (1) that the value of the compensation to the landowner is comparable to the value of the entitlement that was taken, and (2) that the community does not "finance" TDRs by establishing supernormal standards on other identifiable landowners solely for the purpose of giving them in compensation to the first landowner. The taking issue is not settled by robbing Peter to pay Paul.

9.8. ENTITLEMENT PROTECTION AND NEO-GEORGISM

The previous sections developed a set of rules for entitlement protection whose primary objective was to promote economic efficiency. This section will consider the implications of entitlement protection in terms of fairness. Rather than undertake a general survey of the issues, I shall outline proposals and beliefs to which the label "neo-Georgism" is affixed, in honor of their intellectual forefather, Henry George.

The analysis begins with an entitlements diagram, figure 19. Suppose that the initial entitlement point, tested in the courts, is B. Point B may be either normal or supernormal. The landowner wants to move from B to A. Assume that A is consistent with normal behavior in the community. (The argument would not apply if either point were in the subnormal range.) If the community were protected by a liability rule, the landowner would, in principle, have to pay only the amount under the community's benefit schedule labeled X. If the community's entitlement were protected by a property rule, the landowner could be required to pay amount $X + Y$, leaving him only enough return to justify having plighted his own resources in an attempt to obtain the rezoning.

I argued in section 9.5 that the community should, as a matter of efficiency, be protected by a property rule except where point B falls into the supernormal area in figure 19. In most cases the community would extract only amount X or a little more from the bargaining process. The landowner would usually get a substantial fraction, if not all, of amount Y.

But why should the landowner be allowed to obtain amount Y if it were feasible in some situations (where benefits were very clear to all parties) for the community to extract it for the benefit of its current population? The argument that it is *fair* for the community to extract as much of Y as possible I label neo-Georgism. It is an idea that has affected debates about land use policies. I shall mention a few instances.

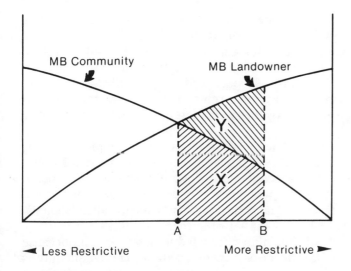

Figure 19. Appropriation of Rents

Law professor Donald Hagman created an elaborate land use reform scheme that he called "windfalls for wipeouts."[12] The basic idea is that public agencies whose regulations cause property value reductions should compensate landowners for such "wipeouts." But to be *fair* about it, public regulations or other government activities that increase property values should be recaptured by the government: the government thus recaptures the "windfalls" *that it creates*.

Another example that evinces a neo-Georgist outlook is the special land gains tax (as opposed to just a capital gains tax on all assets) that real estate developments are subjected to (Glickfeld 1978). This is different from development charges or subdivision exactions insofar as it is not based on arguable costs to the community but is applied generally to all land developments regardless of their impact on the community.

A third area where neo-Georgist ideas were applied was in the New York Court of Appeals decision in the *Penn Central* case (chap. 8, n. 15). In upholding the right of the city of New York to require the owner to maintain Grand Central Terminal in its original condition, New York's highest court had to rule on how much compensation was appropriate.

The state court took the position that a less-than-market-value standard was appropriate because much of the value of the property derived from its location within the city. Since the community at large created this value, there was no need for the city to repay the private owners of the terminal for its loss. The neo-Georgist rhetoric is conspicuous: "It is enough . . . that the privately created ingredient of property receive a reasonable return. It is that privately created and privately managed ingredient which is the property on which the reasonable return is to be based. All else is society's contribution by the sweat of its brow and the expenditure of its funds."[13]

The central idea of neo-Georgism ties these examples together. Because most property is valueless except within a larger society, the members of that society, through government agencies, ought to be entitled to all increments in property value that are not attributable to individual action (labor) or forbearance (capital). For Georgists, this is a matter of fairness as well as efficiency.

Economists are sometimes attracted to neo-Georgism because it appears to be a form of benefit taxation. The community is merely collecting what its actions create. This promotes efficiency insofar as it gives incentives to adopt regulations or undertake projects that increase value. The difference is that a benefit tax would, in terms of figure 19, attempt to see that the community was awarded amount X, the cost to the community of the development (moving from point B to point A). Neo-Georgism, as we have seen, is more than that. It says that the community is entitled to get an amount well in excess of "damages."[14]

9.9. DEFENSES AND CRITICISMS OF NEO-GEORGISM

Sections 1.7–1.9 showed that the proposals of Henry George to expropriate private property through land taxation were based on an economic analysis of the consequences of private ownership of land.[15] Because this analysis is not valid, George's ethical basis for expropriating land is not compelling. The single tax would not right the wrongs that George perceived. Neo-Georgism's moral basis must therefore rest on something other than that of Henry George. In this section I shall outline some alternative defenses of neo-Georgism and examine them.

9.9.1. Increments versus Single Tax

Neo-Georgists might defend their position by pointing to the differences between their proposals and Georgism. Neo-Georgism would let all current land rents accrue to the owners; only *newly created* (by the government or by society at large) rental values are appropriable. If one looks at the history of any parcel of land, though, its present value is the result of a long series of incremental values. If neo-Georgism is right for the present, why is it not right for the past, especially since we can correct all the sins of the past with expropriation of all land values? There is nothing in principle to distinguish contemporary increments to land value from those that began at any moment in the past. (Henry George rejected this proposal for exactly these reasons.)

9.9.2. Efficiency of Land Taxes

Perhaps the strongest argument for neo-Georgism is that a tax on land value increments can be as efficient as a tax on land in general. Even if this is true, one should keep in mind that an efficient tax need not be fair in the most elementary sense. All a tax needs to be efficient is a base that cannot be removed or reduced by the person or thing being taxed. A tax that assessed fifty thousand dollars per year on all people with XY chromosomes and one dollar per year on people with YY chromosomes would be efficient, since one cannot alter that characteristic.

Both neo-Georgist and original Georgist positions may be regarded as second-best methods of income redistribution, given the administrative costs and potential inefficiencies of an income tax or other taxes on wealth. Even if we were confident that such redistribution on balance benefitted the poor—and I am not—the income redistribution argument overlooks the administrative costs of such a system.

Neo-Georgism requires that public officials differentiate increments to land value attributable to pure economic rents from those attributable to labor and capital. This is especially difficult for the return to risk bearing. Most discussions of land taxes and development charges seem to ignore this. They evaluate all increments to land value on an ex post basis, as if there were no risk premium required to induce landowners to undertake development. Moreover, this approach might tempt public officials to differentiate between projects on the basis of the wealth position of their owners. This would involve considerable administrative costs, as well as losses in scale economies from large assemblage.

9.9.3. Who Creates Land Value?

The fall-back argument of neo-Georgists is that regardless of income distribution considerations, it is reasonable that a democratic government reap the values that it creates. It is undoubtedly true that property rights are valuable only insofar as they receive government protection. This is most obvious in the case of rezonings, where a local government's action can mean substantial increases in property values. In the absence of other considerations, it is widely believed that people should get what their actions create. Why hold a different standard for government?

One might first quibble about the meaning of *create*. It is true that landowners do not create the rental values of their land. Government or society did not create the value, either, if the verb *create* is to denote purposeful and directed activity.

Even if we accept that governments do create land values, we cannot move from this to a theory of deservingness. It may be socially useful to reward people in proportion to their creative activity, but that does not make the outcome fair. Even economists who are solicitous of private property rights concede that there is no moral connection between productivity and deservingness (Van den Haag 1976). Why should the notion that government activity might be productive imply a theory of just distribution?

9.9.4. Takings and Neo-Georgism

Ultimately, the problem with neo-Georgism comes back to the original rationale for the taking clause. Applied at the local government level, it simply seems to be a way by which the majority of voters can extract benefits from an identifiable but politically effete minority, the owners of open land. Neo-Georgism would look better in this respect if it subjected *all* owners of land to its standards. Then a suburban government whose restrictive zonings increased the value of *existing* housing would tax away the incremental value of homeowners' land. But even if this were done, the revenues so collected would be spent on activities that typically benefited existing residents. The transfer of wealth from underrepresented owners of undeveloped land to the existing homeowners in the community would still remain.[16]

In sum, lacking the elaborate but erroneous economic and social rationale for the single tax that George advanced, neo-Georgism can only advance its proposals on the argument of expedience: if government can get it, it should get it. This seems inconsistent with ideals of what democratic governments are established to do.

9.10. SUMMARY OF RULES FOR TAKINGS AND ENTITLEMENT PROTECTION

The rules for takings and entitlement protection in this and the previous chapter may be summarized with reference to an entitlements diagram, figure 20. The six numbered arrows in the figure show the changes in zoning restrictions that would be covered by these rules. The back of the arrow represents the original zoning restriction, as yet not tested in the courts. The direction of the arrow indicates the proposed changes, via rezonings, special exceptions, and the like. It is assumed that the only two parties are landowner-developers and community authorities.

An arrow pointing to the right (arrow 1, 2, or 3 in figure 20) means that the community wants to impose more restrictions on undeveloped land. Although I shall speak of these increased restrictions as rezonings, it must be kept in mind that such increased restrictions as often involve changes in zoning administration that cause long delays in granting building permits or subdivision reviews.

Arrow 1 in figure 20 indicates that the community wants to rezone property to a more restrictive use, but one that arguably remains within standards of normal behavior. (The breadth of the normal standard suggests both that it might change over time and that its definition at any moment can be ambiguous.) This rezoning would not require compensation if it could be argued that there was a reasonable relation (rather than full benefit-cost analysis) between it and provision of public goods in the community *and* if the transaction costs of making the compensation would be high relative to the losses sustained by landowners. If either of these failed, the community would have to pay the landowner the *in-*

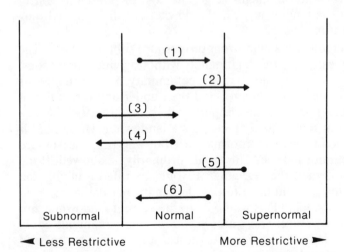

Figure 20.   Summary of Rules for Takings and Entitlement Protection

cremental damages of the restriction, which would be the reduction in market value of his land from its value in the previous entitlement. The landowner is protected only by a liability rule here.

Arrow 2 indicates that the community wants to rezone property to a much more restrictive use, well above standards of normal behavior. This would not be permitted unless the community could show that benefits (public goods) of the regulation exceeded costs to the landowner and that transaction costs of making compensation were prohibitive. The community's desire to impose supernormal standards on the landowner would always provoke greater judicial scrutiny of community motives and in the best situation would reverse the presumption of validity of the ordinance. The community would have to prove that it was acting reasonably and fairly rather than require that the landowner prove the opposite. If the community could not succeed in this argument, it would have to purchase restrictions from the landowner for damages, as in eminent domain proceedings. The landowner enjoys liability rule protection.

Arrow 3 indicates that the community proposes to rezone a subnormal use to normal standards. It would ordinarily be permitted to do so without paying compensation, so long as it could meet the traditional and easy tests of nonarbitrariness and reasonable relation to the public welfare. If the landowner possessed, by grandfather clauses or other conditions, an entitlement to subnormal uses, the community could require higher standards by paying incremental damages (e.g., the cost of pollution control devices) to the landowner. The landowner is still protected only by a liability rule here.

Arrow 4 indicates a landowner proposing a subnormal use. The community can deny this legitimately without giving any reasons. Zoning is fully alienable, but the community may exchange its restrictions only if it wants to, and then under any terms that it wants. The community has property rule protection.[17]

Arrow 5 in figure 20 characterizes a landowner whose land is initially zoned for a "supernormal" use but who proposes a more intensive but normal use. This would ordinarily be allowed. If the community denied the rezoning, it would be ruled a taking and the community would have to pay the landowner damages, as in the case of arrow 2. (This would be to the current landowner, not any previous owners.) There are exceptions. The community could legitimately deny the rezoning request if a long time had passed since the original supernormal standards had been established, unless it had been normal procedure for the community to grant rezonings whenever landowners requested them. If the rezoning were denied and the denial upheld, the landowner still would have the option of paying "damages" to the community in exchange for less restrictive zoning. This is the sole case where the community is protected by a liability rule, not a property rule (section 9.6). It cannot refuse to trade.

Arrow 6 indicates a landowner whose property is currently zoned for normal activity who wants it rezoned for a more intensive but still arguably normal activity. Here the rule is the same as in the case of arrow 4: the community does not have to rezone, and it is protected by a property rule. It does not need to consider any trades if it does not want to. In practice the courts might distinguish this from proposals to adopt subnormal use for the land by closer attention to due process rules and reasonable relation criteria. But ordinarily the community would not be required to rezone the land, and any exchange that occurred would be on its own terms.

9.11. CONCLUSION: FAIRNESS AND EFFICIENCY

I believe that the suggested rules regarding the fairness of land use regulation also promote economic efficiency and, to a certain degree, vertical equity. Reconsider the discussion in chapter 7, in which several causes of excessive restrictions on housing development in suburban areas were identified.

The first cause (sections 7.3 and 7.4) was excessive transaction costs due to legal restraints on trade and public decision making. The rules described in this and the previous chapter address the legal restraints by suggesting that zoning be regarded as perfectly alienable and fungible. Furthermore, by attempting to limit the range of zoning entitlements to the degree that they fall into a normal behavior standard, the cost of beginning trade from an extreme position (which induces rent seeking by special interests) can be reduced.

The second cause of excessive restriction was the wealth effect of initial zoning entitlements (section 7.5). Although initial entitlements as such are not inefficient, the granting of substantial entitlements to initial suburban residents, who may be personally richer than those who follow, could be regarded as inequitable. Once more, the normal behavior standard would limit the amount of wealth that initial residents could appropriate by the more restrictive practices of many suburban communities.

Another problem was monopoly motives by the community

(section 7.7). The rules for takings that I suggest will discourage monopolization in the housing market. It would hardly seem consistent with normal behavior to forbid development of additional suburban housing that was more or less similar to the type of development already in the community. Even if such an entitlement were granted by virtue of longstanding practice, my suggestion that communities be protected only by a liability rule would enable developers to break the monopoly position of the community.

A final cause of excessive restriction was the overbroad and vague definition of zoning entitlements, which made policing of "illegitimate preferences" more difficult (section 7.6). The suggestions for the taking issue may make the definition of zoning more precise insofar as they may increase judicial skepticism about rent seeking, but the normal behavior standard and the rules for entitlement protection cannot by themselves resolve this issue. We need instead to inquire more closely about the meaning of "illegitimate" preferences.

We are agreed, I think, that racial considerations are illegitimate. But what about income, fiscal, or public safety (from criminal acts) considerations? What happens when there is a close correlation between racial or income exclusion and more legitimate considerations? These issues cannot be resolved by the rules suggested in these chapters. We need to develop models of the fiscal functions of local government and location of housing in an urban context before we can readdress this issue in chapter 15.

NOTES

1. Arguments favoring inalienability are discussed at greater length in Calabresi and Melamed (1972) and in Bromley (1978). Section 6.1 explored reasons for hostility to applying economic analysis to land use issues; these are also relevant for inalienability. Attitudes of judges and planners towards contract zoning were noted in section 4.8.

2. Posner (1977, 41) suggests that capitalization makes Michelman's demoralization costs irrelevant, since landowners could insure against it, just as they insure against natural hazards. Aside from the moral hazard of such insurance (why would a government scruple at any taking if it were insured?), this begs the question of why governments should create an artificial hazard to be insured against. Mandelker (1981, 49) also invokes capitalization as a means of disposing of a taking, as does Rose (1983, 908).

3. Ellickson and Tarlock (1981, 587) note that some legal commentary would bar recovery for a nuisance if a plaintiff had purchased the property

knowing of the nuisance's existence. Geller (1983, 134) finds that some courts rule the foreknowledge by a buyer of a lot's physical disabilities will preclude a variance that might have been issued to the former owner. Both arguments are analogous to capitalization arguments, since they assume that compensation was given to the buyer in the form of a lower purchase price. This was specifically invoked (in dictum) in Flynn v. Cambridge, 418 N.E. 2d 335, 339 (Mass. 1981), where it was ruled that those who purchased apartment buildings after rent controls had been imposed could not claim a taking.

4. The barrier here is the transaction costs of dealing with many potential landowner-bargainers, not their monopoly power. If the barrier really were monopoly power, as Posner (1977, 40) suggests, there would be only the agency and the landowner to deal with the problem of dividing up the economic surplus. In this case, we would expect the road to be built regardless of who got the surplus. True monopoly (one seller) would reduce the number of roads built only because the wealth transfer might leave the community poorer and thus less willing to pay for such projects.

5. Local governments sometimes have assembled parcels without resort to eminent domain. The construction of the Los Angeles aqueduct is an example. The city acquired most of the Owens Valley water rights through a private agent. One reason for doing this was that eminent domain proceedings would have been adjudicated in Inyo County (Owens Valley) courts, which were regarded by the city as too sympathetic to local interests (Kahrl 1982).

6. What of my analogy of the community authorities to a private corporation's managers in chapter 5? That was to show that a large number of residents do not foreclose Coasian bargaining. The problem considered here is that community authorities have only the smallest incentive to initiate such exchanges, and even if they had them, the political decision-making process seems to be far slower than the corporate one. Private corporate managers have incentive problems, too, but their devices for dealing with them—stock options, for example—are hardly available to communities.

7. The problem of illegitimate motives was considered in section 7.6. Not all observers regard community monopolies as a bad thing. Finkler, Toner, and Popper (1976, chap. 5) urge cities to think and act as monopolists do.

8. White (1979, 227). The urban economics issues raised in her paper are considered in chapter 12. White contends that Pigovian taxes are superior to Ellickson's proposed remedy because the latter does not deal with monopoly problems. This apparently overlooks all of his section 5 (1977, 424–41) and other parts of his article that explicitly treat the monopoly issue.

9. See Kmiec (1982). One state court case was Burrows v. Keene, 432 A.2d 15 (N.H. 1981), which cited Brennan's opinion as controlling. See also the commentary in Land Use Law and Zoning Digest, May 1981. Ellickson (1977) is the chief article on damages in these situations.

10. This is recommended by Bosselman (1968) and Williams (1982, 240), as well as by other commentators more sympathetic to compensation for regulatory takings.

11. The California appeals courts, grappling with the California Supreme

Court's rejection of monetary damages, seem to have seized upon TDRs as a compromise between invalidation of an ordinance and full money damages. Two cases are discussed in *Land Use Law and Zoning Digest*, April 1983.

12. Hagman and Misczynski (1978, 18) and Hagman (1965). Since I first wrote this I learned that Don Hagman died in an accident. I met him once at a conference, and his good humor, common sense, and sound scholarship inspired me to undertake a more serious look at the neo-Georgist viewpoint. I found his *Windfalls for Wipeouts* sufficiently attractive that I wrote a paper to try to separate the reasonable suggestions from what I regard as the unacceptable (and largely unnecessary) reliance on neo-Georgism (Fischel 1980a). Another proposal evincing a neo-Georgist position is Kmiec (1981).

13. 366 N.E. 2d 1271, 1273 (N.Y. 1977). This argument was not taken up in the U.S. Supreme Court's opinion upholding the city (Marcus 1979). The neo-Georgist argument is similar to a rationale sometimes advanced in defense of the corporate income tax: corporations could not exist without government's granting limited liability and other entitlements. But, as Musgrave and Musgrave (1980, 401) point out, these entitlements are practically costless to society and would not themselves justify a large tax.

14. Does not property rule protection for the community, which I advocate, permit the community to appropriate all landowner surplus also? I argued in section 9.5 that the superior bargaining ability of the landowner ordinarily would afford sufficient protection. But where zoning involves supernormal standards, another reason for permitting the developer to pay only damages is to prevent such extortion. I would also rule out auctions of zoning permits that were divorced from individual parcels as suggested by Clawson (1971, 186). Landowners would have no strategic protection under such terms.

15. It may be pressing the point to suggest that George's belief that most landowners would agree to his proposals if they just understood their consequences is consistent with Michelman's fairness doctrine (George 1880, bks. 7, chap. 3, and 9, chap. 3; Michelman 1967; section 8.1 above). This is consistent with George's forbearance, for the most part, from attacks on "greedy landlords" and other populist villains. He saw the single tax as a policy to enhance total wealth, not just to transfer it.

16. Compare Ellickson's position (1977, 440 and n. 153) that local adoption of Henry George's original policy would not be unfair if it included homeowners as well as other landowners. Hagman's proposal (1978) subjects everyone to the rigors of windfall recapture, though his examples focus largely on developers and landowners.

17. My position differs from that of Ellickson, who would allow the landowner in this situation to acquire an entitlement for subnormal behavior if the landowner could show that prohibiting such uses was "grossly inefficient" (1977, 420–24, 494–95). I believe that explicit fungibility of zoning, combined with the superior bargaining ability of most landowner-developers, makes this unnecessary on either equity or efficiency grounds. It also seems possible that an elastic standard of normal behavior would cover most of the situations about which Ellickson is concerned.

10.

The Political Geography of Zoning

Discussion in previous chapters assumed a generic difference in the political behavior of suburbs and central cities. Suburban jurisdictions are small and homogeneous, which allowed for the application of the majoritarian model of politics and an economic analysis based on the median voter theory. Such a model was central to the analysis of residential restrictions on housing in chapter 7 and the taking issue in chapters 8 and 9.

This chapter will attempt to derive the varying behavior of zoning authorities by type of jurisdiction from a single model of political behavior. In the process, I shall develop intermediate cases between the large central city and the small residential suburb. These include rural jurisdictions and isolated small cities, both of which tend to be less restrictive in their zoning decisions than suburbs. The same model will also be used to examine land use decisions at the state level, with special attention to the new regional land use review boards.

The other issue to be addressed in this chapter is the structure of government. This will allow a look at the monopoly zoning hypothesis from section 7.7. I hope in the process to dissuade my fellow economists from developing models of zoning based on the assumption that a large metropolitan area is subject to a single zoning authority.[1] It just is not so.

10.1. THE ECONOMIC THEORY OF POLITICS

The following sections are based on a model developed by, among others, Downs (1957), Olsen (1965), Stigler (1971), and Peltzman (1976). According to the economic theory of politics, politicians act as if they want to get elected and reelected, and political appointees want to be reappointed. Zoning is a political activity. Politicians will pass zoning laws and administer them in such a way as to improve their chances of reelection or reappointment. If they are not incumbents, candidates will promise to use zoning to maximize political support.

Politicians are constrained by two problems, both of which are related to the cost of information. First, officials may not know what the voters want. Second, voters may not know that a particular politician will serve them better than some other. The latter condition is the result of "rational ignorance." Voters know that their vote is unlikely ever to be the deciding one in an election. Thus even though they may vote, they will not devote much time to informing themselves of the positions of each candidate.

When both voters and politicians are ignorant of one another's preferences and positions, there is an opportunity for special-interest groups to try to influence both of them. Special interests exist because information is costly. They collect selective information and disseminate it to advance their interests. When selective information is given to politicians, the activity is called lobbying. When applied to voters, it is called advertising or electioneering.

Not every interest can be an effective special interest. Organizing and operating a special-interest group are costly. To justify these costs, the members of the group must be able to transfer substantial economic resources to themselves via the public sector. For this reason, most special-interest groups will be organized on the basis of activities that affect their members' major source of income rather than the uses (expenditures) to which they put that income. Dairy farmers will undertake the cost of forming a special-interest group to influence milk prices because a small price increase will have a large effect on their incomes. Milk drinkers will not, because milk is but a small fraction of most families' total expenditures.

The number of people who have a common interest also affects organizing costs. A smaller group of people is more easily organized as a special interest than is a larger one. Smaller size is a disadvantage in some ways, though. The fewer the members, the fewer direct votes they will be able to supply to politicians. To compensate for small size, special interests will have to spend more money on advertising and lobbying. If information costs are high, so that politicians and voters have little information about issues, and if organizing costs for a special-interest group are large, smaller size is an advantage.

10.2. THE POLITICS OF SUBURBAN ZONING

The foregoing model of political activity might suggest that my assumption in earlier chapters that landowner-developers are an effete minority in suburban jurisdictions is badly flawed. But it is not. Landowner-developers might be eager to organize and to lobby politicians and persuade voters, but their lobbying comes to no effect. Voters in small jurisdictions, where the issues are few and well known, are apt to know where their interests lie and which politicians favor them. Similarly, politicians embroiled in local zoning issues get a clear reading of voter sentiment in the numerous public hearings that any change in zoning must undergo. Thus lobbying plays only a minor role in most suburban jurisdictions. This knowledge of official actions by affected voters may also be a reason why suburban zoning is seldom systematically tainted by corruption.[2]

In general, development in suburban areas takes place because existing residents—who are largely homeowners—either seek to have it (for fiscal reasons) or find it sufficiently harmless to their interest that they do not bother to object. This does not mean that all residents are happy with zoning. Instances of neighbors objecting to the actions of zoning authorities who approved intensive development are common in the courts (section 3.2). In most zoning cases, though, the evidence is fairly strong that a relatively small group of neighboring homeowners can succeed in blocking rezonings. Local governments in suburbs are seldom dominated by any interest group other than homeowners, who are almost always a majority. If the majoritarian approach to political economy has any validity, it is surely in the suburbs.[3]

Not all suburbs will respond in the same way to a rezoning request by a landowner-developer. The response will differ according to local geographic conditions, the extent of development that has already occurred, and the personal tastes of residents. The most important determinant of tastes is the average income of the community: the higher the income, the more exclusive the suburb.

There are three other types of communities that may have distinctly different preferences and political controls. I shall apply the political decision model to them to see where they may differ from the suburbs. The taxonomy I use divides the nonsuburban world into (1) rural areas, (2) isolated small cities, and (3) central cities.

10.3. THE POLITICS OF RURAL ZONING

The politics of rural zoning is problematic because people have different ideas about what is rural. I adopt a functional approach to fit the topic at hand. A rural jurisdiction is a sparsely populated one in which most people earn their income from agriculture or industries that are within its borders or in other rural areas. Most residents are not commuters to jobs in cities or suburbs of a metropolitan area; nor are they retirees or vacation homeowners who happen to be in a rural area. This definition thus excludes many jurisdictions that have a great deal of open land, much of it farmed, but are near metropolitan areas. In their zoning laws these "exurban" areas are similar to the suburbs, because the politically dominant groups earn their income from other places. Local development does not increase their wealth or income.

Truly rural areas often have no zoning at all, and those that do are often very permissive.[4] This is partly because of the expenses involved in establishing and administering a zoning ordinance. It is seldom because the rural local government lacks the authority to establish zoning. If the township cannot zone, then the county in which it is located almost surely can. Rural zoning is more common now that the federal government has subsidized its establishment with grants for planning, but it remains more permissive than suburban zoning.

The greater permissiveness of rural zoning has little to do with political ideology. Instead, it is because a significant fraction of the politically active residents stands to gain from development. Some own land—usually farmland—that may be subdivided. Others own or work for businesses that may gain from development. These groups form a special-interest group to lobby both their neighbors and the township or county board.

Because rural communities are even smaller than suburbs, though, lobbying local officials is not likely to be important. Influencing their fellow voters is a more effective strategy. This may take a subtle form.

Even though a majority of rural residents may not own land that could be developed, they are often personally acquainted with someone who does. I think that this is important. It is difficult for people who may be inclined to halt development to despoil someone they see at civic functions, at church, or at work. In situations like this, it is not the force of the law that restrains zoning but the desire to be neighborly. It is hard to raise the cry against greedy landowners and rapacious developers when the landowner is a longtime resident and the developer is the local contractor.

There is another factor in the apparent permissiveness of rural zoning. If rural zoning were quite strict, it would not make much difference except in those areas near growing cities and towns. Urban development pressure acts on only a very small fraction of the land area of the United States. For most Iowa farmers it is no more necessary to zone out housing tracts and shopping centers than it is to ban polar bears. That rural citizens spend little effort in doing so suggests that they know it.

10.4. ZONING IN ISOLATED SMALL CITIES

Isolated small cities (i.e., those that are not suburbs or satellite cities of a larger SMSA) do not usually behave like suburbs. The degree of exclusiveness tends to be less than in suburbs of similar average incomes. These cities have the full array of zoning regulations, but it is usually easier for a developer to build a tract of houses or a factory or a store there than in a suburb. Indeed, in my several years of experience observing this phenomenon, I have noted that such cities often eagerly pursue development.

The main reason for this attitude is that people in these cities tend to live and work in the same jurisdiction. The cost of exclusion or the benefit of development is more likely to be perceived by a significant fraction of the voting population. This makes small cities distinctly different from both suburbs and central cities.

Suppose that an existing firm wants to expand its operations in such a way as to cause some inconvenience to existing residents. In small cities this inconvenience would have an offsetting benefit that would make it more palatable to voters: there would be improved job opportunities. For most proposed developments there would thus be a substantial group of people in favor of development. They might form a temporary special interest by themselves, or they might tip the voting scale towards approval of development.

In a suburb of a larger metropolitan area, though, such offsetting benefits would not be perceived by voters. Relatively few suburban residents are employed in the firms located in their own town. Thus expansion of employment opportunities is irrelevant to the politically active population. Only the possibility of fiscal benefits (e.g., lower property taxes) or similar side payments would persuade them to relent in their opposition to the inconveniences of development.

The same tendencies mark other types of land use. New shopping centers may be more welcome in isolated areas because of improved buying opportunities. In the suburbs such opportunities may be present in neighboring communities, so that the convenience benefit has little weight in offsetting the disamenities of more traffic and noise. In small cities new housing may draw less opposition because residents realize that it is necessary to attract more workers for an expanding industry or because construction creates jobs for some of the politically active residents. Such a possibility is again more remote in suburban areas.

Working and voting in the same district creates some other motives. The most obvious may be called the chamber of commerce effect. Owners of existing businesses may attempt to keep others from entering in order to protect themselves from competition for employees or for customers. But one should not make too much of this. The beneficiaries of additional competition, the employees and customers, also have votes, and they outnumber the business owners in most cases. Moreover, most chambers of commerce are a diverse lot. What might seem like undesirable competition to one firm may seem like a profitable business relationship to another. I have seldom found that general business associations in small towns and cities are vigorously antidevelopment.

10.5. THE POLITICS OF CENTRAL CITY ZONING

Land use controversies in central cities are resolved in favor of developers more frequently than in the suburbs.[5] The political process seems more capable of resolving the issues. I shall explore the reasons for these tendencies in this section.

One reason why central cities are less restrictive is the same as that given for small cities: people who live in central cities most often work in the same jurisdiction. Thus there are voters who will benefit from development as well as those who are harmed by it, and the distribution of voter preferences will be tilted a little more towards development.

Large cities have some suburban tendencies towards zoning because of the ward or alderman method of political organization. Local legislatures in big cities are usually elected so that each legislator represents a contiguous geographic district, which may be as homogeneous as a suburban jurisdiction. Like suburban voters, but unlike voters in small cities, the voters in each ward may expect that development beneficial to them for jobs or shopping may locate elsewhere in the city, so that they can have its benefits without the neighborhood costs. This form of government may offset prodevelopment inclinations in the city at large. We need some additional reasons, then, to explain the differences between central cities and suburbs with respect to attitudes towards development.

One reason why central cities may like development more is because their average level of income is lower.[6] Lower-income people are more pro-development than are affluent voters, in part because they are more concerned about employment opportunities. But lower-income people are less politically active, too, so that central city politics may reflect the preferences of voters with incomes higher than that of the average family. Income differentials cannot be the whole explanation for the relative ease with which development occurs in central cities.

The more convincing reason for the generally pro-development attitude of central cities is the nature of the political process. The conditions that led me to believe that the majoritarian model applies to suburban issues were that politicians know the preferences of voters on each issue, and voters are aware of which politicians favor their interests. Neither is true in large cities. This is because there are more voters per politician and because there are many more issues. Ample opportunity exists for special interests to influence political outcomes by lobbying officials, advertising about particular issues, or electioneering for candidates who favor their interests.

A paradigm of central city zoning decisions was the proposal to develop some industrial property in Manhattan for a forty-three-hundred-unit residential complex called Lincoln West (*New York Times*, 8 November 1982, B1). The neighbors, who had an ongoing political organization, complained that the project would adversely affect them because of increased traffic and other forms of congestion. The local legislator, elected by the immediate geographic district (e.g., the ward), also objected to granting the necessary permits. In most suburbs such objections would dispose of the project. In the city, though, the proposal went through, with modifications and side payments in the form of new neighborhood facilities.

The reasons for the project's approval had to do with the pressures brought to bear on the city legislature and mayor. As everywhere, taxes were an important consideration. In addition, however, real estate interests, contractors, and, more importantly, the members of construction unions who live in the city, appear to have been influential. As one public official put it, "I think it's too big for us to ignore those kind of construction dollars, which translate into more jobs and more tax dollars."

The influence of pro-development groups in big cities is further facilitated by the large number of other issues in which voters are interested. This enables legislators to engage in logrolling or vote trading. A city councilman from a district whose residents oppose the proposed development may favor it (or not vigorously oppose it) because he expects other council members or the mayor to vote for an issue that is even more important to his constituents.

All of this is not to argue that central cities are unambiguously in favor of development.[7] They have plenty of effective neighborhood associations, whose interests are as parochial as suburban homeowners'. They do not, however, own the political machine; compromise is possible. In reporting a zoning controversy in Chicago in which developers complained of the "new" opposition to further development by affluent city residents, the *Wall Street Journal* (30 July 1980, 21) quoted a city alderman as saying, "When developers tell you it can't be done, it really means they haven't tried."

10.6. SUBURBAN GOVERNMENT STRUCTURE AND MONOPOLY ZONING

The four types of local government discussed above constitute an incomplete taxonomy. There are hybrid types, such as very large suburbs (usually counties) that may combine the characteristics of suburb and city or constitute a different type altogether. We might also inquire into the political arrangements of metropolitan federations or statewide controls. Each of these zoning arrangements—large suburbs, metropolitan federations, and state government agencies—raise another concern. Because of the large and valuable land area that they control, local government monopoly might be an important factor in zoning.

Section 7.7 discussed the monopoly control issue in a theoretical context. Now I shall inquire whether it is a realistic problem for metropolitan areas. This involves two questions: (1) Does the economic theory of politics discussed above suggest that a government with monopoly power really will restrict development? and (2) does government structure in the areas where monopoly would seem most effective, the suburban areas of large SMSAs, look at all monopolistic? The tentative answer to both of these questions is no, but there are some other anticompetitive outcomes that might result from suburban government structure.

The economic theory of industrial organization is frequently exposited in terms of a chain of causation. In the first stage the market *structure* is investigated in order to find out how many firms are engaged in it, how large they are relative to one another, and whether there are barriers to potential competitors. The next aspect is the *conduct* of the members or the industry. In this second stage the investigation tries to determine whether the firms collude with one another, adopt unusual pricing policies on their own, or seek special government aid. These two inquiries are then brought to bear on the issue of the *performance* of the market: Are prices too high, and is production too low?

Using a straightforward application of this framework to the monopoly zoning question, we might come up with the following conclusions for at least some metropolitan areas. The *structure* of local governments seems monopolistic in that there are only a few jurisdictions, and often a very large one dominates the rest. Moreover, entry seems to be restricted. It isn't easy to form your own local government. The *conduct* of such governments with respect to their assets, however, suggests an independent attitude towards one another's policies. Though local governments are openly encouraged to collude with one another, most planners decry the lack of cooperation among such governments. The *performance* in many cases nonetheless appears to provide too little development, and at a very high price, at least for many types of activities.

What is wrong with this analogy? For one thing, the statement about structure applies directly to only a few metropolitan areas, as I shall demonstrate. But another flaw is in the area of conduct. Does the local political process lead governments to behave as if they were profit-maximizing firms, paying monopoly dividends to their voter-stockholders?

Assuming no transaction costs, a local government would establish a development permit system for its undeveloped land and sell off the zoning restrictions whose value to the residents seemed lower than the value to developers. The revenues would then be distributed to the local electorate.

This cannot be done to the extent that a business corporation holding the same entitlements could do it. Aside from the legal inhibitions on this practice (section 4.6), municipal corporations, whose "owners" have such varied ideas about the appropriate use of land, seldom agree on price and terms. Stockholders in a firm may differ on how the firm should be run, but they are united in their desire to make money. Such an unambiguous motive is absent in most municipal corporations, which may be why Congress exempted them from liability for damages in the Local Government Antitrust Act of 1984.

Even if we grant that local governments do not consciously act as monopolists, there are reasons to be concerned about their size. A large unit of government that is excessively restrictive for some nonmonopoly reason (e.g., wealth effects, inability to exchange zoning entitlements for preferred goods, or illegitimate motives, as discussed in chapter 7) will have a larger effect on development than will a smaller unit of government.

This concern must be balanced by the conclusion from the previous section that a larger unit of government is more likely to balance competing pro- and anti-development forces. (In this respect, a large suburb may resemble the isolated small city paradigm.)[8] Nonetheless, a large anti-development suburb will have a greater effect on the metropolitan housing market than will a small one. Even when a large suburb does contain both pro- and anti-development forces, the result is more likely to be vacillation between two extremes—zero growth and excessively rapid growth—which is less desirable than a moderate growth policy.

10.7. MEASUREMENT OF SUBURBAN GOVERNMENT FRAGMENTATION

For the reasons given in the last section, it is worth taking an empirical look at the structure of metropolitan political boundaries to see how worrisome suburban monopoly may be in reality. I have done a survey of local government structure in the twenty-five largest Urbanized Areas (Fischel 1981). The results of my survey are that only a few of these metropolitan areas have *suburban* government structures that I would be willing to characterize as monopolistic.

Rather than reproduce my findings here, I will present maps of three UAs that illustrate the range of government structure. Maps 1, 2, and 3 are U.S. Census Bureau maps of the St. Louis, Baltimore, and Milwaukee UAs in 1970. These cities were chosen because they show the range of fragmentation one can expect in

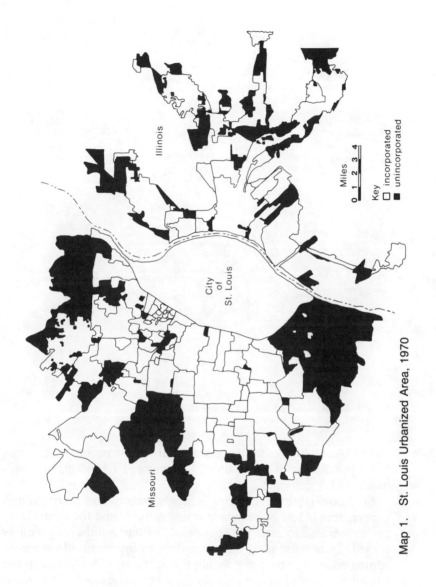

Map 1. St. Louis Urbanized Area, 1970

Key
☐ incorporated
■ unincorporated

Miles
0 1 2 3 4

Illinois

Missouri

City
of
St. Louis

217

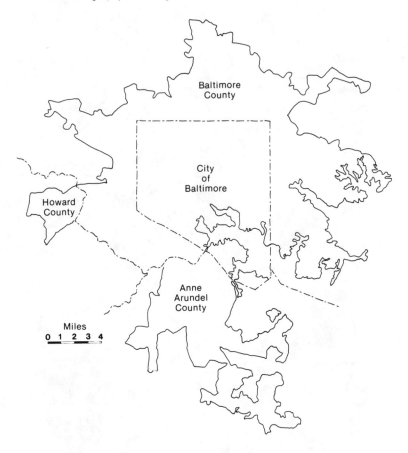

Map 2.   Baltimore Urbanized Area, 1970

large UAs and because they are roughly the same size. (St. Louis
has a population of 1.9 million; Baltimore, 1.6 million; and Milwaukee, 1.3 million.)

St. Louis is an example of a highly fragmented metropolitan
government. Most of its incorporated suburbs and the central city
are authorized to zone independently of one another, as well as
provide certain services. There are thus, by my count, 116 separate
zoning units in or partially within the St. Louis UA. Although the
city of St. Louis is relatively large, it comprises only 13 percent
of the total area of the UA, and no single suburb comes close to
it in size.

Baltimore represents the opposite extreme. There are many
named places around the city, but only four units of government

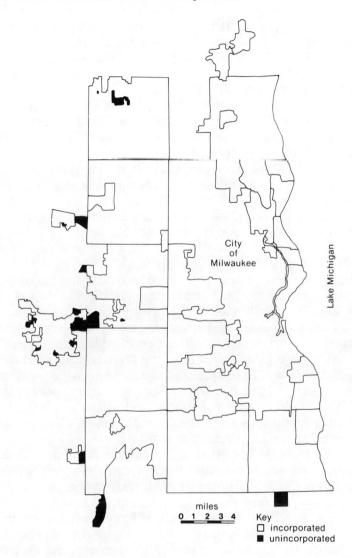

Map 3.   Milwaukee Urbanized Area, 1970

are authorized to zone: the city of Baltimore, Baltimore County (which does not include the city of Baltimore), Howard County, and Anne Arundel County. Indeed, most of the suburban part of the UA is in Baltimore County. The city of Baltimore occupies about 25 percent of the UA land area.

A middle point in the spectrum is represented by the Milwaukee UA. Here the central city is surrounded (within the UA) by forty different local governments with zoning authority, but most of the suburban land area is accounted for by a dozen municipalities. The four largest suburban communities in the Milwaukee UA account for 30 percent of the total UA land area and 38 percent of the suburban land area included in the UA. Development restrictions by any one of these municipalities would have little effect on metropolitan structure, but it would take only a few communities—a half dozen or so—to make an appreciable dent in the supply of suburban land for development.

Using these three cities as benchmarks, we can summarize government structure for the twenty-five largest UAs. Most of the large UAs, especially those in the Northeast and in the north central states, appear to fall between the highly atomistic St. Louis structure and the moderately fragmented Milwaukee example. Only a few large UAs (and none of the seven largest, which hold more than a third of all UA population) fall between the paradigms of moderately fragmented Milwaukee and highly concentrated Baltimore. Indeed, only Washington and Miami can be said to bear an unambiguous resemblance to Baltimore's nearly "monopolistic" suburban government structure.

In the smaller UAs (less than 1 million in population), there are fewer local governments and less fragmentation. A very rough generalization is that the number of local governments is proportional to the population of the UA. This means that the smallest UAs (less than 200,000 population) will have only two or three local governments and so resemble the model of the small isolated city (section 10.4). The fact that their local government structure appears monopolistic is deceptive, since households or firms who want to locate in such urban areas can choose among many similar UAs within a given region of the country. Thus these areas may have little influence on housing and development costs, despite apparent monopolistic structure. (The smaller number of local governments does mean that residents of smaller UAs have less choice with regard to level of local government services. The greater range of choices available in larger UAs appears to be one of the consumer advantages of locating there.)[9]

10.8. STATE AND FEDERAL REGULATIONS AND TAKINGS

The economic model of politics presented earlier in this chapter should be applicable to land use decisions by legislatures other than local governments. This section will use the model to explain the behavior of the federal and state governments. Specialized land use agencies such as regional environmental commissions will be considered in the following section.

10.8.1. Land Use Politics at the Higher Levels of Government

The states' and the federal government's land use decisions should be closer to the behavior of large central cities than to the behavior of suburbs or rural areas. Their populations are large and heterogeneous. The number of issues that voters face is typically very large. Thus politicians have little information about voter preferences, and most voters have even less information about which politicians favor their interests. As a result, special interests will play a crucial role in all political decisions. The economic theory of regulation and its empirical evidence point to this model.

The model suggests that landowners and development interests should fare better, relative to anti-development interests, in the state legislatures and the U.S. Congress. Larger jurisdictions are more likely to include as voters those people who will benefit from development, as well as those who will be harmed by it. The politics of land use at the local level, especially in suburban communities, is a matter of "we against them." At the state or national level, it is more like "we against us."

More important, though, is the cost of organizing national anti-development interest groups. Such groups exist, of course, but they are more likely to confine themselves to specific issues rather than to lobby for general land use restrictions. It is not that such groups do not want state or national land use controls; there is clear evidence that they do (Library of Congress 1973; Reilly 1973). But they meet their match in legislative lobbying and political campaigning from local governments anxious about preemption and from the various beneficiaries of development projects. The success of anti-development interests at the state and national level has largely been limited to legislation that increased their ability to restrict development at the local level. (An example of such legislation is farmland preservation, discussed in chapter 13.)

10.8.2. Takings at the Higher Levels of Government

It is for the foregoing reasons that I proposed in sections 8.10 and 8.11 that the taking issue should be confined largely to local land use controls. Oppression of identifiable minorites is more likely to occur when information costs are low, so that those adversely affected have little opportunity to divert their resources to the political arena to protect their interests. This position on the taking issue implies that one defense of minority interests from excesses of the majority, or one way of registering the intensity of preferences, is to marshal economic resources to thwart the casual will of the majority.

Saying that land use takings should *usually* be invoked only at the local government level should not exclude state and federal legislatures and their agencies from judicial notice. There are several instances in which land use regulations passed by the federal or state government ought to invoke the taking issue.

1. Federal and state regulations that apply only to small, specific geographic areas should be scrutinized. The opportunity for those landowners adversely affected by the regulations to influence legislators is considerably restricted. They cannot as easily band together with other landowners and allies from other areas, since those people are not affected. Morcover, the transaction costs of offering compensation to those adversely affected in a well-defined geographic area would seem to be much lower. Federal or state regulation that restricted development in all flood plains or along the entire coast would not raise the taking issue, but regulations that restricted land use only around Yellowstone National Park or only on the shore of Cape Cod would be suspect.

2. Land use controls established by voter initiative or decided by binding referenda should always be subject to greater scrutiny than those established by normal legislative and administrative processes.[10] This applies to state as well as local governments. Initiatives and referenda are suspect because they bypass one of the means by which strength of preferences may be revealed.

Within normal local council proceedings, a law establishing growth controls would be subjected to vote trading and logrolling among council members who favored or opposed development. Developers and landowners would also find it easier to point out the drawbacks of such legislation. In a popular election, though, vote trading is impossible, and providing information to decision makers is much more costly, even when the decision makers (the voters) are willing to listen, as rational ignorance theory suggests they will not.

Readers who are fond of direct democracy should recall that the taking issue would still be largely confined to immovable resources, or resources made immobile by the regulation. Most referenda and initiatives, including those on general environmental issues, would not be subject to such scrutiny.

The existence of initiatives and referenda may help explain the otherwise paradoxical behavior of some central cities. Several large cities in California have adopted growth controls that are as restrictive as those of the most elite suburban municipality. This is not what we expect from the economic model of this chapter. The explanation may be that the initiative is a widely used device among California local governments. San Jose, formerly eager to develop, adopted strict growth controls as a the result of an initiative that the local legislature opposed (Frieden 1979, 29).

3. Local governments should not escape scrutiny under the taking doctrines simply by pointing out that the state government delegated them the power to enact a specific type of land use control. If this argument were admitted, it would absolve all local governments from such constraints, since all local governments are creatures of the state government.

This should not prevent state governments from requiring local governments to *administer* statewide land use controls. The difference is in the extent of discretion given the local government. Requiring all local governments to establish flood plain controls merely makes the local governments administrative vehicles of the state's legislation. But if the local government has the *option* to enact special restrictions, or has great discretion in administering a statewide program, the likelihood of majoritarian excess is as great as when controls are initiated at the local level.

10.8.3. The Problem of NEPA

The other major federal land use law is the National Environmental Policy Act of 1970 (NEPA), which required all federal government agencies to include in any major development plan a statement of how environmental conditions would be affected by it. It seems to me that no economist can fail to applaud the motives behind such legislation. Protection of air and water quality is the archetypical public good. Even the most elementary view of political economy recognizes that many agencies are either myopic or "captured" by special interests who care little for the provision of environmental amenities.

The problem with NEPA and with analogous state acts is in the enforcement of the Environmental Impact Statement (EIS) provision. Clearly it would not do simply to trust the federal or state agency to enforce its own standards of what an EIS should contain. The agencies' lack of incentive to consider such standards was what prompted the legislation in the first place. The problem is, I believe, that the remedy went too far. It allowed any private citizen, or groups of citizens, to mount a challenge to the content of the EIS.

Combined with the vagueness of what constitutes an acceptable EIS, the citizen participation approach has made it possible for a relatively small group of people with a common interest to deny development both in their own communities and in those in which they do not live. The denial may be a direct defeat of the proposal by making its EIS too embarrassing to the agency, but more frequently developers are simply delayed so long or forced to make so many compromises with so many different parties that they simply give up.

Reform of NEPA procedure to mitigate these problems is beyond the scope of this book. (One attractive reform is outlined by Bardach and Pugliarisi [1977]). In any case, the taking clause would not seem to be the proper focus for reform. Takings apply to government actions; the problem with NEPA is that it has enabled private groups to assume a regulatory function analogous to that of government entities without limiting their entry. A landowner-developer who satisfies the conditions of a local government does not need to contend, for the most part, with other local governments. Satisfying a private environmental organization may invite others to seek additional conditions.

10.9. SPECIAL LAND USE COMMISSIONS

There is another means by which state governments can delegate authority to control land use. In the last few years, state governments have created a number of special commissions that affect land use. Some attempt to control general land use in a large area that cuts across local government borders. The California Coastal Zone Commission is an example. Others, such as Vermont's environmental review commissions, review certain decisions of local governments, providing the double-veto system described in section 2.3. Still others attempt to coordinate local government land use decisions in major metropolitan areas. An example is the Minneapolis and St. Paul Metropolitan Council.

One aim of these entities is to deal with land use decisions whose effects cross municipal boundaries. As section 4.3 showed, zoning law does not give local governments much authority to control nuisances outside their borders. There might be a need for some mechanism other than neighborliness to deal with such spillovers.

It should stand as no criticism by itself to note that these special bodies are often anti-development (Danielson 1976, 286). Some developments whose costs are foisted upon people outside the host community should be restricted if not forbidden. But there is also reason to believe that these bodies are excessively restrictive, preventing development for reasons having little to do with spillovers. There are two reasons for this.

The first is that most of the specialized regional bodies are not general government bodies, so they lack an identifiable constituency and a broad set of powers. For example, Minnesota's Metropolitan Council is appointed by the governor, and the council in turn appoints members to land use committees. Members of Vermont's district environmental commissions and state environmental review board are appointed by the governor and usually hold no state or local office.

This creates a tendency towards restrictiveness, because landowners and developers have no means by which they can buy their way out of restrictions. They cannot engage in political logrolling and vote trading, since there is no alternative issue in which a member of these commissions is interested. Since there is no direct constituency who will benefit by promises of fiscal benefits or employment opportunities, there is no way for developers to compensate voters for their spillover effects. This by itself is a substantial transactions cost that may excessively restrict development.

The second reason for excessive restrictions arises from the procedures of these special bodies. Most of them hold lengthy hearings that are begun *after* the local government has held all its hearings and made a decision. These new hearings give yet another opportunity for anti-development interests to delay, and thus sometimes deny, the necessary permission. Moreover, these additional hearings do not confine themselves to intergovernmental spillovers.

The chief opponents of development in such proceedings are often the commercial competitors of the proposed development, whose protectionist motives are only thinly disguised by references to conservation or the environment. Such motives might be present at the local government level, too, but they are less effective there because the opportunity cost (lower taxes or better jobs) of exclusion of a new enterprise is obvious to local voters and their representatives. The special review commissions have no general constituency, however, and most are not charged with distinguishing the motives of those who oppose development. For this reason, they often decide against development or hold it up to the point where it becomes uneconomical.

One example might help clarify the previous argument. A budget motel chain sought to locate in a Vermont town near the junction of two interstate highways. The town approved its location, but it had to pass the state's review process. A local newspaper reported the outcome: "The small motels in the area form the Independent Motel Owners Association. They got themselves a lawyer and went to the Act 250 hearing and raised all sorts of questions about the suitability of soil on the Motel Six site and the effect the new building would have on soil erosion and water runoff. [The site is in a commercial area in which two other large motels are already located.] The questions they raised helped to draw out the entire Act 250 approval process, and those close to the project think Motel Six just got tired of waiting" (*Valley News* [Lebanon, N.H.], 14 August 1981, 1).

10.10. SPECIAL COMMISSIONS AND THE TAKING ISSUE

The special state and regional review commissions present a difficult intermediate case for the taking clause. They are creatures of specific legislation enacted by the state. Presumably landowners and other development interests are represented in this process insofar as they can lobby on any bill and provide campaign support for friendly legislators. There is some evidence that this process is causing the special commissions to take a more balanced outlook in some states.[11]

Despite this safety valve, the actions of special state commissions ought to receive more attention than general acts of the legislature. The commissions are delegated great authority, and their decisions are often applied to a small set of land uses, often just an individual parcel. While landowners as a group may eventually redress the balance of the commissions by changing the legislation or the membership of the commissions, individual landowners who are adversely affected are not likely to be compensated as a result.

It may appear that I have taken a one-sided view of development issues in that the taking issue is to be invoked when development is unduly retarded but not when there is excessive development. Either outcome is detrimental to society. I submitted that on the state or national level the play of interest group politics would be sufficient to protect minority interests. But this same mechanism may cause *over*protection of minority interests. It is commonplace for a well-organized minority interest group to feed at the public trough at the expense of the unorganized majority. We may at the national or state level produce outcomes that are too favorable to developers.

This possibility seems to be an important component of Joseph Sax's argument that we should disregard the taking issue in a wide range of cases (section 8.2). His reasoning is that those who enjoy a pleasant environment are numerous but unorganized. Those who would incidentally degrade the environment—development interests—are few but well organized. To give the latter group the protection of a broad reading of the Fifth Amendment's injunction against taking property without just compensation further restrains a group—consumers of the environment—that is unorganized relative to development interests.

Bruce Ackerman (1977, 54) has suggested a flaw in Sax's reasoning. Ackerman points out that the political battle over just compensation is not between environmentalists and developers but between environmentalists and taxpayers. The latter must finance the compensation to be paid for regulations that go beyond whatever line the judiciary draws between legitimate police power activity and a taking. They are just as badly organized as Sax believes environmentalists to be. Thus there is no reason to expect that environmental interests would be shortchanged by requiring compensation when transactions costs are not prohibitive.

As I noted in chapter 8, most national and state environmental legislation, with the exceptions enumerated in the previous section, does not need to be subject to the taking clause. Clean air and water legislation would seldom fall into these exceptions. Thus the approach suggested here would not hobble the national and state environmental movement. (Environmentalists also do not seem as poorly organized as other consumer groups. One reason may be that their local organizations form a means by which existing residents' property values may be enhanced [section 13.9].)

10.11. CONCLUSION

The goal of this chapter was to point out the differences in zoning behavior by type of local jurisdiction. I submit that the degree of restrictiveness of a community is greatest for small, homogeneous suburban jurisdictions and least for large, heterogeneous cities and very rural areas. Small cities and the larger suburbs fall in between these extremes. The chief reason for these differences is that size and location have an impact on political organization. In larger places, voters more often live and work in the same jurisdiction, and their political process allows for logrolling, vote trading, and other devices that roughly balance development interests with homeowners' concerns.

Large, homogeneous suburbs would do more damage to suburban housing markets than would a number of small ones, but I find little evidence that such a condition characterizes many large metropolitan areas in the United States. More apt to be anti-development are the special land use commissions that have been created in several states. These control a large amount of land and are the more serious candidates for promoting monopoly zoning.

Taxonomic distinctions like those in this chapter are necessarily arbitrary and incomplete. One might extend them by suggesting that some states are so small that they should be regarded as large suburbs.[12] We do not need to go to that extreme to make use of the distinctions, however. Their major purpose is to emphasize that zoning is a political activity and that politics is not everywhere the same. Remedies to zoning's excesses must take account of this variation. An understanding of jurisdictional variation will also prove essential in evaluating the effect of zoning on housing markets and general locational efficiency. This will be examined in the next two chapters.

NOTES

1. Most general equilibrium models that examine zoning constraints in the urban economics model (chapter 12) make just this assumption. Examples are Carpenter and Heffley (1982) and Stull (1974). Such an assumption may be necessary to derive results of heuristic value to model builders, but it does not simulate policy alternatives currently available in most American metropolitan areas. A more realistic two-government model—central city and unified suburbs—is used by Rubinfeld (1978) and White (1978a) to examine suburban zoning issues.

2. Gardner and Lyman (1978) describe several instances of suburban corruption but find that in most cases the community took steps to preclude its reappearance by mandating more public participation, which in turn made its zoning more restrictive. See also section 4.7.

3. The majoritarian model is regarded as appropriate to suburban jurisdictions by Cooley and LaCivita (1982), Danielson (1976, 4), Ellickson (1977), and Frieden (1979). Note that my theory emphasizes that suburbs are small enough to reduce the information problem and that most voters are homeowners. There is no need to emphasize other aspects of homogeneity of population, such as income or demand for public services, as is done in chapter 14.

4. Siegan (1976, 52) cites several examples of zoning's being defeated at referenda. All were in small rural townships or counties. The International City Managers' Association (1960, 2), noted the lack of rural restrictions, as did Manvel (1968) and Ohio Department of Economic and Community Development (1974). The communities that have huge minimum lot sizes to protect farmland are most often "exurban" areas described in the text. See also chapter 13.

5. Williams (1975, chap. 3) notes the relative lack of zoning cases from central cities. Big cities are apt to be less exclusionary because of heterogeneity of interests, according to Danielson (1976, 4) and Komesar (1978, 223). Komesar seems to have been the first to suggest a shift of zoning behavior from the "majoritarian model" of small jurisdictions to the "influence model" of larger jurisdictions. Much of my present chapter is an attempt to explain this shift. The city of Houston, Texas, serves as an extreme example of the lack of restrictiveness of central city zoning in that it has none, and voters defeated proposals to adopt it (Siegan 1972). Houston is unusual among American cities in that its municipal boundaries encompass most of its suburbs, making for a very heterogeneous population in which the "influence model" of politics (i.e., the high information cost situation) applies well.

6. See section 6.2. The income differences between the suburbs and the central city often seem slight, but Hekman (1980) finds that it is explained by higher labor force participation among low-income families in urban areas.

7. An apparent exception to my theory is rent control, in which the numerous tenants succeed against the concentrated interest of property owners. This may be explained by several factors: (1) rent, unlike most other consumer prices, represents a substantial fraction of tenants' expenditure; (2) rental units are often the majority of units in large cities, so that organizing consumers' interests is easier in these places; and (3) building trades are not allies to landowners once the building is up.

8. A well-documented hybrid is Fairfax County, Virginia, a suburb of Washington, D.C. Fairfax enacted highly restrictive growth controls in the early 1970s which contributed to high housing prices in the metropolitan area as well as to urban sprawl (Peterson 1974b). The growth controls fell to court decisions and to election of a new county government that was responsive

to pro-development interests (Dawson 1976). Fairfax was thus suburban in its adoption of growth controls but like a central city in that internal political pressures from development interests were a balancing factor.

9. These advantages are discussed in chapter 14 in the context of the Tiebout model of local government. That the advantages of this mechanism accrue mainly in large urban areas is confirmed by the findings of Gramlich and Rubinfeld (1982, 556).

10. Hanke and Carbonell (1978) compare the passage of Coastal Zone legislation by initiative with its failure to pass in the legislature in California. The U.S. Supreme Court's upholding of binding local zoning referenda is criticized by Wolfstone (1978). Both invoke arguments in the text below. That the voting in the California Coastal Zone initiative corresponded with the economic interests of the voters is established by Deacon and Shapiro (1975).

11. California's new governor took steps interpreted as attempting to alter the largely anti-development outlook of the California Coastal Zone Commission (*New York Times*, 28 April 1983, A16). For similar reasons, Oregon's Land Conservation and Development Commission has become more receptive to development. Vermont's Act 250 was also an issue in recent gubernatorial elections.

12. In 1980 six municipalities—New York, Chicago, Los Angeles, Philadelphia, Detroit, and Houston—had populations greater than 1 million, while twelve states had smaller populations.

11.

Does Zoning Matter? Empirical Evidence on Zoning, Externalities, and Housing Costs

The reader who has waded through the first ten chapters may be excused for muttering something like, "Zoning had darn well *better* matter." As I shall show, zoning does matter. The real questions are these: In what sense does zoning matter? What is the evidence that zoning influences the market for land and the supply of housing and other activities? Is there further evidence that this influence, if it exists, is undesirable?

The literature addressed to these questions is growing rapidly, and there are a number of seemingly conflicting answers to them. This chapter is an interpretive essay in which my goal is to sort out the implications of these studies rather than to survey them all.

11.1. THE COASE THEOREM AND TWO UNZONED CITIES

There is an obvious answer to the question, Does zoning matter? Of course zoning matters. It matters in the same sense that possession of any entitlement matters. Ask a developer or a landowner or a community resident or a public official whether zoning matters. It would be like asking whether the deed to the land or the title to the car or the employment contract matters. But let us press the case. Suppose that zoning did not exist as an institution. Would not some *other* institution have arisen in its place (private covenants, extended nuisance laws, public acquisition of development rights) that would have accomplished much the same pattern of outcomes that zoning has?

It may help to understand this position to note that the proposition that zoning does not matter, in the sense just described, is a direct application of the Coase theorem. Coase argued that as long as entitlements were fully defined, assigned, and tradeable at zero cost, the allocation that was ultimately reached would be the same regardless of how entitlements were initially distributed. Since zoning is one distribution of land use entitlements, and lack of zoning and reliance on private covenants is a different one, the notion that the ultimate result is the same is an assertion of the Coase theorem.

Consider two sources that suggest that zoning may not have mattered. The first is historical, and it was not intentionally addressed to the question at hand. Sam Bass Warner's (1971) description of the suburbanization of Boston in the late nineteenth century indicates that several suburban land use patterns often attributed to zoning emerged without any zoning at all. The most prominent of these was income segregation among suburban neighborhoods. Small-time, independent developers created these segregated neighborhood patterns. The developers' reasoning was simple. Such patterns allowed for some scale economies by reproducing the same type of house. What is more important, they sold well because of buyers' desire to live near people of the same income class.

Warner's study is useful in showing that income segregation is not caused solely by government controls. The assertions by some of the "open suburbs" advocates would lead one to believe that poor and rich would live side by side in the absence of zoning laws preventing it. Segregation by neighborhoods, though, is quite different from segregation by entire communities. Warner's lace-curtain Irish might not have lived on the same block with their poorer countrymen, but the former could not prevent the latter from living in the same community. Moreover, zoning's major effect is on development of open land. The developers of suburban Boston caused the city to spread out in more or less contiguous districts, usually just ahead of the trolley lines. The ability of preexisting residents or early homebuyers to slam the door on newcomers was nearly nonexistent.

The modern study suggesting that zoning does not matter much for the segregation of commercial from residential districts is Bernard Siegan's (1972) extensive investigation of Houston, Texas. Houston is the only large city in the United States that does not have a zoning ordinance. Despite this, Siegan finds that most business uses segregate themselves from both residential and non-compatible commercial or industrial uses. The difference he does find is in housing: its cost is lower and more plentiful for lower-income people than in comparable cities (Peiser 1981). Otherwise, the supposed benefits of zoning seem conspicuously absent.

Siegan's study has been criticized by pointing out that many Houston residential districts are protected by private covenants, so that zoning is not needed. Thus, it is argued, Houston is not a valid test of nonzoning. This criticism misses the whole point of Siegan's argument. Nonzoning does not mean no regulation. It means simply that landowners must be convinced to enter into regulation (covenants) voluntarily. Whether this is a realistic alternative in other cities is an open question, but the existence of covenants in Houston is an important point supporting Siegan's view, not contradicting it.

Like Warner's study, Siegan's is most useful as an antidote to assertions about the absolute necessity of zoning in our complex, interdependent, urban society. Houston functions well enough to attract plenty of immigrants. Other cities of comparable size seem to have at least as many urban problems.

Yet the real question is not whether Houston works but whether it works as well as it would under zoning. I admit that the question is a very difficult one, but the evidence that Siegan presents is not entirely convincing. Housing prices may indeed be lower in Houston. Maybe that's because of nuisances that zoning would have prevented. We so often concentrate on zoning as excessively raising the price of housing that we forget that housing might be priced too low if it is devalued by the threat of uncompensated nuisances.[1]

The other problem with the study is that Houston is a large central city. For reasons given in section 10.5, central cities generally are less restrictive than suburbs. The more important question about zoning is its effect on the suburbs. Since Houston's municipal boundaries encompass both the downtown and, to an extent unusual among large metropolitan areas, most of its suburbs, it is hard to say what the effect of nonzoning would be in independent suburban districts.

The basic problem in all studies of the effects of zoning and evaluations of its desirability is the lack of modern suburbs that do not have zoning. Investigators are left with indirect techniques to evaluate its effects. The following sections will describe and evaluate three approaches. The first approach is to see whether the objectionable uses that zoning is supposed to control actually have adverse effects on residential land values. The second approach asks whether zoning, or substantial changes in zoning policy, affects the prices of residential housing. A third approach looks at zoning's effects on land values within a community.

11.2. THE EXTERNALITIES AND ZONING STUDIES

The approach of externalities and zoning studies is to take the traditional justification for zoning at face value and see whether its underlying assumptions are valid. The traditional story, at least as it is understood by economists, is that zoning is necessary because in the absence of public controls, activities that adversely affect the value of housing will locate in residential neighborhoods. Other purposes of zoning may be advanced, but preservation of residential amenities appears so often in the literature that it seems reasonable to focus on the apex of the traditional pyramid.[2]

Studies investigating this claim usually find a residential neighborhood that has some nonconforming land use and compare its housing prices with the prices in a similar neighborhood that lacks the nonconforming use. If the first neighborhood's housing prices are lower than those in the second, it means that buyers of housing viewed the nonconforming use as a nuisance to be avoided and lowered their offers for the site. If this effect is found, many researchers conclude that zoning is justified in order to separate nonconforming uses. If there appear to be no systematic differences between the two neighborhoods, zoning is not justified.

Note that I have changed the question around here. "Does zoning have an effect" has been subtly replaced by "Is zoning justified?" Many people seem to think that these are the same questions, and they quote different studies indiscriminately. I will argue that the externalities studies do not conclusively answer *either* question.

It will help nonspecialists to understand my criticism of these studies to learn something about their basic procedure. The technique ordinarily employed is to take a sample of houses or census tracts (at least 40) and employ a statistical technique called multiple regression analysis to determine the "price" of the house. In everyday speech we often refer to the value of a house and its price as the same thing. We speak of a house priced at $80,000, for example. But that is not a satisfactory approach to a good as complex and variable as a house.

A house is a composite of many attributes. These include lot size, number of rooms, square feet of interior space, number of bathrooms, size of the garage, type of flooring, extent of insulation, neighborhood and community characteristics, and proximity to jobs, shopping, and schools. The economists' approach to measuring these attributes is the hedonic price index, in which a house's value is thought to be the sum of the value of each attribute.[3]

The empirical question is how important each attribute is. This is where multiple regression analysis comes in. A simple example would be as follows:

House Value $= a$ (number of rooms) $+ b$ (lot size) $+ c$ (miles to employment) $+ d$ (distance to pulp mill)

The coefficients a, b, c, and d are to be estimated by the regressions, while the attributes (number of rooms, lot size, miles to employment, and distance to pulp mill) constitute the data for the sample. The coefficient estimates impute a dollar value to the attribute. For example, the estimate of coefficient a might turn out to be \$4,129, meaning that at the mean of the sample an extra room adds \$4,129 to the value of the house, other things held constant. Standard statistical tests are applied to the coefficients to see whether they can be accepted as significantly different from zero.

Now consider what one would expect from performing a statistical experiment like this and how the results can be interpreted. We would ordinarily expect coefficients a and b to be positive: more rooms and a bigger lot are attributes that people are willing to pay to have. Coefficient c would usually be negative: as people move farther from their place of employment, they must suffer the increased expense and irritation of long-distance commuting. Coefficient d, the one relevant to the externalities and zoning studies, is expected to be positive: the closer one gets to a pulp mill (or a commercial district, a busy highway, a dilapidated structure, a high-crime neighborhood) the greater is the disamenity effect and the less potential buyers will value the site.

Researchers who undertake these studies are often surprised to find that coefficient d is *not* significantly different from zero or, if it is significant, how small it seems to be relative to the noise made at zoning hearings about such prospective uses.[4] From these results, some investigators have concluded or implied that externalities are not very important. (I use the term "externalities" in this chapter to mean spillovers, regardless of whether property rights in them can be established. This is what most empirical studies take it to mean.) This conclusion is probably not warranted. The next section offers some reasons why empirical studies usually underestimate the importance of negative neighborhood effects.

11.3. INTERPRETATION OF EXTERNALITIES STUDIES

Suppose in the example of the previous section that the employment center is the pulp mill. This creates a conflicting incentive on the part of potential buyers of the house (who plan to work in the pulp mill or in some other firm nearby). They will want to live near the mill in order to reduce commuting costs, but not too near, in order to keep away from its disamenities.[5] It might well turn out that the estimates of both coefficients c and d are very low or insignificant, because one offsets the other. This will not always be the case, though, especially in large urban areas, where jobs may be located in many different places. Moreover, careful sample selection can overcome this problem if the researchers are aware of it.

There are other reasons why coefficient d might be low. Suppose that construction of the pulp mill is proposed after the nearby houses are built. The residents of the neighborhood object to the construction of the mill at a zoning board hearing. As a result, the pulp mill owners take some steps to reduce the nuisances or to compensate the neighbors (as suggested in chapter 5).

There are several methods by which the neighbors might be compensated. The mill might provide a park or some other public facility. It might give money to local charities to finance summer camp programs for children in the area. Alternatively, the community authorities might redirect some of the property taxes paid by the mill for special services for the neighborhood.

Each of the aforementioned compensations is directed at the neighborhood rather than at specific individuals. Compensation thus "runs with the land" (section 6.3). When a prospective buyer (or tenant) arrives, he will perceive the nuisance effects of the mill, lowering his offer to buy, but he will also perceive the compensatory benefits, raising it right back up. Unless the compensations are separated from the nuisance effects—something few studies attempt to do—the estimate of the importance of nuisances will be too low.

I do not want to be nihilistic about studies of the effects of nuisances on surrounding property values. With the right sample and careful specification, the hedonic price index approach should reveal reasonable estimates of willingness to pay for neighborhood and community amenities.[6] Moreover, other techniques, such as interview surveys about prospective changes in land use, can reveal some information. Answers to these questions are surely valuable for planning purposes.

I wish to address a different question now: What do studies of the importance of externality have to do with the justification for zoning? Suppose that a study using impeccable statistical techniques showed that some nonconforming use had no appreciable effect on neighboring property values. Would this be an argument against zoning? Not necessarily; the reason that the nonconforming use had no effect might be that the area in question was subject to zoning. Zoning authorities may have seen to it that it stayed innocuous or that it satisfied neighboring residents that the benefits to them clearly outweighed the costs. The use of zoning (or even the prospect of zoning) might be precisely the reason why spillovers are hard to detect. The real question is whether zoning results in a more satisfactory use of land than does some other system.

If this is the question, would not the discovery that spillovers *do* affect property values be an indictment of zoning? Again, it does not necessarily follow. Just because one land parcel's value is reduced does not mean that total welfare is reduced. Suppose that zoning authorities ignore the objections of neighbors and allow a mill to be constructed on a certain site. Neighbors' property values are reduced by $20,000; however, the utilization of that particular site by the mill allows the value of paper production to rise by $50,000. Is this situation undesirable?

According to the equity standards developed in chapter 8, the neighbors should be compensated if the neighborhood was not already an industrial enclave (where a mill would be normal behavior) and transaction costs of compensation are low relative to the neighbors' loss. But if these conditions are not met, there is no reason to think of this situation as undesirable from either an efficiency or an equity standard. The relevant question is whether zoning, as an institution, is more likely than some other arrangement to lead to a better result.

11.4. HOUSING PRICE STUDIES

Another branch of the empirical evidence addresses the effect of zoning on housing costs. The reasons why zoning might restrict the supply of housing, and thus raise its costs, were explored in chapter 7. To review that chapter, the reasons were: high transaction costs for exchange of zoning entitlements; the wealth effect of initial entitlements; the illegitimate preferences problem; and monopoly control. The important point to recall from the analysis in chapter 7 is that each of these causes was identified within a setting that identified some nonmonopoly, legitimate *benefits* provided by a system of regulation.

I remind the reader of the benefit side of zoning because so many studies of zoning's effects on housing costs seem to neglect it. The most obvious are those that simply add up the costs of regulation (Seidel 1978). Of course there are costs to regulation. Installing effective brakes adds to the cost of an automobile as well. The real question is whether the costs of regulation outweigh its benefits and whether an alternative system could not create the same benefits at a lower cost to society. The studies identifying the costs serve to inform people of the panoply of regulation that exists in our society, but they are not especially useful in evaluating the desirability of zoning as such.

The more sophisticated and informative studies ask whether some novel zoning method increases the market price of housing. It was pointed out earlier that it is nearly impossible to compare housing costs in a zoned community to those in a nonzoned community, because there are no suburbs that lack zoning. A method of overcoming that is to note that some communities are more restrictive than others and that some areas (communities, states, or regions) adopt increasingly restrictive zoning restrictions over time, so that one can compare before and after housing prices.

The problem with the first method—comparing communities for apparent restrictiveness[7]—is that there are very few good quantitative indexes of restriction. Section 4.5 showed that just looking at the zoning laws themselves can give a misleading idea about restrictiveness, since the laws are subject to so much discretion and since other community policies (e.g., limited municipal service hookups) may accomplish the same thing. The second method, which involves calculations of housing prices before and after zoning innovations, will be explained in the context of a policy that has generated a number of empirical studies.

During the 1970s, the state of California adopted many novel and highly restrictive local and regional land use controls. One was the growth management approach pioneered by the city of Petaluma and subsequently adopted, after court certification, by many other cities. Another was the establishment of the California

Coastal Zone Commission, which controlled development along the entire coast of California. (The majority of Californians live within a few miles of the coast.) Still a third was the California Supreme Court's conclusion that the California Environmental Quality Act applied to private as well as public developments. This provided a powerful means by which antidevelopment forces could frustrate local zoning decisions allowing large-scale housing developments. In the background was a longstanding California tradition of electoral initiative and judicial deference to local government authority over land use. This tradition allowed each of these new devices to operate without much interference from the courts and without significant influence by development interests. California thus became the leader in the growth control movement of the 1970s.

One type of experiment using the California data is to see whether the price of housing in the newly restricted area either grew faster after the restriction or was higher after the restriction than prices in nonrestricted places. For example, one might run a regression such as the following:

House Value $= a$ (number of rooms) $+ b$ (lot size)
$+ c$ (miles to employment) $+ d$ (dummy for restriction).

The dummy variable would take a value of one when or where the new restriction applied, and a value of zero when or where the new restriction was not in effect. If the coefficient d were judged significantly different from zero, it could be concluded that the new land use restriction raised housing prices, since other components of house value had presumably been accounted for by the other variables.

11.5. INTERPRETING THE HOUSING PRICE STUDIES

The conclusion of almost all housing price studies is that the new restriction policies do indeed have significant effects on housing prices.[8] These findings ought to quiet the assertions by defenders of such restrictive policies that they will have no effect on housing prices. (One should not expect this to persuade the enthusiasts of such policies to forswear them. The costs of exclusion are usually borne by someone else.)

It will hardly do, however, only to knock down naive arguments. A more sophisticated argument on behalf of the new restrictions admits that there are costs from these policies but says that they are more than outweighed by the benefits provided by the policies. In fact, the rise in housing prices following adoption of these policies might just as well be taken as support for this position. If a community makes itself more attractive as a result of some novel growth control or preservation policy, more people will want to live there, bidding up the price of existing housing and of prospective building lots. In econometric terms, that is an identification problem: Were higher housing prices caused by an inward shift in supply, which seems undesirable, or by an outward shift in demand, which seems innocent if not laudable?

This rejoinder to the housing price studies again reminds us that zoning provides benefits as well as costs. The normative question is, What benefits are legitimate benefits? This question is discussed in sections 7.6, 8.7, 9.6, and 15.8. For now, I will assume that it is not legitimate to use zoning solely to raise the value of one's home by eliminating the competition from new homes (i.e., by shifting the supply curve to the left).

Within this normative framework, we can draw some tentative inferences from the housing price studies. To do this, we must distinguish between studies that focus on housing prices solely within the restricted area and those whose sample of observations includes *other* areas within the same housing market.

A study that finds that housing prices in a restrictively zoned area have increased is perfectly consistent with the idea that zoning is designed to create legitimate benefits for the community. These restrictions will increase the desirability of owning property there. But if one community's land use restrictions cause housing prices *outside* the community (e.g., in the rest of the metropolitan area) to rise, there is cause for some skepticism of the desirability of such restrictions, since we ordinarily expect the nonmonopoly benefits of most zoning restrictions to be fairly localized. If some of the *costs* of zoning are being foisted upon other communities in the form of higher housing prices, we have reason to suspect that the zoning ordinance is excessively restrictive, since the community that enacted them may not take these costs into account.

It may help to understand this argument to consider the conditions under which a community could enact a special zoning ordinance and still have no effect on the housing prices elsewhere in the metropolitan area. One condition would be an ordinance that made the community more attractive but did not impinge on total housing production per year. For example, a new ordinance that redirected growth to contiguous municipal service areas might not affect total production. Another would be an ordinance that allowed many uses but concentrated them so as to minimize spill-overs. Lafferty and Frech (1978) show that reducing the dispersion of incompatible uses raises single-family home values. Adoption of such policies would not cause housing price increases in other communities.

A second condition would be when a community inefficiently restricted growth but constituted such a small part of the metro-politan area that the people who would have lived there caused an imperceptible effect on housing prices in other communities. However, in this situation we would not expect housing prices in the restricted community to rise either. The reason is that the community is too small to have any effect on the housing market.

There is a tendency among economists to regard many zoning restrictions as inherently in the second category. The communities that establish novel restrictions are small, and though the legiti-mate benefits seem illusory, the costs are largely irrelevant because of the number of alternative sites. What is missing from this per-spective is the tendency for other communities to imitate the most restrictive one once the latter's ordinance passes judicial muster. Thus the importance of the novel and highly restrictive growth management policy of Petaluma, California, is not in its direct effect on the housing market north of San Francisco (though it appears to have had such an effect) but in the example that it provided for other communities wishing to establish the same kind of ordinance but wary of the court challenges to it.[9]

11.6. LAND VALUE AS A MEANS OF JUDGING ZONING

There is a way of judging whether a community's new zoning restriction creates benefits in excess of its costs. Assume that the community is small; this will preclude the option of monopoly gains to existing homeowners. Also assume that the community is only partly developed; say, only one-fourth of its land is de-veloped and the rest is largely rural. A new restriction that creates residential benefits in excess of costs will make the entire com-munity—developed and undeveloped—more attractive. Thus the total value of land in the community will rise. It may be a side effect of the ordinance that some, maybe all, undeveloped land will fall in value as a result of the restrictions applied to it, but this will be more than offset by rises in the other land in the community.[10]

Now consider an ordinance that creates benefits smaller in total than its costs. (It may pass because the benefits accrue to existing homeowners, while costs are borne by nonresident landowners.) In this instance, total land values in the community will fall, or at least they will be lower than they would have been had the novel restriction not passed.

The reason why we may be confident that land values will reflect benefits and costs is that we assume, reasonably, I think, that they run with the land. Benefits of zoning, and its costs, are not assigned by individuals or firms. When the people sell their property to someone else and move on, the zoning laws remain. If the benefits and costs are local and the community possesses no monopoly power, the land market is in fact the only place to conclusively judge zoning's relative efficiency.[11]

This analysis indicates a conceptual problem with the housing price studies. By focusing on the price of existing housing rather than on all potential housing, one gets a partial view of zoning's effects. The sample in such studies usually does not include undeveloped land. Thus the major locus of the costs of a typical suburban zoning restriction is overlooked. Even if we do have a small community whose housing prices rise due to zoning and whose effects are confined to the community, we cannot conclude that the regulation in question improves resource allocation. Only if the benefits accrue to both existing residents and potential residents can we make such a conclusion, and the only way that potential residents register their demand is via a developer who bids for the undeveloped land.

If my contention that land values hold the key to evaluating both zoning's effects and its desirability is correct, why have there not been dozens of studies on the effects of zoning on land values? There are a few, but they are rare. One reason is that it is difficult to get a good sample of market sales of land that separate other effects. The other complication is that many of the new zoning restrictions involve potential monopoly effects (sections 7.7 and 10.9). In the context of monopoly control, land value maximization is not consistent with welfare maximization.

Having been critical of the method of many studies, I think it is appropriate to report one that does the job right. George Peterson, of the Urban Institute, undertook a study of the effects of zoning regulations on land and housing prices in several suburban communities in the Boston area (1974a). These communities were small relative to the Boston housing market. Peterson employed regression analysis of a sample of sixteen hundred houses and a study of undeveloped parcels as well. Unlike most other studies, his attempted to estimate both the losses to landowners from being restrained from subdividing their lots or converting their houses to two-family structures and the corresponding gains to the community (fiscal protection and amenity values) from these restraints. He found that the landowner losses exceeded the sum of the community gains.[12]

This study stands in my mind as convincing evidence that conventional suburban zoning is inefficiently restrictive. Landowners could compensate the community or their neighbors and still have an incentive to use their land more intensively. The magnitude of the estimated gains is not trivial, either. The prospective gain in land values averaged around a quarter of the land's total value.

Peterson's study was, of course, limited both in geographic area and in the issues it addressed. It is more properly characterized as a test of the efficiency of subdivision regulations. Its design and outlook, however, should serve as a paradigm for future investigations of the effects of zoning restrictions.

11.7. ARE HIGH HOUSING PRICES BAD?

The preponderance of evidence seems to show that modern zoning restrictions, including the panoply of growth controls, have substantial effects on the supply of housing and the location of economic activities. The evidence suggests that these restrictions, especially the California ones, caused a large net loss in well-being, if we include the welfare of those who did not live in the community.

What persuades me of this more than the occasional study like Peterson's is the structure of decision making in local land use issues. The benefits go to the insiders, the current resident voters. The costs are imposed upon landowner-developers, whose political influence in the suburbs is minor and whose constitutional claims are often rebuffed in the courts. The latter party is usually the only representative of the potential consumers. With this structure of decision making, and with the high transaction costs of landowner-developers buying back development entitlements, it is easy to believe that the dramatic rise in housing prices in California and in some other areas was largely the result of growth controls and that the legitimate public benefits of these controls do not outweigh their costs.

It is doubtful whether most growth control enthusiasts would accept this conclusion. Growth controls, it is sometimes argued, would not have been necessary had it not been for the dramatic increase in demand for housing. This is half-true. This chapter has focused on supply restrictions as causing high prices. Restrictions on new construction are irrelevant if there is no shift in demand for the existing stock of housing to drive prices up.

In one sense this argument is naive: it simply says that communities would not have to exclude anyone if no one wanted to get in. But a more sophisticated version might be advanced. Owner-occupied housing, the main species in the suburbs, gets massive subsidies throughout the United States. The major subsidy, one that dwarfs all others, is the lack of a tax on the services of owner-occupied housing and the effective absence of any capital gains taxes on owner-occupied housing (Aaron 1972).

The absence of such taxes makes owning a house especially attractive during inflationary times. This is because the U.S. Federal tax system does not distinguish between real and inflationary capital gains. Housing is one of the few widely available tax shelters for middle-income people during inflationary times.

The growth control movement might be thought of as an unintentional means of controlling this excessive demand for housing. This has some rough congruence with the facts. The growth control movement did coincide with the most inflationary time in our history, the 1970s. (I shall argue in section 15.3 that inflation was one cause of the movement.) And several respected economists have argued that we do indeed spend too much on housing investment and, as a consequence, not enough on new factories, machinery, and other industrial investment.[13] Even if it is not part of their conscious intention, might we not want to applaud growth controls as a means of staunching overinvestment in housing? Could we regard them as a second-best policy to redirect resources to their proper use?

It may alarm opponents of growth controls to learn that this argument has some theoretical merit. Consider figure 21. Assume that the true, unsubsidized (or optimally subsidized—more on this later) demand curve is D. Subsumed under the supply curve, S, are "reasonable" land use controls, those whose benefits are at least equal to the costs.

This diagram indicates housing in the entire country. The supply curve slopes upward, even in the long run, because resources used in housing are specialized, and those that cost the least are used first. Now suppose that we add to D the net value of all the national subsidies to housing mentioned above, including the increased value of these subsidies during inflation. The new demand curve

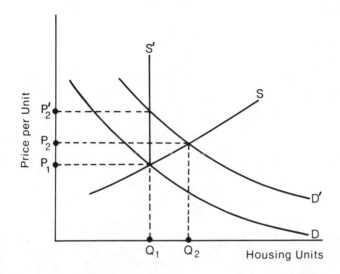

Figure 21. Supply and Demand for Housing with Subsidies and Growth
Controls

is now D'. If we regard the subsidies that account for the difference
between D and D' as socially undesirable, then the new equilibrium quantity, Q_2, must be "too large." Were it not for these
subsidies, the "proper" quantity of housing would be Q_1.

As one learns in elementary economics courses, a given allocation of resources can be attained with either price controls or
direct quantity controls. In figure 22, a production possibility curve
for housing and industrial capital shows the trade-offs. The optimal
allocation of capital between housing (Q_1) and industry (K_1) is
assumed to be known to be point 1 in figure 22. The price dis-
tortions caused by the subsidies cause us to move to point 2 instead, which corresponds with Q_2 units of housing and, necessarily,
less industrial capital (i.e., K_2 instead of K_1).

If we assume that it is politically impossible to end the subsidy
to housing and so dampen demand, then the next best thing may
be to restrict supply to S' in figure 21. This effect will of course
raise the prices of housing to P_2'. In this sense, buyers of housing
will continue to spend too much on housing because of the higher
prices. But the resources that would have been used for producing
the additional housing $(Q_2 - Q_1$ units of housing) will be released
to be used in the industrial sector of the economy.

One might object that the high price of housing will cause

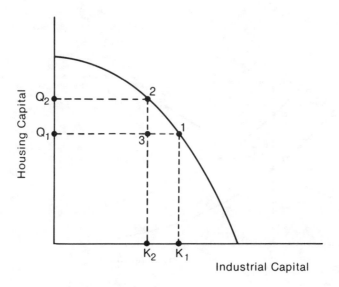

Figure 22. Production Possibility Curve for Housing and Industrial Capital

homebuyers to devote all of their savings to the purchase, so that none of it will be available to be used by the industrial sector anyway. But this misses the other side of the transaction. The *seller* of housing gains in wealth exactly what the buyer loses. He now has the money to invest in the stock market or whatever, which will then purchase for investment the resources that would have been used to produce the additional housing. Housing will continue to be "too expensive," but only because the demand subsidies cause buyers to bid up the price, not because excessive resources are used for housing production. (The same argument is often advanced against land speculation, and it is false for the same reason. That is, land speculation by itself does not reduce capital investment.)

11.8. HIGH HOUSING PRICES ARE BAD

Admitting to arguments like those in the previous section is like conceding the rare valid arguments for protectionism in international trade. The latter are invariably seized upon by protectionist forces as a justification for their position, regardless of whether the arguments are applicable to the types of tariffs or quotas for which they are lobbying. I will point out the fragility of the assumptions on which the foregoing analysis is constructed.

The first problem is knowledge of the optimal degree of housing restriction. Even if we agreed that there was too much housing demanded, it would occur only by the wildest coincidence that the optimal amount corresponded with what local and regional growth controls happened to allow.

Related to the first problem is the question of which subsidies are inappropriate. It may be that we subsidize owner-occupied housing for very good reasons; without the subsidy, too little would be produced. A well-known problem in the real estate market is that one house's deterioration may adversely affect other houses in the neighborhood. Public subsidies may be needed to overcome this. Because owner-occupiers tend to overmaintain their houses, tax subsidies may counter this effect.

Even if one grants the foregoing argument, though, it seems clear that the rate of subsidy to housing ownership did jump during the 1970s because of inflation. This effect was almost surely inadvertent. (One might ask, though, how long homeowning voters would have put up with inflationary policies had they not accrued capital gains from their fixed-rate mortgages.) The introduction of growth controls may have helped offset the overinvestment that may have resulted. Even if this were true, though, one should note that the rate of inflation (at this writing) has dropped and changes in the tax laws have lowered the taxes (by adjusting depreciation schedules) on much industrial capital. Thus even if this rationale for growth controls existed in the past decade, it is less likely to apply to the current one.

The second major problem is that the argument of the last section assumes that quantity constraints—rationing housing development permits—use no more resources than changes in prices by shifting demand inward (i.e., getting rid of the subsidies). This is extremely unlikely. At Q_1 in figure 21, the demand, D', does not go away when supply is fixed at S' by the quantity constraints. There is a strong incentive for developers to get some of that excess profit, $(P_2' - P_1) \times Q_1$, by efforts such as lobbying, lawsuits, and bribes. Even if they are not successful, they have used resources in the process. Moreover, in order to move quickly when an opportunity presents itself, developers may mobilize other resources by offering above-market wages. This, too, would retard their movement into other sectors of the economy.

This process shows the costs of rent seeking (section 6.1). Because rent seeking uses real economic resources, its existence can leave us inside the production possibility curve. In the extreme situation in which the rents are totally exhausted by efforts to obtain them, we are left with a situation shown by point 3 in figure

22. Less housing is produced, but no more industrial capital is made available, because of the additional resources used in rent seeking in the controlled sector.

A final response to this argument is to point out that it requires that all housing development in every section of the country and in every jurisdiction within a state and metropolitan area be similarly restricted. The growth control movement, however, is selective and thus does not correspond to this condition at all. It is more effective in some states than in others. What is more important, its intensity seems to vary by location within the metropolitan area. It is most intense in suburban areas, particularly those suburban areas on the fringe of larger metropolitan areas. It is not very intense in small, isolated cities, in central cities, or in largely rural areas, for reasons discussed in the previous chapter.

The selective application of growth controls means that even if we grant that they could redirect investment to other sectors, there is no assurance that this would happen. This does not mean that suburban growth controls have no effect, though. As development is deflected from suburban areas, it locates in other areas. The resulting pattern of development might cause substantial economic inefficiency as people commute too much, crowd together too much, or lose the advantages of producing and consuming in a metropolitan area. These costs will be explained in the next chapter, in which the urban economics location model is applied to zoning issues. Whatever the form of the cost, it leaves us inside the production possibility curve.

11.9. SUMMARY AND CONCLUSION

The question in the title of this chapter was seen to be two related questions: (1) Does zoning as an institution cause land use to be any *different* from what it would be under some alternative institution? and (2) Does zoning as an institution result in land use that is *better* than it would be under alternatives?

The answer to the first question is almost surely yes. The studies of unzoned areas such as late-nineteenth-century Boston and mid-twentieth-century Houston indicate that basic city land use patterns are not themselves determined by zoning. But these observations are otherwise too special to be taken as guides. The studies suggesting that nonconforming uses have no effect on residential land values are suspect because they overlook possible compensatory adjustments that the nonconformers may have adopted.

These studies also take an old-fashioned view of zoning's effects, viewing it simply as an alternative to nuisance laws.

The modern view, that zoning's objective is to control development of open land, has some empirical support. Modern growth controls have been shown to raise housing prices both within communities and within entire metropolitan areas. In evaluating all of these studies, one must keep in mind that zoning restrictions have become increasingly stringent over time and over the development of any given community (sections 3.4.5 and 4.4). Restrictions also vary by state and by location within a metropolitan area. It may be that zoning has had little effect on land use if one looks at samples (1) prior to 1955; (2) in rural areas or central cities; (3) in regions with little development pressure; and (4) in states such as Illinois and Pennsylvania, where courts have usually looked out for the interests of landowner-developers.

The second question, whether zoning is inefficient, implies both a benefit-cost test and a comparison with feasible alternative institutions. Here the conclusions must be more tentative. Most empirical studies simply look at the costs of zoning. Raising housing prices outside of restricted communities is probably evidence that benefits do not equal costs, so that increases in metropolitan housing prices due to zoning probably cause net welfare losses when the potential land users are counted.

More convincing are the occasional studies of land values within a community that show that the beneficiaries of the restrictions (current owners of developed lots) gain less than is lost by those on whom the costs are imposed (owners of undeveloped land). This finding is consistent with the institutional analysis of land use laws in earlier chapters: the losers have few political defenses (in suburbs), landowners are not afforded much protection by the courts, and there are high legal and institutional transaction costs to buying back development rights. Land value studies must be interpreted, however, in a metropolitan context, to which I will turn in the next chapter.

NOTES

1. A study by Janet Furman (1982) indicates that people in the Houston area are willing to pay a premium to live in districts with covenants or in suburban areas with zoning as compared with uncovenanted, unzoned areas of Houston. (Houston is so large that it encompasses some small municipalities that do have zoning; Furman has discovered that rare sample where

zoned and nonzoned places may be compared.) This affirms Siegan's idea that covenants provide protection as well as zoning. The only problem with Furman's study is that the two zoned communities lack much undeveloped land, on which I argue zoning has its greatest effect.

2. An early paper, whose title is its thesis, is "Nonconforming Uses Destroy the Neighborhood" (Bartholomew 1939). See also section 2.1.

3. The principal article on this method is Rosen (1974). An application of it to the housing market, which finds that the attributes listed in the text have meaningful interpretations, is Grether and Mieszkowski (1974).

4. The first study to suggest lack of systematic external effects was Crecine, Davis, and Jackson (1967) for Pittsburgh. Later studies with largely consistent results are Grether and Mieszkowski (1980, New Haven); Mark and Goldberg (1981, Vancouver); Maser, Riker, and Rosett (1977, Rochester); and Rueter (1973, Pittsburgh). Each of these studies involved central city samples. Those that tend to refute them (i.e., find that nuisances do matter) use suburban samples: Blomquist (1974, Winnetka, Ill.); Crone (1983, Foster City, Calif.); Lafferty and Frech (1978, Boston suburbs); and Stull (1975, Boston suburbs). Jud (1980) shows that spillovers matter in a Charlotte, N.C., central city sample.

5. This is pointed out by Edwin Mills (1979). Stull (1974), among others, shows that central city nuisances may cause suburban land to be more valuable in some areas than land closer to the central business district. See also chapter 12.

6. Probably the most successful attempts to date were by Lafferty (1978) and Lafferty and Frech (1978), who used a detailed land use survey of Boston suburbs. They found that single-family house values are in fact sensitive to nonresidential uses but that the relationships vary by type of use and distance from use. For example, transportation and public buildings such as hospitals reduce land values for neighbors but raise them for the community as a whole. Like others, Lafferty and Frech found generally negative effects from unused land. The reason is probably that neighbors were uncertain about the future use of such land; studies of greenbelts and other permanent open space show positive spillovers to neighboring houses (Correll, Lillydahl, and Singell 1978).

7. An attempt using a cross section of New Jersey communities is Sagalyn and Sternlieb (1973); the authors found that zoning does raise housing costs.

8. To my mind, the most thorough of these studies to date is Schwartz, Hansen, and Green (1981), on Petaluma and its environs. Other regression studies are Mercer and Morgan (1982, Santa Barbara County) and Frech and Lafferty (1976; 1984, southern California coast). Persuasive case studies of the San Francisco area are Frieden (1979); Rosen and Katz (1981); and Stanford Environmental Law Society (1982).

9. On Petaluma's effects see Schwartz, Hansen, and Green (1981; 1984). Petaluma did inspire other communities to copy its ordinance (Ellickson and Tarlock 1981, 853). Their reasoning may have been something like this: "Cities and towns about us are adopting zoning ordinances, and Wakefield [Mass.] will soon become an unprotected district with undesirable building

coming here where the bars are down." (Comey 1925; See also above, chap 7, n. 5.)

10. It is frequently found in land value studies that having a parcel zoned for commercial or manufacturing raises its value (Downing 1970, 1973; Hushak 1975). This in itself does not imply inefficiency, since it may maximize total land values to keep such uses scarce in a residential community (section 4.4.1).

11. The efficiency of a community's maximizing total property value is established by Brueckner (1979; 1982); Lind (1973); and Sonstelie and Portney (1978). Since in the long run nonland property is movable, their results must be consistent with maximizing land values.

12. Another study that undertakes a welfare economics analysis of zoning with similar results for a California sample is Frech and Lafferty (1984).

13. Feldstein (1982). The National Association of Homebuilders opposed Feldstein's appointment as chairman of the Council of Economic Advisors for having advanced such an idea. Kau and Sirmans (1983) demonstrate that the cause of increased housing prices was not, as is often charged, the lack of productivity growth in the home building industry.

12.

Urban Economics and Zoning

The last chapter showed that the effects of zoning must be evaluated in the context of a metropolitan area. The model most useful for this purpose is the urban economics location model. This model will be developed briefly in the first sections of this chapter. Later sections will then examine how zoning can alter the land use patterns that we expect to find in the benchmark model.

The major conclusion of this analysis is that modern suburban zoning most likely causes cities to be too spread out. This in turn induces excessive expenditures on transportation and lower average land values, which may result in excessive expenditures on housing. It also results in a loss of the agglomeration economies that make cities productive places for economic activity.

To put the theory in context, recall that most of the U.S. population, and hence most economic activity, is located in urban areas. Urban activities occupy only a small fraction—about 3 percent—of the total land area. The population distribution of urban areas is highly skewed: the ten largest contain about one-third of SMSA population. Most of the larger metropolitan areas have dozens of small, politically independent suburban jurisdictions surrounding one or two central cities.

12.1. WHY THERE ARE CITIES: AGGLOMERATION ECONOMIES

One way to understand the function of cities is to imagine an extraterrestrial being who arrives and reads about our urban problems. News about racial strife, crime, pollution, congestion, noise, and aesthetic blight fills our city newspapers and most discussions about cities. Our visitor might well observe, "You don't get along very well, yet you crowd into this very small amount of land. Why don't you just spread out into the 97 percent of the country that you hardly use?"

The answer is that on balance, our living standards would decline if we did that. Cities are economic entities. They exist because it is possible to produce or consume many types of goods and services in greater quantity or quality when people are in close physical proximity to one another. These production and consumption advantages are called agglomeration economies.[1] These advantages must outweigh the disadvantages of urban life for most of us.

Agglomeration economies may be illustrated with a few historical examples. Cities first provided for personal security. The fortress cities existed because it was easier for a thousand people to defend themselves in a small area than for those same people to defend themselves individually in the countryside. Medieval market towns grew up because close proximity of many buyers and sellers lowered the transaction cost of traveling from one merchant to another. Agglomeration economies applied most obviously to the industrial cities, in which the economies of scale of large factories required that workers and the firms associated with factories locate nearby to conserve on commuting and transportation costs. Agglomeration applies in a more subtle way to the modern service-producing city. Manufacturing firms have become increasingly decentralized, but their place has been taken by the service sector. Educational, financial, advertising, and managerial activities may locate near one another because the production of their services and the development of innovations in their field are enhanced by their being close to related firms.

Other agglomeration economies highlight the reasons why some cities are larger than others. A larger population allows for greater specialization. This allows for the production of services that would not otherwise yield enough income to their producers. A surgeon, for example, can specialize only to the degree that he or she has enough patients to earn a return on his or her specialty. Only a small fraction of the population will need such a service, so only a large urban area will provide sufficient demand for it. On the other side, people may move to cities to take advantage of such services. One reason why we have such a skewed distribution of city sizes may be that under a more even distribution certain specialized services might not be produced at all.

I mention the agglomeration economies in a loose historical context to suggest a point made by Jane Jacobs (1969). Her view, one often subscribed to by urban economists, is that cities are sources of invention and innovation.[2] She sees those as their primary functions. Thus cities change over time. Once an urban activity becomes mature, it becomes decentralized (to the suburbs, rural areas, or small towns). Other activities, however, move in to take its place. The cities are not left in the same form, but they retain the essential characteristics of large population and high concentration of physical capital in a relatively small space.

This view provides a counterargument to some schemes for urban preservation. If we insist that an activity remain in the central city by denying it a location in a suburb or even farther afield, we not only hobble the production of that particular activity (e.g., manufactured goods), but prevent the city from fulfilling its role as an agent of innovation and change. This is not an argument against preserving fine architecture. It is an argument against subsidizing firms to remain in downtown areas or blocking their removal to suburbs or small towns. The surest way to kill a city, in the long run, may be to turn it into a museum representing someone's static vision of a city.

It is sometimes argued that public land use controls are unnecessary when it is possible to move away from noxious activities (Dahlman 1982). People who do not like smog do not have to live in Los Angeles. Since many people do live there, it must be that the costs of avoiding smog by moving elsewhere do not outweigh the benefits of living in Los Angeles.

This argument would hold true if there were no agglomeration economies. People would remove themselves from proximity to the offending use, and nothing would be lost in the process. This might apply to such noxious activities as cigarette smoking in a large, uncrowded restaurant. Smokers and nonsmokers can voluntarily segregate themselves without much trouble. But in a world where working or consuming close to other people yields significant benefits (i.e., there are agglomeration economies), this solution is suboptimal (White and Wittman 1982).

Even if the process of relocating to avoid nuisances is costless, the relocation may reduce the total value of production. People will either have to commute longer or work in more isolated situations, which means that some of the advantages of cities will be lost. Only in a world where transportation costs were zero (for example, if we had a *Star Trek* technique of "Scottie, beam me down") would this argument apply. Existence of agglomeration economies forms a necessary condition for some kind of land use controls. It is not by itself an argument for zoning, for zoning must be compared with other possible responses to the problems of proximity.

12.2. THE URBAN ECONOMICS MODEL

The urban economics model takes agglomeration economies as given for a particular area, usually called the central business district (CBD), and asks how other businesses and households will be distributed around it.[3] The model is a simplification of reality, but that is the function of all theoretical models.

Because of the advantages of locating near the CBD, firms and households are willing to pay more to locate there. This causes rents or prices of land nearer the CBD to be bid up. Owners of this land discover that they can profit even more from their location by constructing buildings that are taller and closer together.

The extreme of this tendency is found in the downtown areas of the largest cities. Land prices are quoted in thousands of dollars per square foot, and buildings are close together and hundreds of feet tall. As one moves away from the center of the city, both rents and density of buildings (height and closeness) drop rapidly.

Another thing that changes as one moves away from the CBD is the type of land use. Near the CBD are located those uses that find proximity to other firms most useful. In the latter half of this century, CBDs have increasingly been given over to service firms such as banking, insurance, advertising, consulting, and legal services. Farther away from the CBD are the residences of individual households. Individuals find it desirable, other things being equal, to be close to their place of employment. Further away the land is dominated by agricultural uses.

The description is summarized in figure 23. In figure 23 the density of land use, or the capital (building) to land ratio, is graphed against distance from the CBD. The greatest density goes to commercial establishments, which are clustered at the center in tall buildings; then to housing, with high rises close-in and semirural estates farther away; and finally agriculture. Figure 23 shows a vertical cross section of land use. An aerial view of this city would show concentric circles. This is unrealistic in that it does not admit intermixing of land uses within the concentric zones, but as a generalization about the dominant land uses, it is more reasonable.

The theory by which the borders of the concentric zones are determined is summarized in figure 24. A rent-offer curve is the maximum amount a person proposing one of the three types of activities (commerce, housing, or agriculture) will offer to the owner of land at a given distance from the CBD. Rent-offer curves, as they are drawn here, clearly overlap one another. However, only the highest rent offer will dominate at a given distance from the city.

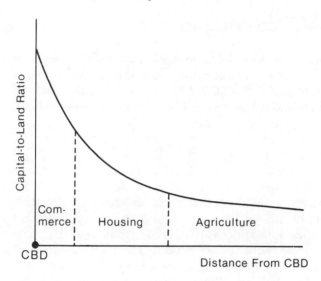

Figure 23. Stylized Model of Urban Land Use

For example, all activities are willing to pay something to be located between points A and D (distances from the CBD in figure 24). But households value that location the most, so they will be the dominant land use there. It is not that the land is uniquely suited for housing; commerce or farming could be located there as well. It is just that the location advantages of housing exceed others in this zone.

The upper "envelope" of solid line in figure 24 represents the rent-distance function. A caveat must be put forth here. The demand for location by each sector affects the demands by all others. There are, therefore, an indefinite number of rent-offer curves possible. However, in equilibrium there is only one rent-distance curve. This interdependence means that if some commercial firms decide to leave the city, rent offers by residential, agricultural, and remaining commercial activities will change. This may alter their pattern of location.

12.3. IMPLICATIONS OF THE URBAN MODEL

12.3.1. Lot Sizes

Consider a family whose house is at point B in figure 24. Clearly, not all families can live exactly B miles from the CBD, so this one

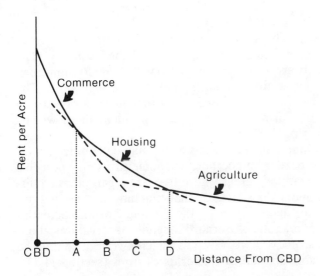

Figure 24.   Rent Offer Curves in the Urban Model

is asked to move farther out, say to point *C*. However, if the family members are to move voluntarily, they must be made no worse off than before. But at *C* they are worse off, since they have to commute longer to get to their jobs (unless they work at home or in agriculture). Thus they must be compensated. It turns out that the best way to compensate them is to give them a larger lot to build their house on. This is logical, because the land is cheaper near *C* than near *B*.

This reasoning shows that large lots in the suburbs are not necessarily caused by higher incomes of the residents (though this is an additional factor) nor necessarily by zoning regulations. The family that we considered was not offered a higher-paying job to move, nor was their decision to buy a house on a larger lot foisted upon them by some minimum lot size requirement. Large-lot zoning may still affect location, though, for it could require lot sizes far larger than people would want. The point is that we should not expect that zoning reforms will equalize lot sizes within a metropolitan area.

12.3.2. Commercial Clustering

Another implication of the urban model is that there is some reason to expect segregation of land uses by activity even in the absence of zoning. This cannot be said to be a result of the rent-distance function, for the theory from which it was derived assumed contiguity. The segregation comes from the existence of agglomeration economies within a sector of the economy. The rents paid in a city are very high compared with those for nonurban land. What makes a firm willing to pay such a high rent? The advantage of conducting activities near other firms is one strong reason. Since like firms will have the same idea, there will be voluntary clustering.

Despite voluntary clustering, there still may be conflicts, since one sector must border on another, and some firms may perceive advantages to locating in areas where they are regarded as a nuisance. The argument does suggest that planning and zoning authorities' jobs are made easier by the tendency of like activities to locate near one another. Bernard Siegan's observations about Houston are instructive here. Even in the city without zoning, he saw a considerable amount of clustering of firms (section 11.1).

12.3.3. Income Segregation

A third implication is that there will be some income segregation based on distance from the CBD. The full explanation is too complicated to deal with here (E. Mills 1980, 230). The gist of it is this. Consider a household that is currently in equilibrium by location—the advantages of a move further out just equal the disadvantages. Suppose now that its permanent income is increased. This will have two consequences. The household's commuting costs will rise, because the value of one's time increases with income. On the other hand, higher-income people generally demand more housing, which is cheaper in the suburbs because of low land prices. If this latter motive (more housing) is stronger than the former one (higher commuting costs), people with higher incomes will tend to live in the suburbs, further from the CBD than lower-income people. As an empirical matter, it does seem that this is the case. Even in the absence of "exclusionary" zoning (section 7.9), there will be a tendency for the outer suburbs to have richer people than the inner ones or the central city.

12.3.4. The Planning Problem

The urban model illustrates the magnitude of the planning problem. This is because the efficient location of every sector (and there are many more than three) depends on the location of every other sector. Once one gets beyond the simplest models, the optimal allocation of activities in an urban setting cannot be solved even by the most sophisticated computer methods.

Cities are immensely complicated machines. Their actual allocation of resources is almost surely not the optimum. But the private or decentralized planning mechanism, the market for land, does have an advantage in one respect: the profit motive of the landowners forces them to consider many alternative uses and to compare each use with the others. No planner has a similarly powerful motive to gather information for each parcel in the city. This is not to argue that government planning is unnecessary; it does militate for confining planning to deal with spillovers, which landowners may have less ability to control, rather than general allocative efforts.

12.4. ZONING CONSTRAINTS AND METROPOLITAN STRUCTURE

Chapter 11 argued that the effects of zoning would show most clearly in the price of land and that a metropolitan (or other land market) context was needed to evaluate the effects of suburban growth restrictions. The urban economics model, particularly the rent-distance (i.e., land price) diagram, can be used to provide this context.

To evaluate the issue at hand, it is necessary to modify the urban model somewhat. This involves adding political boundaries and, to simplify the exposition, dropping the commercial sector. (This is now assumed to be located at a point in the CBD.) The result is shown in figure 25, in which land rent is graphed against distance.

The solid curves in figure 25 are the equilibrium rent-offer curves in the absence of zoning. A digression about this "absence of zoning" condition: Most studies of zoning that examine it in terms of the urban economics model assume as a benchmark a system that has no spillovers or land use conflicts. The basic model is usually exposited in such a context. As a result, zoning must only be a cost-creating device, since there are no benefits.[4] Zoning is represented as a costly cure for which there is no disease. It is hardly surprising, then, that such studies should find the effects of zoning to be undesirable.

To avoid proceeding on these preordained assumptions, I shall explicitly assume that the "absence of zoning" entails a system of regulation with none of the defects of zoning described in chapter 7: all entitlements are freely transferable; there are no initial undesirable wealth effects; illegitimate motives are not a factor; and suburban governments are numerous and uncooperative with one

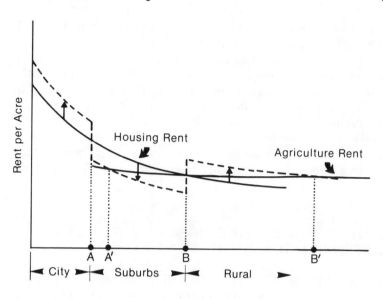

Figure 25.   Effect of Suburban Zoning on Housing Rent Offer Curve

another with regard to restrictions, so that monopoly power is not important. The presence of zoning then involves a system of land use controls that suffers from one or more of these defects. The defect to be examined is that zoning entitlements cannot be transferred from the community to developers when the latter are willing to pay what community residents demand.

The benchmark situation is shown in figure 25. The boundary between the central city and the suburbs is point A, and the boundary between the suburbs and rural townships is point B. The latter jurisdiction is devoted solely to agriculture, but it can become part of the suburbs if enough people move there. Suburban municipalities are numerous, but they imitate one another in their land use controls.

Suppose that every suburban jurisdiction is only partly developed with housing. Each one now adopts large-lot zoning or some other type of growth control that is "too restrictive" in the sense just described. Say the minimum lot size goes from a quarter-acre, to which original residents were subject, to five acres on the undeveloped land. The cost of the five-acre lot, of course, will be higher than that of a quarter-acre lot, but the *average price per acre* will fall in the undeveloped area. This is because the density of development cannot be as great as before; an artificial constraint has been put on the capital-to-land ratio. Land values of already developed lots may rise, but this will be more than offset by reductions in the value of undeveloped land.[5]

This is not the end of the story. People who might have been able to live in the original suburban jurisdictions are displaced. Where do they go to find housing? There are two alternatives within the metropolitan area. (A third is considered in the next section.) They are the central city, which we assume does not adopt restrictive zoning, and the rural townships, which are also permissive as to development. (See chapter 10 for the reasons for this.) Suburban zoning could cause one or both of the following: crowding in the central cities and suburban sprawl in the rural areas. The results are shown in the upward shifts in the housing rent-offer curve in the central city and the rural area in figure 25. As people move to the central city or rural areas instead of the suburbs, land prices are bid up. The metropolitan rent-distance function is the broken line in figure 25.

The land use pattern that results from extensive suburban zoning is also suggested by figure 25. Between points A' and B in the suburbs, agriculture now outbids housing. This is because the market for houses on five-acre lots is rather thin. One does not need to take literally the conclusion that agricultural activities will occupy all the land between A' and B to see that there will be far lower densities in the suburbs now.

As a result of the suburban restrictions, development now occurs in rural townships between B and B' in figure 25. Some of this development will be at higher densities than in the suburbs. Housing densities and hence population densities will rise in the central cities as well. The overall pattern will be a population that is more crowded in the central cities and more widely spread in the suburbs and rural areas.

12.5. OPEN CITIES AND THE LONG RUN

The households displaced by suburban zoning of the type described in the last section have a third alternative. They may move to another metropolitan area rather than put up with the high rents in the central city or the long commute from the rural fringe. This would happen under what urban economists call the open cities model.[6] There are no barriers to migration by any household. Jobs are as easy to find in one metropolitan area as they are in any other. Since the emigrants are dispersed to many different areas, no single area will be much affected by zoning. Land prices in the original suburbs will go down, but they will not rise appreciably in any other place.

The three alternatives considered in evaluating the effects of zoning clearly depend on the assumptions about both intra- and interurban migration. In the case where large-lot zoning caused suburban sprawl and/or central city crowding, it was implicitly assumed that the population of the metropolitan area stayed the same before and after zoning. Those displaced had the intraurban choice between the central city and rural fringe. In the open city case, people migrated to other areas in response to the economic disincentives created by excessive suburban zoning.

Which model applies in reality? I believe that the free migration, open city model applies in the long run and that it applies sooner in small cities than in large ones. How long is the long run? There is little hard evidence, but one anecdote may help to put the process in perspective. The branch of the electronics industry that makes silicon chips for computers flourished in the 1970s. Its geographic locus has been the area of the Santa Clara Valley south of San Francisco Bay that has become known as Silicon Valley. The area is known almost as well for its high housing prices. Whether these are caused by excessive zoning regulations, as many aver, does not concern us. What is important is that the expansion of these industries is being hampered by the inability of the companies to hire workers from outside the state. One corporate recruiter complained, "Housing is by far the greatest deterrent to the job market in California." Several companies are planning expansion in other states instead.[7]

This suggests that the long-run adjustment process may take from ten to fifteen years. For most policy purposes, this a long time. For this reason, one should be able to detect the effects of excessive zoning within a large metropolitan area, as in figure 25. I suggest, though, that smaller urban areas are affected more quickly. Because their industries are often already in competition with firms in several other cities, migration of both firms and households will start soon if one of those cities lowers the real income of immigrants by forcing up housing prices. This fact plus the less fragmented government structure in most small, isolated cities also makes them less inclined to adopt highly restrictive regulations (section 10.4).

Open cities allow for migration, closed cities do not. The latter model thus gives the opportunity for a monopoly. A government that controlled metropolitan land in a closed city would face a downward-sloping demand curve for land uses. It is standard that value maximization under monopoly does not maximize welfare, so land value changes in monopoly zoning situations would not be appropriate guides to efficient zoning.

Economists who examine land use controls and other public policies in a closed city urban model often conclude that land values are not appropriate guides to decisions, because of "general equilibrium conditions" (Pines and Weiss 1976). All this means is that in their models monopoly distorts decisions based on market prices. Monopoly land use authority thus creates secondary effects from land use policies that affect other variables in the model.

The assumption of monopoly control of development by local governments is not realistic in most U.S. cities (sections 10.6 and 10.7). Most large metropolitan areas contain many local governments, and smaller cities may be characterized by free migration, so monopoly would have no effect. Moreover, most rezonings occur one at a time in small parts of a metropolitan area, so effects of a given decision are marginal. For these reasons I submit that market-determined land values are appropriate guides to local land use policies. In particular, the requirement that governments pay market values when a taking of property is found need not be undermined by references to "general equilibrium conditions."[8]

12.6. SUBURBAN ZONING, DECENTRALIZATION, AND HOUSING PRICES

It may come as a surprise that theorists who have tried out the suburban large-lot zoning constraint in the context of the urban economics model have not been able to conclude unequivocably that it is a cause of sprawl, even when the city's population is fixed (White 1975b). The choice of location by households excluded from the suburbs in this case is between the central city and rural areas. The choice is influenced both by the households' preferences and by the method by which housing is produced. Especially important is the nature of the substitution between capital (building) and land (lot size) in both preferences and production functions. Loosely speaking, if capital is a very good substitute for land, in terms of both consumers' preferences and producers' technology, households displaced by suburban zoning will move to the central city, not to the rural fringe.

Despite this possibility, there are reasons to believe that suburban zoning's major deleterious effect is to cause excessive spreading out into the rural fringe—sprawl—rather than high central city housing cost (Moss 1977). The analysis of zoning in the urban model usually ignores the historical development of the central city and the costliness of tearing down or converting old buildings. Central cities have a lot of old housing that is not well suited to middle class tastes. Most builders find the vacant rural acreage far more inviting to build on, and seekers of the suburban way of life appear to be willing to pay the higher cost of commuting rather than accept the central city substitute.

As a result of these considerations, my working hypothesis is that the deleterious effects of large-lot suburban zoning are excessive amounts of suburbanization. The consequence of this for land values (confining the analysis to housing) is that while rural fringe values will rise, they will not rise as much as suburban land values will fall (Peterson 1974b). Thus when both suburbs and rural areas are taken into account, the overall effect of zoning is to lower housing prices, not raise them. (This may induce greater *expenditure* on housing, if housing demand is price-elastic.)

To understand why this peculiar result is obtained, consider an extreme situation. Suppose that the suburban ring around the CBD absolutely forbade any new housing rather than allowed just low-density housing. The value of the land for housing in this ring would now be zero. Suppose that all of the displaced households moved farther out into a rural fringe. Would land prices per acre be as large there as they would have been in the suburbs? Not necessarily. This is because the extra commuting cost associated with living in the rural area would erode the willingness to pay for a unit of land. The land would be cheaper, and conceivably people would then buy more of it, if the income reduction entailed by more transit cost did not outweigh the price reduction effect.

The point is that suburban growth restrictions may, on average, lower metropolitan land rents, not raise them. This lower land rent, of course, is derived from the lower degree of satisfaction (utility) of all households taken together in the metropolitan area. This is derived in turn from the original assumption that growth controls do not confer offsetting benefits to suburban residents.

In this model, the main problem with suburban zoning is that it causes households to live too far away from the city's center. The direct cost of this is excessive commuting. (It is perhaps worth noting that the major component of commuting cost is the time an individual spends on the trip, not the costs of the vehicle.) The indirect cost is loss of agglomeration economies. Both of these costs will be evaluated in the concluding section of this chapter.

12.7. SPECULATION AND SPRAWL

It was argued in the last two sections that excessive suburban-ization—sprawl—was caused by suburban growth controls. (This is ironic, since many growth control plans list sprawl as one of the problems to be cured.) Development is deflected to rural town-ships until they, too, become like suburbs and adopt growth con-trols. Development then goes still further afield to an even more remote area, and the cycle begins again.

The response by growth control advocates might be that the real cause of sprawl is not local controls but federal government tax and spending policies and land speculation. I will delay con-sideration of the former cause until section 13.6. The land spec-ulation argument is dealt with here.

12.7.1. The Function of Land Speculation

Successful land speculation involves holding the land as long as the net growth of its value exceeds the rate of return on another asset (Markusen and Scheffman 1978). When the growth rate of land values slows to the point that it just equals the interest rate, land will be sold and speculators will purchase other assets. If the speculators wait too long, and the growth of their land's value is less than the interest rate, they will lose some or all of their gains.

Speculation involves withholding land from the market for a while. On the suburban rural fringe this may cause some home-builders to be denied building sites and thus may induce them to purchase land and put up houses still farther from the CBD. This creates a pattern called "leapfrog" development.

Does the existence of land speculation in the far suburbs and rural fringe contribute much to sprawl? I suspect that it does not. Consider the position of the speculator. His asset is increasing in value, as is shown by the most recent offer by a homebuilder who wants to put up a tract of houses on one-acre lots. Why might the speculator decide not to accept the most recent offer? Because next year a builder might want to use the land even more inten-sively, say, for half-acre housing rather than one-acre housing, for which he would pay even more. If the speculator guessed right about the next year's prospects, not only would he make a lot of money but he would reduce urban sprawl.

Urban sprawl would be reduced because the later offer involved higher-density housing. If the speculator had sold to the earlier developer, the land would have been used for low-density housing. Other housing demand would have had to go elsewhere, most likely still farther from the central city. Thus a successful land speculator—one who predicts the market trend and therefore makes a lot of money—reduces urban sprawl by creating a *temporary* leapfrog development pattern, which is later filled in with higher-density development.[9]

By the same token, an unsuccessful land speculator contributes to urban sprawl. He can be unsuccessful in one of two ways. He may sell too quickly, allowing his land to be built upon at a lower density than if he had waited. Or he may wait too long, so that the rate of growth of his land's value falls below that of alternative assets. In the previous example, this would mean spurning the first offer only to find that next year the best offer was for a lower-density and lower-value use than that of the year before.

The moral of this analysis is that speculation causes sprawl only when speculators guess wrong. Speculators, it seems to me, guess wrong a lot of the time. But there is one corrective factor: those who guess wrong consistently lose money and are thereby induced to get out of the business.

12.7.2 Antispeculation Policies

It may be that there are feasible public policies to reduce the number of unsuccessful speculators. We need not go into them, however, because almost all suggested public policies regarding speculation have exactly the opposite effect. The most widely adopted response to speculation is to create more land use regulations. The discretion involved in administering these regulations and the prospect of changing them entirely creates uncertainty for landowners. Such uncertainty about the future creates situations analogous to those in which the speculators guess wrong: they may decide to develop too early in order to beat the controls, or the regulations may so delay development that demand is deflected elsewhere (Markusen and Scheffman 1977, chap. 4).

The other antispeculation policy is to tax the speculative gains. Only a few jurisdictions have undertaken this (Glickfeld and Hagman 1978; Smith 1976). It is nonetheless a popular idea and requires some examination. By taxing the after-the-fact gain in land values, these taxes penalize those who sold their land at the right time for the higher-density use and reward (by lower taxation) those who sold too quickly or waited too long.

There are several variations on these taxes. A popular one, enacted in Vermont and considered in other states, is different in that the tax liability is greater for land held for a short period than for land held over a longer period. The obvious incentive is to create long-term speculation rather than short-term. As desirable as this may sound, it may actually contribute to sprawl, not reduce it.

Developers under this tax system are encouraged to deal with owners such as farmers who typically have held the land for a long time. These people may lack the speculators' knowledge of market conditions and thus accept the first offer, which is typically for lower-density housing than later offers would be. These owners are, of course, speculators, but only by default. No one should expect them to be very good speculators.

Special taxes on land speculators are often advocated as if they had no effect on current owners of land. Since selling to speculators is discouraged by such taxes, original landowners have two options: to sell their land at a lower price (reflecting the taxes that the speculator-buyer must pay) or to become speculators themselves. The latter choice has the disadvantage of imposing speculative risks on people who may not be well suited to bear them. Even without land use controls, land speculation is a risky business. Its reputation as a sure thing is engendered by the natural reluctance of those who lose their shirts to proclaim it to the world. Professional land speculators provide insurance for landowners who do not wish to speculate themselves.

Which is the more important cause of sprawl—unsuccessful speculation or excessive suburban zoning? It seems to me that it is the latter. Speculators have a strong incentive to look at both the costs and the benefits of waiting until next year. Suburban zoning authorities do not have this incentive, because the costs of waiting for next year fall on people with little political influence in their community. Individual speculators usually control far less undeveloped land than even a small suburban municipality. Their mistakes are not likely to have metropolitanwide effects. Finally, unsuccessful speculators will allow some development, even if it is not of the optimal density. Mistakes are usually matters of timing rather than determining the ultimate use of the land.

12.8. THE COSTS AND BENEFITS OF SPRAWL

The term "sprawl" is usually pejorative. It means excessive suburbanization. Thus it may seem odd to have a section that mentions the benefits of sprawl. I do this to point out the possibility that what is called sprawl might not deserve the pejorative connotation.

Consider one study of the problem that has been very influential, *The Costs of Sprawl* (Real Estate Research Corporation 1974), commissioned by the President's Council on Environmental Quality. Its approach was to compare several paradigms for suburban housing development. One paradigm was the low-density single-family housing tract, which is the dominant form of suburban housing. Others were apartment units, various mixtures of apartments and single-family units, and higher-density single-family units.

The costs considered included schools, public services, utilities, land, open space, and residential construction. It was found that higher density generally had lower costs than lower density. This was most clearly the case in construction costs and provision of utilities and schools. The last cost was lower for apartments for the unsurprising reason that they were assumed to house fewer children per unit.

Despite the detail of the engineering cost studies, I find it remarkable that anyone should use this as a basis for any policy conclusions.[10] The main problem is that the study made no attempt to determine what suburban pattern would *not* be excessive. How are we to decide how much suburbanization is too much? One standard is to compare it to a situation in which people who live in the suburbs pay all of the costs identified in the study. If they pay all of the costs and still live in the patterns we observe in suburbs, then the benefits must be greater than the costs.

This raises the central problem with the methodology of *The Costs of Sprawl*. Its authors did not ask whether developers or subsequent homeowners pay for such costs via taxes, subdivision exactions, or infrastructure dedications. I earlier suggested that mechanisms to force these payments have long been in place for most community infrastructure (section 4.1). Even if one does not accept this, some inquiry should be made before concluding that the typical American suburb deserves the term "sprawl."

Yet even this approach would not yield fully satisfactory results. This is because much sprawl is caused by local zoning practices rather than by poor municipal pricing policies for infrastructure.

Under local growth controls, displaced homebuyers may pay all municipal costs in the far suburban or rural locations to which they must move. They nonetheless suffer net welfare losses because they are unable to purchase preferred locations closer to the central areas.

12.9. CONCLUSION: THE NET COSTS OF SUBURBAN GROWTH CONTROLS

The previous section is not meant to be a defense of unmanaged suburban development. There are problems with the pricing of municipal services that may cause excessive decentralization (Hirsch 1977). I think, however, that the major cause of sprawl is suburban growth controls. However, to consider sprawl the only cost of these controls would miss some important consequences.

If suburban growth controls do result in sprawl, the most obvious cost is excessive commuting by those who live too far away from their jobs. To excessive commuting one should add the excessive travel to stores, schools, and recreation facilities. Some of these destinations may respond to sprawl by moving out to suburbs. This reduces the direct commuting costs of the households, but it may add to the transportation costs of the firms.

The relocation of firms to suburban areas adds a subtle cost to growth controls. It may be that many firms would have moved to the suburbs even if their employees or customers had not moved so far away. But if sprawl is an additional factor, there is another potential cost: the loss of agglomeration economies. The beginning of the chapter showed that cities exist because of the advantages of physical proximity. I am especially attracted to the idea that such proximity fosters innovation. By inducing firms to sacrifice proximity to one another in order to save on commuting time, we may retard innovation, as well as lose some other agglomeration economies.

Earlier in this chapter I argued that there were two other consequences of excessive suburban zoning. Households and firms might be forced into the central city or, in the open city model, to another metropolitan area. Each of these possibilities has its costs, too.

Forcing development into central cities, which seems to be at least the rhetorical rationale for growth controls, would not cause the loss of agglomeration economies and would involve less commuting. The remaining problem is that too much capital would be used in housing (and perhaps by firms). The unit cost of housing is greater in central cities because it is eventually more costly to build up than out. (The law of diminishing returns applies to growing buildings as well as crops.) This will cause too much capital to be used in housing. Such crowding may have social costs as well; it was not so long ago that reformers decried urban crowding and its consequences. In other words, it seems silly to use scarce private and public capital to provide housing services in central cities when one could substitute the inexpensive land left in the suburbs.

Finally, the development that was excluded from metropolitan suburbs might just go somewhere else entirely. But this, too, costs something in terms of agglomeration economies. The somewhere elses that are eager to get the businesses and households are often rural areas or isolated small towns and cities. While we cannot look at such decentralization as an unmitigated cost, there may still be agglomeration economies that are lost by such a pattern. The computer terminal and the telephone have not entirely replaced the face-to-face meeting.

NOTES

1. On agglomeration economies generally see E. Mills (1980, chap. 1). Evidence on agglomeration is provided in Segal (1976).

2. Economic expositions and evidence for the innovation thesis are Lichtenberg (1960) and Sveikauskas (1979).

3. The exposition of the model in this section is derived from E. Mills (1980, chap. 5). Its most extensive treatment is Henderson (1977). Urban location relationships are more complex than the simple model summarized here largely because of the declining residential neighborhoods in older cities (McDonald 1979). My focus in this work, however, is the expansion of suburban development on the edge of the urban area, so the simple model remains useful if one regards the CBD in the text as being a suburban employment locale or a major highway interchange.

4. Such models characterize zoning simply as a constraint on an otherwise optimal system. Examples are Courant (1976); Moss (1977); Rubinfeld (1978); and White (1975b; 1978a). Each of these articles provides insights on urban location issues if it may be argued, as I do below, that the type of constraint they adopt fails to provide benefits in excess of costs. Even then, however, an analysis based on the assumption that zoning provides no benefits will overstate welfare losses.

5. An urban model with empirical estimates that are consistent with this result is Peterson (1974b). A simulation model showing lower suburban densities is Orr (1975). It is typical for empirical studies to find that parcels

zoned for large lots have lower prices per acre than those zoned for smaller lots (Hushak 1975; Peterson 1978).

6. The distinction between open city and closed city is applied to zoning by Courant (1976), whose results I follow here with some modification.

7. Silicon Valley firms relocated or expanded in Oregon (*New York Times*, 9 August 1980, 25), Taiwan (*Wall Street Journal*, 23 February 1983, 4), and Arizona (*New York Times*, 12 October 1980, 11, sec. 12) in part because of housing prices. The quote in the text is from the last article. On Silicon Valley housing prices, see Frieden (1979) and Stanford Environmental Law Society (1982).

8. This was the focus of White's (1979) critique of Ellickson's (1977) proposal. White's model was of a closed city with a single zoning authority.

9. Ohls and Pines (1975) derive the conditions for leapfrog development's efficiency and note that speculation may contribute to the outcome. A more elaborate model in the same vein is D. Mills (1981b). Their contrasting models of "foresight" and "uncertainty" correspond to the successful and unsuccessful speculators, respectively, in the text. Zeimetz et al. (1976) found that population growth in rapidly developing areas occurred at higher than previous densities. This was the result of filling in areas previously bypassed by developers.

10. The authors of the study noted at the outset that they made no attempt to calculate the benefits of sprawl. *The Costs of Sprawl* is nonetheless widely quoted as if its calculations were net of benefits. See also the critique by Windsor (1979).

13.

Suburban Development and Agricultural Land

In the 1970s a new reason for excluding development in suburban and rural communities appeared: the need to preserve farmland. Although the farmland preservation literature often mentions the aesthetic benefits of farmland, the movement's central tenet is that continued conversion of farmland to urban uses will cause us to run out of agricultural land. The more lurid tracts warn of future starvation from embargoes by food-producing states and disruptions of food supplies by strikes or other calamities. (Even if these were likely, would preservation of local cropland rather than storage of goods be the prudent precaution?)

The more respectable concern is with the export market and the data that showed a greatly increased rate of urbanization of cropland.[1] The United States must preserve farmland, it is argued, to ensure that its chief export does not become too expensive. If this were to occur, our balance of payments would deteriorate, or more generously, the poor in the rest of the world would have less to eat.

As I indicated in section 1.1, the data used to claim that the rate of urbanization of farmland jumped suddenly in the late 1960s are not to be believed.[2] It might also be pointed out that we have had flexible foreign exchange markets since the early 1970s, so the balance of payments is no longer a central policy issue. And it is by no means obvious that underselling the agricultural markets in developing countries is a good way to help the largely rural poor in those places.

Rather than develop these themes, this chapter will evaluate the claim that urban development threatens the stock of farmland. This claim is found to be wanting in both facts and logic. There is no reason to expect the private land market to fail to provide

272

farmland to grow adequate "food and fiber" now and in the future. In showing this, I shall continue the task, begun in the last chapter, of examining the process of land development. Later sections will present more plausible arguments for some public intervention in rural land use. I shall conclude with an inquiry on the political economy of this issue.

13.1. THE FARMLAND PRESERVATION MOVEMENT AND SUBURBAN EXCLUSION

At the federal and state levels the farmland preservation cause has been led by soil conservationists and some environmental groups (Berg 1979). The former are largely allied with the U.S. Department of Agriculture's Soil Conservation Service (SCS) and its numerous state and county extensions. While there has been relatively little federal intervention on this issue,[3] it has been successful at the local government level. It is hard to find a suburban master plan written since 1975 that does not at least mention the need to preserve farmland. This concern has engendered several programs (Coughlin and Keene 1981; Geier 1980). The main ones are listed below roughly in order of their frequency.

1. Property-tax abatements for farmland, usually in exchange for an agreement by the landowner not to develop that land for a certain time period.
2. Identification of especially good farmland and attempts to direct development to other land.
3. Zoning land in agricultural areas to prevent most residential development, usually by adopting minimum lot sizes ranging from 10 to 640 acres.
4. Requiring that farmland preservation be included as a criterion in state (and some federal agency) environmental impact statements.
5. Purchasing development rights from farmland owners.

I shall argue that the farmland preservation movement is successful mainly because it provides a mechanism by which communities can exclude development without bringing down the wrath of the state courts that are concerned about such exclusion. Adoption of the idea that each local government has a public duty to preserve farmland is a way of meeting the due process criterion that regulations bear some reasonable relation to public welfare. It is thus better for the community than simply designating large areas as "open space," which many state courts find unacceptable.

Even the New Jersey Supreme Court, which leads all others in its skepticism of local exclusionary motives, stated in its 1983 *Mount Laurel* decision (section 3.6.2) that "municipalities consisting largely of conservation, agricultural or environmentally sensitive areas will not be required to grow because of *Mount Laurel*" (456 A.2d at 420).

Farmland preservation has the further advantage of excluding from development a far greater amount of land than could be preserved by most environmental, historical, or conservation designations. One example is Olmstead County, Minnesota, which constitutes the Rochester SMSA. Combined with restrictions on flood plains and septic systems, its farmland preservation system restricts development to less than 10,000 of the county's 422,000 acres (Pyle 1982). The argument that this is sufficient supply to satisfy demand manages both to confuse the stock of land with its supply and to be a tautology (section 7.8.1).

13.2. DEFINING FARMLAND: USDA "PRIME"

When it is charged that urbanization is chewing up valuable farmland, one needs some definition of what land is so valuable. The U.S. Census of Agriculture counts all land used in commercial farming. Its definition of commercial farming is based on revenue. One needs to sell only twenty-five hundred dollars' worth of produce to be counted as a farmer (Gardner 1981). Sales from a large backyard garden might qualify some suburbanites as farmers and their lots as farmland. This definition omits much potential farmland and does not distinguish the quality of the land. One cannot infer from it much about the effects of urban development. All one knows is the total acreage in such shifting categories as cropland, pasture, and range.

An alternative approach is to separate land by characteristics that make it attractive for farming. One widely used designation is "prime farmland." The definition was developed by the U.S. Soil Conservation Service (Diderikson, Hidlebaugh, and Schmude 1977). The SCS has promoted this definition as a basis for local preservation programs. A problem with this approach is that it may cause people to overlook the fact that prime farmland is in large measure a produced good. It is easier to produce prime farmland in some locations, such as the middle of Iowa, than in others, such as upland New England. Nonetheless, almost all land requires some initial investment to become "prime" and continuing investment to maintain it in that condition (Simon 1980).

The other problem with the SCS's prime farmland standards is that they are heavily weighted by the ease with which soil conservation can be undertaken. It is called, after all, the *Soil Conservation* Service, not the *Agricultural Production* Service. Soil is necessary to hold up the plant and to provide a medium for the dissolved minerals essential for plant growth. While original topsoils contain some of these nutrients, most do not contain enough to obtain modern commercial crop yields without the addition of fertilizer (Laetsch 1979, 262). This suggests that concern about the original quality of soils, which is the basis for many farmland preservation plans, is misplaced. Other factors such as climate, precipitation, levelness, and proximity to markets are often more important. Even if we were to put all the foregoing criteria into an index of farmland quality, however, we cannot explain away the fact that land is not a very important constraint in agriculture (Schultz 1982).

The real problem with defining farmland by physical characteristic is that all such definitions make static assumptions about the prices of farm products and inputs and about the technology of farming. All of these continually change, and so our inventory of farmland—or any resource, for that matter—continually changes (Raup 1982). For this reason, I have some sympathy with the definition adopted by the National Agricultural Lands Study (1981): all dry land that is not classified as urban or built-up is "agricultural land."[4]

Under the NALS definition, any suburban development necessarily reduces farmland. That is one way to come up with an alarming statistic about "losing farmland to development." But it has the drawback (for preservationists) of indicating how much land is left over. Even if we were to build upon 1 million acres per year (a very generous estimate) until the year 2000, we would still have at least 95 percent of the forty-eight states' land area left over.

The definition of farmland quality may not really matter for local exclusionary interests. They may just come up with a definition that will suit their needs. How this can be done is suggested by a county in Iowa that developed an index of land's suitability to grow corn. Land that exceeded a certain quality level was to be excluded from conversion to other uses. It was discovered that development was not much constrained by this standard, so authorities reduced the threshold quality level until it provided a serious barrier to development (Toner 1978, 23).

13.3. THE DEVELOPER'S CHOICE AND PRIME FARMLAND

This section presents an elementary model to illustrate some points about developers and resource preservation. The model starts from the assumption that there are substitutes for land in the production of crops. All of these substitutes (machinery, buildings, fertilizer, pesticides) are referred to as capital. The other land use is housing, which will be a surrogate for all other urban-produced goods. Like agricultural products, housing is produced with both land and capital. The problem is how best to allocate land and capital so as to produce food and housing at the least cost.

Not all land has the same qualities. Some is especially suited for growing crops. However, this same land may also be good for building houses. The examples below demonstrate two propositions that are either overlooked or denied by farmland preservationists. First, the private market will normally guide developers to use land less suited for crops when it is in society's interest to do so. Second, it may be in society's interest for the developer to use the good farmland and induce the farmer to take up an alternative plot of land, even when such a plot has poorer farming qualities.

Assume only two sites. Suppose that site A has a present value of $10,000 for use in agriculture (i.e., it would sell for that amount if it were forever restricted to agricultural use), while adjoining site B has a present value under the same conditions of $4,000. Site B is less desirable because it is hilly, thereby requiring more capital-intensive conservation and production measures than A to produce the same output. Now assume that a housing developer must choose between A and B.

If the cost of constructing a house is the same on both sites, the developer will choose B, since its cost to him will be lower. It need not be exactly $6,000 lower, for there may be competition among developers. But if only one site will be developed, B will always be cheaper and thus more attractive to the builder. This establishes the first proposition, since society has preserved its resources solely by the actions of profit-seeking developers.[5]

To illustrate the second proposition, take the same situation but suppose that in order to build houses on site B the developer must incur larger capital expenditures for grading, drainage, fuel cost, and sewerage than he would have to endure on site A. If this differential is greater than $6,000, it will be in both the developer's interest and society's interest to acquire site A and build there.[6] For example, suppose that choosing B would cost the builder $8,000 more in capital costs than would choosing A. Since it would cost the farmer only $6,000 to move to B to produce the same goods, society would save $2,000 by allowing the builder to acquire A.

One might object that because the farmer must now move to site B and incur greater expenses in farming there, it is possible that food prices may rise (depending also on demand). But the alternative advocated by farmland preservationists, which would require the builder to go to the less desirable site, would result in an even more damaging increase in housing costs.

Note that this example does not depend on the value of housing itself. It holds regardless of whether the houses built are mobile homes or mansions. It is housing's high value of capital to land that leads many people erroneously to believe that developers can disregard agricultural land values.

The skeptical reader may object that this is not the way it usually happens. More often the farmer goes out of business or retires when he gets a good offer, so that site B is not used anyway.[7] But the argument does not depend on there being a particular alternative site. Site B may be many miles away, and the farmer who is induced to take it up for agriculture may never have met the developer or the farmer who left the business. He only knows that the price of agricultural products has risen sufficiently that this new land is worth the necessary investment to cultivate it. As he does so, he increases the supply of agricultural products and thereby drives the price down again.

There is an even happier scenario than this Ricardian outcome. Most farming is subsidized by the government. The amount of the subsidy is usually tied to agricultural prices (Gardner 1981). The higher the price the less the payment needed to maintain "parity" and the less taxpayers have to hand over to farmers. As land is withdrawn from production, prices go up, but the subsidies go down, leaving the cost to consumers the same. Consumers and farmers are no worse off, and taxpayers are much better off. Although in fact land withdrawals from urbanization are trivial, the reader may want to ponder the paradox of worrying about losing farmland while paying farmers not to use the land they have.

13.4. IRREVERSIBILITY AND FUTURE GENERATIONS

One drawback of the model in the previous section is that it does not address the "irreversibility" of urban development. As I think the data show, even if urban development is irreversible, we are such a long way from having to worry about it that it is hard to take it seriously. But like many other conservation issues, the question of what will happen decades from now requires some response. There are two: questioning the whole idea of irreversible development; or, accepting the concept, drawing analogies to the economics of the depletion of nonrenewable resources.

It would be expensive, but not impossible, to tear down houses and use urban spaces for agriculture (Bradshaw and Chadwick 1980, 261). But this falls into the category of extremist imagery. A more benign view of suburban housing tracts on former cropland is to regard them as conversion from one agricultural use to another. The structures and pavements themselves take up only a fraction of the total area. Much of the rest is in lawns, ornamental shrubs, shade and fruit trees, and flower and vegetable gardens which, if they were grown by commercial enterprises, would be called agricultural uses. One might without being too whimsical point to the suburban backyard as a marvelously decentralized method of hedging against high food prices.[8]

For those who nonetheless wish to take the irreversiblity assumption seriously, there is a simple analogy between "loss" of agricultural land and the exploitation of a finite amount of some nonrenewable resource such as oil. There is an extensive economic literature on this, almost all of it stemming from Harold Hotelling's classic article on the problem (1931).

Hotelling proved that competitive private ownership of a known and nonrenewable resource with fixed extraction costs would result in a socially efficient depletion rate. The optimal path of exploitation would set the growth rate of prices equal to the rate of interest. Private owners of rural land near cities have incentives to follow this path. If prices for urban land grew faster than interest, it would pay owners of rural land to sell less this year and more next year. This would raise prices this year and lower them next year, until the percentage spread between prices now and later equaled the interest rate.

There are, however, a number of factors that might cause farmers in such situations to sell to developers too soon. Interest rates may be "too high" in that the private discount rate may be higher than some ideal social discount rate. This applies to all capital projects as well as resource use. It may be an argument for not taxing interest or other income from savings, for these taxes are the wedge raising perceived interest rates. There is no obvious reason to apply this remedy selectively to farmland and not other assets.

It has also been suggested that property taxes might cause owners of rural land to sell to developers too soon. The economic merits of this argument are still being debated,[9] but nearly every state has gone ahead and reduced taxes on farmland and other open space. If it does turn out that full market value land taxation encourages premature conversion to urban use, it is currently of little policy significance.

A third and usually neglected factor that may cause farmers to sell out too soon is their anticipation of agricultural zoning regulations that would reduce the value of their land. If farmland owners thought that in five years the township in which they resided would adopt zoning ordinances that would not allow them to develop their land, they might hustle to find a developer to sell to right away.

In closing this section, I reemphasize my skepticism of applying the fixed resources model to conversion of farmland. There is nothing wrong with the internal logic of the model; it is just the notion of farmland as a fixed, nonrenewable stock that is unrealistic. Farmland preservationists implicitly agree with this. They express concern about loss of production due to the "impermanence syndrome," in which farmers anticipating development stop maintaining their land. The notion that land needs continuing investment to maintain its value belies the image of farmland as a nonrenewable resource. As for the merits of the concern, should farmers use resources to maintain land that will shortly be out of production?

13.5. FARMLAND CONVERSION IN THE URBAN MODEL

A more useful way to look at the agricultural land issue is in a spatial context. This is provided by the simple urban economics location model from the last chapter. Figure 26 is the same as figure 25 in the last chapter, except that it does not show the effects of suburban zoning. The curve R_u is the rent-distance function for urban land uses. These uses are here assumed to be mutually exclusive with agriculture.

The simple urban model is, as before, constrained at its outer

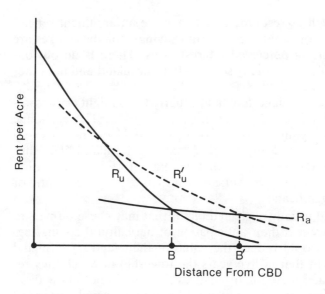

Figure 26. Urban and Agricultural Rent-Distance Curves

boundary by the rent for agricultural purposes, curve R_a in figure 26. Point B is the outer boundary of the urban area. Outside of this boundary, the maximum that households will pay for land is less than what farmers would pay (or accept as payment). A developer would not find it profitable to buy land and put up houses outside B, because households would not pay both the agricultural rent and their increased commuting costs.

This model indicates that farmers can outbid developers. There are two reasons why this contention is not intuitively obvious. One is that most farmland is already owned by farmers. Thus the only transaction that we observe is when developers buy farmland. We do not observe the nontransaction that proves my point: a developer makes an offer for farmland that is refused because it is too low.

The other reason is that average developed land prices are so high compared with farmland values. The average is deceiving here as elsewhere in economics. At the margin of development a subdivider must decide how large a lot to sell. Where land is cheap, he will follow consumer tastes for larger lots. Where it is dear, he will put the houses on small lots. The relatively small lots in many suburban developments in California's Central Valley, whose farmland is among the most valuable, is consistent with this result.

There is more systematic evidence on the constraining effects of agricultural land rents on the amount of suburbanization. Edwin Mills (1972) used a numerical analysis of an urban economics model of a city of 1 million to test the sensitivity of various constraints on it. He found that a 20 percent increase in agricultural rents caused a 9 percent decrease in the land area of the city, while a 20 percent decrease in R_a caused a 24 percent increase in urban area. Brueckner and Fansler (1983) found that the density of small Urbanized Areas varied directly with the value of farmland in the counties in which the UAs were located. While the simplifying assumptions of the urban model and data limitations preclude confidence in the exact magnitudes of these results, they show that the role of agricultural rents in determining the extent of urban development should not be ignored, since national variations in average farmland prices surrounding metropolitan areas are substantial.

The dramatic difference between average urban and average agricultural land prices probably contributes to the widespread belief that rising urban land values affect the value of *all* farmland. It is clear that rural land values *near* large urban areas are affected by the potential for development (Chicoine 1981; Peterson 1978). Farmland value may also rise because proximity to urban areas enables farm families to commute more easily; most farm households have at least one member who has a nonfarm job. But given that urban areas occupy only 3 percent of U.S. land area, it is implausible that all farmland should be affected by development potential. This is consistent with the data of Smith and Raup (1982, 10), which show that the greatest gains in Minnesota farmland values during the 1970s were *not* near large or growing urban areas and that the most valuable farm tracts were in rural areas, not near Minneapolis and St. Paul.

13.6. SUBURBANIZATION AND SUBSIDIES

The principal value of the urban model is not its static equilibrium conditions but the insights that it can provide into the process of suburbanization. Suburbanization has induced a relative shift in land values, with greater growth in the suburbs than in the center of the urban area. This shift is shown by the broken line designated R_u' in figure 26. The new equilibrium border between suburban and agricultural uses is now B'. Within this context we can discuss the issue of subsidies and sprawl.

13.6.1. Subsidies to Suburbanization

Has suburban development been subsidized to the extent that it takes a significant amount of agricultural land, thereby making B' farther out than it would be in a market in which all prices equaled marginal social cost? The literature on farmland preservation lists all manner of subsidies to suburban development (Raup 1975). In the context of figure 26 the result of these subsidies ought to be that the urban-rural boundary B' would be too far away. That is, we would have urban sprawl.

It is generally recognized that the two most important areas of subsidy are transportation and housing. Suburban housing is subsidized insofar as federal and state income tax provisions do not tax the imputed rent from owner-occupied housing, and ownership of these assets is further encouraged by making it easy to avoid capital gains taxes. Various mortgage guarantee programs of the federal government are also mentioned, but the magnitude of these programs is dwarfed by the tax subsidy (Aaron 1972). The net effect of these provisions has been to encourage ownership of suburban housing and so to contribute to an urban-rural border farther from the center than that which would have obtained in the absence of such a subsidy.

The effect of housing subsidies on the areal size of metropolitan areas probably is not large. The subsidy is to ownership of both land and capital, not just land; indeed, the subsidy can be had without even owning the land on which one's structure is located (as in condominiums and mobile homes). Even if the subsidy resulted in every U.S. household's consuming about a third more than current gross suburban lot sizes, this would take up an area equal to less than 4 percent of current cropland or less than 1 percent of the U.S. land area.

Federal highway programs are said to make decentralization more attractive. They are financed largely by motor fuel taxes, which fall short of the ideal user fee. It is nonetheless doubtful that marginal cost pricing of transportation facilities would have prevented much decentralization. Such hypothetical fees could hardly have been double the real price of fuel in 1970; yet real fuel prices nearly doubled during the 1970s, with little effect on long-term decentralization trends. There is thus little reason to believe that such subsidies have had an important effect on the amount of agricultural land converted to other uses.[10]

Suburbanization has been proceeding at least since the 1880s (Mills 1972; Warner 1971). Cities were spreading out before zoning was widespread, before the income tax made homeownership more attractive than renting, and before automobile ownership was widespread. This does not absolve these as potential causes of sprawl, but it does suggest that there is more behind the desire to live or operate in the suburbs than possibly perverse public policies.

13.6.2. Subsidies to Agriculture

I have so far discussed the subsidies for suburbanization and other forces that might push the ultimate urban-rural boundary out too far. But this falls into a one-sided approach. We should also ask whether the various subsidies to agriculture have not raised agricultural rents (R_a in figure 26) to the degree that B' might be too *close* to the center of the city.

This possibility was candidly suggested by Secretary of Agriculture Bob Berglund: "I see the benefits of many of our farm programs going not to improve the incomes of rural families needing help but contributing, instead, to higher and higher land prices" (Reinsel and Reinsel 1979). Among the programs that may boost farmland prices are tax breaks to farmers, price supports for farm commodities, and low-interest loans from the Federal Land Bank, whose real rates during parts of the 1970s were negative (Smith and Raup 1982). A serious evaluation of the role of the land market in determining the urban-rural boundary would have to account for such programs that may more than offset the subsidies to suburban development.

Another concern about the urban-rural boundary is that it may now be too far out because of the dramatic rise in housing prices in the 1970s. Real prices of housing did indeed rise, which would push out the boundary, other things equal. The trouble with this argument is that it, like the subsidies argument, neglects the other side of the boundary. During the 1970s, farmland and farm real estate prices rose even faster than did housing prices (Gardner 1977, Smith and Raup 1982). The reason was the dramatic and, it now seems, transitory increase in the world price of grain. This drove up the price of all farmland and may even have been part of the reason why housing prices rose (Ozanne and Thibodeau 1983, 65). There is no a priori reason to believe that inflation's effects have left the suburban boundary too far out.

13.7. URBAN-RURAL LAND USE CONFLICTS

The arguments of the previous sections indicate that there is no reason to be concerned about preserving farmland for its services in producing agricultural goods; that is, farmland is not a resource issue. But there are conflicts between farmers and residents who are not farmers in both suburban and rural areas. There may be reasons to be concerned about preserving farming in such areas even if farmland preservation is not a serious issue.

13.7.1. Moving to the Nuisance

Mixing residential and agricultural activities in the same area can produce conflicts. One cannot come up with an exhaustive list of such conflicts, since farming encompasses many different activities. Some crops may be damaged by air pollution. Traffic on rural roads is a hazard for moving farm equipment and animals. The presence of many nonfarming neighbors may increase vandalism—motorbikes going through fields, children harassing livestock.

The nuisances have their converse. Farming may interfere with residential activities. Pesticides may drift onto residential areas; livestock may get loose or be an attractive nuisance that endangers children; farm machinery and livestock are road hazards; the smell of manure piles may not be much admired; and the noise of early morning or late evening farm machinery may annoy residents.

The list of mutual incompatibilities raises a question: Why would the two activities ever locate near one another? In particular, why would a sensitive person "move to the nuisance" of commercial farming? A number of reasons will be suggested below, and within the context of these reasons, I shall discuss the role of zoning for agriculture.

One reason may be that the nuisances are not very substantial. It is my casual impression that farmers and nonfarmers in truly agricultural areas generally get along. In any event, given the small number of the parties involved, it would seem easy to make informal agreements to deal with various nuisances. Neighborliness is, after all, a prized virtue in rural areas.

13.7.2. Right-to-Farm Laws

A less benign view is that the newcomers are aware of the nuisances prior to arrival but believe that they can have them abated, at the farmers' expense, by nuisance suits or zoning laws. How often this occurs is not clear, but the problem has generated a legislative response in many states. "Right-to-farm" laws have been adopted in seventeen states and are a growing phenomenon (Coughlin and Keene 1981, chap. 5). These laws protect farmers from nuisance suits and regulations that would restrict their operations.

Right-to-farm laws provide unconscious confirmation of Coase's (1960) approach to the externalities problem. He suggests that it is normatively arbitrary and analytically counterproductive to identify one party in nuisance disputes as a "perpetrator" and the other as a "victim." Most zoning law is founded on the notion that homeowners are would-be victims of commercial establishments and other nuisance perpetrators. Right-to-farm legislation turns this notion upside down, making the commercial establishment—the farm—the victim of regulations passed by homeowners. Some polluters, it seems, are more equal than others.

Right-to-farm legislation may, however, have a role in resolving these conflicts. This is because most disputes in truly rural areas involve small numbers of people; thus the transaction costs of agreement seem lower. Bargaining may be facilitated in such a setting by a clear establishment of initial entitlements. Under right-to-farm legislation, it becomes clear that the developer or subsequent buyer must put up with the open manure pile (or other farm nuisance) unless he strikes a bargain with the farmer. This will save the cost of going to court and arguing about what really constitutes a nuisance.[11] It also will not make isolated rural sites artificially attractive.

Right-to-farm laws should not be adopted without some attention to their possible abuse. One can imagine, for example, a commercial developer bargaining for a rezoning for some subnormal use by threatening to establish an even more noxious farm use that is protected by right-to-farm legislation. The real-life example occurred in Stowe, Vermont, where a landowner's proposal for a motel was defeated after neighbors protested at state land use hearings. The landowner then established a pig farm on the site, piling manure close to the neighbors (*Burlington Free Press*, 10 November 1982, 1A). To guard against such strategies, three limitations are proposed.

First, the right to farm ought to be protected by a liability rule, not a property rule. Farmers ought to be forced to abate nuisances if neighbors or the local government unit is willing to pay for the cost of doing so. (This is consistent with the discussion of liability rules in section 9.5.)

Second, the right to farm should involve a flexible definition of normal farming operations. What is normal farming practice in viticulture is apt to be different from that in dairying and cotton growing. This suggests that a good deal of local control is necessary in designing such laws.

Third, right-to-farm legislation should apply to isolated rural areas, not to rural areas adjacent to towns and cities. In the latter places, the number of people affected by the nuisance is much greater and the gains to be had from strategic threats to use noxious activities are larger. Such a rule could be extended to all subnormal activities. Moving to the nuisance could be a defense for truly isolated or rural noxious activities but not for those immediately adjacent to expanding urban areas. This defense could reconcile requiring discontinuance of the polluting brick factory or dangerous quarry adjacent to the city with the greater judicial toleration of the smelly rural cattle feed lot.[12]

13.7.3. Agricultural Zoning

The other reason why suburban residents might move to rural nuisances is because they are unable to locate on open sites in the suburbs nearer to urban areas. As I indicated in the previous chapter, the most probable cause of this discontiguous development and excessive decentralization is the highly restrictive growth controls of many suburban communities.

Developing suburbs may use the farmland preservation arguments as an excuse to take large amounts of land off the market, putting it in a permanent agricultural zone and "guiding" growth to remote or costly sites. The irony is that this ultimately causes real conflicts between those who are displaced by this zoning and farmers in rural areas. The policy to prevent the conflicts between residents and farmers is to disallow the use of such zoning in areas that are appropriate for residential development.

This does not mean that all agricultural zoning should cease. In isolated rural areas such zoning may be appropriate to prevent damage by residents to farming operations. The type of nuisances foisted upon farmers by residential developments may be less amenable to nuisance laws and individual negotiation than nuisances emitted by farming. Agricultural districting could help to cluster new development. This in itself would shorten the perimeter between farms and residences and thus would reduce nuisance conflict. This may provide a rationale for zoning exclusively for agriculture in a large part of some *truly rural areas*.

It is important to recall that in these places, farmers are an influential minority if not a majority, so that the typical exclusionary interests of nonfarming homeowners are diluted and there is less of a possibility of legislation that especially burdens landowners. In such cases, commercial farming forms the standard of "normal behavior," and activities that impinge upon it may rightfully be regarded as "subnormal" (section 8.9).

This argument does not apply to most developing suburbs and

small towns. In these places, farmland owners are a small minority, and the use of strict agricultural zoning may be a means of preventing farmers from disposing of their land for developments similar to those occupied by the politically dominant homeowners. Like right-to-farm legislation, agricultural zoning improves land use only in areas that are in fact remote from areas of urban development.

13.8. AMBER WAVES OF GRAIN

The more plausible argument for agricultural land preservation is that it looks nice. This economic benefit conferred by farmers on passers-by and neighbors is not reflected in the prices they receive for their output. Thus they will fail to take this into account when responding to a developer's offer to purchase the land.

This view of farmland may provide a rationale for some type of public intervention. The benefits of looking at farmland are perceived by many people, but each one may understate his individual willingness to pay for such benefits. A collective arrangement may be required to overcome this free rider problem when the beneficiaries are numerous.

The marginal valuation of all goods, public as well as private ones, tends to decline as we have more of them. As a nation, we are in no sense running out of farmland; thus even if we agree that farmland looks nice, a tiny percentage loss should hardly require national responses. The issue is largely a local one. How does a residential community manage to persuade the owner of an attractive hillside apple orchard to leave it the way it is?

The way not to do it, if one accepts the taking criteria from chapter 8, is to zone the land exclusively for agriculture. The orchard is clearly supernormal land use, the orchard owner is easily identified, and the land is already being used for the activity in question, so transaction costs are low.

Compensation of the orchard owner does not require fee simple acquisition. One means of providing payment is to offer property-tax abatements for farmers or other landowners whose open space is deemed by the community to be a public good. There are a wide variety of such programs in nearly every state.

Under these tax abatement programs, some attractive farmland will continue to be converted to urban uses, despite all the encouragement not to. This conversion is often taken as evidence that such programs are failures, but this is not necessarily correct. The idea behind such subsidies to agricultural land is to make farmers perceive an additional opportunity cost to conversion to reflect the public's aesthetic regard for agriculture. Some farmers will thereby be induced to keep farming, but others will not. In order to keep more farmers in business, a larger subsidy would be required, and this is a cost that legislators seem reluctant to pay in most cases. Permitting exclusive agricultural zoning would reduce the cost to the legislature but not the cost to society as a whole.

Another means of compensating landowners is to lower their costs of operation by allowing them to continue locally offensive operations (say, using smudge pots). This may seem inconsistent with my previous recommendation that right-to-farm legislation should be limited to remote rural areas. In the present case, however, residents are assigned the initial entitlement to be free of nuisances. Such entitlements should be alienable. If resident-voters collectively want to sacrifice some of their local air quality for a nice view, that is their business.

The final means of preserving attractive land is to buy the development rights. A few exurban counties and communities have tried this (Wolfram 1981). Preservationists usually claim that development rights are too expensive, but in fact they may be too cheap. Public funds to purchase development rights are raised through the tax-exempt bond market, whose interest rates are lower than others. The community then repays the interest on the bonds from local property taxes, which are deductible from the federal income tax base. Hence, buying development rights is not as expensive for the average voter as it is for the average developer. That voters are nonetheless reluctant to do so suggests that the local benefits of farmland may not be very large.

13.9. FARMLAND PRESERVATION AS AN ENVIRONMENTAL ISSUE

It seems strange that many environmental organizations should actively promote farmland preservation. Few activities are more antithetical to the values expressed by these organizations than commercial farming. A modern farm is an applied chemical factory, and commercial farmers seldom tolerate the intermixing of other plants and wildlife that interfere with their crop or livestock. Farming is a major source of water and air pollution. By most environmental standards, the typical suburban tract is more benign than a commercial farm.

The answer to this puzzle may be that environmental organizations want to preserve existing farmland so that farmers will not elsewhere convert wildlands to farming. Although this effect must be on the second order of smalls compared with other factors in such decisions, it is at least consistent with environmental goals. A policy that would further this would urge "infilling" of bypassed suburban tracts. Some national environmental organizations, such as the Sierra Club, in fact support this policy.

The problem is that the local chapters of these organizations, as well as independent local environmental groups, often end up opposing all development, including infill development. The reason, I submit, is that the local groups are influenced by people who stand to gain from prevention of development in or near their communities. For these people, the environmental movement provides a useful legal organization and a high-minded rationale for excluding development (Frieden 1979).

This view of the function of local (as opposed to national) environmental organizations is relevant to a point I made in section 10.10. Some argue that environmentalism is politically far weaker than development interests because it is like a consumer movement: everyone benefits a little bit from environmental improvements, so few are willing to form a special-interest group to lobby for them. This is true for such widespread environmental improvements as reductions in water and air pollution and preservation of large tracts of scenic or wild areas.

It is not true, however, for many local land use issues. Homeowners in suburban areas have a financial interest in some aspects of local environmental issues. The equity in their homes represents a substantial fraction of their personal wealth. It is worth time and money to support organizations that will protect or increase it. Thus at the local level, one should expect environmental groups to be as well organized as developers and considerably more numerous, the ranks of the true believers being augmented by homeowner interests. This is not necessarily a criticism of such organizations. It may be that the only way to organize groups that will support national environmental goals is to tie these goals to the more parochial concerns.

13.10. CONCLUSION: GROUNDLESS CLAIMS

Farmland preservation is a canard. The farmland preservation movement's allegations about the amount of farmland lost to development are false, as are its assumptions about the nature of farming and the operation of the land market. There is no more reason for concern about the future stock of farmland than for other renewable resources.

The issue that deserves some public attention is not farmland but farming. Conflicts between farming and other activities may call for some public regulation. Exclusive agricultural zoning, with the possible exception of agricultural areas far from any centers of development, is inappropriate. Regulations specific to the nuisances and benefits involved are generally more efficient and equitable.

My opening contention was that the real purpose served by agricultural land protection is the rationalization of local restrictions on new development that would otherwise not pass judicial scrutiny. My method so far is to cast doubt about the explicit and implicit public justifications for these policies. I shall conclude this chapter by asking more directly about motives.

It is, of course, hazardous to impute motives to groups. One must rely on circumstantial evidence: those who most vigorously argue for agricultural land preservation also press for other exclusionary devices. The principal local method of preserving farmland is the same as that historically used to exclude development: the large minimum lot size, ranging up to 640 acres. This seems largely preferred to the idea of clustering rural developments, which would be better for farmers and would allow more housing.

The movement seems most vigorous in those affluent suburban and exurban areas that historically have been most exclusive. The local leaders of the movement are seldom full-time farmers. Some may pass for farmers, since it is so easy to qualify as one, but their main source of income is plainly from nonfarm sources. Landowners who are full-time farmers are usually opposed to regulations that would restrict the disposal of their major asset.[13] (Some of them may, however, be delighted to sell to local governments development rights that they are confident they will never use.)

The purveyors of the data and ideology of farmland preservation are largely soil conservationists. They are undoubtedly sincere. It must be especially encouraging that preservationism is so much more popular than traditional soil conservation issues. I believe that it is a major mistake to succumb to this popularity. It will reduce the scientific credibility of the real issues of soil conservation (Brown et al. 1982). Controlling wind- and waterborne soil erosion is an important public good.[14] Its importance ought not to be diminished by promoting unfounded fears about paving over America.

NOTES

1. In 1977 one-third of all U.S. cropland was used for exported crops (Berry 1983, 188). Protecting this was the major focus of the National Agricultural Lands Study (1981). A rebuttal of its *Final Report* by the research director of the NALS is Brewer and Boxley (1981). Brewer and Boxley are especially critical of projections of demand and supply that neglect prices as equilibrators (see also Raup 1982). A number of papers by members of the NALS research group (which had little influence on the *Final Report* and attendant publicity) also question some of the assumptions. These are published in Brewer (1981). Especially useful essays are those by Brown and Beale and by Boxley.

2. See Fischel (1982) and chap. 1, n. 1. Supporting my conclusion are Dunford (1983); Frey (1982); Hart (1984); Lee (1984); and Simon and Sudman (1982).

3. The Farmland Protection Policy Act of 1981 requires federal agencies to develop guidelines for evaluating their impacts on farmland. Whether this will evolve into a farmland equivalent of the National Environmental Policy Act is not clear at this writing.

4. The study actually counted only land not owned by the federal government, but ownership has little to do with physical standards of land quality.

5. For other models like the above see Gardner (1977) and, more technically, Arnott and Lewis (1979). The outcome in the text is consistent with Pyle (1982), which reports that 45 percent of the rural land in Olmstead County, Minnesota (Rochester SMSA), was in the top agricultural class, but only 28 percent of new development occurred on such land in the early 1970s, prior to farmland preservation efforts.

6. Two studies suggesting that such a differential may be very large are described in Dillman and Cousins (1982). On the other hand, homebuyers may prefer the hilly or scenic sites less suited for farming (Hart 1984).

7. A fine study of the Baltimore fringe areas by Peterson (1978) shows that life-cycle considerations are important in the decision to sell to non-farmers. But this does not negate the previous argument; Peterson's regressions show that "poor quality farmland, ceteris paribus, will be converted to alternative uses before top quality farmland" (p. 71). Sale of land to non-farmers does not mean conversion to urban uses. Brown, Phillips, and Roberts (1981) indicate that most urban fringe land changes from farm operator ownership to other owners twenty years prior to development.

8. An organization called Gardens for All (1981) conducts an annual poll of home gardeners. It found that in 1980, 43 percent of all households grew backyard vegetables, whose average retail value was about $460. Over the period 1970–80 the number of household gardens was found to be closely correlated with average food prices.

9. Bentick (1979) and D. Mills (1981a) find that land taxes are not neutral in this situation, but this is disputed by Tideman (1982).

10. This appears also to be the case for the other "subsidy," the lack of a congestion toll within urban areas (E. Mills 1980, 212).

11. For a skeptical view of such an approach see Bromley (1978). Why

not make the farmer liable for all nuisances, since he has better information about how to reduce them? The answer may be just that farmers are better represented in state legislatures, for reasons discussed in section 10.1.

12. The first two cases are Hadecheck v. Sebastian 239 U.S. 394 (1915), in which Los Angeles moved out to the brickyard, and Goldblatt v. Town of Hempstead 369 U.S. 590 (1962), involving a New York City suburb's gravel pit. The third case is Spur Industries v. Del Webb Development Co., 494 2d 700 (Ariz. 1972), involving a development near but not contiguous to Phoenix. The argument may be couched in terms of which party is better able to avoid the nuisance costs. When housing developers go to rural areas, they have many site options not available for development close to existing urban centers. The Arizona court's opinion suggests this line of reasoning.

13. The National Farm Bureau Federation and the National Cattlemen's Association, whose members are full-time commercial farmers, opposed national legislation to preserve farmland for this reason (Hite and Dillman 1981).

14. McConnell (1983) shows that farmland owners have sufficient incentives to prevent soil erosion to maintain productivity but not to prevent spillover effects. Swanson and Heady (1984) conclude that soil erosion is not likely to constrain agricultural production.

14.

Zoning, Property Taxes, and the Tiebout Model

A Pure Theory of Local Expenditures," by Charles Tiebout (1956), has become the touchstone of much of the theoretical and empirical literature in local public finance.[1] Although Tiebout mentioned zoning only in passing and the property tax not at all, his approach provided a framework for integrating analyses of property taxation, zoning, and location choice. The role of zoning cannot be understood without some knowledge of what is known as the Tiebout model. This chapter will describe this model and explore the implications of adding to it zoning and property taxation. The major implication is that the Tiebout model can promote efficiency in the provision of local public services, but it does not allow for local income redistribution. I shall also consider the effects of local competition for commercial and industrial property. Perhaps surprisingly, such competition may promote location efficiency without having adverse effects on income distribution.

14.1. THE TIEBOUT HYPOTHESIS

The problem that Tiebout addressed had been posed by Musgrave (1939) and Samuelson (1954). They had shown that no theoretical market solution existed to establish an efficient level of public goods. The failure of the market in their model was due to the absence of a mechanism to exclude people from enjoying the benefits of such public goods as national defense. Without such a mechanism, people who benefit from expenditures on defense have no incentive to reveal their true preferences for it.

Tiebout's response to this was to divide public expenditures into national public goods and local public goods. This is an important division. Aggregate state and local expenditures are about as large as federal government nondefense expenditures. Tiebout's objective was to present a model in which the provision of *local* public goods overcame the problem posed by Samuelson and Musgrave.

The model that Tiebout outlined corresponds to the highly fragmented government structure that one sees in most large metropolitan areas. His model requires many local governments among which well-informed consumers are fully mobile. These communities provide a predetermined package of public services—schools, parks, police services, roads, libraries—that consumers can obtain only by living there. Intermunicipal spillovers were assumed away, though Tiebout noted that even where they existed, the problem might be small because of a tendency for similar communities to be contiguous.

Tiebout's insight is that such a system potentially provides a market for public services. The marketlike behavior is that people will migrate among communities to select their preferred bundle of services. They will, in other words, vote with their feet. The trip to market to buy private goods is replaced by a trip to a community to buy or rent housing and jointly consume local public goods.

14.2. CONGESTION COSTS AND ZONING
IN TIEBOUT'S MODEL

The analogy between selecting a preferred community and selecting a market basket of goods was not enough, however, to get the efficient alternative that Tiebout sought. One problem was that communities might become inefficiently crowded, because Tiebout's local public services were not true public goods in the sense described by Samuelson and Musgrave.

Tiebout's goods were equally available to all in the community, but the cost of providing a given level of service per capita at first fell with community size and then rose because of congestion. This is a reasonable assumption, but its adoption makes suspect Tiebout's argument that he had found an alternative to the public goods problem. His alternative depended in part on changing the nature of the good.

Tiebout's community cost curve is illustrated in figure 27. The curve AC is cost per household for the provision of a *given level* of services, say, a local park. At populations less than N_1, the

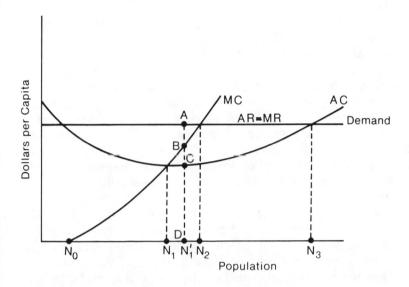

Figure 27.   Community Size and Location Rents

average cost of accommodating additional households declines. This is because for small populations the park is a pure public good: an additional household's enjoyment of the park does not detract from another's, nor does such use add to the costs of maintaining the park.

If the park were a pure public good, the per capita cost of providing parks, AC, would continue down towards the horizontal axis. There would be no reason to attempt to exclude anyone and no reason to have more than one community. This discussion does not address the issue of how big or how good a park is to be provided. A bigger community might decide to provide a better park for its residents as the cost per household fell. This does not affect the result we are aiming at here, though.

Empirical evidence indicates that most local services are not really pure public goods (Bergstrom and Goodman 1973; Gramlich and Rubinfeld 1982). Eventually the presence of more people does lower the enjoyment of the park by others. This point does not mean that population growth should stop. If the new people make an equal contribution to the average cost (assuming that all pay AC), the payment may outweigh the disadvantages of congestion. In figure 27, the initial congestion population is N_0, where additional people impose costs on others. But assuming that costs are spread around so that everyone pays AC, they are still welcome, as long as congestion costs (MC, marginal cost) are less than AC. Where $MC = AC$, AC is minimized at N_1.

Tiebout regarded N_1 in figure 27 as the optimal size of the community in that it minimized the cost of local services. This result is analogous to that obtained from the theory of the firm in a competitive market. To be efficient, firms should produce at minimum average cost. Recall, though, that Tiebout's minimum average cost implies a certain level of population for a given community. How is this level of population to be attained?

Tiebout's answer was that community authorities would encourage immigration at a population less than N_1, but would discourage, by the use of zoning, population growth beyond N_1. Tiebout was not explicit about how costs were shared among residents, but one can easily see why residents should want to get to N_1 if everyone shared equally in the financing of the services.

Thus the role of zoning in Tiebout's original formulation was to promote cost minimization in the supply of public goods. Despite its simplicity, the model provides an explanation for the tendency of suburban communities to adopt increasingly restrictive zoning ordinances. Rural communities near urban areas that are just beginning to develop may be below N_1, and their zoning laws reflect a willingness to accommodate development. As such communities grow and approach N_1, their zoning laws become more stringent.

14.3. LOCATION RENTS AND THE TIEBOUT MODEL

This section will amend Tiebout's formulation to accommodate location rents in an urban area.[2] I shall show that in some situations adherence to Tiebout's minimum AC condition does not promote efficiency. This will also enable me to point out the relationship between Tiebout's approach and the property rights approach.

Let us assume that the suburban community is but one of many in a large metropolitan area (e.g., a western suburb of St. Louis, as shown in map 1 in section 10.7). Thus it has no monopoly power. Let us assume, furthermore, that there is only one land use in the community, residential housing, and that the community's zoning laws are constrained by a rigid rule, namely: all new housing is on quarter-acre lots, which corresponds exactly to all developers' demands, or new housing is not permitted at all. The costs of a given level of local public goods are just as they were described in the previous section, which implies the U-shaped cost curve.

This situation is illustrated in figure 27 by the horizontal demand curve, AR. The demand is willingness to pay for the right to occupy a site in a suburban community. It is horizontal because there are a large number of communities like this one equidistant from the CBD, so that the supply of sites in any one has but a trivial effect on the total supply of sites in the area. Thus each new household is willing to pay average revenue (AR), which is also equal to marginal revenue (MR), since demand is perfectly elastic, for permission to locate in the community.

Given this situation, N_1 is no longer the efficient level of population for the community.[3] The efficient level is N_2, at the point where the MC curve intersects MR and AR. This means that the last household to move in is willing to pay exactly the amount that it costs the community in additional local services.

Consider a population less than N_2, such as N_1' in figure 27. At N_1' the community would be too small because the costs imposed on the whole community by the new resident would be the amount BD, while the perceived benefit of location by the prospective resident is AD. If the new resident could be induced to pay at least BD (but not more than AD), the community would not be worse off and the new resident would be better off. In other words, there are Pareto improvements in social welfare to be had at N_1' by increasing community size.

If it were the rule that all residents must share costs equally, meaning that all would pay their average cost, then population growth would not exceed N_1. (Uniform assessment of property values would correspond to such a rule in the present model, since everyone owns the same amount of housing in the community.) The reason is this: at N_1' the new residents pay average cost (CD), while they impose larger marginal costs equal to BD. The rest of the community loses (via the subsidy to the new development) amount BC, the difference between average and marginal cost. Faced with such a possibility, the community will zone out all development after achieving N_1.

Thus minimum average cost per capita may not correspond with the optimal community size where there are location rents, which includes most suburban locations. The analysis also shows why equal cost-sharing arrangements within such communities might cause zoning to be too restrictive. We can also see why some public controls may be necessary. Without them, new residents would make their location decision based on AC. Thus community growth would only stop at N_3 in figure 27. The community would be inefficiently large in this case.

14.4. TIEBOUT, PROPERTY RIGHTS, AND MONOPOLY ZONING

This section will point out the formal similarities between the modified Tiebout analysis in the last section and the property rights approach developed in chapters 5–7.[4] Refer to figure 28, which reproduces the marginal cost curve and the marginal revenue line from figure 27. The marginal cost curve is relabeled as the marginal benefit (MB) to the community (of excluding residential sites). Community benefit is maximized at N_0 and minimized at the far right border. The horizontal marginal revenue curve is relabeled as the marginal benefit to landowners (of developing additional sites). We assume that the benefit accrues to the owners of the sites, since new residents must pay them to locate in the community. Total benefits to landowners increase with population, but at a constant rate, so that their MB "curve" is horizontal.

The maximum total benefit to the community and landowners taken together is at N_2. This is for reasons identical to those used in the analysis of the Coase theorem in section 5.2. A move to the right or the left of N_2 causes one party to lose more than the

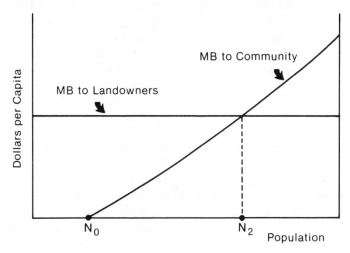

Figure 28. Community Size and Property Rights

other gains. Thus our analysis of the Tiebout model with rents is formally identical to the property rights approach.

There are expositional differences between the present analysis of residential development and the analysis of suburban behavior in section 7.2. Here we assume a special situation, where only one intensity (quarter-acre lots) of land use is demanded, so the landowners' MB curve does not decline with development. Moreover, we are dealing here with many landowners rather than with a single, representative site. The formal results are nonetheless the same. The optimal population of the community is the point at which the two MB "curves" intersect, N_2.

The omission of the AC curve in figure 28 is intentional. It is not important for a general analysis, for it assumes a particular cost-sharing scheme. The general question for attaining optimal community size is, Are there institutional devices by which newcomers can pay their full marginal costs to the current residents, who are entitled to limit development? Any limitation on such transactions, whether it is the requirement that there be average cost pricing or inability to charge for rezonings, will tend to make the population too small, just as I argued in section 7.3.

The analogy of the Tiebout model to the property rights model may illuminate the issue of monopoly zoning from section 7.7. I argued there that a community that possessed a monopoly position in the metropolitan area could potentially perceive an additional gain to restraining development. However, this was difficult to show in an analysis that focused on a single, representative landowner. Now, however, land use in an entire community is shown, albeit under restrictive institutional assumptions.

Assume that the demand for locating in a community is downward-sloping, as shown in figure 29.[5] This demand is the marginal benefit to prospective households of locating in that community rather than somewhere else. This benefit will be reflected in bids for the land and thus will accrue to competitive landowners. A monopolist, however, perceives that demand is downward-sloping, and thus it is seen as its average revenue curve rather than as the marginal revenue curve. If the community is in this monopoly position, its authorities perceive a marginal revenue curve (MR) *below* the demand curve. In the monopoly situation, community authorities will see that the profit-maximizing point is the intersection of the MR and MC curves. This occurs at population N_1 in figure 29. This is below the optimal population, N_2.

Population N_1 in figure 29 does not necessarily correspond with

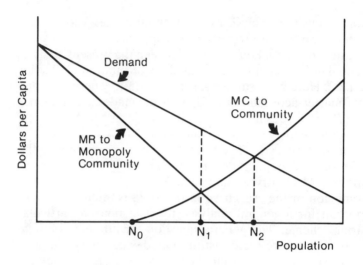

Figure 29.   Monopoly Community's Size

the suboptimal population N_1 in figure 27. In the earlier analysis, N_1 was too small because the community had to charge average costs rather than marginal costs to newcomers and thus admitted too few. In the present situation, the community can charge newcomers whatever it wants, but with its monopoly position it charges too much. It is of course empirically difficult to distinguish between the two reasons for excessive growth controls or to discern which effect is worse as far as prospective residents are concerned. The analysis reinforces the conclusion from section 7.9 that economists ought not to jump to the conclusion that monopoly motives are involved when communities restrict growth excessively.

The Tiebout model, then, is a special version of the property rights model developed earlier. Tiebout's approach has the advantage of showing the analogies between the local public sector and other branches of economics and of dealing with them in terms familiar to other economists. But it has the disadvantage of causing researchers to focus on a narrow set of municipal finance considerations. This in turn encourages them to think in terms of "fiscal" zoning as opposed to some other kind, a distinction that is not especially useful (section 2.4). It also has led to a line of research that has attempted to evaluate zoning's effectiveness solely in terms of fiscal considerations. As I argued in section 7.1, such considerations explain only partly why a community might adopt a particular zoning policy. Nonetheless, one result of this line of inquiry is sufficiently intriguing to merit more extensive discussion in the following section.

14.5. HAMILTON'S HYPOTHESIS: THE PROPERTY TAX IS EFFICIENT

An important extension of the Tiebout model was made by Bruce Hamilton (1975). Tiebout's approach emphasized the problem of supplying public goods at minimum cost. The role of zoning was to prevent these costs from rising beyond that which they would be at the optimal community size. Implicit in this approach was the assumption that each person in the community contributed the same amount to finance these goods. Tiebout never mentioned the property tax, which is in reality the mainstay of local government finance.

Hamilton introduced the property tax into Tiebout's basic model and came up with a remarkable result. When combined with a plausible species of zoning behavior, the property tax is an efficient tax, at least in suburban communities.[6]

To be efficient a tax must gather into the public sector exactly the resources that are withdrawn from the private sector. The cause of inefficiency in taxation is the incentive for those who are taxed to modify their behavior so as to avoid paying so much tax. In the Tiebout-Hamilton model, inefficient avoidance behavior is made impossible through the judicious use of zoning.

Rather than focus on some generalized municipal service subject to congestion, Hamilton looked at the real world and noted that the principal local public service is education. A good argument can be made that the cost per pupil of a given level of education is constant, at least in the long run. Thus the problem of exclusion is not related so much to overall size of the jurisdiction as it is to the arrangements for financing the goods in question.

The suburban residential community of Richdale, for example, has houses whose average value is $100,000. They are assessed at full market value. Each household has one child in school in a given year, and school expenditures per child are $3,000. The tax rate per house is thus 3 percent. The school quality is excellent. A family of more modest means sees this and buys some land in Richdale and builds a modest house valued at $50,000. With the 3 percent tax, the newcomer pays only $1,500 in school taxes but receives $3,000 in school services. There is a transfer of $1,500 from the affluent citizens of Richdale to the less affluent.[7]

The means by which Richdale residents can avoid this transfer is to zone any undeveloped land in such a way that a house valued at no less than $100,000 can be built. While no zoning law explicitly can set a minimum value, section 4.4 showed that such devices as minimum lot sizes and floor area ratios can see to it that this standard is met.

Consider the efficiency implications of this practice. Zoning has established a minimum standard for new housing equal to the current average of the community. If this minimum is not exceeded, the new residents must pay in property taxes an amount exactly equal to their household's consumption of school services. In the current example that is $0.03 \times \$100,000 = \$3,000$, but the result in no way depends on a particular value for tax rates, house value, or school services.

The property tax is thus perfectly efficient under Hamilton's model. People cannot avoid paying for the local public services they get, since zoning requires a minimum house value. But is not the inefficiency just pushed on to another sector of the economy? Suppose that a family willing to pay $3,000 per year for education is not willing to pay $100,000 for a house. Hamilton's answer is to go back to Tiebout's voting-with-one's-feet market place and modify it slightly. If there are enough communities, there will be a wide variety of houses and local services among them. Thus a household that demanded a $3,000 education but only a $50,000 house could live in the town of Academia, where taxes are 6 percent, instead of Richdale. Similarly, those who demand only minimum educational expenditure and low-cost housing could live in Poorville, where both house values and tax rates are low.

Hamilton's shopping trip would seem to require many more communities than Tiebout's. This problem is mitigated in that demand for education and demand for housing are likely to be closely correlated. Thus if a household seeks a community with houses of a certain value, it is likely that educational and other local government services will be close to the amount that the household would have demanded had they been offered as separate bundles of goods.

14.6. THE TIEBOUT MODEL AND THE SUBURBAN WALL

There is now an extensive empirical literature on the Tiebout hypothesis and Hamilton's extension of it. Much of it asks whether the basic assumptions of Tiebout's model are met. It is clear that many large metropolitan areas have enough local governments to provide several choices for households (section 10.7). The model also assumes that households must be mobile among communities. This does not require that they be willing to move at a moment's notice; most people move in response to employment and life-cycle changes. At each of these moves comes the opportunity to select not just housing but also a community. Many empirical studies have established that housing purchasers are aware of differences in taxes and the quality of services among communities.[8]

Many studies of the Tiebout model founder on what the appropriate comparison is. Should the standard be a world in which all local public services are provided on the private market or one in which all local public services are provided by a single level of government? Most studies that use the former model as a benchmark find the Tiebout model wanting (Epple, Zelenitz, and Visscher 1978). However, it would seem that for most policy purposes it is the second comparison that is appropriate. Tiebout's original question aside, his model seems to ask whether centralized or fragmented local government structure is preferable.

A direct approach to testing the Tiebout-Hamilton model is to ask whether suburban communities are in fact stratified by economic characteristics of their households. Hamilton's theory emphasized the connection between household income and demand for local public services. This leads us to expect that a system of locally provided public services financed by the property tax would result in each community's being homogeneous with respect to household income and other characteristics. We would expect this to happen in part because zoning regulations make it possible to exclude housing for lower-income people.

This empirical test is discussed at greater length here because it is related to the charge that suburban zoning contributes to income and social segregation within the metropolitan area. I refer to this charge as the "suburban wall" theory because it sees the suburbs surrounding central cities as a wall that excludes the central city poor. Such income segregation, however, seems to be a necessary condition of the Tiebout hypothesis.

There is a difference between the Tiebout hypothesis and the suburban wall theory. The Tiebout hypothesis requires a large number of different suburbs. The suburban wall theory requires only two different communities, a central city and an independent suburban jurisdiction. The Tiebout model would actually mitigate the suburban exclusion process. This is because when there are many suburban communities, they may have different packages of housing and public services and thus different zoning standards. In a fragmented metropolitan area, some suburbs may exclude the poor, but others may not, or they may at least be less vigorous in their exclusion.

Yet the possibility of choosing among several communities will not really answer the charge that suburban zoning excludes the poor. A crucial consequence of the Tiebout-Hamilton model is that it is not possible to redistribute income from the rich to the poor through a local government except insofar as the rich communities want to do some voluntary redistribution. For this reason we must consider the evidence that suburban zoning really results in substantially homogenized communities.

14.7. EVIDENCE OF SUBURBAN HOMOGENEITY

Much of what is written on suburban homogeneity often better serves as evidence of statistical illiteracy. More than once have I read that the suburbs must be exclusionary because the average price of a new house there is clearly beyond the 25 percent of annual income most households spend on housing.[9] Let us enumerate the statistical sins: (1) An average means that some are higher and some are lower. One surely wants to know something about the variation in housing values. (2) Twenty-five percent or any other percent of current income is not a moral or legal constraint (Weicher 1980, 22). Many young couples spend much more on their first house, confident that as their incomes rise and their equity grows, mortgage payments and property taxes will shrink to more manageable proportions of their income. (3) Not everyone lives in a new house. Given how long they last, houses are usually best built expensively so that they do not deteriorate too fast. (4) A house's value, which is what is invariably quoted, is not the same as its price (section 11.2). If price went down, expenditure would go up if demand were price-elastic, so that high values in the suburbs might be consistent with lower prices.

Despite their reliance on dubious statistics, open-suburbs advocates are correct in that suburban zoning does exclude at least some of the poor from areas where they would otherwise have chosen to live. There is, however, a serious challenge to the idea that zoning promotes income or class segregation. Janet R. Pack and Howard Pack (1977; 1978) developed a statistical test for homogeneity for a sample of Pennsylvania suburbs. They then determined whether the communities seemed homogeneous with respect to several demographic variables, such as education, income, household type, occupation, and age. Their findings indicate that suburbs are far more heterogeneous than most people who address either the exclusionary zoning issue or the Tiebout model would lead one to expect. If suburban zoning is intended to preserve a homogeneous community population, it does not appear to work very well.

Two responses may reconcile the Packs' findings with the widely perceived notions of suburban zoning's effects. First, the heterogeneity they detected may be more statistical than real. This is caused by life-cycle considerations. A community composed of people with identical lifetime incomes might nonetheless appear at a given time to have a substantial amount of variation in annual incomes. This is caused by temporary gains or losses in income by people of the same age and by the fact that in any community there will be people of different ages. By making dwellings sufficiently expensive to construct, suburban authorities can exclude people with low lifetime earnings. But a fledgling doctor with low current earnings will surely be able to borrow money to buy a house there on the strength of future income. A retired person with low current income but no mortgage or childcare expenses may continue to maintain a home there.[10]

The other way to reconcile the Packs' results with the Tiebout model is to look more closely at the process of zoning. Zoning is not a static device. Suburban communities become increasingly restrictive as they develop (section 4.4.2). The increasing tendency of zoning to exclude lower-income people is difficult to determine by looking at the overall pattern, which is the product of a history of changing land use controls. The Packs have discovered that average homogeneity is not strong, but that may still be consistent with considerable marginal homogeneity enforced by current zoning laws.

14.8. COMMERCIAL AND INDUSTRIAL PROPERTY IN THE TIEBOUT MODEL

My extension of the Tiebout model introduces commercial and industrial land uses.[11] This adds a new dimension to the issue of zoning, property taxation, and local environmental quality. Section 4.3 showed that community authorities must be satisfied that prospective commercial or industrial firms will compensate residents for nuisances that they do not find profitable to abate. In suburban communities, the main means by which such compensation can be made is payment of property taxes in excess of services directly consumed. My basic proposition is that at least part of the property taxes paid by firms represents side payments for neighborhood effects and that such a system of side payments promotes economic efficiency both in the location of firms and in the provision of local environmental quality. In short, the property tax is partly a local tax on pollution.

My model for business location assumes that firms behave as households do in Tiebout's model. They are mobile and capable of shopping around various suburban communities to find the best mix of local services, in addition to desirable sites on which to conduct their operations. However, firms differ from households in two important respects. First, they usually create more nuisances in the community. These include traffic congestion, unattractive structures and parking lots, and perhaps additions to litter, crime, fire hazards, and pollution. Second, because they do not come with school children attached, they are capable of paying more in property taxes than they receive in local services. The second feature makes it possible for firms to compensate local residents for the first feature, the nuisances. This creates another marketlike situation.

Communities may be thought of as suppliers of sites to the firms. The firms are willing (not eager) to pay the communities for the local nuisances they create because they value permission to locate there. Because there are many communities, the firms can shop around among them to ensure that they will not have to pay too much for their use of the community's environment. The community's right to exclude the firms (by zoning) ensures that they will not pay too little.

Thus there is competition for the firms among communities in the metropolitan area. The nature and outcome of this is often misunderstood. The competition among communities eliminates *excessive* compensation by firms to the community. There are still gains to the community from the exchange of a development permit for taxes or other perceived benefits from industry. Of course, all communities would like to get more fiscal benefits from firms for the same or less sacrifice of residential amenities, but that is true in any market. The question is whether some sort of monopoly or cartel of communities would be preferable to this competitive process.

The advantage of competition among communities is that it keeps the cost of producing the firms' goods low. If the cost of any factor of production that the firms use is raised, the cost of the goods they produce will be increased. The use of the local environment is a factor of production, just like labor, raw materials, and machinery. For efficiency, it should be paid for, not given away for free. But the community should not, on the other hand, be overpaid for use of its environment. Imposing a price higher than marginal cost (to residents) for community environment will cause the value of the firm's production to fall by more than the value of local amenities will increase.

14.9. FISCAL BENEFITS FROM BUSINESS PROPERTY

It is often argued that fiscal benefits from firms are not empirically evident. This section will show why the benefits may be difficult to detect. Figure 30 represents the trade-off that a voter in a community perceives between private goods (assumed to be income after federal and state taxes) and local public services (Bradford and Oates 1971). In the initial situation, the voter perceives a budget line AB between these two types of goods. Assume that point W is chosen. The voter gets OE in local public services and pays AD in local property taxes. (This means that amount OD is left over for private goods.)

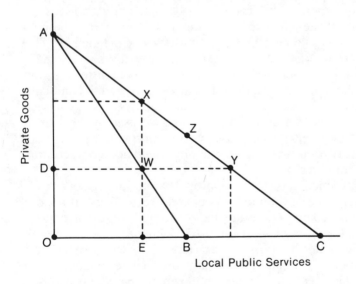

Figure 30.   Effects of Nonresidential Tax Base

In the comparison situation, a large amount of commercial and industrial property is allowed into the community. Suppose for simplicity that its aggregate assessed value exactly equals the former residential assessed value. This changes the perceived budget line of the representative voter. For the same amount of taxes that he paid in the initial situation (AD), he can now get twice as many public services. His new budget line is AC, where C is twice as far from the origin as B. Because of uniform assessment rules, voters must tax residential property to get any benefits from business property. In other words, the perceived "tax price" of local public services has been cut in half.

We cannot tell what voters will choose in this new situation. They could have the same level of local services as before and just lower their taxes. This would be point X. Thus the fiscal benefits would appear to be amount XW, the reduction in property taxes. (The firms would like this, too, but we assume that they knew what would happen to taxes once they made their decision to locate in the community.)

At the other extreme, the voter may prefer to keep taxes the same and move to a point such as Y, getting WY in additional local public services. In this case, a researcher who focused exclusively on local tax rates might conclude that firms convey no benefits. But it is not so: the voters simply chose to take benefits in additional public services—say, better schools, a public swimming pool, a new park—instead of additional private goods.

Faced with new industrial or commercial property, the community will most likely choose a point such as Z in figure 30. They will take some of the fiscal benefits as lower taxes and some as more local public services. Point Z is not all benefit for the community, though. It has sacrificed some of its residential ambiance to have the firms locate there, and some of the local public services may go simply to offset the local nuisances caused by these firms. Nonetheless, it seems safe to assume that most voters prefer point Z to point W; otherwise the community would not have permitted the firms to enter.

The introduction of business property into the Tiebout model may offset some of the model's apparent regressivity. It appears that lower-income people are more inclined to accept nonresidential property, particularly industrial activities, than are wealthier people. Thus one offset to the Tiebout system's exclusion of income transfers is that it does allow low-income communities to increase their tax (and perhaps employment) base by being more accommodating to industry (Fischel 1976; Ladd 1976). Such activity was endorsed in dictum by the U.S. Supreme Court in a case upholding local financing of public schools: "Changes in the level of taxable wealth within any district may result from any number of events, some of which local residents can and do influence. For instance, commercial and industrial enterprises may be encouraged to locate within a district by various actions—public and private" (San Antonio Independent School District v. Rodriquez, 411 U.S. 1, 54 [1973]).

There is another advantage of community homogeneity. Since the nuisance effects of business uses are perceived equally within a neighborhood or community, it is preferable to have people with similar tastes grouped by geographic areas. If the rich and poor lived together in the same community, one or the other probably would be dissatisfied with the industrial zoning policies.

This approach also indicates that studies that focus on the effects of local tax rates on business location are not likely to turn up significant effects, not because tax rates are irrelevant, but because they are only part of the location decision. They affect a firm's demand for location in a community, but they do not directly affect the willingness of communities to supply (by zoning) sites to businesses. Noxious firms may end up in communities with high tax rates because they are unable to compensate residents in low-tax communities for their neighborhood effects.

14.10. COMPETITION FOR FIRMS AND LOCATION DISTORTIONS

This section evaluates some of the problems associated with the process described in the last two sections.

14.10.1. Central Cities' Losses

Competition in the supply of sites is said to be undesirable because it encourages the loss of firms from central cities, thus contributing to the decline in the tax base and employment opportunities there. This is a value judgment, since it indicates that tax base and employment are more important in central cities than elsewhere. But more is involved than that. It is worth asking *why* a firm might want to leave a central city location for a suburban location. There are two general categories of reasons.

The first is the general location advantage of the suburbs. For commercial firms this may be nearness to customers and the work force. For industrial firms this may mean easier access to highways or airports (as opposed to central city ports or railroads) and cheaper land on which to spread out continuous assembly lines. Preventing firms from leaving central cities denies them these cost-reducing advantages.

The other reason might be just that central cities demand taxes from the firms in excess of their social costs. Given the subsidies and tax breaks often offered to businesses by central cities, it is not clear that this is in fact the case. But if it is, forcing them to stay there may harm the consumers of their products, since they will have to pay higher prices as a result.

14.10.2. Limiting Subsequent Residential Development

A problem with the property tax as a means by which firms can compensate the community is the fiscal incentive for communities to become more exclusive with respect to housing when new industry arrives. A simple example will show the problem. A community with property tax base per household of $40,000 gets a large industrial plant that raises the tax base to $60,000 per household (that is, the plant pays one-third of the town's taxes). Now the fiscal incentive for the community is to allow only houses worth $60,000 to be developed, so as not to dilute the tax base. But since few such houses would be developed, this prevents workers in the factory from locating there.

Is this such a bad result? The literature on externalities has been concerned with the problem of people's moving to the nuisance. Here is a process that prevents it. The real problem with the process is that the firm has not been permitted to compensate only the preexisting residents with a lump sum. By paying for their nuisance effects with a stream of taxes, the firms pay all subsequent residents as well as the residents present when a decision was made to allow the firm in.

This represents a defect in the assignment of property rights. Communities have the right to exclude new residents, but if they allow them in, they cannot prevent them from enjoying the stream of income provided by the firms. Voters may, as a result, choose to exclude new residents unless they pay more in taxes to offset the dilution of the tax base.

Some reform proposals that have addressed this issue suggest that communities that get industry should also be required to zone for new housing for workers (Bergman 1974). The idea is that people who work in a community ought to be able to live there too. This would seem to deny communities the advantages of specialization; each would, over time, have to mimic the land use patterns of the entire metropolitan area. However one feels about this, the proposed reform may not accomplish its desired end. Rather than accept firms with workers, suburban communities would simply rezone the land to prevent firms from entering at all.

There is something suspect in the assumptions of this policy, too. Why would firms locate in places where their employees could not? If they were to do so, they would have to pay higher wages to attract the workers there (section 5.6). Presumably they take this into account when they relocate their facilities.

14.10.3. Moving away from Employees

There is one possible exception to the aforementioned rule that firms' self-interest can be relied upon to keep them from choosing remote locations where their employees are not permitted to live. This may occur when the firm must pay its workers a wage in excess of the value of their marginal product. Such a constraint may be imposed on the firm by effective labor unions or by government regulations.

A firm faced with such a wage constraint has a number of options. One is to move its plant to a nonunion area within the United States or abroad. But some firms might be especially tied to a particular metropolitan area. One way they can adjust is to move to a remote suburban location. This move does not reduce the nominal wages that the firm must pay, but it does reduce the real wages of the workers, because they must commute more. If the commute is long enough, the workers' real wages will be cut to the competitive wage rate.

The firm does not cut its workers' real wages for spite. It moves to economize on land rents. Although it loses some of the advantages of being in a central location, the decentralization enables it to substitute low-cost land for high-cost labor. (It may also have the further advantage of economizing on commuting costs of executives.) It would be even better, from the firm's point of view, if the community did not allow its workers to live there, for then the firm would save on taxes as well as land costs. The process might be called the "Mahwah effect," after the far suburban New Jersey community in which a Ford assembly plant located and which resisted efforts by the auto workers to rezone for moderate-cost housing.[12]

This process is wasteful. It results in excessive commuting and the loss of agglomeration economies in the urban area, since the firm is no longer near others. This hypothesis might form an efficiency-based rationale for metropolitan zoning programs designed to prevent firms from leaving central cities for the suburbs. But there are numerous barriers to such a program. The foremost is the absence of empirical studies to discover whether this motive is important. Moreover, it would be very difficult to distinguish between firms that wanted to move for the reason suggested here and those that wanted to move for efficiency reasons. Reducing the firm's mobility also affects its ability to negotiate more reasonable labor contracts. The threat of closing down or relocation is one bargaining device that management may use to keep a powerful union's (or government regulator's) demands in line with reality.

14.10.4. Intermunicipal Spillovers and Tax Base Sharing

A final objection to the competitive location process is that it does not account for intermunicipal spillovers. That is, a community that gets the firm and receives its tax benefits is satisfied with the compensation, but a neighboring community that endures some of the costs of the firm does not, under a purely local system, receive any compensation for the spillovers.

It should be pointed out that it is a problem in two ways. A community that creates benefits for people in other communities, such as improved employment and shopping opportunities, does not get compensated by the others. If we are going to be concerned with spillovers, we ought to look at beneficial as well as cost-creating spillovers of business.

Interjurisdictional spillovers are efficiency problems, but it is easy to exaggerate their importance. As I pointed out in section 5.6, most nuisances are fairly localized. The effects of industrial and commercial spillovers are likely to be perceived in but one or two jurisdictions. Thus one could expect that bilateral or trilateral arrangements could be made to compensate the communities not compensated via the property tax.

The existence of these spillovers requires compensation from one community to another, if the administrative costs of such a scheme do not consume most of the potential gains. It does not follow that *all* other communities ought to share in one community's fiscal gains. The latter objective motivated, in part, a Minnesota program that shares a portion of each community's new commercial or industrial tax base with other jurisdictions in the Minneapolis and St. Paul area (Fischel 1976; Fisher 1982). The present analysis suggests that most of these fiscal gains are not windfalls in the sense that the host community surrenders nothing to obtain them.

14.11. CONCLUSION AND RESEARCH NOTE

This exposition of the Tiebout model and its variations has been intended to show that the pattern of metropolitan land use engendered by the independent decisions of local governments may not be as irrational or chaotic as its many detractors would have one believe. The system of autonomous local governments, local property taxation, and zoning combine for some efficiency advantages in the production of local services and amenity values that may be lost in a more centralized system. The results of such a system may displease those with a desire for tidiness in the layout of cities, but they may conform reasonably well to the demands of those who live there. This is not to say that the system is beyond reform; it does suggest that the reforms that involve more centralization will involve a loss of some efficiency from local government.

This and previous chapters indicate that the economists' debate about the merits of the Tiebout model can be sharpened by narrowing the variety of institutional arrangements in the model. I suggest the following:

Most large metropolitan areas have a fragmented government structure. There are many communities from which to choose. However, the number is not indefinitely large. It is not easy to form one's own community. Models that rely entirely on a perfectly elastic supply of communities are suspect, and some types of communities may be scarce.[13]

All communities are subject to zoning. Models that seek to criticize the Tiebout model on migration grounds cannot ignore the possibility that zoning can control entry of firms and, less perfectly, households.[14] If excessive immigration is to be the focus of the critique of the Tiebout model, one must explain the defect with zoning that allows this to occur.

Finally, the mechanism by which public decisions are made in suburban communities closely approximates the conditions of the median voter model. One cannot assume without more specific information that the level of public services is exogenous to the model or that there will be persistent divergences between private demand for local services and their public supply.[15] Given the homogeneity of the population—evaluated in a way that accounts for life-cycle considerations—the Tiebout model gives an efficient level of public services within each community (Brueckner 1979; Edelson 1976). The critiques of the Tiebout model may be valid, but most rely on the failure of local governments' most pervasive institution—zoning—to get their results. How zoning fails in these models is largely an unexplored topic.

NOTES

1. An extension of the Tiebout model to broader governmental issues is Oates (1972). Reviews with extensive references are Henderson (1979) and Inman (1979).

2. This section is based largely on Fischel (1978). A parallel and more rigorous development of the argument is Sonstelie and Portney (1978). Both have antecedents in Davis (1963).

3. The issue of optimal community size in this chapter is different from the question of optimal size of the metropolitan area addressed by Tolley (1974). The reason for the difference is that most metropolitan areas have many local governments, and the optimal size for each may not sum to the optimal size for all. The relationship between community size and area size remains unexplored in the literature, though there is work on the optimal degree of fragmentation of metropolitan areas (McGuire 1974; Oates 1972; Rothenberg 1970).

4. This formal identity was originally suggested by a student, Jonathan Bain. This may have been obscure to me (and perhaps the reader) because the left side of the entitlements diagram corresponds to maximum development, while the left side of the community cost curve (figure 27) corresponds to minimum development.

5. A similar graphical analysis of this situation is Sonstelie and Gin (1982).

6. Hamilton's result is not to be confused with the contemporaneous discovery that the property tax might well be viewed as a tax on capital and hence less regressive than originally thought. The latter idea was developed by Mieszkowski (1972) and exposited by Aaron (1975).

7. Hamilton (1976) points out that as a result of the transfer, the poor families' housing values are raised and the rich families' are reduced. This would be merely a transfer if the gain by the poor were equal to the loss to the rich. Equality of gain with loss is unlikely because the transfers come in the form of changes in the tax price of local public services rather than cash. In any event, it is the capitalization itself—the devaluation of their property—that the original residents seek to prevent by zoning.

8. This is the minimum interpretation of the pioneering empirical study of the Tiebout hypothesis by Oates (1969). The study has been replicated

many times (e.g., Rosen and Fullerton 1977). For a review of the question of what capitalization implies see Hamilton (1976) and Yinger (1982)

9. The *Mount Laurel II* opinion (sections 3.6.2 and 15.2.2) makes all of the errors in the text below (456 A.2d 390, 417 n. 6 and 421 n. 8). The court is not alone; the *Wall Street Journal* (7 November 1983, 1) labels a chart that records average expenditures on new single-family homes "U.S. Home Prices."

10. However, Janet Pack has pointed out to me in a personal communication that their results indicated much intracommunity variation in house values, which are a reasonable proxy for permanent income. Another reason for their results may be that the Packs' sample was entirely in Pennsylvania, whose courts have long been hostile to the kind of zoning envisioned in this chapter (Ellickson and Tarlock 1981, 793). This may explain why results contrary to the Packs' were found by researchers using other samples (Eberts and Gronberg 1981; Hamilton, Mills, and Puryear 1975).

11. Fischel (1975). Works in a similar vein are Fox (1978); Ladd (1975); and White (1975a). Empirical evidence supporting the basic hypothesis is in McGuire (1983).

12. The problem has generated litigation: U.A.W. v. Township of Mahwah, 291 A.2d 847 (N.J. App. Div. 1972), dismissed for lack of jurisdiction, and Urban League of Essex County v. Township of Mahwah, 377 A.2d 682 (1977), which was decided for plaintiffs as part of the *Mount Laurel II* decision, 456 A.2d at 483 (N.J. 1983).

13. Edel and Sclar (1974) and Epple, Zelenitz, and Visscher (1978) indicate that capitalization of fiscal differences should disappear in an efficient Tiebout model, but both rely on community formation or annexation to obtain this.

14. Examples of models that overlook or dismiss zoning as an effective migration control and thus find the Tiebout model deficient are Buchanan and Goetz (1972); Flatters, Henderson, and Mieszkowski (1974); and Rose-Ackerman (1979).

15. It is on such grounds that Yinger (1982) finds the Tiebout model wanting. Political scientists are less enamored of the Tiebout system because of the lack of attention to the political mechanism (Miller 1981). Attempts by economists to remedy this are and Epple and Zelenitz (1981) and Rose-Ackerman (1979).

15.

Opening Up the Suburbs and Growth Controls

Just as economists were discovering that fragmented local government structure in metropolitan areas may have some efficiency advantages, a new reform movement attempted to eliminate most of the supposed advantages because they appeared unfair. The open-suburbs movement grew out of the urban concerns of the 1960s.[1] It appears to have been a loose amalgam of social scientists, lawyers, and advocacy groups. Its main goal was to break down the regulatory barriers that excluded low-income housing in the suburbs.

Following close on the open-suburbs movement in the 1970s was the growth control movement (sections 7.1 and 11.4). Growth controls are said to have grown out of environmental concerns. My thesis in this chapter is that growth controls may have borrowed from the ideology of the environmental movement, but three other reasons account for their existence in the 1970s: (1) growth controls resulted from the method of financing local utilities which made current residents reluctant to accept development whose nominal costs were higher due to inflation; (2) growth controls were a rational suburban response to courts that would no longer tolerate selective exclusion of the poor; and (3) the decline in local variations in property taxes reduced the opportunity cost of excluding development that was formerly fiscally profitable to accept.

This thesis is developed by limning the development of both the open-suburbs and the growth control movements. I then argue that opening the suburbs by requiring them to accept publicly supported low-income housing may have more costs than benefits as a way of helping the poor. Reforms along these lines are prob-

316

lematic because of the larger social function now served by land use controls.

15.1. THE POLITICS OF OPENING UP THE SUBURBS

The problem of suburban exclusion of low-income housing has provoked much academic commentary and a large number of reform proposals (Babcock and Bosselman 1973). These issues arc of more than just academic interest; there have been real attempts to reform them.

Consider the several ways in which suburban zoning is alleged to harm the poor:

1. Income-based exclusion is often simultaneous with or a surrogate for racial segregation.

2. The poor are denied convenient access to employment in the suburbs, which is where most of the new jobs are.

3. The poor are required to pay high central city taxes for their local services.

4. Housing costs for the poor are raised by forcing them into fewer communities.

5. The poor are deprived of the opportunity to attend the better public school systems.

6. The poor are deprived of the advantages of living in safer, more pleasant neighborhoods.

I shall consider some reforms that have been proposed to rectify these problems. The most thoroughgoing of these regards suburban exclusion as a major social problem requiring substantial public outlays and aggressive regulatory reform. This program is best set forth by Anthony Downs in *Opening Up the Suburbs* (1973). Downs foresaw two major tactical problems to be overcome by his proposal. First, the poor would not move without subsidies, and the subsidies had to be large enough to build housing acceptable to the host community. Second, all suburbs had to agree to their fair share of low-income housing; otherwise no single suburb would accept such housing for fear that it would end up with all of it.

Federal funding for new, low-income housing units was cut back soon after Downs's proposal appeared, so it never had a serious trial. Nonetheless, the open-suburbs movement did have an effect on housing policy in the 1970s. The U.S. Department of Housing and Urban Development (HUD) tried to redirect public housing to suburban jurisdictions and attempted to use federal subsidies as a bargaining tool to get suburbs to accept such housing (Danielson 1976, chaps. 8 and 9). The problem with the first attempt was lack of money. The second foundered because most of HUD's programs were aimed at poorer communities anyway. They had little leverage in the affluent suburbs.

More successful were the attempts to create some metropolitan governing bodies to coordinate land use policies. These would ostensibly give central city residents some say in the area's land use policies. They might also have played a part in allocating low-income housing around the entire metropolitan area, to avoid the suburban "floodgates" fear. But neither of these had much effect, probably because most such metropolitan bodies were federations of local governments. They may have served as a means of communication among governments, but they had little power to coerce an individual community to change its zoning laws.

There is a subtle reason why the open-suburbs movement has not succeeded politically. This has to do with the objectives of elected officials and the purposes of public housing projects. Politicians like to get elected; they especially like to get elected to higher office or to have the office to which they are elected grow in importance. Thus there is a basic conflict between the open-suburbs movement and the motives of central city politicians.

If the movement were to succeed, the central cities might lose population even faster than they do now.[2] While this might not affect a mayor's chance of reelection, it would affect the importance of his or her office within the state and the nation. More importantly, the central city members of the U.S. House of Representatives *would* find their electoral chances reduced as their constituents moved away and they were redistricted. Even if we assume, in other words, that politicians look after their constituents, they want them to remain *their* constituents.

This political focus also may explain the role of public housing. Economists largely agree that low-income housing projects are an inefficient way to redistribute income. As a transfer within our geographically based political system, however, they are very attractive. Voting to give cash or other portable benefits to a group of constituents may earn their undying political gratitude, but it will not do the politician much good if the beneficiaries move to another jurisdiction. It is thus preferable to transfer income to constituents in a way that will guarantee that they will be around to vote for those responsible for the transfer.

15.2. THE JUDICIAL ATTACK ON EXCLUSIONARY ZONING

The open-suburbs movement is currently moribund in the legislatures.[3] It continues to be played out in the courts, as advocacy groups such as the NAACP and Suburban Action attempt to persuade the courts to take up the cause. Two general legal areas bear upon this problem. The first one, public school finance litigation, is seldom considered an attack on zoning, but it may have a substantial effect on community behavior.

15.2.1. School Finance and Fiscal Zoning

One of the frequently cited causes of suburban exclusion of the poor was that the suburbs realized that the poor would dilute the property-tax base while raising school costs (Hirsch and Hirsch 1979). This is the heart of Bruce Hamilton's (1975) exposition of how zoning was necessary for the efficient operation of the Tiebout model. Without the local financing of different levels of school expenditures, there is little reason to exclude people for fiscal reasons. (This would be true whether the state government provided equalizing matching grants to communities or simply undertook to run the school systems directly.)

Judicial activism at the state level in the 1970s had a dramatic effect on the system of local government school finance (Carroll 1979; Herman 1980). Two of the more influential cases were Serrano v. Priest, 487 P.2d 1241 (Cal. 1971) and Robinson v. Cahill, 303 A.2d 273 (N.J. 1973). While the legal grounds for these and other suits varied and their remedies are not uniform, the outcome of all of them is a substantial reduction in the *variation* in local property-tax burdens for education among communities. This means that communities in many—perhaps most—states now have substantially less incentive to zone out the poor for fiscal reasons.

15.2.2. Suburban Zoning and the Mount Laurel Case

The more direct legal assault on the exclusionary suburbs comprised suits by advocacy groups that sought to overturn suburban zoning regulations. These were different from the usual developer's cases, where the landowner-developer sought a change in a community's zoning in order to get his project approved. The new litigants were sometimes allied with developers and landowners, but their approach was different. They sought court review of a whole class of zoning ordinances based on arguments analogous to the equal protection clause of both the federal and state constitutions (section 3.6). The federal cases never got anywhere, but the state cases have, in a few instances, had a substantial nominal effect. We will focus on the most sweeping of them, the *Mount Laurel* case in New Jersey.[4]

Mount Laurel is a twenty-two-square-mile township on the fringe of the Philadelphia Urbanized Area. Its zoning regulations are typical of other New Jersey municipalities in a similar situation. Most of its land was zoned for single-family homes, agriculture, and industry; there was no provision for low-cost or subsidized housing.

The suit against the township was brought by the local NAACP chapter and various co-plaintiffs. The allegation was that Mount Laurel had injured low- and moderate-income people both inside and outside its borders by zoning standards and practices that effectively denied them the opportunity to occupy acceptable housing there. The New Jersey Supreme Court upheld the plaintiffs' contention in 1975. It ordered the township to rezone to accommodate low-income housing and to accept its "fair share" of the region's poor. It also directed the state government to come up with a formula to determine what "fair share" means.

If the wood fiber in all the books and papers written about the original Mount Laurel decision were converted into construction materials, it would conceivably amount to more low-income housing than was built as a result of the decison. To make a long story short, Mount Laurel dragged its feet, other communities adopted a wait-and-see attitude, the legislature was not enamored with the role the court had cast for it, and the court itself equivocated in subsequent cases. Other state courts mention the *Mount Laurel* doctrine favorably, but none has yet adopted the remedial approach boldly embarked upon by the New Jersey court. Eight years after its original decison, the court was candid about the ineffectiveness of its original approach: "Mount Laurel remains afflicted with a blatantly exclusionary ordinance. Papered over with studies, rationalized by hired experts, the ordinance at its core is true to nothing but Mount Laurel's determination to exclude the poor."[5]

The New Jersey court in its 1983 decision issued a sweeping order to try to enforce its original decision on Mount Laurel. The court will appoint three judges, one for approximately each third of the state, to hear all subsequent appeals and develop a consistent doctrine to enforce the *Mount Laurel* requirements on all communities. These requirements involve having all communities take affirmative steps to build their "fair share" of their region's low-income housing. Remedies for not meeting the *Mount Laurel* standard include requirements to apply for existing state and federal housing programs and special requirements on developers to build low-income housing as a price for allowing higher-income housing to be built. The latter is known as "inclusionary zoning" (discussed in section 15.5).

The *Mount Laurel II* opinion is more than ninety pages long, and all its implications have yet to be sorted out. My concern with it in this chapter is as a document representing major tenets of the open-suburbs movement. This will stand in contrast to the "deregulation of housing" approach exemplified by the President's Commission on Housing, discussed in the conclusion of chapter 7. In this regard the following features of the decison seem most important (references are to pages in the *Mount Laurel II* opinion in 456 A.2d).

1. The case in no way questions the traditional tenets of zoning and the basis for planning. To the contrary, the opinion goes out of its way to praise the role of planning in rectifying the evils of the private market and speculators, who are regarded with more than a little suspicion. For example, the "builders' remedy," a court order to allow a proposal to go through, is not to be granted by the trial courts when there are "environmental or other substantial planning concerns" (p. 452). Aesthetic considerations, open-space requirements, preservation of agricultural lands, and other broad zoning purposes likewise are not questioned as acceptable goals.

2. The court expressed little if any concern with the total production of housing. Its goal is to get every community in the state to have its "fair share" of low- and moderate-income housing; after this the court would not inquire into other exclusionary devices: "Once a community has satisfied its fair share obligation, the Mount Laurel doctrine will not restrict other measures, including large-lot and open area zoning, that would maintain its beauty and communal character" (p. 421). Moreover, the builders' remedy is restricted to those that will advance the community's march toward its fair share of low-income housing. It cannot be used solely as a bargaining chip in building other types of projects (p. 452).

3. Limiting the *Mount Laurel* requirement to developing municipalities, which was the court's earlier standard, was reversed. In *Mount Laurel II*, the court's primary location consideration was

whether the community was in the boundaries of the State Development Growth Plan (SDGP), a state document that outlined where sewers and water mains generally should be built. (The plan's authors apparently did not intend it for the use to which the court put it, and this has become a political issue in itself, as the court anticipated [p. 433 n. 16].) Its intention is to channel low-income housing growth to these areas. (Communities outside the SDGP area are not subject to the same requirements, but if they do grow at all, they are subject to them [p. 432].) There seems to have been no thought given to any other intrametropolitan location considerations that might have contributed to the patterns of location by income class.

4. Damages or other monetary awards were not considered either as a final remedy or as a means of compelling compliance by communities. Use of the taking clause as a remedy is rejected in a brief footnote (p. 477). Only injunctive types of remedies were recommended. These involve invalidation of the ordinance, appointment of special masters to oversee reformulating zoning standards, and, in the extreme, a builder's remedy requiring the community to approve particular projects.

5. Standing to sue is open to nearly anyone. The basis for the original claim may even be moot: the shutdown of the Ford plant in Mahwah was deemed not to have affected the standing of plaintiffs who had sued on the basis of job location (p. 483; see section 14.10.3 above on the "Mahwah effect"). The concern expressed by the U.S. Supreme Court in Warth v. Selden (section 3.6) that such a policy would overtax judicial resources is not echoed in this opinion.

6. The court would not be satisfied by free-market outcomes. No distinction was made between income segregation fostered by zoning and that achieved by private covenants or other private development processes. The market "filtering" of housing, whereby low-income residents indirectly benefit from new construction by having more used housing available (section 15.6), was rejected as a remedy (p. 451). Communities found wanting under the *Mount Laurel* doctrine must take affirmative steps to get new, low-income housing; just getting out of the way is not an acceptable response.

The overall impression of the decision is quite contrary to the "deregulation of housing" approach, which sees the major problem with zoning as restrictions on total production (Johnson 1982; President's Commission on Housing 1981). In *Mount Laurel II*, developers appear to be regarded as a necessary evil whose motives must constantly be monitored and whose interests are to be considered only when they correspond with achieving the low-income housing goals. Particular outcomes, not reformed processes, are the objective of the remedies. The open-suburbs movement, at least as manifested in this document, is an exercise in social engineering. Its connection with the deregulation of housing advocates is based only on an occasional congruence of interests, not on fundamental similarity of goals. Its adherents are not especially concerned with overall production and are profoundly skeptical of free-market processes.

15.3. THE GROWTH CONTROL MOVEMENT AND INFLATION

15.3.1. Growth Controls

Parallel to the assault on suburban exclusion of the poor was a movement that was more successful on its own terms. This movement criticized the system of local government zoning for not being exclusionary enough.[6] There were two charges: (1) that within the municipality, existing zoning law did not provide enough protection for the natural environment, historic and scenic areas, and aesthetic values; and (2) that intermunicipal spillovers were pervasive and undesirable. Communities that properly protected their environmental, historic, and scenic areas were nonetheless degraded by the failure of their neighbors to do so.

I described the growth control movement in section 11.4 in the context of studies of the effects of zoning on housing prices in California. There is evidence, however, that this movement is a nationwide trend; it has shown up in nearly every region subject to development pressure (Frieden 1979). The techniques of this movement were described in earlier chapters (sections 4.5, 7.1, 10.9, and 11.4). The question I shall begin to address in this section is why growth controls became so popular during the 1970s.

One answer to this question might be that the techniques for controlling growth were a new product in the 1970s. The most obvious example is the National Environmental Policy Act of 1970, an important means by which undesired community growth could be slowed down.[7] But the development and use of new legal devices does not necessarily make them causes of growth controls. They may have arisen because there was a shift in demand for controls. They may not have been exogenous events.

15.3.2. Inflation and Efficient Community Size

One exogenous event of the 1970s that did change the demand to restrict new developments was inflation. Between 1970 and 1980 the Consumer Price Index rose by 112 percent. Contrast this to the rises of 31 percent between 1960 and 1970 and 23 percent between 1950 and 1960. By most accounts, the acceleration in inflation in the 1970s was unexpected.

To understand how inflation affects the demand for growth controls, consider the following example. Suppose that there is a community of 100 identical households that have made an infrastructure investment in sewers, water mains, and so on, that costs them a total of $10,000 annually in repayments to municipal bondholders. This cost is shared equally among the households via a uniform property tax, so that each pays $100 a year for interest and amortization costs.

Now suppose that another 100 households want to move in, occupying new houses identical to those of the original inhabitants. Suppose that the additional infrastructure costs $10,000 annually for them, too. The marginal cost of development in this dimension is thus equal to $100 per person, the same as the average cost for previous development. Thus if all costs are pooled in the municipal treasury, they will total $20,000. They will now be spread among 200 households, so that annual taxes will remain at $100.

Assume now a scenario for new development that differs from the previous one only by inflation. We assume that the *nominal* annual infrastructure cost of new development doubles. (This could be due to inflation of the physical capital costs or higher interest rates.) Thus the nominal cost for the 100 additional residents is $20,000, or $200 per person. But the previous residents made a fixed charge in the bond market: they are each still paying the luckless bondholders $100 per year, even though under today's conditions they would have to pay $200. The latter is the true opportunity cost of the capital.

Like homeowners who prior to the early 1970s got low-interest, long-term, fixed-rate mortgages, the original residents in the second example reaped a sizable capital gain. However, if new residents move in, they will lose some of that capital gain if the costs of the new infrastructure are paid for out of equally shared property taxes. The average tax payment in our example would be ($10,000 + $20,000)/200, or $150 per person. If this situation cannot be mitigated by charging more to the newcomers, the original residents have a strong incentive to adopt growth controls to prevent newcomers from entering at all.[8]

Suppose that in the last situation original residents were forced to accept the new development and equally share the cost of $150. The problem now is that the price faced by new residents may be *too low*. The replacement cost of new infrastructure is $200 at current prices. If the infrastructure is at all congestible, either there will be too many new residents or they will overuse the facilities, since the price is too low. In short, for economic efficiency, there should be nominal price discrimination against newcomers: each should pay $200, regardless of what the original residents paid (section 4.1).

This inequality seems unfair. But it is no more or less unfair than other capital gains achieved by all borrowers through unanticipated inflation. This capital gain just happens to occur through the public sector. The problem, egalitarian qualms aside, is that our institutions for charging marginal cost prices in the public sector are very imperfect. Most states have uniform residential property-tax rules in their constitution. Thus only special assessments and fees, which are naturally resisted by developers and new residents, are available to pay the additional costs.

There used to be a way of getting around this problem: the local assessor simply never revalued old houses, but he did assess new construction at its market value. New residents thus paid more in property taxes than did old residents. If the prices of everything—houses, sewers, water mains—doubled, new residents would end up paying their full marginal cost even under a nominally uniform property tax. This practice has been substantially reduced in the past two decades, often under court orders to reassess everyone (Inman and Rubinfeld 1979, 1701). These decisions may have resulted in a change in community behavior that promoted growth controls.

Inflation may raise new development costs sufficiently that the community may lose the advantage of scale economies from sharing the cost of a fixed infrastructure (section 14.2). Even though it may be the case in a partially developed community that the addition of residents reduces the per capita costs in real terms, the losses involved in having to share in the additional nominal costs of infrastructure could outweigh the gains from economies of scale. A community that would otherwise have been eager to have development might adopt growth restrictions if inflation were severe enough.[9]

This effect of inflation is consistent with the recent tendency of communities on the exurban fringe to adopt highly restrictive zoning. These communities used to welcome development, in part because it reduced the cost per capita of major infrastructure projects. Such scale economies may still exist, but the benefits do not redound to the voters when new development is not charged its marginal costs.

It must be recalled that this argument applies only to fixed capital costs. Variable costs such as the salaries of teachers and police would rise at the rate of inflation. Capital costs are only about 10–20 percent of the local tax bill, so their overall impact on local decisions may be small. Moreover, there are a number of devices, such as subdivision exactions, by which new developments may be charged more (section 4.1). While I suspect that inflation explains some of the growth control movement, it is not sufficient to explain all of it.

15.4. COURT-ORDERED EQUALITY AS A CAUSE OF GROWTH CONTROLS

It is my contention that the judicial decisions promoting equality in local school financing and combating suburban exclusion of low-income households have had the perverse effect of promoting growth controls. This was a revolution of the late 1960s and 1970s, so it may be regarded as something unique to this period and hence an exogenous cause.

A frequently stated objective of the school finance reforms was that educational resources per student should not depend on the "arbitrary" factor of the value of real property available for taxation. Regardless of the merits of this goal, achieving it would mean that the additional property-tax base from new development would have no effect on the fiscal resources (for schools, at least) of a given community.

The ideal outcome would eliminate the fiscal incentive to selectively exclude low-income housing. If a family with five children moves into town and lives in a new mobile home, state aid to the district is expanded to cover the additional costs of education not covered by the small increase in the property-tax base.

An unanticipated outcome of such a reform is that it eliminates the fiscal incentive to accept housing that does pay its own way.[10] If a developer proposed a tract of homes that would have a higher than average property-tax base per pupil, the community would be no better off, since it would *lose* state aid. If such development is inconvenient to current residents for any nonfiscal reason, there is no reason to have to put up with it. One might as well exclude both high-income and low-income housing, as well as all commercial and industrial development (Rosner and Barrows 1977).

Court-ordered school finance reforms have not completely equalized the fiscal capacities of local governments. There is evidence, however, that the more successful aspect of these reforms is in that direction (Carroll 1979). The point is that the property-tax system provides an institution by which developers could compensate community residents for putting up with the loss of amenities from development. Even though the property-tax system encourages communities to discriminate against low-income housing, it provides a means by which some housing could be built. It is not the only means by which this transaction could be made, but eliminating it or reducing its local variation may add to the transaction costs of developers.

More important than the school finance cases was the impact of *Mount Laurel* and other cases that directly attacked suburban practices. None of these cases, however, has attacked the foundations of zoning; indeed, the *Mount Laurel* court vigorously affirmed them. They have unconsciously allowed zoning to remain a community property right. These cases have tried, instead, to differentiate between good motives and bad motives on the part of the community.[11]

Thus the combined effect of these two movements may account for the rise of growth controls in the 1970s. The argument may be couched in terms of a benefit-cost calculus for the median voter. Reducing reliance on local property taxes to finance important local services such as schools causes the costs of excluding all development to go down. There is no longer as much gain from getting commerce, industry, or high-value housing. On the other hand, judicial and legislative insistence that any growth that does occur must accommodate low-income housing, which suburban voters dislike, causes the benefits of excluding all growth to go up. The result is much more restriction than before.

15.5. HOW INCLUSIONARY ZONING CAN BE EXCLUSIONARY

It would be erroneous to conclude from the last section that communities can ignore cases like *Mount Laurel*. Even if they could, internal guilt pangs in many suburbs would require some response. Fortunately for such communities, a device has been developed that meets the appearance of equity while in fact excluding most development. It is called, ironically, "inclusionary zoning." In a town with inclusionary zoning, the landowner-developer is required to construct units reserved for lower-income residents as a price for being permitted to develop higher-income units.

This requirement amounts to an in-kind tax on the landowner-developer. The proceeds are earmarked for subsidized housing rather than for general municipal uses. If the tax rate is set high enough, say, by requiring the developer to provide a subsidy for low-income housing that exceeds the profits obtained from the unsubsidized housing, the developer will not undertake the project.

The irony of this is that the more vigorously the community pursues low-income housing through inclusionary zoning the higher the tax is, and the more development is discouraged. In his analysis of inclusionary zoning, Robert Ellickson (1981) notes two apparent puzzles. First, it is often employed by communities that are otherwise quite exclusionary. Second, the community residents do not demand that the revenues that developers are willing to pay be converted to uses that benefit voters.

The answer to both of these puzzles may be that the purpose of inclusionary zoning is to fend off legal attacks aimed towards opening these communities to low-income housing. Thus the revenues that are diverted—when any development does take place—to low-income housing do in fact benefit the resident voters in the community. They get to maintain an exclusive suburban community by getting the landowner-developer to pay for the appearance of complying with orders to open up the suburbs.

Inclusionary zoning has some other advantages as an exclusionary device. First, it removes the private landowner-developer as co-plaintiff with groups that represent poor people in zoning litigation. This was formerly a frequent alliance.[12] Under inclusionary zoning, their interests are now opposed; the more low-income housing is required the greater the tax on the developer.

Second, inclusionary zoning puts much of the cost of social integration on prospective residents rather than on existing residents. Most inclusionary zoning requires that new housing involve closely mixed high- and low-income units. This both dampens the demand for high-income units, which is part of the tax on the developer, and ensures that low-income units will not be in close proximity to existing neighborhoods.

The efficacy of an inclusionary zoning program in actually building houses will vary according to the "monopoly power" of the jurisdiction that adopts such a plan. Inclusionary zoning is an avoidable tax on developers: if just one small jurisdiction adopts it, developers will simply move to other sites in other communities to avoid the tax (Clapp 1981). (It is not a classical tax on land rent, since it is contingent on developer activity [section 1.4].) If there are no alternative sites, because the jurisdiction is large or because the jurisdiction has some unique characteristics that make it more attractive than nearby communities, developers will be willing to pay at least some of the tax (i.e., they will build un- profitable low-income housing) in order to build more profitable housing. Thus, to the extent that the *Mount Laurel II* remedy relies on the uniform application of inclusionary zoning, it may be successful in inducing developers to erect at least some low- income housing. The substitute sites for developers are in other states. (New Jersey's major metropolitan areas are, however, im- mediately adjacent to Philadelphia and New York, so substitutes may be easier to find than one might think.)[13]

15.6. GROWTH CONTROLS AND FILTERING OF HOUSING

My argument has been that the attack on exclusionary zoning has in part led to the growth control movement. If selective ex- clusion is unenforceable, then the next-best approach may be wholesale exclusion. The growth that is allowed as a result of inclusionary zoning or other remedial devices may be balanced in terms of type and income mix, but it is smaller than the increase in housing units that would have been obtained under zoning that allowed only the usual single-family units. As I mentioned in sec- tion 15.2.2, such an outcome seems to be acceptable to the *Mount Laurel II* court. It was willing to let communities adopt large-lot zoning and other exclusionary devices once they had reached the judicially acceptable mix of housing types.

This outcome might be defended by advocates of low-income housing. They argue that the old system did nothing for the poor, since only expensive units that paid their own way were allowed. The *Mount Laurel* remedy might restrict total housing production somewhat, but at least some units are built for the poor.

I wish to argue in this section that this turn of events may not be beneficial to the poor or to housing consumers in general. By making the developing suburbs even more exclusive, one reduces the overall supply of new housing. This means that existing units will rise in price, and there will be less turnover in the housing stock and less *used* housing available for the poor. The effect is to slow down the "filtering" process by which affluent homes eventually reach the poor.

The filtering *process* is often confused with a filtering *policy*. A filtering policy is one that subsidizes construction of new homes for the affluent. This is a feature of the U.S. federal income tax system (section 11.7). Even in the absence of such subsidies, however, the filtering process would continue. Because this process is often misunderstood, I shall explain it by analogy to another durable asset, automobiles.

Most new cars are too expensive for low-income people. True, those with a strong taste for such goods may purchase them at considerable sacrifice, but for the most part, new cars are for the affluent. After they are driven for a few years, the cost of maintaining them and general obsolescence induce the original owners to sell them. The next purchasers are likely to be poorer than the first owners. They have a deteriorated car, but one within their means. Its useful lifetime has been shortened, but it provides service at reasonable cost during the time it is owned by subsequent drivers, especially if its owner applies some of his own maintenance services. The used car, like the used home, is an example of "filtering."

Suppose that the government decided that the poor would be better served by new car ownership and undertook to have new cars built that the poor could afford. It would be politically difficult, however, to subsidize the purchase of ordinary brand-new cars by the poor. Middle-income voters would notice that the poor were driving cars generally in better shape than theirs, and they would wonder what their legislators were doing with their tax money (Welfeld 1977). So the wise program would be to *build new, substandard cars*.

The problem with such cars would be that they would wear out more quickly. Once the poor were done with them, there would be no one to sell them to. The years of service per dollar invested in new cars might be reduced by such a program. One could make the obvious point that the poor could be made better off by a similar expenditure on a more widely available welfare program.

The essential difference between used cars and used houses is that hardly anyone gets upset about parking next to a deteriorated automobile, while people do get upset about deteriorating houses next door. Moreover, because of the alleged difficulty in controlling the quality of old housing, one deteriorating house may cause others to become worse too. It is a *non sequitur*, though, to argue that this shows that the filtering process is a social failure and new housing for the poor is justified, for the same problem also applies to government-sponsored housing. What it calls for, if the argument is valid, is some incentive to maintain old housing at reasonable quality levels.

Filtering is a means of providing low-income people with housing at a lower cost than that for similar-quality housing built specifically for the poor.[14] This process may leave the suburbs more segregated by income class than would a policy of opening up the suburbs with new, subsidized housing for the poor. The problem is that attempts at the latter program may retard the filtering process by inducing suburbs to adopt the egalitarian policy of slowing *all* housing development. Less than 3 percent of all new housing starts between 1961 and 1977 were of federally sponsored low-income units (Murray 1983). Even under a more ambitious program of housing the poor, the plain fact is that most of the poor will continue to live in old, privately built housing. Reducing the overall production of new housing for the affluent will cause them to hold onto their existing housing for a longer time and thus lower the amount that becomes available to the poor.

15.7. IS OPENING UP THE SUBURBS WORTHWHILE?

In the previous sections I questioned whether the means by which the open-suburbs advocates pursue their goals will have the intended effects and whether some unintended side effects might frustrate other worthy goals. It is possible, however, that the means may work to the satisfaction of the advocates or that they may be adjusted to overcome their shortcomings. Even if they can be made to work, though, we should at least question whether the goals are worth the considerable effort being devoted to them. In this section I shall argue against a concerted campaign to induce the construction of low-income housing in the suburbs. I shall do this by arguing, first, that the putative benefits of such programs are smaller than is usually claimed (Glazer 1974) and, second, that the costs of this method of redistributing income are much higher than those of most other methods.

The benefits of such programs are to reduce the harms enumerated in section 15.1. Thus the benefits would be to (1) reduce racial segregation, since many poor are black; (2) put the poor closer to suburban jobs; (3) lower their local tax burdens; (4)

reduce their housing costs; (5) enable them to attend better suburban schools; and (6) obtain better neighborhood and social amenities. I shall deal with these in turn.

1. It is neither correct nor good tactics for open-suburbs advocates to equate black with poor. The incidence of poverty is higher among blacks, but the majority of the poor are white. If suburban residents equate blacks with the occupants of low-income housing projects, they may well intensify efforts to discriminate against blacks in the private housing market. Aversion by sellers and subtle forms of discrimination by real estate agents are largely accepted as the main causes of racial segregation patterns (Yinger 1979). If we are to use public resources to their best effect, they should be aimed at reducing these influences.

2. Physical access to suburban jobs is not an important constraint on the poor. The main cause of poverty is the lack of ability (for educational or family reasons) to get and hold a steady job. Once it is obtained, the person is no longer poor, and he or she can obtain transportation to the job. Being housed right next to high-tech suburban industry will not make one employable by those firms.

3. It is not necessarily true that the poor would pay less in taxes in most suburbs than they do in central cities. Many suburbs have property-tax rates substantially higher than those of central cities. The latter often have a number of other revenue sources. The possibility of "exporting" taxes by taxing nonresidential activities and commuters is greater in most central cities than in most suburbs (Fischel 1976; Ladd 1976).

4. Housing costs may be lower in the suburbs, but they are lower in part because of the higher transportation costs one must ordinarily endure in suburban locations. The urban economics model (chapter 12) suggests that it is myopic to look only at housing costs and that there may be rational reasons for the poor to choose to live in central cities.

5. Access to better public school systems would benefit low-income children. The question is whether this necessarily means that the poor should be housed in the suburbs. Suburban school systems are often oriented to the aspirations (and whims) of middle-class parents. Whether these jibe with the educational demands of the poor might be an open question.

6. There is little doubt that poor families would benefit from safer, cleaner, more pleasant neighborhood environments. This

seems to me to be the most unambiguous benefit to the poor. The problem is that it is widely perceived by suburban voters that this is a zero sum proposition: what the poor gain by living near them the suburban middle class loses by living near the poor. (I shall expand upon this in the next section.)

Proposals to open up the suburbs continue to insist that this means public housing in the suburbs. Proponents often admit, of course, that previous public housing might not have been successful, but their promises to rectify the problem with scatter-site, low-rise apartments only suggest to suburban residents that a new and even worse policy error may be foisted upon them.

Regardless of whether these fears are well founded, public housing in the suburbs is a very costly way to make the poor better off. Economists are well aware of the drawbacks of transfering income by goods in kind: in exchange for an apartment whose market value is $400, most people would accept as little as $300 in cash (Aaron 1972, 47). This may not be the major inefficiency in producing low-income housing. Additional costs of the production and administration of public housing are substantial (Weicher 1979).

The other cost of the open-suburbs strategy is that it encounters suburban resistance, and that can be very costly. The fees of lawyers and planners and expert witnesses for both sides can be substantial, and the opportunity cost of judges and other public officials involved in adversary proceedings is not trivial. Attempts by the community to avoid low-income housing also involve costs. They may adopt strategies that restrict all development.

15.8. LAND USE CONTROL AS SOCIAL CONTROL

The puzzle about the desire of suburbs to exclude the poor is that it does not exist as much in other societies, and it does not seem to have occurred very much in earlier days in the United States. Neighborhood segregation by income is common throughout the world, and it was common even in the nineteenth century in the United States; but deliberate attempts to exclude low-income people from the entire community seem to have arisen in the latter half of this century in the United States. What has brought this about?

Suburban antipathy to low-income housing has little to do, I believe, with the physical characteristics of the structures themselves (though mobile homes may be an exception to this). This is suggested by the fact that low-income housing for the elderly is not much resisted. Instead, it is fear of crime and generally disorderly and threatening conduct by the occupants of such housing that motivates the communities. By focusing on the poorest of the poor, public housing has brought together people with the most serious social problems and the least means for dealing with them. Proximity to such housing lowers property values, because prospective buyers of nearby homes regard the public housing's occupants as dangerous.[15] I have found no academic study as convincing as a *New York Times* article that began with the following paragraphs:

> He is a successful Suffolk County lawyer who went into the Deep South to struggle for the civil rights of blacks before it became fashionable to do so. . . .He finds no comfort in speaking—anonymously as he and so many others feel they must—against the growing pressure for subsidized, low-income public housing in Suffolk County. As the courts, the federal Government and civil rights groups move in new directions to provide public housing for the poor in the middle class suburbs, his words betoken the resistance that these efforts are meeting.
> "It's a terrible tragedy," he said. "Poor people certainly need decent places to live. I understand it is a social necessity. But the terrible dilemma is that if we provide for the honest, working poor, we must accept the leavening of undesirables who can simply pollute the community."
> "For all of the nice suburbanites like me who go to New York City and cringe at the fall of night," the lawyer continued, "who go to matinees instead of evening performances, the thought that we may one day have to start cringing at home is just unacceptable" (25 April 1977, 33).

My hypothesis is that the principal reason for suburban aversion to low-income residents is that as a society we have forgone much of our ability to control public behavior. In the old days, public behavior of "undesirables" was controlled with the nightstick and a host of laws that made it relatively easy for public officials to exert prior restraint on those deemed likely to commit some public offense. These were not, of course, the good old days, for the laws and methods were often arbitrary and unjust.

The injustice of these methods has been gradually remedied by legislation and constitutional interpretation. One example of the latter is Papachristou v. City of Jacksonville [Fla.], 405 U.S. 156 (1972). In this case the Supreme Court struck down an ancient ordinance that permitted police to harass, among others, suspected vagrants and loiterers. That the administration of such laws was arbitrary and discriminatory cannot be doubted. The result of the decision, however, is that police have less ability to control behavior that local residents do not like. Police in these situations did not, I submit, harass people because the officers themselves enjoyed acting mean. They did so because that was what the majority of community residents wanted them to do.

Constitutional and legislative acts that eliminate these arbitrary social controls do not make the purposes they served go away. People who benefitted from their protection seek alternative ways of accomplishing them. One means would be to hire more and better-trained police. That is costly. A cheaper alternative is to keep those who might commit such acts out of the community entirely. Suburbs and, increasingly, semirural small towns have discovered that land use controls are an inexpensive means of achieving social controls.[16]

15.9. CONCLUSION: EFFICIENCY VERSUS EQUITY?

Chapters 8 and 9 outlined an approach to zoning laws that I argued would promote efficiency and individual fairness. The two keys to the suggested approach were assignment of land use entitlements along the lines of a standard called "normal behavior" and adoption of rules that would facilitate the exchange of such entitlements. This would protect the community from inappropriately located noxious uses and would facilitate orderly and attractive development. It would also protect the property rights of landowners and allow efficient operation of the land market. In subsequent chapters, I argued that the free market will normally allocate land uses in such a way as to avoid inefficient suburban sprawl. I also argued, however, that suburban zoning was a necessary condition for the efficient allocation of local public goods via the Tiebout model. The latter efficiency result comes, however, at the expense of equity considerations.

The open-suburbs movement can be regarded as an attack on the Tiebout model. In this chapter I have argued that this attack not only forgoes the efficiency advantages of suburban zoning in providing for local public goods but also loses the efficiency advantages of the private market in general. This is caused by the method of reform, which is outcome- rather than process-oriented.

By attempting to force communities to achieve certain goals, these reforms encourage them to adopt growth controls that are both inefficient and harmful to the poor.

It would be pleasant to conclude this chapter and the book with a proposal that would reconcile both efficiency and equity in land use reform. I have previously addressed this issue (Fischel 1979b), but I have since become convinced that the problem is less tractable than I suspected. The previous section suggested why: suburban exclusion of the poor is rooted in a larger social problem whose dimensions transcend the realm of land use controls.

Despite this, I do not want to conclude on an altogether pessimistic note. The trade-off between efficiency and equity need not be as severe as it currently seems to be. Reforms that focus on landowner rights via the taking clause may promote the interests of the poor more effectively than those that focus on the rights of the poor themselves.

If the approach to the taking issue suggested in this work were adopted, the question of "normal behavior" would arise. This would provide an opportunity to ask whether suburban rules that preclude low-income housing are normal activities for local governments: Should a developing suburban community be permitted to argue that it is normal to exclude or severely limit apartments in which low-income people might live? Two suggestions might help answer this question without excessively emotional and subjective argumentation.

First, the type of proposed low-income housing probably exists in a similar form in several other places. Its effects on neighborhood property values and community character might be determined with the aid of expert testimony.[17] If such units have adverse effects analogous to subnormal uses such as noxious industries, the community could argue that they may be excluded. Agents for such housing would then be in a situation analogous to that of an industrial developer, and they could respond similarly with offers to redesign the project and compensatory side payments. Such side payments are routinely paid by the federal government to facilitate local acceptance of tax-exempt military facilities.

Second, the right to exclude any land use from the entire community should vary by the land area of the community in question. If the land area is small, there is little harm in such exclusion, since other communities can accommodate such development. But if the suburb is a large one, controlling a significant fraction of undeveloped land near a metropolitan area, then its restrictions should be more closely scrutinized. Municipalities should not replicate the land use patterns of the region in which they are located, but in those communities with many square miles of undeveloped land a variety of land uses is necessary to avoid excessive commuting and to combat the potential for monopoly land use.

The second rule might induce some large communities to split up into smaller ones. There is nothing wrong with that. Aside from the Tiebout advantages of such a system (section 14.1), having more independent communities increases the chances that developers of low-income housing or other nonstandard land uses will be able to strike a satisfactory agreement with one of them.

The other advantage of using the taking clause as a basis for attacking exclusionary zoning is that it offers a more effective remedy. Suppose a community's zoning of a parcel is considered to be illegal because it involves supernormal standards. How does the court see to it that the zoning is changed without having the community frustrate the developer's intentions with its arsenal of delaying tactics? The surest way is to award a payment of damages for profits lost due to delay after the order is given. It is hard to believe that the Township of Mount Laurel would have been willing to accumulate a bill for forgone development over a period of eight years (the time between *Mount Laurel I* and *Mount Laurel II*). They of course received no such bill. The plaintiff was not a landowner claiming a taking, and the New Jersey court did not order the township to rezone a particular parcel or to pay damages. Consequently, the court has had to take on what are normally legislative functions to fashion a remedy.

It should be clear that the property rights approach suggested here will probably not lead to the outcomes that are sought by the open-suburbs movement. Landowner-developers will most likely seek to develop relatively costly housing, and communities might in any case succeed in arguing that low-income housing projects are "subnormal" land uses in the suburbs by pointing to studies that show that they lead to reduced property values in the neighborhood. But there will be exceptions to either outcome: Developers may find it profitable to erect low-cost, attractive housing, especially if it is built with the new "manufactured housing" techniques. Low-cost public housing might be found not to have much nuisance effect if it is not concentrated in one area and if applicants are screened. In any event, construction of any type of housing will eventually help the poor by increasing the national stock of housing and thus keeping its price down, wherever it is located.

This approach may turn out to be far more beneficial to the poor than ideologically pure reforms that ignore production considerations and inadvertently promote growth controls.

NOTES

1. The idea of a housing "crisis" and responses to it were set in motion by two government reports issued in 1968. The President's Committee on Urban Housing (the Kaiser Committee) and the U.S. National Commission on Urban Problems (the Douglas Commission) both focused on the inadequacies of urban housing for the poor. The Douglas Commission was especially critical of suburban zoning, and the open-suburbs movement may be said to have stemmed from its report, *Building the American City*, 1968. A discussion of the advocacy groups' role in this process is in Danielson (1976, chap. 5).

2. Loss of city population assumes that a successful open-suburbs plan would not induce business and the middle class to move back to central cities as they find that the suburbs offer no haven from low-income housing and as the central cities become more attractive as a result. The *Mount Laurel II* opinion (n. 4 below), citing Downs (1973), expresses this hope without citing any evidence that it is more than that (pp. 415–16 n. 5). See section 12.3 for reasons why suburbanization by the middle class and industry may be caused by factors other than local public policies. On the *Mount Laurel II* opinion's hope see below, n. 13.

3. Danielson (1976, chap. 10) notes that only two states made serious legislative attempts to place low-income housing in the suburbs. New York's law was soon repealed, but the Massachusetts "Anti-Snob Zoning" law had some effect (Schafer 1974).

4. As of this writing there are two *Mount Laurel* cases: Southern Burlington County NAACP v. Township of Mount Laurel, 336 A.2d 713 (N.J. 1975), and 456 A.2d 390 (N.J. 1983). They are referred to as *Mount Laurel I* and *Mount Laurel II*, respectively.

5. *Mount Laurel II*, 410. Critiques of *Mount Laurel I* that anticipated its remedial problems are Ellickson (1977); Komesar (1978, 243); Rubinfeld (1979, 43); and Wolfstone (1978, 73). An approving study by an economist is Vogel (1980).

6. See, e.g., Mandelker (1981, chap. 1) and Natural Resources Defense Council (1977). The growth control movement is ably described by Frieden (1979).

7. Several legal cases involving a conflict between the EIS and low-income housing are discussed by Komesar (1978). Marcus (1980) expresses concern that the new zoning devices, of which he generally approves, will be perfected as instruments of suburban exclusivity.

8. The influence of higher nominal interest rates on growth controls is suggested by White (1978b). White also advances the idea that judicial hos-

tility to selective exclusion may have promoted growth controls. Cooley and LaCivita (1982) demonstrate in a more rigorous model that inflation will hasten adoption of growth controls in a given community.

9. In terms of figure 27 (section 14.2), the problem is that the AC and MC curves may be shifted up in nominal terms, so that the existing residents may want to halt development to the left of the minimum-cost community size. Generally, if the post-inflation marginal cost of additional households exceeds the pre-inflation average cost for existing households, existing residents will oppose growth unless newcomers pay more than the old average cost.

10. Mace and Wicker (1968) argued that single-family homes paid their own way in local taxes, largely because of subdivision requirements. But according to Muller and Dawson (1972), residential development did not pay because of high capital outlays. White (1975a) wonders why suburbs ever accepted development that only paid its own way; why not adopt a "fiscal squeeze" strategy to extract some rents from developers? The answer may be that prior to 1968 (when the open-suburbs movement and inflation both began) there was little harm in allowing new development and consequently little net benefit in risking litigation by aggrieved landowner-developers.

11. Section 7.6 discussed the difference between good and bad motives on the community's part as a reason why zoning might be said to be too restrictive. The problem is that it is difficult for an outsider to differentiate among motives because of the many acceptable goals under zoning enabling acts. A more general reason is offered by Wittman (1977), who notes that control of inputs allows more latitude of purpose than does control of outputs. Zoning controls land, an input, while nuisance law controls outcomes and thus allows for less substitution of other community goals. See also section 2.2.

12. The alliance of landowners and low-income groups was suggested by a footnote in Construction Industry Association v. City of Petaluma, 522 F. 2d 897 (9th cir. 1975). Dismissing the construction association's contention that Petaluma's building permit quota hurt not only the association but also the poor, the court noted: "Contrary to the picture painted by appellees, the Petaluma plan is 'inclusionary' to the extent that it offers new opportunities, previously unavailable, to minorities and low and moderate incomes persons." Schwartz, Hansen, and Green (1984) found that several years after this decision Petaluma's percentage of "affordable" housing had dropped precipitously.

13. It is the existence of such substitutes, among other factors, that seems likely to frustrate the Mount Laurel II hope that the middle class will move back to the central cities once they find that they cannot escape having to live near the poor in the suburbs (n. 2 above). While the New York and Pennsylvania courts have favorably noted the Mount Laurel I doctrine, their remedies have been far more modest, so that their suburbs are unlikely to face the same judicial pressures as those in New Jersey.

14. The benefits of the filtering process for the poor depend on housing's durability. Those who find that filtering does not reduce the price for the

poor assume that housing capital is highly malleable, so that the poor get
exactly the amount that they pay for (Lowry 1960; Olsen 1969). Those finding
the opposite assume that the housing stock does not deteriorate quickly in
response to a downward shift in demand (Ohls 1974; Sweeney 1974; Weicher
1980). The latter assumption seems more realistic because of the structural
rigidity of housing capital and because zoning regulations retard the conversion of older housing to other uses. The "chain of moves" studies, such
as Lansing, Clifton, and Morgan (1969), illustrate the process but do not
prove that filtering is efficient, since they usually neglect marketwide price
effects, demolition, and costs of alternative approaches.

15. Grether and Mieszkowski (1980) found that New Haven public housing projects lowered neighborhood residential values. Nourse (1963) found
that replacing slum housing with public housing for low-income people had
no effect on nearby property values in St. Louis, suggesting that occupants
are more important than type of housing. Rabiega, Lin, and Robinson (1984)
found, however, that Portland, Oregon's policy of scattered, low-rise public
housing had no deleterious effects on neighboring property values.

16. This is my interpretation of a theme developed by Oates (1977).
Downs (1973) regarded fear of crime as a major reason for suburban resistance to low-income housing, but he offered no evidence that the crime rate
could be reduced by scattering the low-income projects.

17. Expert testimony could include econometric studies but not be limited
to them. My previously expressed skepticism of quantitative studies (in sections 8.4, 9.6, and 11.3) should be kept in mind, though studies of neighborhood effects of specific projects are likely to be easier to do correctly
than studies of entire metropolitan areas.

Bibliography

Aaron, Henry J. 1972. *Shelter and Subsidies.* Washington, D.C.: Brookings Institution.

———. 1975. *Who Pays the Property Tax?* Washington, D.C.: Brookings Institution.

Ackerman, Bruce A. 1977. *Private Property and the Constitution.* New Haven: Yale University Press.

———, ed. 1975. *Economic Foundations of Property Law.* Boston: Little, Brown.

Adelstein, Richard P., and Noel M. Edelson. 1976. "Subdivision Exactions and Congestion Externalities." *J. Legal Studies* 5 (January): 147–63.

Alchian, Armen A., and Harold Demsetz. 1972. "Production, Information Costs, and Economic Organization." *Am. Econ. Rev.* 62 (December): 777–95.

Allensworth, Donald T. 1974. *The Political Realities of Urban Planning.* New York: Praeger.

American Law Institute. 1975. *A Model Land Development Code.* Philadelphia.

Andreano, Ralph L. 1965. "Trends and Variations in Economic Welfare in the United States before the Civil War," in *New Views on American Economic Development,* edited by R. L. Andreano. Cambridge, Mass.: Schenkman.

Arnott, Richard J., and Frank D. Lewis. 1979. "The Transition of Land to Urban Use." *J. Pol. Econ.* 87 (February): 161–70.

Babcock, Richard F. 1966. *The Zoning Game.* Madison: University of Wisconsin Press.

———. 1976. "The Deplorable States." *Center Magazine* 9 (September/October): 23–29.

Babcock, Richard F., and Fred P. Bosselman. 1973. *Exclusionary Zoning: Land Use Regulation and Housing in the 1970s.* New York: Praeger.

Baden, John, and Richard Stroup. 1981. "Saving the Wilderness: A Radical Proposal." *Reason,* July, 29–36.

Bardach, Eugene, and Lucian Pugliaresi. 1977. "The Environmental Impact Statement vs. the Real World." *Public Interest* 49 (Fall): 22–38.

Barker, Charles A. 1955. *Henry George*. New York: Oxford University Press.

Bartholomew, Harland. 1937. "Non-Conforming Uses Destroy the Neighborhood." *Land Econ.* 15 (February): 96–97.

Bassett, Edward M. 1936. *Zoning: The Laws, Administration, and Court Decisions during the First Twenty Years*. New York: Russell Sage Foundation.

Baumol, William J. 1969. *Welfare Economics and the Theory of the State*. Cambridge, Mass.: Harvard University Press.

————. 1974. "Environmental Protection and Income Distribution," in *Redistribution Through Public Choice*, edited by Harold M. Hochman and George E. Peterson. New York: Columbia University Press.

Baumol, William J., and Wallace E. Oates. 1975. *The Theory of Environmental Policy*. Englewood Cliffs, N.J.: Prentice-Hall.

Becker, Gary S. 1976. *The Economic Approach to Human Behavior*. Chicago: University of Chicago Press.

Bender, Bruce, and Steven Shwiff. 1982. "The Appropriation of Rents by Boomtown Governments." *Econ. Inquiry* 20 (January): 84–103.

Bentick, Brian L. 1979. "The Impact of Taxation and Valuation Practices on the Timing and Efficiency of Land Use." *J. Pol. Econ.* 87 (August): 859–68.

————. 1980. "Capitalized Property Taxes and the Viability of Rural Enterprise Subject to Urban Pressure." *Land Econ.* 56 (November): 451–56.

Berg, Norman A. 1979. "Evolution of Land Use Policy in USDA," in *Farmland, Food, and the Future*, edited by Max Schnepf. Ankeny, Iowa: Soil Conservation Society of America.

Berger, Lawrence. 1974. "A Policy Analysis of the Taking Problem." *N.Y.U. Law Rev.* 49 (May/June): 165–226.

Bergman, Edward M. 1974. *Eliminating Exclusionary Zoning: Reconciling Workplace and Residence in Suburban Areas*. Cambridge, Mass.: Ballinger.

Bergstrom, Theodore C., and Robert P. Goodman. 1973. "Private Demands for Public Goods." *Am. Econ. Rev.* 63 (June): 280–96.

Berry, David. 1983. "Threat to American Cropland: Urbanization and Soil Erosion," in *Beyond the Urban Fringe*, edited by Rutherford H. Platt and George Macinko. Minneapolis: University of Minnesota Press.

Bhagwati, Jagdish N. 1982. "Directly Unproductive, Profit-Seeking (DUP) Activities." *J. Pol. Econ.* 90 (October): 988–1002.

Blomquist, Glenn. 1974. "The Effect of Electric Utility Power Plant Location on Area Property Value." *Land Econ.* 50 (February): 97–100.

Blume, Lawrence E., Daniel L. Rubinfeld, and Perry Shapiro. 1984. "The 'Taking' of Land: When Should Compensation Be Paid?" *Q. J. Econ.* 99 (February): 71–92.

Bosselman, Fred P. 1968. *Alternatives to Urban Sprawl: Legal Guidelines for Government Action*. Washington, D.C.: U.S. Government Printing Office for the National Commission on Urban Problems.

Bosselman, Fred P., and David Callies. 1971. *The Quiet Revolution in Land Use Control*. Washington, D.C.: Council on Environmental Quality.

Bosselman, Fred P., David Callies, and John Banta. 1973. *The Taking Issue*. Washington, D.C.: Council on Environmental Quality.

Bowen, Howard R. 1943. "The Interpretation of Voting in the Allocation of Economic Resources." *Q. J. Econ.* 58 (November): 27–48.

Bradford, David F., and Wallace E. Oates. 1971. "The Analysis of Revenue Sharing in a New Approach to Collective Fiscal Decisions." *Q. J. Econ.* 85 (August): 416–39.

Bradshaw, A. D., and M. J. Chadwick. 1980. *The Restoration of Land*. Berkeley: University of California Press.

Brenner, Joel F. 1974. "Nuisance Law and the Industrial Revolution." *J. Legal Studies* 3 (June): 403–34.

Brewer, Michael F., ed. 1981. *Agricultural Land Availability*. Washington, D.C.: U.S. Senate Committee on Agriculture, Nutrition and Forestry.

Brewer, Michael F., and Robert F. Boxley. 1981. "Agricultural Land: Adequacy of Acres, Concepts, and Information." *Am. J. Ag. Econ.* 63 (December): 879–87.

Bromley, Daniel W. 1978. "Property Rules, Liability Rules, and Environmental Economics." *J. Econ. Issues* 12 (March): 43–60.

Brown, David L., and Calvin L. Beale. 1981. "Sociodemographic Influences on Land Use in Nonmetropolitan America," in *Agricultural Land Availability*. See Brewer 1981.

Brown, David L., Michael F. Brewer, Robert F. Boxley, and Calvin L. Beale. 1982. "Assessing Prospects for the Adequacy of Agricultural Land in the United States." *Internat. Reg. Sci. Rev.* 7 (December): 273–84.

Brown, H. James, Robyn S. Phillips, and Neal A. Roberts. 1981. "Land Markets at the Urban Fringe." *J. Am. Plan. Assoc.* 47 (April): 131–44.

Brueckner, Jan K. 1979. "Spatial Majority Voting Equilibria and the Provision of Public Goods." *J. Urban Econ.* 6 (July): 338–51.

———. 1982. "A Test for Allocative Efficiency in the Local Public Sector." *J. Pub. Econ.* 19 (December): 311–21.

Brueckner, Jan K., and David A. Fansler. 1983. "The Economics of Urban Sprawl: Theory and Evidence on the Spatial Sizes of Cities." *Rev. Econ. & Stats.* 65 (August): 479–82.

Buchanan, James M. 1973. "The Coase Theorem and the Theory of the State." *Nat. Res. J.* 13 (October): 579–94.

Buchanan, James M., and Roger L. Faith. 1981. "Entrepreneurship and the Internalization of Externalities." *J. Law & Econ.* 24 (April): 95–112.

Buchanan, James M., and Charles J. Goetz. 1972. "Efficiency Limits of Fiscal Mobility: An Assessment of the Tiebout Model." *J. Pub. Econ.* 1 (February): 25–43.

Buchanan, James M., and William Craig Stubblebine. 1962. "Externality." *Econ. J.* 29 (November): 371–84.

Calabresi, Guido. 1965. "The Decision for Accidents: An Approach to Nonfault Allocation of Costs." *Harvard Law Rev.* 78 (February): 713–31.

——. 1968. "Transaction Costs, Resource Allocation, and Liability Rules—A Comment." *J. Law & Econ.* 11 (April): 67–74.

Calabresi, Guido, and A. Douglas Melamed. 1972. "Property Rules, Liability Rules, and Inalienability: One View of the Cathedral." *Harvard Law Rev.* 85 (April): 1089–1128.

Callies, David. 1980. "The Quiet Revolution Revisited." *J. Am. Plan. Assoc.* 46 (April): 135–44.

Carpenter, Bruce E., and Dennis R. Heffley. 1982. "Spatial Equilibrium Analysis of Transferable Development." *J. Urban Econ.* 12 (September): 238–61.

Carroll, Stephen J. 1979. *The Search for Equity in School Finance: Summary and Conclusions.* Santa Monica: Rand Corporation for the National Institute of Education.

Chapin, F. Stuart, Jr., and Edward J. Kaiser. 1979. *Urban Land Use Planning.* Urbana: University of Illinois Press.

Cheung, Steven N. S. 1970. "The Structure of a Contract and the Theory of a Non-Exclusive Resource." *J. Law & Econ.* 13 (April): 49–70.

——. 1973. "The Fable of the Bees: An Economic Investigation." *J. Law & Econ.* 16 (April): 11–34.

Chickering, A. Laurence. 1975. "Land Use Controls and Low Income Groups: Why Are There No Poor People in the Sierra Club?" in *No Land Is an Island*, edited by Benjamin Bobo. San Francisco: Institute for Contemporary Studies.

Chicoine, David L. 1981. "Farmland Values at the Urban Fringe: An Analysis of Sale Prices." *Land Econ.* 57 (August): 353–62.

Clapp, John M. 1981. "The Impact of Inclusionary Zoning on the Location and Type of Construction Activity." *Am. Real Est. & Urban Econ. Assoc. J.* 9 (Winter): 436–56.

Clawson, Marion. 1968. *The Land System of the United States.* Lincoln: University of Nebraska Press.

——. 1971. *Suburban Land Conversion in the United States: An Economic and Government Process.* Baltimore: Johns Hopkins Press.

Coase, Ronald H. 1937. "The Nature of the Firm." *Economica* 4 (November): 386–405.

——. 1959. "The Federal Communications Commission." *J. Law & Econ.* 2 (October): 1–40.

——. 1960. "The Problem of Social Cost." *J. Law & Econ.* 3 (October): 1–44.

——. 1972. "Durability and Monopoly." *J. Law & Econ.* 15 (April): 143–50.

——. 1981. "The Coase Theorem and the Empty Core: A Comment." *J. Law & Econ.* 24 (April): 183–87.

[Coase, Ronald H.] 1973–74. "Coase Theorem Symposium." Pts. 1 and 2. *Nat. Res. J.* 13 (October): 557–716 and 14 (January): 1–86.

Coke, James G., and Charles S. Liebman. 1961. "Political Values and Population Density Control." *Land Econ.* 37 (November): 347–61.

Colwell, Peter F., and James B. Kau. 1982. "The Economics of Building Codes and Standards," in *Resolving the Housing Crisis. See* Johnson 1982.

Comey, Arthur C. 1925. *Report of the Planning Board to the Citizens of the Town of Wakefield.* Wakefield, Mass.

Cooley, Thomas F., and Charles J. LaCivita. 1982. "A Theory of Growth Controls." *J. Urban Econ.* 12 (September): 129–45.

Cooter, Robert. 1982. "The Cost of Coase." *J. Legal Studies* 11 (January): 1–34.

Cordes, Joseph J., and Burton A. Weisbrod. 1979. "Government Behavior in Response to Compensation Requirements." *J. Pub. Econ.* 11 (February): 47–58.

Correll, Mark R., Jane H. Lillydahl, and Larry D. Singell. 1978. "The Effect of Greenbelts on Residential Property Values." *Land Econ.* 54 (May): 207–17.

Coughlin, Robert E., and John C. Keene. 1981. *The Protection of Farmland: A Reference Guidebook for State and Local Governments.* Washington, D.C.: U.S. Government Printing Office for the National Agricultural Lands Study.

Courant, Paul N. 1976. "On the Effect of Fiscal Zoning on Land and Housing Values." *J. Urban Econ.* 3 (January): 88–94.

Crecine, John P., Otto A. Davis, and John E. Jackson. 1967. "Urban Property Markets: Some Empirical Results and Their Implications for Municipal Zoning." *J. Law & Econ.* 10 (October): 79–100.

Crone, Theodore M. 1983. "Elements of an Economic Justification for Municipal Zoning." *J. Urban Econ.* 14 (September): 168–83.

Dahlman, Carl J. 1979. "The Problem of Externality." *J. Law & Econ.* 22 (April): 141–62.

———. 1982. "An Economic Analysis of Zoning Laws," in *Resolving the Housing Crisis. See* Johnson 1982.

Danielson, Michael N. 1976. *The Politics of Exclusion.* New York: Columbia University Press.

Davidoff, Paul, Linda Davidoff, and Neil Gold. 1970. "Suburban Action: Advocate Planning in an Open Society." *Am. Inst. Planners J.* 36 (January): 12–21.

Davis, Otto A. 1963. "Economic Elements in Municipal Zoning Decisions." *Land Econ.* 39 (November): 375–86.

Dawson, Grace. 1976. *No Little Plans: Fairfax County's PLUS Program for Managing Growth.* Washington, D.C.: The Urban Institute.

Deacon, Robert, and Perry Shapiro. 1975. "Private Preference for Collective Goods Revealed through Voting on Referenda." *Am. Econ. Rev.* 65 (December): 943–55.

Demsetz, Harold. 1964. "The Exchange and Enforcement of Property Rights." *J. Law & Econ.* 7 (October): 11–26.

———. 1969. "Information and Efficiency: Another Viewpoint." *J. Law & Econ.* 12 (April): 1–22.

———. 1972. "Wealth Distribution and the Ownership of Rights." *J. Legal Studies* 1 (June): 223–32.

Devarajan, Shantayanan, and Anthony C. Fisher. 1981. "Hotelling's 'Economics of Exhaustible Resources': Fifty Years Later." *J. Econ. Lit.* 19 (March): 65–73.

Diamond, Douglas G., Jr., and George S. Tolley, eds. 1982. *The Economics of Urban Amenities.* New York: Academic Press.

Dideriksen, Raymond I., Allen R. Hidlebaugh, and Keith O. Schmude. 1977. *Potential Cropland Study.* Washington, D.C.: U.S. Department of Agriculture, Soil Conservation Service, Statistical Bulletin 578.

Dillman, B. L., and Charles F. Cousins. 1982. "Urban Encroachment on Prime Agricultural Land: A Case Study." *Internat. Reg. Sci. Rev.* 7 (December): 285–92.

Dorfman, Robert. 1977. "Incidence of the Benefits and Costs of Environmental Programs." *Am. Econ. Rev.* 67 (February): 333–40.

Downing, Paul B. 1970. "Estimating Residential Land Value by Multivariate Analysis," in *The Assessment of Land Value. See* Holland 1970.

———. 1973. "Factors Affecting Commercial Land Values: An Empirical Study of Milwaukee, Wisconsin." *Land Econ.* 49 (February): 44–56.

———. 1977. "Suburban Nongrowth Policies." *J. Econ. Issues* 11 (June): 387–400.

Downs, Anthony. 1957. *An Economic Theory of Democracy.* New York: Harper and Row.

———. 1973. *Opening Up the Suburbs: An Urban Strategy for America.* New Haven: Yale University Press.

Dunford, Richard W. 1983. "An Overview of the Farmland Retention Issue." Report 83–635 ENR. Washington, D.C.: Congressional Research Service.

Dunham, Allison. 1958. "A Legal and Economic Basis for City Planning." *Columbia Law Rev.* 58 (May): 650–71.

———. 1965. "Promises Respecting the Use of Land." *J. Law & Econ.* 8 (October): 133–65.

Dunlap, Riley E., and Michael P. Allen. 1976. "Partisan Differences on Environmental Issues: A Congressional Roll-Call Analysis." *Western Pol. Q.* 29 (September): 384–97.

Eberts, Randall W., and Timothy J. Gronberg. 1981. "Jurisdictional Homogeneity and the Tiebout Hypothesis." *J. Urban Econ.* 10 (September): 227–39.

Edel, Matthew, and Elliot Sclar. 1974. "Taxes, Spending, and Property Values: Supply Adjustment in a Tiebout-Oates Model." *J. Pol. Econ.* 82 (September): 941–54.

Edelson, Noel M. 1976. "Voting Equilibria with Market-Based Assessments." *J. Pub. Econ.* 5 (April/May): 269–84.

Ellickson, Robert C. 1973. "Alternatives to Zoning: Covenants, Nuisance Rules, and Fines as Land Use Controls." *U. Chicago Law Rev.* 40 (Summer): 681–782.

———. 1977. "Suburban Growth Controls: An Economic and Legal Analysis." *Yale Law J.* 86 (January): 385–511.

———. 1979. "Public Property Rights: A Government's Rights and Duties When Its Landowners Come into Conflict with Outsiders." *Southern Cal. Law Rev.* 52 (September): 1627–70.

———. 1981. "The Irony of 'Inclusionary' Zoning." *Southern Cal. Law Rev.* 54 (September): 1167–1216.

———. 1982. "Cities and Homeowners Associations." *U. Pa. Law Rev.* 130 (June): 1519–80.

Ellickson, Robert C., and A. Dan Tarlock. 1981. *Land Use Controls: Cases and Materials.* Boston: Little, Brown.

Ely, John Hart. 1980. *Democracy and Distrust: A Theory of Judicial Review.* Cambridge, Mass.: Harvard University Press.

Epple, Dennis, and Allan Zelenitz. 1981. "The Implications of Competition among Jurisdictions: Does Tiebout Need Politics?" *J. Pol. Econ.* 89 (December): 1197–1217.

Epple, Dennis, Allan Zelenitz, and Michael Visscher. 1978. "A Search for Testable Implications of the Tiebout Hypothesis." *J. Pol. Econ.* 86 (June): 405–25.

Epstein, Richard A. 1982. "Not Deference but Doctrine: The Eminent Domain Clause." *Supreme Court Review*, 351–80.

Feldman, Roger. 1974. "Liability Rules and the Transfer of Economic Rents." *J. Legal Studies* 3 (June): 499–508.

Feldstein, Martin. 1982. "Inflation, Tax Rules, and the Accumulation of Residential and Nonresidential Capital." *Scandinavian J. Econ.* 84:292–311.

Finkler, Earl, William J. Toner, and Frank J. Popper. 1976. *Urban Nongrowth: City Planning for People.* New York: Praeger.

Fischel, William A. 1975. "Fiscal and Environmental Considerations in the Location of Firms in Suburban Communities," in *Fiscal Zoning and Land Use Controls*, edited by Edwin S. Mills and Wallace E. Oates. Lexington, Mass.: Heath-Lexington Books.

———. 1976. "An Evaluation of Proposals for Metropolitan Sharing of Commercial and Industrial Property Tax Base." *J. Urban Econ.* 3 (July): 253–63.

———. 1978. "A Property Rights Approach to Municipal Zoning." *Land Econ.* 54 (February): 64–81.

———. 1979a. "Determinants of Voting on Environmental Quality: A Study of a New Hampshire Pulp Mill Referendum." *J. Env. Econ. & Mgmt.* 6 (June): 107–18.

———. 1979b. "Equity and Efficiency Aspects of Zoning Reform." *Public Policy* 27 (Summer): 301–32.

———. 1980a. "Zoning and Land Use Reform: A Property Rights Perspective." *Va. J. Natural Res. Law* 1 (Spring): 69–93.

———. 1980b. "Externalities and Zoning." *Public Choice* 35: 37–43.

————. 1980c. "Zoning and the Exercise of Monopoly Power: A Reevaluation." *J. Urban Econ.* 8 (November): 283–93.

————. 1981. "Is Local Government Structure in Large Urbanized Areas Monopolistic or Competitive?" *National Tax J.* 34 (March): 95–104.

————. 1982. "The Urbanization of Agricultural Land: A Review of the National Agricultural Lands Study." *Land Econ.* 58 (May): 236–59.

Fisher, Peter S. 1982. "Regional Tax Base Sharing: An Analysis and Simulation of Alternative Approaches." *Land Econ.* 58 (November): 497–515.

Flatters, Frank, J. Vernon Henderson, and Peter Mieszkowski. 1974. "Public Goods, Efficiency, and Regional Fiscal Equalization." *J. Pub. Econ.* 3 (May): 99–112.

Forstall, Richard L., and Richard A. Engels. 1984. "Growth in Nonmetropolitan Areas Slows." Washington, D.C.: U.S. Bureau of the Census.

Fox, William F. 1978. "Local Taxes and Industrial Location." *Pub. Fin. Q.* 6 (January): 93–114.

Frech, H. E., III. 1973. "Pricing of Pollution: The Coase Theorem in the Long Run." *Bell J. Econ.* 4 (Spring): 316–19.

————. 1979. "The Extended Coase Theorem and Long Run Equilibrium: The Nonequivalence of Liability Rules and Property Rights." *Econ. Inquiry* 17 (April): 254–68.

Frech, H. E., III, and Ronald N. Lafferty. 1976. "The Economic Impact of the California Coastal Commission: Land Use and Land Values," in *The California Coastal Plan: A Critique*, edited by M. Bruce Johnson. San Francisco: Institute for Contemporary Studies.

————. 1984. "The Effect of the California Coastal Commission on Housing Prices." *J. Urban Econ.* 16 (July): 105–23.

Freund, Ernst. 1904. *The Police Power: Public Policy and Constitutional Rights*. Chicago: Callaghan.

Frey, H. Thomas. 1979. *Major Uses of Land in the United States: 1974*. Agricultural Economic Report 440. Washington, D.C.: U.S. Department of Agriculture, Economics, Statistics and Cooperatives Service.

————. 1982. "Farmland Conversion: Some Comments on the Potential Cropland Study." *Professional Geographer* 34 (August): 342–45.

————. 1983. "Expansion of Urban Area in the United States: 1960–1980." Economic Research Service Staff Report AGES830615. Washington, D.C.: U.S. Department of Agriculture.

Frieden, Bernard J. 1979. *The Environmental Protection Hustle*. Cambridge, Mass.: MIT Press.

Friedman, Milton, and Dennis Robertson. 1973. "A Milton Friedman-Sir Dennis Robertson Correspondence." *J. Pol. Econ.* 81 (July): 1033–39.

Furman, Janet L. 1982. "Responses to Uncertainty in the Market for Neighborhood Characteristics." Ph.D. diss., Johns Hopkins University.

Furubotn, Erik G., and Svetozar Pejovich, eds. 1972. "Property Rights and Economic Theory: A Survey of Recent Literature." *J. Econ. Lit.* 10 (December): 1137–62.

Gaffney, Mason. 1970. "Adequacy of Land as a Tax Base," in *The Assessment of Land Value. See* Holland 1970.

Gardens for All. 1981. *The Impact of Home and Community Food Gardening on America.* Burlington, Vt.: Gardens for All.

Gardner, Bruce L. 1981. *The Governing of Agriculture.* Lawrence: Regents Press of Kansas.

Gardner, B. Delworth. 1977. "The Economics of Agricultural Land Preservation." *Am. J. Ag. Econ.* 59 (December): 1027–36.

Gardner, John A., and Theodore R. Lyman. 1978. *Decisions for Sale: Corruption and Reform in Land Use and Building Regulation.* New York: Praeger.

Geier, Karl E. 1980. "Agricultural Districts and Zoning: A State-Local Approach to a National Problem." *Ecology Law Q.* 8:655–96.

Geller, Leslie M. 1983. *Strategy Zoning.* Englewood Cliffs, N.J.: Prentice-Hall.

George, Henry. 1880. *Progress and Poverty.* New York: Appleton.

Glazer, Nathan. 1974. "On 'Opening Up' the Suburbs." *Public Interest* 37 (Fall): 89–111.

Glickfeld, Madelyn. 1978. "Sale of Development Permission: Zoning on the Auction Block," in *Windfalls for Wipeouts. See* Hagman and Misczynski 1978.

Glickfeld, Madelyn, and Donald G. Hagman. 1978. "Special Capital and Real Estate Windfalls Taxes (SCREWTS)," in *Windfalls for Wipeouts. See* Hagman and Misczynski 1978.

Goetz, Charles J., and Gordon Brady. 1975. "Environmental Policy Formation and the Tax Treatment of Citizen Interest Groups." *Law & Contemporary Probs.* 39 (Autumn): 211–31.

Goetz, Michael L., and Larry E. Wofford. 1979. "The Motivation for Zoning: Efficiency or Wealth Redistribution?" *Land Econ.* 55 (November): 472–85.

Goldberg, Victor P. 1976. "Regulation and Administered Contracts." *Bell J. Econ.* 7 (Autumn): 426–48.

———. 1981. "Pigou on Complex Contracts and Welfare Economics." *Res. in Law and Econ.* 3:39–52.

Goodchild, Barry. 1974. "Class Differences in Environmental Perception: An Exploratory Survey." *Urban Studies* 11 (June): 157–69.

Gramlich, Edward M., and Daniel L. Rubinfeld. 1982. "Micro Estimates of Public Spending Demand Functions and Tests of the Tiebout and Median Voter Hypotheses." *J. Pol. Econ.* 90 (June): 536–60.

Grether, David M., and Peter Mieszkowski. 1974. "Determinants of Real Estate Values." *J. Urban Econ.* 1 (April): 127–46.

———. 1980. "The Effects of Nonresidential Land Uses on the Prices of Adjacent Housing: Some Estimates of Proximity Effects." *J. Urban Econ.* 8 (July): 1–15.

Haar, Charles M. 1953. "Zoning for Minimum Standards. The Wayne Township Case." *Harvard Law Rev.* 66 (April): 1051–63.

——. 1954. "Wayne Township: Zoning for Whom?—In Brief Reply." *Harvard Law Rev.* 67 (April): 986–93.

Hagman, Donald G. 1965. "The Single Tax and Land-Use Theory: Henry George Updated." *UCLA Law Rev.* 12 (August): 762–88.

——. 1971. *Urban Planning and Land Development Control Law.* St. Paul: West Publishing.

——. 1978. "Compensable Regulations," in *Windfalls for Wipeouts. See* Hagman and Misczynski 1978.

Hagman, Donald G., and Dean J. Misczynski, eds. 1978. *Windfalls for Wipeouts: Land Value Capture and Compensation.* Chicago: American Society of Planning Officials.

Hamilton, Bruce W. 1975. "Zoning and Property Taxation in a System of Local Governments." *Urban Studies* 12 (June): 205–11.

——. 1976. "Capitalization of Intrajurisdictional Differences in Local Tax Prices." *Am. Econ. Rev.* 66 (December): 743–53.

——. 1978. "Zoning and the Exercise of Monopoly Power." *J. Urban Econ.* 5 (January): 116–30.

Hamilton, Bruce W., Edwin S. Mills, and David Puryear. 1975. "The Tiebout Hypothesis and Residential Income Segregation," in *Fiscal Zoning and Land Use Controls*, edited by Edwin S. Mills and Wallace E. Oates. Lexington, Mass.: Heath-Lexington Books.

Hanke, Steve H., and Armando J. Carbonell. 1978. "Democratic Methods of Defining Property Rights: A Study of California's Coastal Zone." *Water Supply & Mgmt.* 2:483–87.

Hanke, Steve H., and John T. Wenders. 1982. "Costing and Pricing for Old and New Customers." *Public Utilities Fortnightly*, 29 April, 423–47.

Hart, John Fraser. 1984. "Cropland Change in the United States, 1944–78," in *The Resourceful Earth*, edited by Herman Kahn and Julian L. Simon. Oxford: Basil Blackwell.

[Harvard Law Rev.]. 1978. "Developments in the Law—Zoning." *Harvard Law Rev.* 91 (May): 1427–1708.

Healy, Robert G., and John S. Rosenberg. 1979. *Land Use and the States.* 2d ed. Baltimore: Johns Hopkins University Press for Resources for the Future.

Healy, Robert G., and James L. Short. 1981. *The Market for Rural Land: Trends, Issues, Policies.* Washington, D.C.: The Conservation Foundation.

Hekman, John S. 1980. "Income, Labor Supply, and Urban Residence." *Am. Econ. Rev.* 70 (September): 805–11.

Henderson, J. Vernon. 1977. *Economic Theory and the Cities.* New York: Academic Press.

——. 1979. "Theories of Group, Jurisdiction, and City Size," in *Current Issues in Urban Economics. See* Mieszkowski and Straszheim 1979.

——. 1980. "Community Development: The Effects of Growth and Uncertainty." *Am. Econ. Rev.* 70 (December): 894–910.

Herman, John H. 1980. "Ad Valorem Property Taxation and Public School Financing." *Urban Law Annual* 20: 261–72.

Hess, David. 1977. "Institutionalizing the Revolution: Judicial Reaction to State Land-Use Laws." *Urban Lawyer* 9 (Winter): 183–94.

Hirsch, Werner Z. 1977. "The Efficiency of Restrictive Land Use Instruments." *Land Econ.* 53 (May): 145–56.

Hirsch, Werner Z., and Joel G. Hirsch. 1979. "Exclusionary Zoning: Local Property Taxation and the Unique-Ubiquitous Resource Distinction." *Southern Cal. Law Rev.* 52 (September): 1671–1726.

Hite, J. C., and B. L. Dillman. 1981. "Protection of Agricultural Land: An Institutionist Perspective." *Southern J. Ag. Econ.* 13 (July): 43–53.

Hochman, Harold M., and James D. Rodgers. 1969. "Pareto Optimal Redistribution." *Am. Econ. Rev.* 59 (September): 542–57.

Holcombe, Randall G. 1980. "An Empirical Test of the Median Voter Model." *Econ. Inquiry* 18 (April): 260–74.

Holland, Daniel M., ed. 1970. *The Assessment of Land Value*. Madison: University of Wisconsin Press.

Hollenbeck, Kevin. 1979. "The Employment and Earnings Impacts of the Regulation of Stationary Source Air Pollution." *J. Env. Econ. & Mgmt.* 6 (September): 208–21.

Hoppe, Arthur. 1975. "A License to Steal," in *Economic Foundations of Property Law*. *See* Ackerman 1975.

Horwitz, Morton J. 1982. "The History of the Public/Private Distinction." *U. Pa. Law Rev.* 130 (June): 1423–28.

Hotelling, Harold. 1931. "The Economics of Exhaustible Resources." *J. Pol. Econ.* 39 (April): 137–75.

Hushak, Leroy J. 1975. "The Urban Demand for Urban-Rural Fringe Land." *Land Econ.* 51 (May): 112–23.

Inman, Robert P. 1978. "Testing Political Economy's 'As If' Proposition: Is the Median Income Voter Really Decisive?" *Public Choice* 33:45–65.

———. 1979. "The Fiscal Performance of Local Governments: An Interpretative Review," in *Current Issues in Urban Economics*. *See* Mieszkowski and Straszheim 1979.

Inman, Robert P., and Daniel L. Rubinfeld. 1979. "The Judicial Pursuit of Local Fiscal Equity." *Harvard Law Rev.* 92 (June): 1662–1750.

International City Managers' Association. 1960. *Urban Fringe Areas: Zoning, Subdivision Regulations, and Municipal Services*. Chicago: ICMA.

Jacobs, Jane. 1969. *The Economy of Cities*. New York: Random House.

James, Franklin J., Jr., and Dennis Gale. 1977. *Zoning For Sale: Transferable Development Rights*. Washington, D.C.: The Urban Institute.

James, Franklin J., Jr., and Oliver D. Windsor. 1976. "Fiscal Zoning, Fiscal Reform, and Exclusionary Land Use Controls." *J. Am. Inst. Planners* 42 (April): 130–41.

Johnson, Corwin W. 1955. "Constitutional Law and Community Planning." *Law & Contemporary Probs.* 20 (Spring): 199–217.

Johnson, M. Bruce, ed. 1982. *Resolving the Housing Crisis: Government Policy, Decontrol, and the Public Interest*. Cambridge, Mass.: Ballinger.

Jud, G. Donald. 1980. "The Effects of Zoning on Single-Family Residential

Property Values: Charlotte, North Carolina." *Land Econ.* 56 (May): 142–54.

Kahrl, William L. 1982. *Water and Power.* Berkeley: University of California Press.

Kau, James B., and C. F. Sirmans. 1983. "Technological Change and Economic Growth in Housing." *J. Urban Econ.* 13 (May): 283–95.

Keiper, Joseph S., Ernest Kurnow, Clifford D. Clark, and Harvey H. Segal. 1961. *Theory and Measurement of Rent.* Philadelphia: Chilton.

Kenyon, Daphne A. 1984. "Preference Revelation and Supply Response in the Arena of Local Government." *Public Choice* 42:147–60.

King, A. Thomas. 1973. *Property Taxes, Amenities, and Residential Land Values.* Cambridge, Mass.: Ballinger.

Kmiec, Douglas W. 1981. "Deregulating Land Use: An Alternative Free Enterprise Development System." *U. Pa. Law Rev.* 130 (November): 28–130.

———. 1982. "Regulatory Takings: The Supreme Court Runs Out of Gas in San Diego." *Indiana Law J.* 57:45–81.

———. 1983. "Manufactured Home Siting: A Statutory and Judicial Overview." *Zoning and Planning Law Report* 6 (March): 105–10.

Kneese, Allen V., and Karl Goran Maler. 1973. "Bribes and Charges in Pollution Control: An Aspect of the Coase Controversy." *Nat. Res. J.* 13 (October): 705–16.

Knetsch, Jack L., and J. A. Sinden. 1984. "Willingness to Pay and Compensation Demanded: Experimental Evidence of an Unexpected Disparity in Measures of Value." *Q. J. Econ.* 99 (in press.).

Knight, Robert L., and Mark D. Menchik. 1974. *Residential Environmental Attitudes and Preferences: Report of a Questionnaire Survey.* Madison, Wis.: Institute for Environmental Studies.

Komesar, Neil K. 1978. "Housing, Zoning and the Public Interest," in *Public Interest Law*, edited by Burton Weisbrod. Berkeley: University of California Press.

Krueger, Anne O. 1974. "The Political Economy of the Rent-Seeking Society." *Am. Econ. Rev.* 64 (June): 291–303.

Krumholz, Norman. 1982. "A Retrospective View of Equity Planning: Cleveland, 1969–1979." *Am. Plan. Assoc. J.* 48 (Spring): 163–74.

Kuznets, Simon. 1966. *Modern Economic Growth.* New Haven: Yale University Press.

———. 1977. "Two Centuries of Economic Growth: Reflection on U.S. Experience." *Am. Econ. Rev.* 67 (February): 1–14.

Ladd, Helen F. 1975. "Local Education Expenditures, Fiscal Capacity, and the Composition of the Property Tax Base." *National Tax J.* 28 (June): 145–58.

———. 1976. "State-Wide Taxation of Commercial and Industrial Property for Education." *National Tax J.* 29 (June): 143–54.

Laetsch, Watson. 1979. *Plants: Basic Concepts in Botany.* Boston: Little, Brown.

Lafferty, Ronald N. 1978. "Neighborhood Land Use and Housing Values:

Hedonic Price Indexes of Single-Family Homes in Eastern Massachusetts with Special Reference to the Spatial Effects of Non-Residential Land Use." Ph.D. diss., University of California, Santa Barbara.

Lafferty, Ronald N., and H. E. Frech III. 1978. "Community Environment and the Market Value of Single Family Homes: The Effect of the Dispersion of Land Uses." *J. Law & Econ.* 21 (October): 381–94.

Lamb, Charles M., and Mitchell S. Lustig. 1979. "The Burger Court, Exclusionary Zoning, and the Activist Restraint Debate." *U. Pittsburgh Law Rev.* 40 (Winter): 169–226.

Langley, C. John, Jr. 1976. "Adverse Impacts of the Washington Beltway on Residential Property Values." *Land Econ.* 52 (February): 54–65.

Lansing, John B., Charles W. Clifton, and James M. Morgan. 1969. *New Homes and Poor People: A Study of the Chain of Moves.* Ann Arbor: University of Michigan Institute for Social Research.

Lee, Linda K. 1984. "Urban and Built-up SCS Data—-An Historical Perspective." Washington, D.C.: U.S. Soil Conservation Service.

Leopold, Aldo. 1949. *A Sand County Almanac, and Sketches Here and There.* New York: Oxford University Press.

Library of Congress, Environmental Policy Division. 1973. *National Land Use Policy Legislation.* Washington, D.C.: U.S. Government Printing Office.

Lichtenberg, Robert. 1960. *One-Tenth of a Nation.* Cambridge, Mass.: Harvard University Press.

Liebermann, Nancy H. 1981. "Contract and Conditional Rezoning: A Judicial and Legislative Review." *Urban Land* 40 (November): 10–12.

Lind, Robert C. 1973. "Spatial Equilibrium, the Theory of Rents, and the Measurement of Benefits from Public Programs." *Q. J. Econ.* 87 (May): 188–207.

Lindert, Peter H. 1974. "Land Scarcity and American Growth." *J. Econ. Hist.* 34 (December): 851–84.

Linowes, R. Robert, and Don T. Allensworth. 1973. *The Politics of Land Use: Planning, Zoning, and the Private Developer.* New York: Praeger.

Lowry, Ira. 1960. "Filtering and Housing Standards: A Conceptual Analysis." *Land Econ.* 36 (November): 362–70.

McConnell, Kenneth E. 1983. "An Economic Model of Soil Conservation." *Am. J. Ag. Econ.* 65 (February): 83–89.

McDonald, John F. 1979. *Economic Analysis of an Urban Housing Market.* New York: Academic Press.

Mace, Ruth L., and Warren J. Wicker. 1968. *Do Single Family Homes Pay Their Way?* Washington, D.C.: Urban Land Institute.

McGuire, Martin. 1974. "Group Segregation and Optimal Jurisdictions." *J. Pol. Econ.* 82 (January): 112–32.

McGuire, Therese J. 1983. "Essays on Firm Location in a Metropolitan Area." Ph.D. diss., Princeton University.

McKean, Roland. 1972. "Property Rights within Government and Devices to Increase Governmental Efficiency." *Southern Econ. J.* 39 (October): 177–86.

McMichael, Stanley L., and Robert F. Bingham. 1923. *City Growth and Values*. Cleveland: Stanley McMichael Publishing Organization.

Mandelker, Daniel R. 1971. *The Zoning Dilemma*. Chicago: American Society of Planning Officials.

————. 1976. "The Role of the Local Comprehensive Plan in Land Use Regulation." *Michigan Law Rev.* 74 (April): 899–973.

————. 1981. *Environment and Equity: A Regulatory Challenge*. New York: McGraw Hill.

Manne, Henry G., ed. 1975. *The Economics of Legal Relationships*. St. Paul: West Publishing.

Manvel, Allen D. 1968. *Local Land and Building Regulation*. National Commission on Urban Problems Research Report 6. Washington, D.C.: U.S. Government Printing Office.

Marcus, Norman. 1979. "The Grand Slam Grand Central Terminal Decision: A Euclid for Landmarks, Favorable Notice for TDR, and a Resolution of the Regulatory/Taking Impasse." *Ecology Law Q.* 7: 731–52.

————. 1980. "A Comparative Look at TDR, Subdivison Exactions, and Zoning as Environmental Preservation Panaceas: The Search for Dr. Jekyll without Mr. Hyde." *Urban Law Annual* 20:3–74.

Mark, Jonathan H., and Michael A. Goldberg. 1981. "Land Use Controls: The Case of Zoning in Vancouver." *Am. Real Est. & Urban Econ. Assoc. J.* 9 (Winter): 418–35.

Markusen, James R., and David T. Scheffman. 1977. *Speculation and Monopoly in Urban Development: Analytical Foundations with Evidence for Toronto*. Toronto and Buffalo: University of Toronto Press for the Ontario Economic Council.

————. 1978. "The Timing of Residential Land Development: A General Equilibrium Approach." *J. Urban Econ.* 5 (October): 411–24.

Maser, Steven M., William H. Riker, and Richard N. Rosett. 1977. "The Effects of Zoning and Externalities on the Price of Land: An Empirical Analysis of Monroe County, New York." *J. Law & Econ.* 20 (April): 111–32.

Mercer, Lloyd J., and W. Douglas Morgan. 1982. "An Estimate of Residential Growth Controls' Impact on House Prices," in *Resolving the Housing Crisis*. *See* Johnson 1982.

Michelman, Frank I. 1967. "Property, Utility, and Fairness: Comments on the Ethical Foundations of 'Just Compensation' Law." *Harvard Law Rev.* 80 (April): 1165–1258.

————. 1969. "On Protecting the Poor through the Fourteenth Amendment." *Harvard Law Rev.* 83 (November): 7–59.

————. 1971. "Pollution as a Tort: A Non-Accidental Perspective on Calabresi's Costs." *Yale Law J.* 80 (January): 647–86.

Mieszkowski, Peter. 1972. "The Property Tax: An Excise Tax or a Profits Tax?" *J. Pub. Econ.* 1 (April): 73–96.

Mieszkowski, Peter, and Mahlon Straszheim, eds. 1979. *Current Issues in Urban Economics*. Baltimore: Johns Hopkins University Press.

Miller, Gary J. 1981. *Cities by Contract: The Politics of Municipal Incorporation*. Cambridge, Mass.: MIT Press.

Mills, David E. 1979. "Segregation, Rationing, and Zoning." *Southern Econ. J.* 45 (April): 1195–1207.

———. 1980. "Transferable Development Rights Markets." *J. Urban Econ.* 7 (January): 63–74.

———. 1981a. "The Non-Neutrality of Land Value Taxation." *National Tax J.* 34 (March): 125–29.

———. 1981b. "Growth, Speculation, and Sprawl in a Monocentric City." *J. Urban Econ.* 10 (September): 201–26.

Mills, Edwin S. 1972. *Studies in the Structure of the Urban Economy*. Baltimore: Johns Hopkins Press.

———. 1979. "Economic Analysis of Urban Land-Use Controls," in *Current Issues in Urban Economics*. See Mieszkowski and Straszheim 1979.

———. 1980. *Urban Economics*. 2d ed. Glenview, Ill.: Scott, Foresman.

Moss, William G. 1977. "Large Lot Zoning, Property Taxes, and Metropolitan Area." *J. Urban Econ.* 4 (October): 408–27.

Muller, Thomas, and Grace Dawson. 1972. *The Fiscal Impact of Residential and Commercial Development: A Case Study*. Washington, D.C.: The Urban Institute.

Munch, Patricia. 1976. "An Economic Analysis of Eminent Domain." *J. Pol. Econ.* 84 (June): 473–97.

Murray, Michael. 1983. "Subsidized and Unsubsidized Housing Starts: 1961–1977." *Rev. Econ. & Stats.* 65 (November): 590–97.

Musgrave, Richard A. 1939. "The Voluntary Exchange Theory of Public Economy." *Q. J. Econ.* 52 (February): 213–17.

Musgrave, Richard A., and Peggy B. Musgrave. 1980. *Public Finance in Theory and Practice*. 3d ed. New York: McGraw Hill.

Muth, Richard F., and Elliot Wetzler. 1976. "The Effect of Constraints on House Costs." *J. Urban Econ.* 3 (January): 57–67.

National Agricultural Lands Study. 1981. *Final Report*. Washington, D.C.: U.S. Government Printing Office.

Natural Resources Defense Council. 1977. *Land Use Controls in the United States: A Handbook on the Legal Rights of Citizens*. New York: Dial Press/James Wade.

Nedelsky, Jennifer. 1982. "Confining Democratic Politics: Anti-Federalists, Federalists, and the Constitution." *Harvard Law Rev.* 96:340–60.

Nelson, Robert H. 1977. *Zoning and Property Rights*. Cambridge, Mass.: MIT Press.

New Hampshire League of Women Voters. 1975. *New Hampshire's Land*. Concord.

New Jersey Bureau of Local Planning. 1967. *Zoning in New Jersey*. Trenton: New Jersey Division of State and Regional Planning.

Nordhaus, William D., and James Tobin. 1972. *Economic Growth*. National Bureau of Economic Research Fiftieth Anniversary Colloquium, 5. New York: Columbia University Press.

Nourse, Hugh O.   1963. "The Effect of Public Housing on Property Values in St. Louis." *Land Econ.* 39 (November): 433–40.

Oates, Wallace E.   1969. "The Effects of Property Taxes and Local Public Spending on Property Values: An Empirical Study of Tax Capitalization and the Tiebout Hypothesis." *J. Pol. Econ.* 77 (November): 957–71.

———. 1972. *Fiscal Federalism.* New York: Harcourt Brace Jovanovich.

———. 1977. "The Use of Local Zoning Ordinances to Regulate Population Flows and the Quality of Local Services," in *Essays in Labor Market Analysis*, edited by Orley Ashenfelter and Wallace E. Oates. New York: Wiley.

Ohio Department of Economic and Community Development.   1974. *Local Land Use Controls in Ohio: Their Extent and Effectiveness.* Columbus: Ohio Land Use Policy Work Group.

Ohls, James C.   1975. "Public Policy toward Low Income Housing and Filtering in Housing Markets." *J. Urban Econ.* 2 (April): 144–71.

Ohls, James C., and David Pines.   1975. "Discontinuous Urban Development and Economic Efficiency." *Land Econ.* 51 (August): 224–34.

Olsen, Edgar O.   1969. "A Competitive Theory of the Housing Market." *Am. Econ. Rev.* 59 (September): 612–21.

Olson, Mancur.   1965. *The Logic of Collective Action.* Cambridge, Mass.: Harvard University Press.

Orr, Larry L.   1975. *Income, Employment and Urban Residential Location.* New York: Academic Press for Wisconsin Institute for Research on Poverty.

———. 1976. "Income Transfers as a Public Good: An Application to AFDC." *Am. Econ. Rev.* 66 (June): 359–71.

Ozanne, Larry, and Thomas Thibodeau.   1983. "Explaining Metropolitan Housing Price Differences." *J. Urban Econ.* 13 (January): 51–66.

Pack, Howard, and Janet R. Pack.   1977. "Metropolitan Fragmentation and Suburban Homogeneity." *Urban Studies* 14 (June): 191–202.

———. 1978. "Metropolitan Fragmentation and Local Public Expenditures." *National Tax J.* 31 (December): 349–62.

Peiser, Richard B.   1981. "Land Development Regulation: A Case Study of Dallas and Houston, Texas." *Am. Real Estate & Urban Econ. Assoc. J.* 9 (Winter): 397–417.

———. 1983. "The Economics of Municipal Utility Districts for Land Development." *Land Econ.* 59 (February): 43–57.

Peltzman, Sam.   1976. "Toward a More General Theory of Regulation." *J. Law & Econ.* 19 (August): 211–40.

Peterson, George E.   1974a. "The Influence of Zoning Regulations on Land and Housing Prices." Working Paper 1207–24. Washington, D.C.: The Urban Institute.

———. 1974b. "Land Prices and Factor Substitution in the Metropolitan Housing Market." Washington, D.C.: The Urban Institute.

———. 1978. "Federal Tax Policy and Land Conversion at the Urban Fringe," in *Metropolitan Financing and Growth Management Policies*, edited by George Break. Madison: University of Wisconsin Press.

Pigou, A. C. 1932. *The Economics of Welfare*. 4th ed. London: Macmillan.

Pines, David, and Yoram Weiss. 1976. "Land Improvement Projects and Land Values." *J. Urban Econ.* 3 (January): 1–13.

Polinsky, A. Mitchell. 1979. "Controlling Externalities and Protecting Entitlements: Property Right, Liability Rule, and Tax-Subsidy Approaches." *J. Legal Studies* 8 (January): 1–48.

———. 1980. "Resolving Nuisance Disputes: The Simple Economics of Injunctive and Damage Remedies." *Stanford Law Rev.* 32 (July): 1075–1112.

Pollard, W. L. 1931. "Outline of the Law of Zoning in the United States." *Annals* 155, no. 2 (May): 15–33.

Poon, Larry C. L. 1978. "Railway Externalities and Residential Property Prices." *Land Econ.* 54 (May): 218–22.

Portney, Paul R. 1981. "Housing Prices, Health Effects, and Valuing Reductions in Risk of Death." *J. Env. Econ. & Mgmt.* 8 (March): 72–78.

Posner, Richard. 1977. *Economic Analysis of Law*. 2d ed. Boston: Little, Brown.

President's Commission on Housing. 1982. *Report*. Washington, D.C.: U.S. Government Printing Office.

Pulliam, Mark S. 1983. "Brandeis Brief for Decontrol of Land Use: A Plea for Constitutional Reform." *Southwestern U. Law Rev.* 13:435–76.

Pyle, Lizbeth A. 1982. "New Homes in the Countryside: Prime Farmland for Residential Development?" *Center for Urban and Regional Affairs Report* (University of Minnesota) 12 (September): 9–13.

Rabiega, William A., Ta-Win Lin, and Linda M. Robinson. 1984. "The Property Value Impacts of Public Housing Projects in Low and Moderate Density Residential Neighborhoods." *Land Econ.* 60 (May): 174–79.

Rabin, Edward H. 1984. "The Revolution in Residential Landlord-Tenant Law: Causes and Consequences." *Cornell Law Rev.* 69 (March): 519–84.

Randall, Alan. 1974. "Coasian Externality Theory in a Policy Context." *Nat. Res. J.* 14 (January): 35–54.

Rashid, Salim. 1981. "Public Utilities in Egalitarian LDC's: The Role of Bribery in Achieving Pareto Efficiency." *Kyklos* 34:448–60.

Raup, Philip M. 1975. "Urban Threats to Rural Lands: Background and Beginnings." *J. Am. Inst. Planners* 41 (November): 371–78.

———. 1982. "An Agricultural Critique of the National Agricultural Lands Study." *Land Econ.* 58 (May): 260–74.

Rawls, John. 1971. *A Theory of Justice*. Cambridge, Mass.: Belknap.

Raymond and May Associates. 1968. *Zoning Controversies in the Suburbs: Three Case Studies*. U.S. National Commission on Urban Problems Research Report 11. Washington, D.C.: U.S. Government Printing Office.

Real Estate Research Corp. 1974. *The Costs of Sprawl*. Council on Environmental Quality. Washington, D.C.: U.S. Government Printing Office.

Reichman, Uriel. 1976. "Residential Private Governments: An Introductory Survey." *U. Chicago Law Rev.* 43 (Winter): 253–306.

Reilly, William K., ed. 1973. *The Use of Land: A Citizens Policy Guide to Urban Growth*. New York: Thomas Y. Crowell.

Reinsel, Robert D., and Edward I. Reinsel. 1979. "The Economics of Asset Values and Current Income in Farming." *Am. J. Ag. Econ.* 61 (December): 1093–97.

Rose, Carol M. 1983. "Planning and Dealing: Piecemeal Land Controls as a Problem of Local Legitimacy." *Cal. Law Rev.* 71 (May): 837–912.

Rose-Ackerman, Susan. 1979. "Market Models of Local Government: Exit, Voting, and the Land Market." *J. Urban Econ.* 6 (July): 319–37.

Rosen, Harvey S., and David J. Fullerton. 1977. "A Note on Local Tax Rates, Public Benefit Levels, and Property Values." *J. Pol. Econ.* 85 (April): 433–40.

Rosen, Kenneth T., and Lawrence F. Katz. 1981. "Growth Management and Land Use Controls: The San Francisco Bay Area Experience." *Am. Real Est. & Urban Econ. Assoc. J.* 9 (Winter): 321–44.

Rosen, Kenneth T., and Mitchel Resnick. 1980. "The Size Distribution of Cities: An Examination of the Pareto Law and Primacy." *J. Urban Econ.* 8 (September): 165–86.

Rosen, Sherwin. 1974. "Hedonic Prices and Implicit Markets: Product Differentiation in Pure Competition." *J. Pol. Econ.* 82 (January/February): 34–55.

———. 1979. "Wage-Based Indexes of Urban Quality of Life," in *Current Issues in Urban Economics.* See Mieszkowski and Straszheim 1979.

Rosner, Monroe H., and Richard L. Barrows. 1977. "School Finance Reform and Rural Land Use Policy Incentives." *Land Econ.* 53 (August): 288–97.

Rothenberg, Jerome. 1970. "Local Decentralization and the Theory of Optimal Government," in *The Analysis of Public Output,* edited by Julius Margolis. New York: National Bureau of Economic Research.

Rubinfeld, Daniel L. 1977. "Voting in a Local School Election: A Micro Analysis." *Rev. Econ. & Stats.* 59 (February): 30–42.

———. 1978. "Suburban Employment and Zoning: A General Equilibrium Analysis." *J. Reg. Sci.* 18 (April): 33–44.

———. 1979. "Judicial Approaches to Local Public Sector Equity: An Economic Analysis," in *Current Issues in Urban Economics. See* Mieszkowski and Straszheim 1979.

Rueter, Frederick J. 1973. "Externalities in Urban Property Markets: An Empirical Test of the Zoning Ordinance of Pittsburgh." *J. Law & Econ.* 16 (October): 313–50.

Sagalyn, Lynne B., and George Sternlieb. 1973. *Zoning and Housing Costs.* New Brunswick, N.J.: Rutgers Center for Urban Policy Research.

Sager, Lawrence G. 1969. "Tight Little Islands: Exclusionary Zoning, Equal Protection, and the Indigent." *Stanford Law Rev.* 21 (April): 767–800.

———. 1978. "Insular Majorities Unabated: Warth v. Selden and City of Eastlake v. Forest City Enterprises, Inc." *Harvard Law Rev.* 91 (May): 1373–1425.

Samuelson, Paul A. 1954. "The Pure Theory of Public Expenditures." *Rev. Econ. & Stats.* 36 (November): 387–89.

————. 1976. *Economics*. 10th ed. New York: McGraw-Hill.

Sax, Joseph. 1964. "Takings and the Police Power." *Yale Law J.* 74 (November): 36–76.

————. 1971. "Takings, Private Property, and Public Rights." *Yale Law J.* 81 (December): 149–86.

Schafer, Robert. 1974. *The Suburbanization of Multifamily Housing*. Lexington, Mass.: Heath-Lexington Books.

Schelling, Thomas C. 1980. "The Intimate Contest for Self-Command." *Public Interest* 60 (Summer): 94–118.

Schultz, Theodore W. 1982. "On the Economics of Agricultural Production over Time." *Econ. Inquiry* 20 (January): 10–20.

Schumpeter, Joseph A. 1954. *History of Economic Analysis*. New York: Oxford University Press.

Schwartz, Seymour, David Hansen, and Richard Green. 1981. "Suburban Growth Controls and the Price of New Housing." *J. Env. Econ. & Mgmt.* 8 (December): 303–20.

————. 1984. "The Effect of Growth Control on the Production of Moderate Priced Housing." *Land Econ.* 60 (February): 110–14.

Scott, Randall W., ed. 1975. *Management and Control of Growth*. Washington, D.C.: Urban Land Institute.

Segal, David. 1976. "Are There Returns to Scale in City Size?" *Rev. Econ. & Stats.* 53 (August): 339–50.

Seidel, Stephen. 1978. *Housing Costs and Government Regulations: Confronting the Regulatory Maze*. New Brunswick, N.J.: Rutgers Center for Urban Policy Research.

Shavell, Steven. 1979. "Risk Sharing and Incentives in the Principal and Agent Relationship." *Bell J. Econ.* 10 (Spring): 55–73.

Siegan, Bernard H. 1972. *Land Use without Zoning*. Lexington, Mass.: Heath-Lexington Books.

————. 1976. *Other People's Property*. Lexington, Mass.: Heath-Lexington Books.

————. 1980. *Economic Liberties and the Constitution*. Chicago: University of Chicago Press.

Simon, Julian L. 1980. "Are We Losing Ground?" *Illinois Bus. Rev.* 37 (April): 1–6.

Simon, Julian L., and Seymour Sudman. 1982. "How Much Farmland Is Being Converted to Urban Use? An Analysis of Soil Conservation Service Estimates." *Internat. Reg. Sci. Rev.* 7 (December): 257–72.

Smith, James D., and Stephen D. Franklin. 1974. "The Concentration of Personal Wealth, 1922–1969." *Am. Econ. Rev.* 64 (May): 162–67.

Smith, Lawrence B. 1976. "The Ontario Land Speculation Tax: An Analysis of an Unearned Increment Land Tax." *Land Econ.* 52 (February): 1–12.

Smith, Matthew G., and Philip M. Raup. 1982. *The Minnesota Rural Real Estate Market in 1981*. Economic Report ER 82–4. St. Paul: University of Minnesota Department of Agricultural and Applied Economics.

Smith, Vernon L. 1982. "Markets As Economizers of Information: Experimental Examination of the 'Hayek Hypothesis.' " *Econ. Inquiry* 20 (April): 165–79.

So, Frank S., Israel Stollman, Frank Beal, and David S. Arnold, eds. 1979. *The Practice of Local Government Planning*. Washington, D.C.: International City Management Association.

Sonstelie, Jon C., and Alan Gin. 1982. "Residential Development and the Cost of Local Public Services," in *Resolving the Housing Crisis. See* Johnson 1982.

Sonstelie, Jon C., and Paul R. Portney. 1978. "Profit Maximizing Communities and the Theory of Local Public Expenditure." *J. Urban Econ.* 5 (April): 263–77.

———. 1980. "Take the Money and Run: A Theory of Voting in Local Referenda." *J. Urban Econ.* 8 (September): 187–96.

Stanford Environmental Law Society. 1982. "Land Use and Housing on the San Francisco Peninsula." *Stanford Environmental Law Annual.*

Stigler, George J. 1971. "The Theory of Economic Regulation." *Bell J. Econ.* 2 (Spring): 3–21.

Stone, Christopher D. 1972. "Should Trees Have Standing?—Toward Legal Rights for Natural Objects." *Southern Cal. Law Rev.* 45 (Spring): 450–501.

Stull, William. 1974. "Land Use Zoning in an Urban Economy." *Am. Econ. Rev.* 64 (June): 337–47.

———. 1975. "Community Environment, Zoning, and the Market Value of Single-Family Homes." *J. Law & Econ.* 18 (October): 535–57.

Sussna, Stephen. 1961. "Zoning Boards: In Theory and In Practice." *Land Econ.* 37 (February): 82–87.

Sveikauskas, Leo. 1979. "Interurban Difference in the Innovative Nature of Production." *J. Urban Econ.* 6 (April): 216–27.

Swanson, Earl R., and Earl O. Heady. 1984. "Economics of Soil Erosion in the United States," in *The Resourceful Earth*, edited by Herman Kahn and Julian L. Simon. Oxford: Basil Blackwell.

Sweeney, James L. 1974. "A Commodity Hierarchy Model of the Rental Housing Market." *J. Urban Econ.* 1 (July): 288–323.

Tabors, Richard D., Michael H. Shapiro, and Peter P. Rogers. 1976. *Land Use and the Pipe*. Lexington, Mass.: Heath-Lexington Books.

Tarlock, A. Dan. 1973. "Toward a Revised Theory of Zoning," in *Management and Control of Growth. See* Scott 1975.

———. 1975. "Consistency with Adopted Land Use Plans as a Standard of Judicial Review: The Case Against." *Urban Law Annual* 9:69–109.

———. 1982. "Euclid Revisited." *Land Use Law & Zoning Digest* 34 (January): 4–8.

———. 1983. "Land Use Issues in Hazardous Waste Facility Siting." *Land Use Law & Zoning Digest* 35 (April): 4–10.

Tideman, T. Nicolaus. 1969. "Three Approaches to Improving Urban Land Use." Ph.D. diss., University of Chicago.

————. 1982. "A Tax on Land Value *Is* Neutral." *National Tax J.* 35 (March): 109–12.

Tiebout, Charles M. 1956. "A Pure Theory of Local Expenditures." *J. Pol. Econ.* 64 (October): 416–24.

Toll, Seymour. 1969. *Zoned American.* New York: Grossman.

Tolley, George S. 1974. "The Welfare Economics of City Bigness." *J. Urban Econ.* 1 (July): 324–45.

Toner, William. 1978. *Saving Farms and Farmland: A Community Guide.* Planning Advisory Service Report 333. Chicago: American Society of Planning Officials.

Turvey, Ralph. 1963. "On Divergences between Social Cost and Private Cost." *Economica* 30 (August): 309–14.

U. S. Department of Agriculture, Economic Research Service. 1972. *Rural Zoning in the U.S.: Analysis of Enabling Legislation.* Misc. Publication 1232. Washington, D.C.: U.S. Government Printing Office.

U. S. Department of Agriculture, Soil Conservation Service. 1984. *Preliminary Data, 1982 National Resources Inventory, Executive Summary.* Washington, D.C.

U. S. Federal Insurance Administration. 1976. *Statutory Land Use Control Enabling Authority in the Fifty States.* Washington, D.C.: U.S. Department of Housing and Urban Development.

U.S. National Commission on Urban Problems. 1968. *Building the American City.* Washington, D.C.: U.S. Government Printing Office.

Van den Haag, Ernest. 1976. "Economics Is Not Enough—Notes on the Anticapitalist Spirit." *Public Interest* 45 (Fall): 109–22.

Vogel, Kenneth R. 1980. "Exclusionary Zoning and the Provision of Education: An Effect of Southern Burlington County NAACP v. Township of Mount Laurel." *J. Urban Econ.* 8 (November): 294–312.

Wagner, Richard E., and Warren E. Weber. 1975. "Competition, Monopoly, and the Organization of Government in Metropolitan Areas." *J. Law & Econ.* 18 (December): 661–84.

Warner, Sam B. 1971. *Streetcar Suburbs: The Process of Growth in Boston, 1870–1900.* New York: Atheneum.

Weicher, John C. 1979. "Urban Housing Policy," in *Current Issues in Urban Economics.* See Mieszkowski and Straszheim 1979.

————. 1980. *Housing: Federal Policies and Programs.* Washington, D.C.: American Enterprise Institute.

Welfeld, Irving. 1977. "American Housing Policy: Perverse Programs by Prudent People." *Public Interest* 48 (Summer): 128–44.

White, Michelle J. 1975a. "Firm Location in a Zoned Metropolitan Area," in *Fiscal Zoning and Land Use Controls,* edited by Edwin S. Mills and Wallace E. Oates. Lexington, Mass.: Heath-Lexington Books.

————. 1975b. "The Effect of Zoning on the Size of Metropolitan Areas." *J. Urban Econ.* 2 (October): 279–90.

————. 1978a. "Job Suburbanization and the Welfare of Urban Minority Groups." *J. Urban Econ.* 5 (April): 219–40.

————. 1978b. "Self-Interest in the Suburbs: The Trend toward No-Growth Zoning." *Policy Analysis* 4 (Spring): 185–203.

————. 1979. "Suburban Growth Controls: Liability Rules and Pigovian Taxes." *J. Legal Studies* 8 (January): 207–30.

White, Michelle J., and Donald Wittman. 1982. "Pollution Taxes and Optimal Spatial Location." *Economica* 49 (August): 297–311.

Williams, Norman, Jr. 1975. *American Planning Law: Land Use and the Police Power.* Chicago: Callaghan.

————. 1982. "Planning Law in the 1980s: What Do We Know About It?" *Vermont Law Rev.* 7 (Fall): 205–47.

Williams, Oliver T. 1965. *Suburban Differences and Metropolitan Policies: A Philadelphia Story.* Philadelphia: University of Pennsylvania Press.

Windsor, Duane. 1979. "A Critique of the Costs of Sprawl." *Am. Plan. Assoc. J.* 45 (July): 279–92.

Wittman, Donald. 1977. "Prior Regulation vs. Post Liability: The Choice between Input and Output Monitoring." *J. Legal Studies* 6 (January): 193–212.

————. 1984. "Liability for Harm or Restitution for Benefit?" *J. Legal Studies* 13 (January): 57–80.

Wolfram, Gary. 1981. "The Sale of Development Rights and Zoning in the Preservation of Open Space: Lindahl Equilibrium and a Case Study." *Land Econ.* 57 (August): 398–413.

Wolfstone, Jeff C. 1978. "The Case for a Procedural Due Process Limitation on the Zoning Referendum: City of Eastlake v. Forest City Enterprises, Inc., Revisited." *Ecology Law Q.* 7:51–99.

[*Yale Law J.*]. 1979. "Note, State Economic Substantive Due Process: A Proposed Approach." *Yale Law J.* 88 (June): 1487–1510.

Yinger, John. 1979. "Prejudice and Discrimination in the Urban Housing Market," in *Current Issues in Urban Economics. See* Mieszkowski and Straszheim 1979.

————. 1982. "Capitalization and the Theory of Local Public Finance." *J. Pol. Econ.* 90 (October): 917–43.

Zeimetz, Kathryn A., Elizabeth Dillon, Ernest E. Hardy, and Robert C. Otte. 1976. *Dynamics of Land Use in Fast Growth Areas.* Agricultural Economic Report 325. Washington, D.C.: U.S. Department of Agriculture, Economic Research Service.

Zumbrun, Ronald A., and Thomas E. Hookano. 1977. "No Growth and Related Land-Use Legal Problems: An Overview." *Urban Lawyer* 9 (Winter): 122–56.

Table of Cases

NOTE: Italic numbers refer to pages in this volume. Page numbers followed by note numbers refer to textual discussion. Numbers within parentheses following such entries provide the page on which the note itself, and often more discussion, can be found.

Index

Ackerman, Bruce, on Sax's theory of takings, 227
Advocacy planning, 33
Aesthetics, as purpose of zoning, 48
Agglomeration economies, 270
    defined, 252–54
    urban model and, 257–58
Agricultural land
    farmland preservation movement and, 273–74, 276, 287, 288–90
    market for, 276–77, 281
    as open space, 69, 287
    ownership of, 11, 290
    rate of conversion of, 2, 272, 275
    urban development on, 276–77, 279–81, 283
Agricultural zoning, 69, 273, 286–87
Air pollution, valuation of, 83–86
Alienability of property. See Inalienability; Selling zoning
Annexation policy, 68
Anti-Snob Zoning Act (Mass.), 138

Balancing means tests. See Benefit-cost criterion
Baltimore Urbanized Area, 218, 220
Benefit-cost analysis, in due process, 47
Benefit-cost criterion, 154, 157, 162–63
Boston, 232, 242
Brandeis, Justice Louis, on takings, 50, 51

Brennan, Justice William, on damages remedy, 193
Bribery, 134, 209
    and selling zoning, 72
Building code, 24
Bulk requirements, 61
Burden of proof, 49, 167–68, 202

Calabresi, Guido, entitlement protection theory of, 112, 113, 179
California
    courts, 49, 239
    growth controls in, 238–39, 262
    planning for low-income housing, 63
    referenda and initiatives in, 223
California Coastal Zone Commission, 224
Capitalization, 184–86, 301 n. 7, 303 n. 8
Central business district (CBD), 255–58, 264, 265
Central city zoning, politics of, 126, 212–24
Civil rights movement, 334
    and equal protection, 54
Coase, R. H.
    on Coase theorem, 117
    theory of the firm, 115
Coase theorem
    air pollution and, 82–87
    assumptions of, 90–91
    bargaining in, 111–12
    criticisms of, 109–16
    entitlement protection and, 112

365